JUSTICES AND PRESIDENTS

JUSTICES AND PRESIDENTS

A Political History of Appointments to the Supreme Court

Second Edition

Henry J. Abraham

New York Oxford
Oxford University Press
1985

Oxford University Press
Oxford London New York Toronto
Delhi Bombay Calcutta Madras Karachi
Kuala Lampur Singapore Hong Kong Tokyo
Nairobi Dar es Salaam Cape Town
Melbourne Auckland
and associated companies in
Beirut Berlin Ibadan Mexico City Nicosia

Library of Congress Cataloging in Publication Data
Abraham, Henry Julian, 1921–
Justices and presidents.
Bibliography: p.
Includes index.
1. United States. Supreme Court–History.
I. Title.
KF8742.A72 1985 347.73'2634 84-825
ISBN 0-19-503479-1 347.3073534
ISBN 0-19-503480-5 (pbk.)

Printing (last digit): 9 8 7 6 5 4 3 2

Printed in the United States of America

TO MY FAMILY:
Mil, Phil, and Pete

Preface to the Second Edition

A dozen years have gone by since the publication of this work's first edition–years that not only witnessed the departure of several members of the Court, including one of its most influential figures, William O. Douglas, but the arrival of the first woman Justice of the Supreme Court of the United States, Sandra Day O'Connor. They constituted years, moreover, that were characterized by the continuing recognition of the verities of the Court's role as a policymaker, of its tripartite role as a legal, a governmental, and, yes, a political institution. Those years also demonstrated that, contrary to the expectations, hopes, or fears of those who profess to understand the Court and its role best, the Burger Court and its Justices did not–with the arguable exception of aspects of the realm of criminal justice–"undo" the jurisprudence of the Warren Court and its Justices. Indeed, the Court has continued to manifest its embrace of an activist role, of judicial legislating, of lawmaking, of judicial activism, even if some of its nuances may well be distinguished from its predecessor tribunals.

Far more than merely a revision, let alone a mere updating, of the first *Justices and Presidents,* the second edition is essentially a new book. Not only has it been expanded by more than a third in terms of its coverage, but it also features two brand-new, additional chapters: one (Ch. 1) discusses the criteria, evaluations, and judgments that constitute the basic model, the theme of the work; the other (Ch. 11) treats the Burger Court and its Justices (the first edition having gone only as far as Justice Thurgood

Marshall) through the 1983–1984 term. Chapters 9 (F.D.R. and Truman) and 10 (from Ike to L.B.J.) have been totally rewritten, and Chapter 8 (from Theodore Roosevelt to Herbert Hoover) almost entirely. Chapters 3 and 4—the *how* and *why* Supreme Court Justices are nominated and appointed—have also been thoroughly restructured and redesigned, and all of the several remaining chapters reflect the myriad changes and new data that have come to life since the earlier version of this tome. Additional appendixes, dealing with diverse statistics and rankings of both Presidents and Justices, augment the textual materials, as do an extensive bibliography and two indexes.

Once again I am delighted to acknowledge, with abiding gratitude, the manifold kindness and assistance by a host of colleagues, members of the Court, research assistants, and graduate students—far too generously numerous to identify. But I should like to express particular appreciation to Chief Justice Burger and Associate Justices Brennan and Powell; to my colleagues Dennis D. Dorin, David Fellman, Robert J. Harris, Dick A. E. Howard, David M. O'Brien, John R. Schmidhauser, Lane Sunderland, and Tinsley E. Yarbrough; to Susan Rabiner and Henry Krawitz of Oxford University Press; to my erstwhile students and now members of the worlds of academe and/or law in their own right, Gary J. Aichele, Vincent M. Bonventre, Stanley C. Brubaker, Peter M. Dodson, Jan Horbaly, Francis Graham Lee, Gary L. McDowell, James J. Magee, Walter R. Markham, Gary E. Mullin, and Bruce A. Murphy; and to my faithful, tireless, devoted research assistants, Barbara A. Perry (who also compiled the index) and James S. Todd—without whom this book would not have been completed. I am also profoundly grateful for the generous financial aid extended to me by the Mayer & Arlene Mitchell and Abraham A. Mitchell Fund, the Robert W. and Patricia T. Gelfman Fund, and the Earhart Foundation.

And while the first edition's dedicatees, like the author, are now twelve years older, the dedication is restated with much love.

Charlottesville, Virginia H.J.A.
November 1984

Preface to the First Edition

This work has its genesis in a series of graduate seminars in constitutional law and the judicial process that I conducted at the University of Pennsylvania in the mid- and late 1950s. The subject matter had always fascinated me, and while I lay aside writing this book in favor of other publications during the ensuing years, the project was never dormant. I gathered a host of data, developing a separate file for each of the one hundred individuals that have served on the highest court of the land, until the end of the Warren Court era in 1969 determined me to write what had been gestating for almost two decades.

What I had initially conceived as a fairly straightforward analysis of Presidential motivations in the appointment of the several Chief Justices and Associate Justices of the Supreme Court of the United States, gradually evolved into a far more ambitious undertaking as the book took shape. Backed by the advice and counsel of sundry colleagues, it seemed almost artificial merely to cite reasons for an individual's selection without concurrently evaluating his subsequent performance on the bench. Thus, the book addresses itself also to the nominee's work on the Court, both in terms of Presidential expectations and in those of my own perception of his performance. Quite naturally the book expanded further by comprising what, in effect, is a "mini-history" of the Court itself—and an attempt briefly to encapsulate and categorize the Presidential performance as well as that of his nominees.

Inexorably, aspects of the book are subjective: judgment of

performance inevitably involves value orientation. Yet I have endeavored to be objective and scholarly in my analyses and evaluations. Temptations to be "cute" are omnipresent; but they serve little purpose in what, after all, is a historical-political account of the reasons why Justices were appointed and how they lived up to their nominators' expectations. What follows, then, represents serious judgment based on carefully gathered and pondered evidence. Admittedly, perhaps many of the explanations and evaluations will prove to be at once controversial and less than astonishing or thrilling. Yet they are based on more than two decades of teaching and research in the field and on lasting interest as well as fascination with an exciting aspect of our system of government.

My research was conducted in the traditional mold of going to the most reliable sources available. That meant both primary and secondary written data; but it also meant personal interviews with a great many individuals in and out of government, including a number of Justices of the Supreme Court, who were truly helpful. Some of the gathered information developed diametrically opposite assertions or evidence (for example, the real reasons for Mr. Justice Goldberg's decision to relinquish his post on the Court) necessitating the kind of judgment Mr. Justice Frankfurter was fond of styling as "inescapable." Accordingly, the book contains numerous such judgments; but they are judgments based on carefully weighed conclusions. As the Bibliographical Note indicates, the sources of my information were indeed broad and numerous, yet—given the unavailability of the papers of many among the Justices—new or different revelations may well lie in the future. In the meanwhile I hope that my account will shed at least some light on a subject that continues to prove to be at once intriguing and challenging.

No work of this kind could have been written without the deeply appreciated aid and comfort of my colleagues in the disciplines of government and politics, history, and law. So many have been of so much help that it would be presumptuous to attempt to list them all. But I should like to acknowledge specifically, and with particular gratitude, the unfailingly wise counsel and support extended to me through the years of gestation by Professors Robert J. Harris, David Fellman, Wallace Mendelson,

Alpheus Thomas Mason, and William M. Beaney. They were always there—be it for a quick quaere or as a sounding board, or as a critic. For invaluable aid in the formative stages of the project I am lastingly indebted to my former student and subsequent colleague, René Peritz, without whose tireless efforts it would never have gotten under way and without whose dedication it would never have come to fruition.

Acknowledged with genuine affection are the research assistants who do the legwork and the typists who produce the manuscript. The research assistants were Peter B. Harkins, Rocco D'Amico, Robert G. Badal, Paul Lutzker, Judith F. Lang, Gilbert E. Geldon, Steven S. Fadem, Norman H. Levine, Mark A. Aronchick, Frank C. Lindgren, Andrew B. Cohn, Perri Beth Madow, Susan J. Dlott, Michael E. Marino, James J. Magee, Michael K. Duffey, John W. Epperson, and Eston E. Melton. Those who so faithfully did the typing were, above all, Rosemary Cicchetti, and Theresa L. Brunson, Marie M. Cross, Bonnie L. Foster, Edna C. Mitchell, Cora L. Pitts, and Lena G. Garrison.

There remains a special thank you to two mainstays at the Oxford University Press: to my superb editor, James C. Amon, whose expertise, encouragement, and insight were essential; and to Joyce Berry, whose sensitivity, literateness, and intelligence atoned for her omnipotent red pencil. I could not have written the book without their dedication.

More than in any other of my writings to date I hasten to post the obvious caveat: that all errors are my own responsibility.

Keswick, Virginia H. J. A.
January 1974

Contents

JUSTICES
AND
PRESIDENTS

1

Introductory Reflections:

Of Criteria, Evaluations, and Judgments

Any effort, such as this work, to establish criteria for standards of merit as a basis for selection of individuals qualified to serve on our courts is not only difficult, it is definitionally controversial. The same fact of life applies to an attempt to evaluate a jurist's performance and to render a judgment in terms of both the jurist-nominator's perception and the perceptions of qualified Court watchers. Still, establishment of criteria for qualification and selection and for bases for evaluative judgments of performance cannot be escaped, and the ensuing pages will endeavor to meet the challenge.

Notwithstanding vast differences in approaches to perceived standards of qualification for judicial office and in ultimate verdicts of performance in that office, any examination of published (or verbalized) analyses demonstrates a remarkable degree of agreement, both as to definitions of what constitutes merit and to on-bench performance judgments. Although prescription of merit may well lie, like smut, in the eye of the beholder, and judgments of performance may well be tailored to the observer's *Weltanschauung,* demonstrable consensus exists in both realms.

It is, hence, not at all impossible to advance certain standards that, at least in theory, ought to govern eligibility, regardless of the degree to which a President's motivation may permit such standards to play a governing role in his decision to make a particular appointment. Thus, Professor Sheldon Goldman, a close observer of the judicial selection process—particularly at the trial and intermediate appellate levels—identified, in a recent *Annals* article,[1] "eight qualities, characteristics, or traits that most," or so he argued warmly, "would agree are associated with the ideal type of a judge." The eight are, in his language: "1. Neutrality as to the Parties in Litigation. 2. Fair-mindedness. 3. Being Well Versed in the Law. 4. Ability to Think and Write Logically and Lucidly. 5. Personal Integrity. 6. Good Physical and Mental Health. 7. Judicial Temperament. 8. Ability to Handle Judicial Power Sensibly." It is hard to argue with the octet. To apply it to specific instances of selection, however, makes for considerably more complexity and introduces controversy in at least some of the stated components. The same observation may well apply to the somewhat shorter roster of six components of merit I had suggested as *de minimis* qualification guidelines in the Seventh Annual Address to the Supreme Court Historical Society in 1982:[2]

> One, demonstrated judicial temperament. Two, professional expertise and competence. Three, absolute personal as well as professional integrity. Four, an able, agile, lucid mind. Five, appropriate professional educational background or training. Six, the ability to communicate clearly, both orally and in writing, especially the latter.[3]

Others have amply voiced similar requirements and qualifications.

And that the above may be broadly attainable in whole or in part is demonstrated by the composite of the 101 men and the lone woman who have to date sat on our Supreme Court of the United States. If the Holmesian tongue-in-cheek aphorism that the job of a jurist requires a "combination of Justinian, Jesus Christ and John Marshall"[4] may not always have been attainable—it is apposite to note that with one possible exception even that trio may not have been perfect! If political party affiliation has almost always played a role—well, there are but nine positions on the highest bench—F.D.R. had to wait four and one half years ere a vacancy occurred at last!—and there are just as many qualified Democrats as there are qualified Republicans, and just as many qualified Republicans as there are qualified Democrats. Nor is there any gainsaying a nominator's justification to select a nominee with whom he or she is ideologically and jurisprudentially comfortable, always assuming the presence of threshold merit.

It may be helpful to identify what history demonstrates as the ascertainable decisional reasons or motivations for the Presidential selections of members of the Supreme Court. A quartet of steadily occurring criteria would appear to emerge quite clearly, notwithstanding specific assertions or analyses to the contrary. In no particular order of avowal or significance, that quartet embraces: first, objective merit; second, personal friendship; third, balancing "representation" or "representativeness" on the Court; and fourth, "real" political and ideological compatibility.[5] Obviously, more than one of these factors—and, indeed, sundry others—were present in most nominations to the Court, and in some cases all four were. Yet it is entirely possible to point to one as the overriding one. Thus, a classic and well-known illustration of Presidential selection based purely on the first category, objective merit *qua* merit, is that of Democrat Benjamin Nathan Cardozo by Republican Herbert Hoover to succeed Justice Holmes early in 1932. That public opinion and Senatorial insistence practically had to put the President on a rack to prompt him to choose Cardozo is beside the point. He did—and he would ultimately be credited for it as "the finest act of his career as President."[6]

Examples that point to the second category, that is, personal and political friendship as the overriding causation for Presidential choice, abound. Among the several illustrations that come to mind quickly, yet were nonetheless unquestionably characterized by merit, is President Andrew Jackson's selection—or, more accurately, selections—of Roger Brooke Taney for Associate Justice (unsuccessful) and Chief Justice (successful). Taney had been Jackson's long-time close friend, loyal adviser, and confidant. President Truman's four appointments (Harold H. Burton, Fred M. Vinson, Tom C. Clark, and Sherman Minton) fall into this category, as do, to cite three other Chief Executives: those by

William Howard Taft of Horace H. Lurton, by John F. Kennedy of Byron R. White, and by Lyndon B. Johnson of Abe Fortas.

The third category, the "representation" or "representativeness" of a putative selectee, has become increasingly prevalent. Thus, such "representative" or "equitable" factors as race, gender, religion, and geography never fail to be advanced as a major consideration, sometimes as the controlling one. Among a host of illustrations are the recent selections of Thurgood Marshall (race) and Sandra Day O'Connor (gender) by Presidents Lyndon B. Johnson and Ronald W. Reagan, respectively; President Lincoln's fruitful search for "an outstanding trans-Mississippi lawyer" (he found him in Samuel F. Miller); President Cleveland's insistence on "geographic appropriateness" in the person of his new Chief Justice, Melville W. Fuller of Illinois (to date thirty-one of the fifty states have been "represented"–see Table 4, Ch. 4, *infra*); and President McKinley's choice of Joseph McKenna (religion–see Table 5, Ch. 4, *infra*).

The fourth, political and ideological compatibility, has arguably been *the* controlling factor. It has been that demonstrably in a large majority of instances, and understandably so. The legion of examples includes, for one, President Harding's Chief Justice Taft-inspired selection of ex-U.S. Senator and Congressman George Sutherland from Utah (one of the very few of foreign birth–England–to reach the Court). An experienced lawyer as well as legislator, Sutherland allied himself with Harding when the two served together in the U.S. Senate, the association culminating in the role of brain-truster to the President. He could have had any position in the latter's Administration; but he preferred to accept spot trouble-shooting assignments at home and abroad–in the frank anticipation of a Court vacancy.

Perhaps one ought to recognize a fifth factor: speaking to a capacity audience at the Annual Dinner of the American Law Institute on May 19, 1983, Justice O'Connor chose as her topic the processes of selection of Supreme Court Justices. Rather than offering her personal impressions of how these processes worked with respect to herself, she, instead, provided a lively survey of their historical development. Her conclusion was that:

> while there are many supposed criteria for the selection of a Justice, when the eventual decision is made as to who the nominee will be, that decision from the nominee's viewpoint is probably a classic example of being thc right person in the right spot at the right time. Stated simply, you must be lucky.

She added:

> That certainly is how I view my nomination, and I think that would be the view of most or at least many of those who have preceded me in their appointment to the Court. I never thought about it as a possibility. It is something you do not seek. It comes or it does not. However, despite what has often been the virtual accidental choice of Justices, the Court has been, by and large, in Madison's words, "a bench happily filled."

As subsequent discussion will demonstrate, it is axiomatic that far more than any other nominations to the federal bench, those to the highest tribunal in the land are not only theoretically, but by and large actually, made with a considerable degree of *scienter* by the Chief Executive. This may well not be true with regard to the initial "fingering" of the candidate, but once the percolating nominating process of a Supreme Court aspirant has reached its penultimate stage, the President–twenty-three of our thirty-nine presidents (sixty percent) were lawyers–*knows* the person he is about to submit to the Senate's confirmation tasks. Even President Harding knew something about his nominees–although a good case could be made for the contention that his selections were in effect made, cleared, or at least not vetoed, by his Chief Justice, William Howard Taft. As President, the latter was intimately acquainted with the profiles of the six he sent to the Court–three of whom, incidentally, were avowed Democrats. President Washington insisted on a veritable Wassermann test *cum smorgasbord* of six essential criteria for his record-setting number of Supreme Court appointments. After having made what he would later categorize as "my two biggest mistakes–and they are both on the Supreme Court,"[7] President Eisenhower insisted on being fully *au courant* of the characteristics and qualifications-in-his-image of the other three appointments fate permitted him. Although President Nixon fortunately did not get what he wanted by way of his ill-fated nominations for the second vacancy on the Court, it was assuredly not for lack of trying. Although the Nixon tapes record Keystone Cops-like references to "Renchquist" and "Renchburg,"[8] the President was fully alive to the cosmos of nominees Rehnquist and Powell. President Truman knew very well why he chose his four arguably less-than-jurisprudentially-distinguished appointees, Burton, Vinson, Clark, and Minton: he knew them well personally and professionally; they were his friends; they were political allies; they were tried-and-true Democrats—or, in Senator Burton's case, a compatible and reasonable Republican. With the exception of aspects of Justice Clark's on-bench performance, Truman would not be disappointed in his expectations. President Kennedy, aided and encouraged by his Attorney General brother, personally selected his two appointees, Byron R. White and Arthur J. Goldberg. This was not the case with President Ford's sole designee, John Paul Stevens, but Ford's faith in the judgment of his able Attorney General, Edward Levi, was abiding. President Reagan had neither met nor heard of Sandra Day O'Connor—nor, for that matter, had anyone else close to him—but she was highly recommended by two sitting Justices he could trust eminently, namely Chief Justice Burger and Justice Rehnquist, and she richly fitted the prescriptive needs of the contemporary political scene. In sum, in more or less understandable, indeed, all but necessary, contrast to lower federal bench selections, a President makes a reasonable effort to know *who* he is about to send to the Supreme Court, *why* he is doing so, and what he *expects* of his choice's performance once on the highest court—to which the sage Alexis de Tocqueville had commented a century and a half ago that "no other nation ever constituted so powerful a judiciary as the Americans[9] . . . [without which] the Constitution would be a dead letter."[10] De Tocqueville was fully alive to Hamilton's famed *Federalist Papers'* (No. 78) half-accuracy, namely, that because the Court's only power is the power to persuade, the purse and sword being in other hands, the Court constitutes government's "least dangerous branch." Yet he correctly perceived the Court's powerful claims not only to authenticity, but to its very real clout–as history has amply demonstrated.

An examination of how the members of the Supreme Court have been ranked or rated by informed Court watchers points to the complexities of establishing agreed-on criteria, yet as contended earlier, it also indicates a remarkable degree of agreement–which is especially remarkable given the subjectiveness of judgments based on elusive criteria. One of the first formal professional attempts to organize an evaluation of the performance of the first ninety-six individual Justices (through Thurgood Marshall) was designed by law professors Albert P. Blaustein of Rutgers University and Roy M. Mersky of the University of Texas in 1970. Enlisting sixty-five law school deans and professors of law, history, and political science (of whom I was privileged to be one), the project asked each participant–all of whom were presumed to be experts on the Court and its personnel–to "grade" each of the ninety-six Justices on a continuum from "great" (A), through "near great" (B), "average" (C), "below average" (D), and "failure" (E). Other than these five categories, neither criteria, yardstick, nor measuring rods were provided to the participants to assist in making the appraisals. We were left to our own judgmental devices within the self-perceived parameters of those five adjectives, although we were invited to provide supplementary explanatory remarks. The undertaking (published as Appendix A, *infra,* and also in 1978 in book form by the coauthors of the project)[11] produced twelve "greats," fifteen "near greats," fifty-five "average," six "below average," and eight "failures." Only one, Chief Justice John Marshall, received all sixty-five votes under the rubric of "great"; next came Justice Brandeis with sixty-two, followed in third place by Justice Holmes with sixty-one; Justice Black was a distant fourth with forty-two. The remaining eight of the twelve ranked as "great" were, in chronological order, Story, Taney, Harlan I, Hughes, Stone, Cardozo, Frankfurter, and Warren.

Despite the amorphousness and disputability of the notion of "greatness" in a Justice–a century ago, Chief Justice Horace Gray of the Supreme Court of Massachusetts deliberately used the adjective "great" to characterize John Marshall as "the greatest Judge in the language"[12]—those categorized as such by the sixty-five raters had, in their considered judgment, made significant, readily recognizable, indeed, seminal contributions to the development or identification of constitutional law. There was wide agreement that a mark of "greatness" on the Supreme Court was, as Blaustein and Mersky put it well several years later, the combined result of several qualities:

> Scholarship; legal learning and analytical powers; craftsmanship and technique; wide general knowledge and learning; character, moral integrity and impartiality; diligence and industry; the ability to express oneself orally with clarity, logic, and compelling force; openness to change, courage to take unpopular decisions; dedication to the Court as an institution and to the office of Supreme Court justice; ability to carry a proportionate share of the Court's responsibility in opinion writing; and finally, the quality of statesmanship.[13]

It is noteworthy that thirteen years earlier than the above-described project, Justice Felix Frankfurter offered *his* list of "greats" (even so precise a linguist as he offered no substitute for that categorization!) on the occasion of a celebrated address at the University of Pennsylvania, "The Supreme Court in the Mirror of Justices."[14] He excluded all those appointed *after* 1932, and, thus, three F.D.R. appointees who would be listed as "great" in the Blaustein and Mersky rankings, namely, Black, F.F. himself, and Stone, plus the one Eisenhower appointee, Warren. Frankfurter's rather more generous roster comprised the other eight "greats" from the Blaustein and Mersky group, to which he added eleven others: Justices W. Johnson, Curtis, Campbell, Miller, Field, Bradley, Matthews, Brewer, Brown, E. D. White, and Moody (of whom six—W. Johnson, Curtis, Miller, Field, Bradley, and E. D. White—would be rated "near great" in the 1970 Blaustein and Mersky study and the other five "average"). Four years after F.F.'s list, Judge Jerome Frank, another ardent Supreme Court scholar-observer, issued his list of rank-perceptions, which was a somewhat longer one still, but which also excluded all post-1932 appointees. The Frank list's top choices included, as had

Frankfurter's, all of the *pre*-1932 "greats" designated by the Blaustein and Mersky poll, and it embraced all of Frankfurter's additional eleven except Matthews, Brown, and E. D. White, none of whom, it will be recalled, had been among the twelve "greats" of the Blaustein and Mersky group.

That there is indeed a rather wide, general index of agreement on what constitutes "greatness" on the Court, in terms of its individual members, is demonstrated by several considerably more recent roster-polls, for example, in 1978,[15] 1979,[16] and 1983,[17] that relied on Court experts. As had the aforementioned earlier ones (and some others in the interim[18]), they patently confirm the now evidently well-established and recognized roster of "greats." That evidence prompted the *American Bar Association Journal* to publish its authoritative list. In a gaily colored article in 1983, entitled "The All-Time All-Star All-Era Supreme Court,"[19] its "Supreme Court Nine" of "greats" comprised, in chronological order, John Marshall, Story, Taney, Holmes, Hughes, Brandeis, Cardozo, Black, and Warren.

One may grant that "greatness" is not quantifiable, yet the evidence is persuasive that the term or concept is not only a meaningful one in the eyes of qualified observers of the judicial function at its apex, but that there is something closely akin to consensus among them—observers who represent the gamut of the sociopolitical and professional spectrum. Those at the seat of power of the nominating and appointment process will, in other words, be in a position to opt for merit, the highest form of which will be along the lines outlined earlier in these pages. Should the decision be for something less than that, as it has been indubitably from time to time, that is of course attainable too. Although it is impossible to foretell future on-bench performance—as so many Presidents have found out, often to their chagrin and sometimes to their delight—an established record and profile of *potential* appointees is assuredly not unattainable. Simply to brush off clarion calls for merit-basis appointments on the grounds of eye of the beholder is at best a crude oversimplification and at worst intellectually dishonest.

The ensuing chapters represent an attempt to analyze and

evaluate the motivations that underlie the process of Presidential selection and appointment, the degree and kind of fulfillment of Presidential hopes or expectations, and the professional performance of those entrusted with the responsibilities of the business of judging.

2

The Nixon Era:
A Turbulent Case Study

For three and one-half years, from June 1968 until December 1971, the attention of the American public was drawn to the highest court of the land more closely than at any time since the epic Court-packing battle between Franklin D. Roosevelt and the U.S. Senate in 1937. On June 26, 1968, President Lyndon B. Johnson announced Chief Justice Earl Warren's intention to resign from the seat he had occupied since 1953 and the nomination of Associate Justice Abe Fortas as his successor. It was a historical event, the start of a fascinating epoch of political maneuvering that would not be resolved until December 10, 1971, when William H. Rehnquist was confirmed as an Associate Justice of the Supreme Court 68:26, a less than overwhelming margin. When the Senate, after more than three months of partisan and often acrimonious debate, had defeated a motion to terminate floor debate to vote on the Fortas nomination in the fall of 1968, Fortas requested the President to withdraw his name from further consideration. In turn, the Chief Justice withdrew his resignation, commenting: "[S]ince they wouldn't confirm Abe they will have me." And so "they" did for another full term of Court until late May 1969, when Earl Warren did step down and was replaced by Warren Earl Burger, a judge of the U.S. Court of Appeals for the District of Columbia. Burger's investiture was President Richard M. Nixon's first of four successful nominations–but the four came from a total of eight attempts.

Judge Burger, sixty-one years old at the time of his appointment and of impeccable Republican credentials, was the prototype of the kind of individual Presidential candidate Nixon had promised the country he would nominate to the bench on his election: one whose work on the Court would "strengthen the peace forces as against the criminal forces of the land"; one who would have an appreciation of the basic tenets of "law and order," being "thoroughly experienced and versed in the criminal laws of the country"; one who would see himself as a "caretaker" of the Constitution and not as a "super-legislator with a free hand to impose . . . social and political view-points upon the American people"; one who was a "strict constructionist" of the basic document; and one who had had broad experience as an appeals judge on a lower judicial level. Burger's confirmation by a vote of 74:3 was both speedy and decisive. The President was jubilant: not only had *his* candidate overcome the hurdle of Senate confirmation with all but *pro forma* ease, but he now had a second vacancy to fill.

Earlier, in May of 1969, Justice Fortas, under intense public and private attack as a result of revelations concerning his relationship with convicted financier Louis E. Wolfson, had resigned from the Court–the first Supreme Court jurist to do so under that type of pressure. Fortas had broken no law, and he fervidly protested his innocence; but his highly questionable judgment and the integrity and prestige of the Court had clearly mandated his move. The not-inconsiderable number of Warren Court haters in the Senate were delighted, and the President–again publicly citing his criteria for Supreme Court nominees–accepted Attorney General John N. Mitchell's suggestion of Chief Judge Clement F. Haynsworth, Jr., of the U.S. Court of Appeals for the Fourth Circuit. Haynsworth was a native of South Carolina and a Harvard Law School alumnus. To his basic specifications Mr. Nixon had added the desire of choosing a Southern jurist of conservative judicial bent. Of course the Court already had at least one Southern strict constructionist, indeed a constitutional literalist of the first magnitude, in the person of the distinguished Justice Hugo Lafayette Black of Alabama, but that was not exactly what the President had in mind. Judge Haynsworth, an able jurist meriting a *"B"* in the minds of most Court watchers, fit all of the President's specifications to date and, perhaps even more significantly, those of such influential incumbent Southern Senators as Strom Thurmond (R.-S.C.), James O. Eastland (D.-Miss.), and John L. McClellan (D.-Ark.).

Indeed, most of the Senate seemed disposed to confirm Judge Haynsworth for the Fortas vacancy. But to the President's anger, frustration, and embarrassment, the hearings of the Senate Committee on the Judiciary provided clear evidence of the nominee's patent insensitivity to some financial and conflict-of-interest improprieties. Apparently, as with Fortas, no actual legal infractions had taken place–but how could the Senate confirm Haynsworth when it had played such an admirable activist-moralist role in causing Fortas's resignation? It could not, and among those who vocally opposed the South Carolinian and voted against his confirmation were such anti-Fortas, "strict-constructionist" leaders as Senators Robert Griffin (R.-Mich.) and Jack Miller (R.-Iowa). Down went the Haynsworth nomination by a vote of 55:45 on November 21, 1969–largely for the reasons indicated, although the candidate had also drawn considerable fire from labor and minority groups for allegedly anti–civil libertarian and anti–civil rights stands. A livid President Nixon, however, chose to lay the blame for his nominee's defeat on "anti-Southern, anti-conservative, and anti-constructionist" prejudice. He vowed to select another "worthy and distinguished protagonist" of Southern, conservative, and strict-constructionist persuasion.

To the dismay of those Senators who had counseled confirmation of Judge Haynsworth, lest a successor-nominee be even less worthy of the high post, the President–again on the recommendation of his Attorney General–quickly countered by nominating Judge G. Harrold Carswell of Florida, a little-known and little-distinguished ex-U.S. District Court judge with six months of experience on the U.S. Court of Appeals for the Fifth Circuit. "He is almost too good to be true," Mr. Mitchell was reported to have said.[1] The appointment was an act of vengeance—one intended to teach the Senate a lesson and to downgrade the Court. The Senate, intimidated by the President and the Attorney General, was clearly disposed to confirm him. But suspicious reporters and researchers soon cast serious doubt on that "almost too good to be true" rating of the nominee. Immediately damaging was the discovery of a statement Carswell made to a meeting of the American Legion on August 2, 1948, while running for a seat in the Georgia legislature: "I yield to no man as a fellow candidate or as a fellow citizen in the firm, vigorous belief in the principles of White Supremacy, and I shall always be so governed."[2] To be sure, the nominee, pointing to his youth and inexperience (he was twenty-eight at the time), now disavowed that statement and any racism as well. But an examination of his record on the bench cast further doubt on his objectivity in racial matters: while serving as U.S. Attorney in Florida, Carswell had been involved in the transfer of a public, municipally owned Tallahassee golf course, built with $35,000 of federal funds, to the status of a private club. The transfer was obviously designed to circumvent a contemporary Supreme Court decision proscribing segregation in municipal recreation facilities.

Still, the Administration appeared to have the votes for Senate confirmation, given the vivid memories of the Haynsworth battle, the intensive wooing of doubtful Senators by the White House and the Justice Department, and the natural predisposition to give the President his choice, all things being equal. But things were far from equal, for as the Carswell opponents continued their attack, it became apparent that—quite apart from the controversy surrounding his civil rights record—the candidate was patently inferior, simply on the basis of fundamental juridical and legal qualifications. If Judge Haynsworth had merited a "*B*," Judge Carswell scarcely merited a "*D*" on the scale of relevant ability. Nonetheless, Senator Roman Hruska (R.-Neb.), the President's floor manager of the nomination, made a pathetic fumbling attempt to convert the candidate's mediocrity into an asset: "Even if he is mediocre there are a lot of mediocre judges and people and lawyers. They are entitled to a little representation, aren't they, and a little chance? We can't have all Brandeises, Cardozos, and Frankfurters, and stuff like that there."[3] Hruska's remarkable assertion was seconded by Carswell-supporter Senator Russell Long (D.-La.), who observed: "Does it not seem to the Senator that we have had enough of those upside down, corkscrew thinkers? Would it not appear that it might be well to take a B student or a C student who was able to think straight, compared to one of those A students who are capable of the kind of thinking that winds up getting us a 100-percent increase in crime in this country?"[4]

This line of argument failed to convince the doubtful Senators. Instead, they became increasingly aware of the lack of ability of the nominee—who, among other debilitating features, held the dubious record of having been reversed by appellate courts more than any of the other then-sitting federal jurists except seven! Yale Law School Dean Louis H. Pollak styled the Carswell nomination as one of "more slender credentials than any Supreme Court nominee put forth in this century."[5] Perhaps even more tellingly, the distinguished legal scholar William Van Alstyne, Professor of Law at Duke University, opposed the nomination. Van Alstyne, an ardent and vocal backer of the Haynsworth nomination, now testified: "There is, in candor, nothing in the quality of the nominee's work to warrant any expectation whatever, that he could serve with distinction on the Supreme Court of the United States."[6] When the final vote on confirmation came on April 9, 1970—three months after the nomination—the President's choice went down by a vote of 51:45. Among the noes were such significant Republican votes as those of Margaret Chase Smith of Maine, Winston L. Prouty of Vermont, Marlow W. Cook of Kentucky, and Richard S. Schweiker of Pennsylvania.

It was indeed a bitter defeat for the President. Not only had he seen two nominees rejected within less than five months, but his carefully devised "Southern strategy" had suffered a serious blow. His reaction was swift and vitriolic. Conveniently ignoring the basic issues for his candidates' defeat, he blamed it instead on sectional prejudice, abject politics, and philosophical negations. And he told the country:

> I have reluctantly concluded that—with the Senate as presently constituted—I cannot successfully nominate to the Supreme Court any federal appellate judge from the South who believes as I do in the strict construction of the Constitution. . . . Judges Carswell and Haynsworth have endured with admirable dignity vicious assaults on their intelligence, their honesty, and their character. . . . When all the hypocrisy is stripped away, the real issue was their philosophy of strict construction of the Constitution—a philosophy that I share.[7]

Quite to the contrary, several distinguished federal jurists in the South were eminently qualified to serve, jurists who, indeed, shared the President's philosophy of government and politics and whom the Senate assuredly would have confirmed. It could not, in good conscience—given the Fortas precedent, the public concern, and the nature and role of the Supreme Court—have confirmed Haynsworth and Carswell, especially not Carswell. The latter, in an ironic footnote, was soon to be defeated by his constituents in the Florida Senatorial primary, during which he was photographed with a lettered sign around his neck, "Heah Come de Judge." It is an intriguing thought that had Haynsworth been nominated *after* Carswell he might well have been confirmed. Indeed, whereas Carswell—who resigned his judgeship to enter private law practice—would within a few years find himself in several brushes with the criminal law, Judge Haynsworth continued to provide distinguished service in the Fourth U.S. Court of Appeals as its Chief Judge for sixteen years, until he assumed senior status in 1981.

President Nixon followed up his blast against the rejections with the petulant suggestion, in a publicized letter to Senator William B. Saxbe (R.-Ohio), that the Senate had denied him the right to see his choices appointed. That right, he insisted, had been accorded all previous presidents—a patently false statement: since 1789, 27 of the 139 nominees formally sent to the Senate for confirmation have been rejected—close to 1 out of 5 candidates (1 out of 3 in the nineteenth century). Moreover, the President's collateral suggestion to Saxbe and the nation that Senatorial advice and consent to nominations (expressly provided for in ARTICLE II, SECTION 2, PARAGRAPH 2 of the Constitution) is merely a *pro forma* requirement, is utterly incorrect with regard to nominations to the judiciary. Mr. Nixon, who was fully familiar with the contrary judgment of practically all students of constitutional law and history as well as with Hamilton's equally contrary assertions in *The Federalist Papers* (No. 76 and No. 77), must have known how wrong he was. His anger and frustrations were understandable, but his historical misstatement was a distinct disservice to country, Constitution, and Court. Three years after his enforced resignation from the Presidency in 1974, Nixon conceded publicly that it had been a mistake to push the Carswell nomination through. But he insisted that the former federal judge had shown "no hint of racism in his decisions" and that it had been unfair for critics to attack Carswell for a racist speech he had made twenty-two years earlier, which, the former President added in Nixonese language, "he should have made which most Southerners were making at that time."[8]

In the early spring of 1970, announcing that the Senate would never confirm a Southern strict constructionist, President Nixon now turned to a Northerner, Harry A. Blackmun, sixty-one, of Minnesota, judge of the U.S. Court of Appeals for the Eighth Circuit. An old and close friend and presumed ideological ally of Chief Justice Burger, Blackmun had served for eleven years on the federal bench. His nomination was as anticlimactic as it was noncontroversial. To the relief of the Senate he appeared to have impeccable credentials and, although he did not rank with the country's most distinguished jurists, he was quickly confirmed on May 12 by a vote of 94:0.

It was too late for Blackmun to participate in the remaining decisions of the 1969–1970 term of Court, which had functioned with but eight Justices since May 1969, but at last the Fortas seat had been filled! There would be no further vacancies for fifteen months, but when they came, President Nixon would find himself in another and multiple imbroglio.

In September 1971 terminal illness compelled the retirements of Justices Hugo Lafayette Black and John Marshall Harlan II, the two most influential figures then serving on the highest bench. Both were veritable giants of the law, often on different jurisprudential tracks, but imbued with dedication, intelligence, and judicial excellence. Their places would be incredibly hard to fill, and the President would have to search long and diligently for worthy successors. Yet he did neither. Instead, he resorted to the trial-balloon method and had names leaked to the press.

Thus, in early October it became apparent that his first choice was Republican Representative Richard H. Poff of Virginia. Although Poff had less than two years' experience in legal practice, he was an able and fair member of the House Committee on the Judiciary and apparently filled the President's "Southern seat" prescriptions. But reporters were quick to uncover civil rights skeletons in the Poff closet—such as his signature on the anti-*Brown* v. *Board of Education of Topeka*[9] decision by 101 members of Congress from the eleven Southern states, known as "The Southern Manifesto: Declaration of Constitutional Principles."[10] Although the Senate might have confirmed him given his overall ability and his popularity among his colleagues, it would not have done so without a battle. Poff asked the President to withdraw his name from consideration to save his family and himself from an embarrassing, damaging experience. (In 1972 he resigned from Congress to become a Justice of the Supreme Court of Virginia, that state's highest tribunal.)

The President now decided to send for appraisal a list of six potential nominees to the Committee on Judiciary of the American Bar Association (A.B.A.), the influential group that had endorsed the Haynsworth and Carswell candidacies. The list, which was widely publicized in the media, was singularly marginal in terms of distinction and stature. It was headed by California State Court of Appeals Judge Mildred Lillie (the first woman to be considered formally for a Supreme Court nomination) and Arkansas municipal-bond lawyer Herschel H. Friday, a good friend of Attorney General and Mrs. John N. Mitchell, and recommended by Chief Justice Burger and Justice Blackmun. The other four potential nominees were Sylvia Bacon, a judge on the Superior Court of the District of Columbia (seven months of bench experience) and part-author of the no-knock search and preventive-detention provisions of the District of Columbia's crime bill of 1967–1968; Senator Robert C. Byrd (D.-W.Va.)—then (although later in his career in the upper house no longer) a long-time opponent of civil rights legislation and an ex-member of the Ku Klux Klan—although a graduate of night law school, he had never practiced law and had not been admitted to the bar; and two recent Nixon appointees to the U.S. Court of Appeals for the Fifth Circuit, Charles Clark of Mississippi and Paul H. Roney of Florida, with a combined total of three years of judicial experience. It is not surprising that the President's selections were widely criticized as manifesting a "relentless pursuit of mediocrity," triggering a nationwide uproar, with thirty-four members of the Harvard Law School faculty signing a petition protesting the nominees. The A.B.A., in an uncharacteristically frank statement, urged the President to "add some people with stature," and its Committee on Judiciary quickly ranked the Administration's two top choices, Judge Lillie and Mr. Friday, "unqualified" (11:1) and "not opposed" (6:6), respectively. When the Committee's action became public—it and the Department of Justice accused each other of leaking the data to the media—the President angrily withdrew the list of "The Six," and the Attorney General announced that the President—who had exclaimed "- - - - the A.B.A.!"[11]—would no longer submit Supreme Court nominees (as contrasted with lower federal judicial candidates) to the Committee for rating purposes. The Committee, in turn, announced that it would not be prevented from issuing evaluative postnomination commentaries on its own motion.

In a dramatic television broadcast President Nixon subsequently revealed to the country his "formal" nominees, whom he had evidently held in reserve. Possibly, as a number of commentators charged, he had not really expected support of his initial slate and assuredly not of the first two—although the Administration indignantly and conceivably quite truthfully denied any such assumption. There is, indeed, little if any doubt that he wanted to send Lillie and Friday to the Court! The two new selectees were of infinitely higher caliber than "The Six." This was especially true of the person the President identified first, Lewis F. Powell, Jr., of Richmond, Virginia. Powell—who had repeatedly declined the proffered nomination—was a past-President of the A.B.A., a distinguished member of the legal profession in the Harlan II mold, with recorded views on criminal justice and governmental "paternalism" akin to those of the President. Here then was the President's "Southern strict constructionist"! And not only was his designation received enthusiastically, but it was confirmed rapidly by a vote of 89:1, the sole negative vote being cast by maverick Senator Fred R. Harris (D.-Okla.). It was, thus, crystal clear that the Senate would not refuse to confirm a qualified nominee from the South.

For the second vacancy Mr. Nixon nominated a far more controversial figure: the relatively youthful (forty-seven) William H. Rehnquist of Arizona, a U.S. Assistant Attorney General. Rehnquist was a brilliant ideological conservative who had been one of Senator Barry Goldwater's chief aides in the latter's unsuccessful 1964 campaign for the Presidency. Rehnquist's career had been chiefly political, but his legal credentials were considerable, including graduation at the top of his class at Stanford University School of Law and a stint as a law clerk on the Supreme Court to Justice Robert H. Jackson—one of the truly coveted posts for a young attorney. A fine lawyer with a quick, lucid mind, he stood considerably to the right of both Powell and perhaps the President himself. It was, thus, not surprising that his nomination would engender opposition from a number of segments in and out of the Senate—including the American Civil Liberties Union, which for the first time in its fifty-two-year history formally fought a nominee for public office. Rehnquist came under strong attack, especially for his championship of such law-and-order issues as preventive detention, limited immunity against compulsory self-incrimination, no-knock police entries, and wiretappng and eavesdropping; for his hawkish defense posture and advocacy of broad-gauged Presidential war powers; and for his tough stance against street demonstrators. But these were, after all, ideological commitments shared by a great many members of the body politic—quite conceivably by a plurality. Thus, although his confirmation was delayed for a number of weeks, it came with a margin of forty-two votes in December 1971.

The country seemed to breathe a sigh of relief at being spared another Haynsworth/Carswell episode, which almost certainly would have resulted had the President persisted in selecting a nominee, let alone nominees, from "The Six." Had it not been for the many wounds sustained by the governmental and confidence process and had the preceding two years not been so potentially damaging to the prestige and posture of the Supreme Court, one might have regarded these struggles as a salutary educational experience for America's citizenry. They had certainly served to alert the public to both the substance and the procedure of the power struggle that periodically brushes the system of separation of powers and its attendant checks and balances. No such controversy would engulf the only two other subsequent Supreme Court nominations to date, President Ford's of John Paul Stevens in 1975 and President Reagan's of Sandra Day O'Connor in 1981.

3

How They Get There:
Appointing Supreme Court Justices

The question of the principles that govern the selection of the men and women who sit on our judicial tribunals is both a moral and a political one of the greatest magnitude. Their tasks and functions are awe inspiring, indeed, but it is as human beings and as participants in the political as well as the legal and governmental process that jurists render their decisions. Their position in the governmental framework must assure them of independence, dignity, and security of tenure. And at no other level is that more apposite than at the highest: the Supreme Court of the United States.[1]

No mystery, confusion, or *double entendre* obtains with respect to the intention of the Founding Fathers regarding the agreed-on language of the Constitution's ARTICLE II, which governs the mode of selection of jurists. It is in fact crystal clear: ARTICLE II, SECTION 2, PARAGRAPH 2 states crisply that the President

> . . . shall nominate, and, by and with the Advice and Consent of the Senate, shall appoint . . . Judges of the supreme Court. . . .

The provision means exactly what it says: it is the President's duty and responsibility to find and *nominate* candidates for the Supreme Court of the United States (as well as, of course, all lower federal judges) and that of a simple majority of the Senate to *consent* to such nominations (presumably, but not necessarily, having tendered *advice* along the way); or, failing to grant such consent, to reject, or to refuse to take action on, a Presidential nominee.

Although the question of the *methodology* to be employed for judicial appointments was subjected to intensive floor debate at the Constitutional Convention during twelve days spread over June, July, August, and September of 1787, be it noted that *criteria* for such appointments were neither debated nor did they appear to loom as a matter of either significance or puzzlement. Those few delegates who vocalized the issue of criteria at all, did so by assuming *viva voce* and *sub silentio* that *merit,* as opposed to favoritism, should and, indeed, would govern quite naturally. The central issue *cum* controversy concerned the degree of power to be vested in the executive and/or the degree of legislative participation. The above-quoted provision, finally agreed on as a result of debates on September 6, 7, and 15, represented a compromise between those who, like Benjamin Franklin, James Madison, and John Rutledge, feared "monarchical" tendencies in strong solo executive prerogatives on the issue and called for a potent legislative role, and those who, like James Wilson, Alexander Hamilton, and Gouverneur Morris, favored broadly independent executive appointive powers. It was the latter group that did most of the compromising, resulting in the largely James Madison-fashioned ultimate adoption of ART. II, SEC. 2, the provision having remained unchanged to this day. Nor is it likely to be changed.

If it may be validly considered as having been raised at all, the issue of judicial qualifications was addressed, however briefly, on June 5 by Doctor Franklin, who pointed to the Scottish mode of appointment "in which the nomination proceeded from the lawyers, who always selected the ablest of the profession in order to get rid of him, and share his practice among themselves."[2] If any concern about qualifications was subsequently expressed by delegates, it came all but inevitably in connection with the controversy over the role of the participatory political branch, ultimately the agreed-on Senatorial one, about which James Madison, for example, notwithstanding his support of legislative input, raised questions of "partiality." Delegates simply assumed, perhaps a mite naïvely, albeit quite understandably, that those selected as federal jurists would be chosen on the basis of merit. Period.

It is thus clear—with convenient 20/20 hindsight—that the Founding Fathers down on Fifth and Chestnut Streets in Philadelphia did not foresee the role political parties would soon come to play in the appointment process. Only John Adams among the notable contemporary statesmen—and he of course was not a member of the Constitutional Convention—visualized clearly the future rise of political parties and, as Joseph P. Harris put it well, "that partisan considerations rather than the fitness of nominees would often be the controlling consideration of the Senate in passing on nominations."[3] Historical dénouement has continued to underscore that political *raison d'être.*

Although many forces influence the judicial selection process today, the developing politics of federal judicial selection emphasize three major factors or considerations: (1) the need to take into account the wishes and the influence of public and private leaders with interests in a nomination; (2) the influential role of the American Bar Association's (A.B.A.'s) Standing Committee on Federal Judiciary (established 1945–1946), which has assumed a controversial, yet professional, evaluative posture in the nomination process and which has demonstrated considerable clout in that process since the mid-1950s; and (3) the advisory role played by sitting (and even retired) members of the bench, especially members of the Supreme Court, who would appear to be taking an increasingly influential part behind the scenes. Rare is the appointment in which these three factors do not now play a significant role.

The *first*-mentioned is the one most apparent to the general public. As a practical matter it is almost impossible for the Chief Executive to select and see confirmed a candidate for the federal bench without the approval of the political leaders of the candidate's own party. Approval by the home-state Senators of the nominee's political party is especially important, although under certain circumstances an influential home-state Senator of the opposite party—for example, an Everett McKinley Dirksen in the L.B.J. Administration or an L.B.J. in the Eisenhower Administration—may well be able to swing some weight too. The President might succeed in seeing his choice confirmed (absent outright Senatorial hostility) for the highest bench, which has always been regarded as the President's personal appointment preserve, but practically no such allowance is made for designees on the lower rungs of the judiciary. Should the President nonetheless persist in submitting a name that is not at least marginally acceptable to the candidate's home-state Senators, almost certainly the latter will invoke Senatorial courtesy, which means rather certain death to the candidacy. Senatorial courtesy dates back to the first years of the Republic when the Senate recognized the need for solidarity to prevent a President from appointing a Senator's political adversary to high office. Actually, it began in the very first session of Congress when George Washington nominated Benjamin Fishbourn as a naval officer in the Port of Savannah, Georgia. Although qualified, Fishbourn was opposed by Georgia's two U.S. Senators, and President Washington withdrew Fishbourn's nomination when it became apparent that the Senate would side with its Georgia colleagues. Subsequently Washington successfully nominated someone favored by the two legislators. Senatorial courtesy is, thus, based on the assumption that the Senate will jointly condemn an affront to one of its members by defeating the measure before it—provided, however, that the aggrieved member offers a reasonably cogent explanation. When the defeat of a judicial nominee is at stake, the condemnation customarily issued is that the nominee, or the manner in which he was chosen, is "personally obnoxious."

Numerous instances of the application of Senatorial courtesy are on record, with the practice at least partially accounting for rejection of several nominations to the Supreme Court. It appears to have been the sole factor in Grover Cleveland's unsuccessful nominations of William B. Hornblower (1893) and Wheeler H.

Peckham (1894), both of New York; the Senate successively rejected them by votes of 24:30 and 32:41, respectively. In each instance David B. Hill, Democratic Senator from New York, invoked Senatorial courtesy; Cleveland had snubbed Hill in his quest for a replacement for the seat vacated by Justice Samuel Blatchford of New York. Cleveland then had his revenge when he refused to name a third New Yorker to the vacancy–instead, he turned to the Democratic Majority Leader in the Senate, Edward D. White of Louisiana. Senatorial courtesy had also figured prominently in the defeat of Reuben H. Walworth of New York, a Tyler (Whig) nominee, in 1844 (21:26) and, although somewhat less so, in that of George W. Woodward of Pennsylvania, a Polk (Democrat) nominee, in 1845 (20:29). Both Senators from New York, Democrats Silas Wright, Jr., and Nathaniel P. Tallmadge, had opposed Walworth, and Independent Democratic Senator Simon Cameron had declared his fellow Pennsylvanian "personally objectionable."

Even so reasonable and eminently fair a public figure as Senator Paul H. Douglas (D.-Ill.) successfully invoked the spirit, if not the letter, of Senatorial courtesy in his 1951 battle to block Harry Truman's nominations of Illinois State Judges Joseph P. Drucker and Cornelius J. Harrington to two newly created judgeships in the Northern District for Illinois of the U.S. District Court. Although the matter involved lower federal court judges rather than appointments at the Supreme Court level, it well illustrates the potential clout of the concept of Senatorial courtesy. Douglas objected to both men chiefly on qualifications but also on other grounds. As the Senator explained to his colleagues:

> . . . Great as the knowledge of a President may be, he cannot, in the nature of things, in the vast majority of instances, know the qualifications of the lawyers and local judges within a given state as well as the Senators from that state. However excellent his general knowledge, the President does not have the detailed knowledge of the qualifications, background, and record of judges in a particular State. . . . I must reluctantly raise my objection to the appointment of these candidates because of the manner and method of their selection, and because the result

> would, in my judgment, be antagonistic to the cause of good government and the maintenance of a strong, independent judiciary.[4]

Backed by an overwhelming referendum in support of his position (and his own candidates) by the Illinois bar, he, thus, appealed to the courtesy of the Senate; its Judiciary Committee supported him unanimously, and the Senate itself sustained his position without even a roll call. Douglas had won his fight, but he had failed to convince the President to send up *his* two nominees, whose names he had "cleared" with Democratic party leaders and members of the Illinois bar six months earlier and forwarded to Attorney General J. Howard McGrath. The result was stalemate and a compromise candidate for one of the three existing vacancies—with Illinois being the loser by the presence of two continuing vacancies. Thus, it is clear that the Senate's power is a veto power—an awesome weapon, to be sure, but a negative one. True, some Senators of the President's own political party are possessed of such influence and power that often they will insist not only on the right of prior consultation and approval of the Presidential choice, but also on the right to choose lower federal judicial candidates. Yet it takes two to dance that particular political tango—and other interested parties are inevitably waiting to cut in. Still, the President courts defeat of his selection if he designedly antagonizes or deliberately fails to consult the fellow-party Senators concerned. Senatorial courtesy may well no longer be used as crassly and as indiscriminately as it once was, but it remains one of the three key considerations in the judicial nominating process.

A second factor—one that has gained recognition only in recent years—is the incontrovertible evidence of the influence of sitting (and retired) members of the judiciary. It has been apparent for some time that incumbents in district courts and in courts of appeal have been consulted about their possible future colleagues. Studies of biographical and autobiographical data, which have become increasingly available during the past two or three decades, make it clear that Presidents do also sporadically consult with Supreme Court Justices—most frequently with the Chief Justice—

for advice on future appointments. The initiative usually lies with the Chief Executive; yet it may also emanate from the Justices, as a mid-nineteenth-century event illustrates: in 1853 Associate Justices John Catron and Benjamin R. Curtis not only personally urged President Pierce to nominate John A. Campbell, but accompanied their plea with supportive letters from all of the remaining sitting Justices (regardless of political or sectional persuasion). Other Justices who lobbied prominently and successfully with Presidents in the last century include Robert C. Grier (for William Strong, 1870); Noah H. Swayne (for Joseph P. Bradley, also 1870); Morrison R. Waite (for William B. Woods, 1880); Samuel F. Miller (for David J. Brewer, 1889); and Henry B. Brown (for Howell E. Jackson, 1893). The Presidents involved were, respectively, Ulysses S. Grant (twice), Rutherford B. Hayes, and Benjamin Harrison (twice).

The champion influencer to date has unquestionably been William Howard Taft, the only person to have served both as President (1909–1913) and as Chief Justice of the United States (1921–1930). Taft actually coveted the latter post more than the Presidency—he was, in fact, infinitely happier as Chief Justice than as Chief Executive—but he was not about to relinquish his place as a leader of America's bar simply because of his elevation to the highest court. He had, after all, appointed six of its members while he was President, two of whom were still serving when he reached the Court. And Chief Justice Edward D. White, whom Taft ultimately succeeded, had been elevated by him to that post in 1910. Taft, on leaving the Presidency in 1913, began to establish a long record of rendering both solicited and unsolicited advice on judicial candidates, literally bombarding the Executive Branch with suggestions, and he assuredly did not stop when President Harding nominated him as Chief Justice in 1921.

Indeed, it is no exaggeration to maintain that Taft rather than Harding was basically responsible for selecting—or at the very least approving—three of the four individuals Harding sent to the Supreme Court before his death in 1923: George Sutherland (1922), Pierce Butler (1922), and William Howard Taft! Taft merely acquiesced in the President's choice of the fourth, Edward

T. Sanford. Taft's lobbying activities in his own behalf were perhaps matched only by his efforts on behalf of Pierce Butler—a classic illustration of Taft's influence over Harding, who seemed almost to fear him at times. Harding's Attorney General, Harry M. Daugherty, a Taft ally and no mean special-interest lobbyist himself, thus told Taft's brother, Henry, that the President "would not approve of anybody for appointment who was not approved by [the Chief Justice]."[5] And among those Taft successfully blocked as not having "sound views" or being of "our kind" was the great Judge Learned Hand of New York, whom Harding wanted to appoint to the Supreme Court in 1922. Taft himself had appointed Judge Hand to the U.S. District Court in 1909 (and would back his promotion by President Coolidge to the U.S. Court of Appeals for the Second Circuit in 1924). Another Taft victim was Benjamin N. Cardozo, who might "herd," or so Taft feared, with Justices Holmes and Brandeis. Cardozo did become a Supreme Court Justice—but not until 1932, after Taft's death. On the other hand, despite Herculean (and nasty) efforts, Taft failed to block President Wilson's contentious appointment of Louis Dembitz Brandeis in 1916.

Although Taft's power to influence the selection of jurists has been unmatched, other Justices have also been influential, notable among them four "Chiefs": Hughes, Stone, Warren, and Burger. Thus, Charles Evans Hughes successfully urged F.D.R. to promote Associate Justice Harlan F. Stone to Chief Justice when he stepped down in 1941. And President Truman asked Hughes (then retired) to come to the White House to talk with him about a successor to Stone when the latter died in 1946. When Oliver Wendell Holmes, Jr., stepped down in 1932, President Hoover consulted him on the candidacy of Stone's fellow New Yorker, Judge Benjamin N. Cardozo. Hoover, a reluctant dragon indeed on the Cardozo nomination, also asked Justice Stone for additional names, "just in case." Judge Learned Hand and Woodrow Wilson's Secretary of War, Newton D. Baker, were Stone's alternate choices. But Stone was convinced of Cardozo's superior qualifications and, suspecting the President's motives, sent him a string of memoranda and editorials extolling Cardozo in preference to the other two. He also tried hard to allay Hoover's political reservations concerning another "Brandeis co-religionist" on the Court. In fact, Stone went so far as to offer to resign from the Court to make room for Cardozo! But Hoover yielded. F.D.R. consulted with Stone before selecting Professor Felix Frankfurter, and Truman did likewise before he named Senator Harold H. Burton (R.-Ohio). Chief Justice Earl Warren was an influential participant in President Kennedy's decision to nominate Secretary of Labor Arthur J. Goldberg to succeed Justice Frankfurter on the bench—a choice evidently discussed with, and fully approved by, Frankfurter as well. Warren was also heavily involved in President Johnson's unsuccessful selection of Abe Fortas to succeed him in 1968—although L.B.J. was so completely committed to his longtime friend and confidant that any adverse reaction from the outgoing Chief would hardly have deterred him. Chief Justice Burger had a hand in both the successful and unsuccessful Nixon nominations to the Court, from his own in 1969 through those of Justices Powell and Rehnquist in 1971. He also was a partisan to the selection of the first woman to be sent to the highest tribunal, President Reagan's choice of Sandra Day O'Connor in 1981.

A third major factor to influence the process of judicial selection is the enormously influential role played by the Standing Committee on Federal Judiciary of the A.B.A. Established during President Truman's initial incumbency in 1945–1946 as the Special Committee on Federal Judiciary, its role in the selection of jurists was more or less formalized at the end of the Truman Administration through the determined efforts of Deputy Attorney General Ross B. Malone. The Committee has been utilized in varying degree by all Presidents since then. Its work represents a significant attempt to complement, if not replace, the "political" aspects of judicial selection with "professional" input, that is, input from the organized bar. The attempt has been crowned with considerable success. An obvious measure was Deputy Attorney General Richard Kleindienst's announcement to the A.B.A. convention in August 1969 that the Nixon Administration had "accorded" the Association's Federal Judiciary Committee absolute veto power over all federal candidates to the bench (Supreme Court excepted) it considered unqualified.[6] The Administration—which would quickly change its mind after the Haynsworth/Carswell episode![7]—even offered the same concession with respect to local judgeships in Washington, D.C., if the A.B.A. wanted it. The Kleindienst disclosure marked the high point of the A.B.A.'s effort formally to influence the selection of federal judges. It also signified an extraordinary delegation of executive constitutional power to a private agency, a delegation of executive responsibility that might well be questioned by students of the judicio-governmental process. Consultation with legal or other professional groups is a valid function, but the responsibility for choosing the candidates for judicial office is clearly delegated to the President in ART. II and ART. III of the Constitution.

The A.B.A. represents fewer than half of the nation's lawyers, and a relatively narrow segment of the "legal establishment" demonstrably dominated its Committee on Federal Judiciary for a good many years. Its members tended to be characteristically men; successful lawyers; partners in large, big-city firms; veterans of local bar-association politics. But the egalitarian pressures that crested in the late 1960s and the 1970s resulted in major changes in the Committee's composition. Not only did it expand its membership to make room for a black attorney-educator, Charles L. Smith of the University of Washington School of Law, in 1976, it also named a woman, Brooksley E. L. Born, to be its Chairperson in 1980. Clearly, no longer is the erstwhile factual tag of establishmentarian justified. A genuine and broadly based measure of diversification has become evident, and it may be confidently expected to continue.[8]

There is no gainsaying the power and influence of the fourteen-member Committee: representatives are one from each of the eleven numbered judicial circuits (but two from the Ninth and more from the Thirteenth, as of late 1984), one from the District of Columbia circuit, plus a chairperson; the three-year term of office is renewable once. It has become a respected, often-crucial vehicle in the appointment process, especially in the vital initial selection stages and particularly at below–Supreme Court federal judiciary levels. It does *not* generate names for judicial vacancies, but it evaluates the qualifications of actual and putative nominees. After an investigation, customarily lasting from six to eight weeks,[9] it reports to the Justice Department on the perceived qualifications of the prospective nominee, rating him or her in one of the four following categories in the instances of *below*–Supreme Court federal judicial candidates: "not qualified" (NQ); "qualified" (Q); "well qualified" (WQ); and "exceptionally well qualified" (EWQ)–with the last used very sparingly. These ratings are subject to change annually, but they seem to have become standard for lower courts. A different evaluation method, to be described later, is utilized for Supreme Court nominees.

The Committee sensibly assumes that it must consult with the executive branch of the government before a public announcement is made concerning a judicial nominee. Although this procedure does not prevent leaks, it does minimize them, assuming full cooperation between the government and the Committee. Thus, when the Attorney General submits a nominee or a list of nominees to the Committee, its investigatory work commences *in camera*. The first step is to submit a detailed questionnaire, often running from fifteen to twenty pages and covering some thirty points of inquiry. One of the questions asks the candidate's judgment and evaluation of the ten "most significant" cases at law the candidate has litigated. A candidate is usually interviewed at length by a Committee member, one from the candidate's judicial circuit if possible. Through interviews with lay and professional individuals–including all pertinent federal judges in the candidate's area, top state judges, local law school deans, lawyers, and certain nonlawyers–the Committee member becomes familiar enough with the candidate's qualifications and character to render a presumably useful appraisal of his ability. The information thus gathered is then passed on in an informal report to the Committee Chairperson, who subsequently submits a complete report to the entire Committee; the data are also sent to the Attorney General, who must decide if he wishes the A.B.A. to render a formal report. If he requests one, it is circulated for a formal vote to all members of its Committee on Federal Judiciary, each acting independently and by mail. The F.B.I. at the request of the Justice Department then makes a painstaking investigation, the results of which are submitted to the Attorney General, who makes the ultimate recommendation to the President. If the President approves of the candidate, the nomination and the complete dossier are sent to the Senate Judiciary Committee for its action—which in the interim will also have received a full appraisal report from the A.B.A. Committee directly and *independently*.

As already indicated, the role of the A.B.A. Committee differs materially in the case of potential Supreme Court nominees, who have always been regarded as the President's own choice. Consequently, the procedures just described seldom have been applied to Supreme Court candidates. Indeed, the Committee's services were not enlisted in that connection until President Eisenhower nominated William J. Brennan, Jr., to the Court in 1956, and only then *after* the nominee's identity had been made public and transmitted to the Senate Judiciary Committee for action. Thus, the A.B.A. Committee preferred to commit itself only to the rankings of "qualified" or "unqualified." This procedure was followed in each of the Supreme Court nominations after Brennan's, until Blackmun was appointed in the spring of 1970, hence embracing the following: Whittaker, Stewart, Byron R. White, Goldberg, Fortas, Thurgood Marshall, Fortas again (the aborted promotion), Thornberry (not acted on by the Senate because its refusal to promote Fortas resulted in Warren's withdrawal of his resignation, hence negating the vacancy), Burger, Haynsworth, and Carswell (the last two rejected). The Committee stuck to the classification of "qualified" in all but a few instances: thus, in 1963 it ranked Goldberg "highly acceptable" but considered it inappropriate to express ". . . an opinion to the degree of qualification."[10] Yet it did express just such an opinion in the case of Judge Haynsworth in 1969—first and unanimously "highly qualified," then on reconsideration "highly qualified," but only by an 8:4 vote. In the Carswell case the Committee returned to its "qualified" designation (although more than a few observers wondered how he merited that).

In response to a storm of criticism following its actions in endorsing Haynsworth and Carswell (the former twice), the Committee's chairman, Lawrence E. Walsh, a Nixon ally—and the President's number-two representative at the Paris Peace Talks on the Vietnam War for some months—announced an impending change in the Committee's Supreme Court nomination classification system. Beginning with the selection of Judge Blackmun early in 1970, the Committee adopted a new top classification of "high standards of integrity, judicial temperament, and professional competence" and substituted categories of "not opposed" and "not qualified" for the erstwhile dichotomy of "qualified" and "unqualified." It signified a tacit admission that under the latter system almost anyone could have been rated as "qualified." Evidently pleased with the Committee's new classification and its endorsement of Blackmun with the new top category, Attorney General Mitchell yielded to the importunities of Chairman Walsh: on July 23, 1970, Mitchell wrote him that henceforth the Nixon Administration would allow the A.B.A. Committee to screen potential nominees for the Supreme Court *in advance* of their submittal to the Senate Judiciary Committee. Considerable approbation in otherwise critical circles followed the announcement, for it also had become evident that its investigation of Blackmun, in sharp contrast to the sketchy report the Committee had rendered to the Senate in just six days in the Carswell case, had been rigorous: it had interviewed some 200 presumably knowledgeable individuals, including upward of 100 judges and lawyers, and had reviewed all of Judge Blackmun's court opinions in an effort to determine the candidate's qualifications in terms of "integrity . . . judicial temperament and professional competence. . . ."

Yet the era of "good tone" was destined to be short lived. When Justices Hugo L. Black and John Marshall Harlan II announced their resignations in September 1971, the Administration moved rapidly to submit possible nominees to the A.B.A. Committee, starting with Richard H. Poff, Republican Congressman from Virginia. The A.B.A. Committee, after interviewing almost 400 individuals, awarded Congressman Poff the A.B.A.'s highest recommendation. After Poff withdrew there came the much-publicized, aforementioned candidacy of "The Six," whose names reached the press and public even before the Walsh Committee went to work on them. The Attorney General in submitting the names of "The Six" urged speed—the Court had already begun its October 1971 term with but seven sitting members—and requested concentration on the Administration's two top choices, Judge Lillie and Mr. Friday. Apparently little or no work was done on the other four candidates, giving rise to later suspicions that they were decoys.

The A.B.A. Committee, now working almost constantly, interviewed another 400 people in connection with each of the two nominees. The results were distressing. Whatever qualifications Judge Lillie and Lawyer Friday possessed, they were at best marginal in terms of what is required for service on the Supreme Court of the United States. The Committee responded with a unanimous vote for "not qualified" for Judge Lillie and a 6:6 tie (6 votes "not qualified," 6 votes "not opposed") for Mr. Friday. The fat was in the fire. When the A.B.A.'s actions, complete with votes, reached the news media only an hour or so after the Attorney General had received them, the Administration barely attempted to conceal its anger. Just who was responsible for the leak is difficult to establish, but this observer, for one, is satisfied that it did not come from the A.B.A. Committee itself: either it was from personnel in the Justice Department or from members or staff of the Senate Judiciary Committee. There is some evidence that it came from both sources, with the initial divulgence made by the Justice Department. Within a matter of days Attorney General Mitchell addressed a sizzling letter to A.B.A. President Leon Jaworski and Chairman Walsh of the Committee informing them that at least the incumbent Administration would no longer apply to the Committee for its advice on nominees to the Supreme Court, that it would return to the practice of sending nominees directly to the Senate.

> The events of the past week have made it clear that our concern of confidentiality of communications between Justice and the Committee was well founded, and I can only conclude that there is no practical way to avoid unauthorized disclosure of the names submitted and the advice of your committee with respect

> thereto despite the best efforts of the committee. . . . Like you, I had hoped that the new procedure would be useful and productive. However, under the circumstances, I have concluded that the only fair and proper course is to resume the long-standing practice of submitting the Attorney General's recommendations directly to the President. . . .[11]

The letter ended on a conciliatory note in recognizing the Committee's "wholehearted cooperation" and was signed "Yours sincerely, John," but there was no mistaking its bitter tone. The Committee was equally bitter. It would neither simply accept the blame nor cease its evaluations of Supreme Court nominees—even though that would have to be made at the Senate stage once again. A plainly miffed Chairperson Walsh made the latter quite clear: when the President subsequently announced his selections of Messrs. Powell and Rehnquist for the two vacancies (he did not send the Lillie and Friday nominations to the Senate at all), the A.B.A. Committee sprang to action. After its normal investigation it submitted its report to Chairman Eastland of the Senate Judiciary Committee: Powell, unanimously approved with the highest of the three classifications; Rehnquist, with eight votes for the highest classification and four "not opposed" votes. As already noted,[12] their confirmation by the Senate in December 1971 came by votes of 89:1 and 68:26, respectively. One year later the A.B.A. formally requested Mr. Mitchell's successor, Richard Kleindienst, to revert to the Department's arrangements with the Committee that had existed prior to "The Six" affair. No action was taken then by Mr. Kleindienst, nor by his immediate successor, Elliot L. Richardson, but matters had been restored to the *status quo ante* by the time President Ford's Attorney General, Edward H. Levi, commenced the search for a replacement for the retired Justice Douglas in the fall of 1975. The ultimate selectee, John Paul Stevens, received the A.B.A.'s top rating. Sandra Day O'Connor, with whom President Reagan replaced the retired Justice Stewart in the fall of 1981, was then not at all well known and was accorded a somewhat guarded rating of "highest standards of judicial temperament and integrity" and "qualified from the standpoint of professional competence for appointment to the Supreme Court."

The work of the A.B.A. Committee is but one piece–albeit a prominently perceived one–in a rather large mosaic. Its contribution is indeed essential, yet it should never become controlling. One of its most distinguished contemporary members noted perceptively that the Committee "performs a very significant function of saying 'no' to the political muscleboys . . . and it also plays an enormously important one in taking flak for the Senators."[13] But as the Committee sheepishly conceded in its Carswell report, "many other factors of a broad political and ideological nature" remain outside its competence. In sum, the bar can be of inestimable help in assessing professional qualifications of judicial nominees, but it must not, on any level, be accorded a veto power. For there remains the crucial constitutional *cum* political fact of governance under our representative democracy that judicial nominations are the President's to make and the Senate's to confirm.

That the Senate takes its confirmation role seriously is documented by its refusal to confirm 27 of the 139 Supreme Court nominees forwarded to it in the less than two centuries of our history as a nation. True, even when counting the Senate's refusal to vote on the Fortas promotion, only 4 have been voted down during the current century, but, as the experiences of the Nixon Administration demonstrate, the possibility is ever present. Yet a return to the nineteenth-century record of 1 rejection for every 3 nominees is highly unlikely.

Just why were the twenty-seven rejected either outright or simply were not acted on by the Senate? Among the more prominent reasons have been: (1) opposition to the nominating President, not necessarily the nominee; (2) the nominee's involvement with a visible or contentious issue of public policy or, simply, opposition to the nominee's perceived political or sociopolitical philosophy (i.e., "politics"); (3) opposition to the record of the incumbent Court which, rightly or wrongly, the nominee had presumably supported; (4) Senatorial courtesy (closely linked to the consultative nominating process); (5) a nominee's perceived "political unreliability" on the part of the party in power; (6) the evident lack of qualification or limited ability of the nominee; and (7) concerted, sustained opposition by interest or pressure groups.

Usually several of these reasons–not one alone–figure in the rejection of a nominee. The purpose of this list is merely to suggest some applicable prototypes.

Thus, a number of candidates were rejected because of Senate opposition to the nominating Chief Executive. For example, John Quincy Adams's nomination of John J. Crittenden in 1828 was "postponed" by the Senate in a strictly partisan vote of 23:17 two months after the nomination. The "loyalist" Democrats in the Senate thereby foiled Adams's last-minute Whig appointment and preserved the vacancy so that it could be filled instead by the President-elect, strong party Democrat Andrew Jackson. In 1844 Whig President John Tyler sent six nominations to the upper house–which disapproved five and confirmed but one, the outstandingly qualified Samuel Nelson, Chief Justice of New York's highest court. Of the others, John C. Spencer, an erstwhile Whig who had accepted high Cabinet posts under Tyler and whom the "loyalist" Whig followers of Henry Clay regarded as a traitor, was rejected by a formal roll-call vote of 21:26; and action regarding Edward King–who was nominated twice and holds the sole distinction of being rejected twice!–Reuben H. Walworth, and John M. Read was postponed by the Senate, chiefly because of the mistaken expectation of the Clay Whigs that their revered leader would defeat James K. Polk in the Presidential election of 1844. In 1852 action on George E. Badger, one of Whig President Millard Fillmore's nominees, was postponed indefinitely (despite the fact that he was then a Whig Senator from North Carolina) and no action at all was taken on his two other nominees, Edward A. Bradford and William C. Micou. The purpose of the anti-Fillmore maneuvers was to preserve court vacancies for incoming Democratic President Franklin Pierce, yet Pierce succeeded in filling only one of them, he, too, falling victim to similar Senate tactics. Democrat James Buchanan's nomination of Jeremiah S. Black in December 1860, one month before his term ended, fell 25:26, chiefly because Republican Senators wanted to hold the seat for Abraham Lincoln to fill. In 1866 Union President Andrew Johnson nominated his gifted Attorney General, Henry Stanbery, but the Senate's hostility to Lincoln's successor was such as to frustrate every attempt he made to fill a Supreme Court vacancy. Congress even went so far as to *abolish* the vacancy (thus "icing" Johnson's nominating impotence). A century later in 1968 the Senate refused to approve Lyndon B. Johnson's simultaneous attempt to promote Abe Fortas to Chief Justice and to replace him with Judge Homer Thornberry of the U.S. Court of Appeals for the Fifth Circuit. Johnson failed largely because most members of the Senate "had had it" with the lame-duck President's nominations. Victory-scenting Republicans also wanted such plums as Supreme Court appointments for themselves; they had not had an opportunity to fill a vacancy on the bench since President Eisenhower's appointment of Justice Potter Stewart ten years earlier.

A good many illustrations are on record in which nominees failed to receive Senatorial confirmation because of their involvement with public issues. Thus, in 1795 the Senate rejected John Rutledge as Chief Justice by a vote of 10:14 (although he had been serving as such for four months on a recess appointment while Congress was not in session). Rutledge had asked President Washington for the appointment on John Jay's resignation but now found his fellow Federalists voting against him because of his vigorous opposition to the Jay Treaty of 1794. The Federalist Senators refused to confirm a public figure who actively opposed the Treaty they had championed so ardently–even though he was able to meet Washington's stiff criteria for service on the highest bench. Their cause was aided by an all-but-unanimous denunciation by the Northern Federalist press. In 1811 James Madison's nomination of Alexander Wolcott fell 9:24 because the Federalist Senators, eagerly backed by the press, opposed Wolcott's vigorous enforcement of the embargo and nonintercourse acts when he was U.S. Collector of Customs in Connecticut. There was, however, also some genuine question as to Wolcott's legal qualifications.

The rejection of James K. Polk's nomination in 1845 of fellow Democrat George W. Woodward of Pennsylvania–although in part owing to opposition by Pennsylvania's Independent Senator Simon Cameron on the basis of Senatorial courtesy–was largely a result of what was termed Woodward's "gross nativist American sentiments." Chiefly because of these alleged sentiments, which were particularly offensive to Irish-Americans, five Democratic Senators joined Cameron and a phalanx of Whigs to defeat the nomination by a vote of 20:29. The President, however, saw the action as a power play calculated to weaken his Administration at the very outset. On December 15, 1869, Republican President Ulysses S. Grant nominated his eminently qualified and popular Attorney General, Ebenezer R. Hoar. The debate over his nomination dragged on for seven weeks until February 3, 1870, when Hoar was finally rejected by a vote of 24:33. He had antagonized most of the Senators by his consistent refusal to back Senatorial nominations for judgeships, by his publicly uncompromising insistence on "nonpolitical" appointments throughout the government, and by his early championship of civil service reform. Moreover, he had made enemies of fellow Republicans by his outspoken opposition to the proposed impeachment of President Andrew Johnson. Few professional politicians appreciated Judge Hoar's high standards of excellence and assertive political independence, and the Court was deprived of an unusually promising candidate.

Another issue-oriented rejection was that of Chief Judge John J. Parker, of the U.S. Fourth Circuit Court of Appeals (Hoover, 1930). A prominent and distinguished Republican leader in North Carolina for many years and an outstanding jurist, Judge Parker fell victim to the sustained opposition of the American Federation of Labor (A.F.L.) and the National Association for the Advancement of Colored People (N.A.A.C.P.)–a pertinent illustration of the power and influence that interest and pressure groups may be able to wield in the confirmation process. Still, the Senate would not have had the votes to defeat the nomination–Parker lost by a two-vote margin, 39:41–had it not been aided by the anti-Hoover Progressive Republicans, including such prominent and influential Senators as Robert M. La Follette, Jr., of Wisconsin, Hiram Johnson of California, and George W. Norris of Nebraska. The A.F.L.'s chief grudge against the nominee stemmed from the impression that he was "unfriendly" to labor and that it was he who had handed down an opinion affirming a lower-court decision upholding yellow dog contracts.[14] A close reading of Judge Parker's opinion in the case indicates neither approval nor disapproval of yellow dog contracts; rather, it reflects the responsible jurist's belief that he was bound by a U.S. Supreme Court precedent.[15] Yet the impression of antilabor bias lingered, fostered by A.F.L. President William Green and other influential labor spokespersons–who, on the other hand, did concede that Judge Parker's integrity, high standards, and professional qualifications were not in question. The N.A.A.C.P. contended that the nominee was generally opposed to black participation in politics and especially to black suffrage. Thus, Walter White of the N.A.A.C.P. leadership pointed out that Judge Parker, while stumping North Carolina as a gubernatorial candidate in 1920, had indeed made an unfortunate remark: "The participation of the Negro in politics is a source of evil and danger to both races and is not desired by the wise men in either race or by the Republican Party of North Carolina."[16] Parker had uttered the statement in response to repeated taunts and charges by his Democratic opponents that he intended to enfranchise blacks and to alter the North Carolina Constitution to accommodate "them." Ironically, it would be Judge Parker (he continued to sit on the Fourth Circuit bench after his rejection) who would write some of the earliest and most significant problack opinions on desegregation. Among them were *Rice* v. *Elmore* in 1947, in which he sustained U.S. District Court Judge J. W. Waring's outlawing of South Carolina's machinations to bar blacks from primary elections,[17] and his 1955 remand opinion in *Briggs* v. *Elliott,* in which he rejected "massive resistance."[18]

The next outright rejections were Judges Haynsworth and Carswell almost forty years later. Although their involvement with civil rights did play a considerable role in their rejections, especially in that of Carswell, the margin of defeat lay elsewhere: in Haynsworth's case in the question of judicial ethics, in Carswell's case in the demonstrable lack of professional qualification.

The Senate's refusal to accept cloture in 1968 in order to vote on the promotion of Justice Fortas has also been variously attributed to his "record" on the high bench on such contentious issues as obscenity and criminal justice. In fact, although the issues were dramatically vocalized by such powerful and committed opponents to the nomination as Senators Strom Thurmond (R.-S.C.)

and John L. McClellan (D.-Ark.), they were not an important reason for the nomination's failure. It was fought with such ardor largely because of deep-seated opposition to the jurisprudential philosophy of the Warren Court—an approach to constitutional interpretation that resulted in the inevitable disaffection of numerous groups and individuals, both public and private. The Court's stance and record of judicial activism on such emotion-charged issues as desegregation, reapportionment and redistricting, criminal justice, separation of Church and State, civil disobedience, and freedom of expression was bound to offend as well as to please.

Coming, as it did conveniently, at the close of the Johnson Administration, the Fortas nomination readily served as target and symbol of the pent-up frustrations against the Warren Court—but against the Court as a unit rather than against the individuals. One of the famous episodes surrounding the attacks against Fortas occurred early in the hearings of the Senate Judiciary Committee when Senator Thurmond shouted at Fortas: "Mallory! Mallory! I want that name to ring in your ears." Thurmond's reference was to Andrew Mallory, a nineteen-year-old black from South Carolina who was arrested in 1954 on a charge of choking and raping a thirty-eight-year-old Washington, D.C., woman while she was doing her laundry. After a seven-hour interrogation by the police *prior* to his arraignment, Mallory had confessed. The trial was delayed for a year because doubts had been raised that he understood the proceedings against him, but ultimately Mallory was sentenced to the electric chair. He appealed to the Supreme Court, alleging a coerced confession. In what became the celebrated case of *Mallory* v. *United States* in 1957,[19] the Court unanimously reversed Mallory's conviction on the grounds that the failure of the police to bring him before a magistrate forthwith constituted an "unnecessary delay" (in violation of federal rules of criminal-law procedure) thereby giving "opportunity for the extraction of a confession." Released, Mallory resumed a life of drifting and crime, culminating in his 1960 arrest in Philadelphia and subsequent apprehension for burglary, assault, and rape. He was convicted on the assault count and served eleven years in jail, but barely six months after his release in 1971 he attacked and robbed a couple in a Philadelphia park. When discovered by two police officers, he aimed a gun at one and was killed by the other in the process. It was the so-called Mallory Rule, as pronounced by the Supreme Court, that Senator Thurmond referred to in his outburst at Justice Fortas. Yet the latter had never been connected with the case and had not even been appointed to the Court until 1965, eight years *after* the Mallory decision! (The Mallory Rule itself was modified by Congress in the Omnibus Crime Control Act of 1968.) Other similar charges were leveled at the nominee, some of them concerning decisions in obscenity cases rendered long before Fortas ever sat.

Senatorial courtesy, fourth in the list of reasons for Senate refusal of Supreme Court nominations, has already been discussed. A fifth one is broadly stylable as "political unreliability," as perceived by the Senate. Perhaps the most obvious example of the application of this reason is another among the several unsuccessful Grant nominations–that of former Attorney General Caleb Cushing (who was the President's third choice) to assume the Chief Justiceship in 1874, following the death of Salmon P. Chase. (Senator Roscoe Conkling of New York, a close political and personal friend, had been Grant's first choice. But Conkling turned down the offer, and the Senate refused to act on Grant's second choice, his Attorney General, George H. Williams.) Cushing's age–seventy-four–was noted prominently during debate, but the real reason for his rejection was the Senate's not entirely erroneous belief that Grant's close personal friend was a political chameleon. Indeed, Cushing had been, in turn, a Regular Whig, a Tyler Whig, a Democrat, a Johnson Constitutional Conservative, and finally a Republican. He had proved himself a first-rate legal practitioner and scholar; nevertheless, with opposition from almost all political factions augmenting daily, Grant withdrew Cushing from consideration.

A final reason for Senate refusal of a nominee is simply real or apparent lack of qualification to sit on the Supreme Court. Of course the concepts of "quality" and "ability" are subject to diverse analysis; yet a number of ascertainable standards and criteria clearly exist. A nominee's age, experience, and record in and out of public life are all available guidelines. Ulysses S. Grant, in choosing his Attorney General, George H. Williams, to fill the vacancy caused by the death of Chief Justice Salmon P. Chase, thus evoked an entirely justifiable storm of adverse reactions. Williams had seen service in the Senate and had been territorial Governor of Oregon; but his record as Attorney General was undistinguished and his talents as a lawyer were clearly mediocre (it was alleged that he had unnecessarily lost several important cases in private as well as public litigation). Both the bar and the press were severely critical of his achievements and his promise. Stunned and hurt by this reaction and despairing of a lengthy confirmation battle, Williams asked President Grant to withdraw his nomination in early January 1874.

It is fair to conclude that Presidents have avoided nominating patently unqualified individuals to the high tribunal (see Appendix A, *infra*), although a number of rather weak nominations have slipped past the Senate, such as James C. McReynolds (Wilson), Pierce Butler (Harding), Sherman Minton (Truman), and Charles E. Whittaker (Eisenhower).[20] The one nominee on whose lack of qualification almost all fair-minded observers now agree is G. Harrold Carswell. With the calm hindsight of history, President Nixon's choice still merits the characterization of a spite nomination. It is to its credit that the Senate simply would not accept Carswell.

Would any of the twenty-seven who failed in being confirmed have been approved had they been members of the Senate at the time of their nomination? The evidence is persuasive that they would have: the Senate almost invariably treats as a *cas d'honneur* the Presidential designation of a sitting member and normally also, although not so predictably, of a past colleague in good standing. Among the many telling illustrations are Senators James F. Byrnes (D.-S.C.) and Harold H. Burton (R.-Ohio). Byrnes, highly respected and very much a member of the Senate's "inner club," was confirmed unanimously without even being scrutinized by its Committee on the Judiciary when President Roosevelt nominated him in 1941.[21] Burton's nomination, although that of a Republican by a Democratic President (Truman), was unanimously confirmed in 1945 on the same day it reached the Senate, then controlled by a Democratic majority.

That the special treatment accorded Senatorial colleagues is normally reserved to those actually serving is demonstrated by the case of *ex*-Senator Sherman Minton of Indiana. Minton, who had been defeated for reelection in 1940, largely because of his ardent espousal of the New Deal, was serving as a judge on the U.S. Court of Appeals for the Seventh Circuit when President Truman selected him for the Court in 1949. In part because of his support of Roosevelt's Court-packing bill, the Senate Judiciary Committee voted 5:4 to ask him to testify before it. Minton refused, pointing to his position as a jurist and questioning the propriety of testifying, lest conflicts arise concerning pending litigation. The Committee relented and reported his nomination favorably, 9:2. Still, led by prominent Republicans, the Senate took a formal vote on recommittal of Minton's nomination—which was defeated 45:21; thereafter, he obtained quick confirmation, 48:16.

A notable exception to the unwritten rule of the all but automatic approval of Senatorial colleagues was Franklin D. Roosevelt's controversial nomination of Senator Hugo Lafayette Black (D.-Ala.) in August 1937. Black's nomination was referred to the Judiciary Committee for full hearings, an action that had then not been taken since 1888! The initial reasons for that move, over the strong objections by the Chairman of the Committee, Senator Henry Ashurst (D.-Ariz.), were Black's strong support of the President's Court-packing bill, his ardent New Deal partisanship, and his ruthless public investigations of the utility lobby. Roosevelt's attempt to increase the size of the Court was anathema to a majority of the Senate as well as the bar. And the controversy was compounded and exacerbated by rumors that Black had once been—and some alleged still was—a member of the Ku Klux Klan (K.K.K.) in his native Alabama. Even so, the Committee ultimately approved the nomination by a vote of 13:4 (2 Democrats and 2 Republicans voting against him), and the Senate confirmed him 63:16 (10 Republicans and 6 Democrats voting nay). Meanwhile reporter Ray Sprigle of the *Pittsburgh Post-Gazette* came up with evidence that Black had indeed belonged to the K.K.K. Black faced the charges squarely: in a candid dramatic broadcast to the American people he admitted a two-year K.K.K. membership in the mid-1920s but pointed to his established liberal record and vowed to be a fair and impartial jurist. During a tenure on the Court lasting more than a third of a century he kept his word.[22]

The last test of the Senate's refusal to refer nominations to the Judiciary Committee came with Burton in 1945; no U.S. Senator has since been nominated. It was precisely the recognition of that rule that prompted leading supporters of President Nixon to urge him to nominate a Senator after Judge Haynsworth's rejection in 1969. Evidently the President briefly toyed with the idea of nominating John Stennis (D.-Miss.) or Sam Ervin (D.-N.C.), both Southern Senators generally supportive of his strict-construction views, but in his determination to teach the Senate a lesson, he chose Carswell. Yet it will be recalled that one of the six he had under consideration in 1971 was Senator Robert C. Byrd (D.-W.Va.)—a man arguably less qualified to serve on the Supreme Court than his colleagues Stennis and Ervin. Whether or not Nixon seriously contemplated the Byrd nomination, there is little doubt that his colleagues would have given their approval. Yet those same colleagues would have been far less likely to approve of someone of equally marginal qualifications from outside the halls of the Senate.

4

Why They Get There:
Qualifications and Rationalizations

It may astonish some to learn that no legal or constitutional requirements for a federal judgeship exist. This is especially surprising in that each state in the union has such requirements for at least some judicial posts. There does exist, however, an *unwritten* prerequisite for a place on the federal bench—a bachelor of laws or *juris doctor* degree. No one can become a member of the Supreme Court today without one of these degrees, although it is not necessarily mandatory either to have practiced law or to have been a member of the bar. Yet, as observed earlier, the American Bar Association (A.B.A.) Standing Committee on Federal Judiciary not only stresses trial experience of a candidate for the judiciary, it also normally requires years of legal practice to qualify the candidate for a passing rating. As a matter of historical record, no non-lawyer has ever served on the Supreme Court of the United States—and it is all but certain that none ever will.

To date all except four presidents—William Henry Harrison (1841), Zachary Taylor (1849–1850), Andrew Johnson (1865–1869), and James E. Carter (1977–1981)—have succeeded in appointing at least one of their nominees to the highest court, although ten appointed but one each: James Monroe (1817–1825), John Quincy Adams (1825–1829), John Tyler (1841–1845), Millard Fillmore (1850–1853), Franklin Pierce (1853–1857), James

TABLE 1

Number of Presidential Appointments of Supreme Court Justices Actually Serving on the Court (1789–1984)

PRESIDENT	PARTY	DATES SERVED	NUMBER OF APPOINTEES WHO ACTUALLY SERVED*
Washington	Federalist	1789–1797	10
J. Adams	Federalist	1797–1801	3
Jefferson	Democrat–Republican	1801–1809	3
Madison	Democrat–Republican	1809–1817	2
Monroe	Democrat–Republican	1817–1825	1
J. Q. Adams	Democrat–Republican	1825–1829	1
Jackson	Democrat	1829–1837	6 (5)†
Van Buren	Democrat	1837–1841	2 (3)†
W. H. Harrison	Whig	1841	0
Tyler	Whig	1841–1845	1
Polk	Democrat	1845–1849	2
Taylor	Whig	1849–1850	0
Fillmore	Whig	1850–1853	1
Pierce	Democrat	1853–1857	1
Buchanan	Democrat	1857–1861	1
Lincoln	Republican	1861–1865	5
A. Johnson	National Union	1865–1869	0
Grant	Republican	1869–1877	4
Hayes	Republican	1877–1881	2
Garfield	Republican	1881	1
Arthur	Republican	1881–1885	2
Cleveland	Democrat	1885–1889 1893–1897	4‡
B. Harrison	Republican	1889–1893	4
McKinley	Republican	1897–1901	1
T. Roosevelt	Republican	1901–1909	3
Taft	Republican	1909–1913	6
Wilson	Democrat	1913–1921	3
Harding	Republican	1921–1923	4
Coolidge	Republican	1923–1929	1
Hoover	Republican	1929–1933	3
F. D. Roosevelt	Democrat	1933–1945	9
Truman	Democrat	1945–1953	4
Eisenhower	Republican	1953–1961	5

TABLE 1 (*continued*)

PRESIDENT	PARTY	DATES SERVED	NUMBER OF APPOINTEES WHO ACTUALLY SERVED*
Kennedy	Democrat	1961–1963	2
L. B. Johnson	Democrat	1963–1969	2
Nixon	Republican	1969–1974	4
Ford	Republican	1974–1977	1
Carter	Democrat	1977–1981	0
Reagan	Republican	1981–	1
			105

* Robert Hanson Harrison (1789), Levi Lincoln (1811), William Smith (1836), and Roscoe Conkling (1882) were nominated and confirmed but declined to serve; hence, they are not counted here; nor are those who died before they could take office, for example, Edwin M. Stanton, who lived only four days beyond his confirmation.
† President Jackson nominated Catron, but he was not confirmed until Van Buren had taken over.
‡ 2 in each term.

Buchanan (1857–1861), James A. Garfield (1881), William McKinley (1897–1901), Calvin Coolidge (1923–1929), and Gerald Ford (1974–1977). Of the four who appointed none at all, William Henry Harrison and Zachary Taylor died soon after reaching office; Andrew Johnson, who saw several nominees blocked by the Senate, was the victim of an implacably hostile Congress; and Carter–the only one of the four to serve a full term–was simply not fated to have a vacancy on the Court during his four years.

Table 1 lists the number of justices who were confirmed by the Senate *and actually served* on the Supreme Court and the Presidents who appointed them. If we count Justices Edward D. White, Charles Evans Hughes, and Harlan F. Stone once (each served as both Associate Justice and as Chief Justice), and do *not* count the recess appointment, ultimately Senate-rejected, of John Rutledge as *Chief Justice* (he had been confirmed as *Associate Justice* earlier but resigned), exactly 102 Justices had served on the Court as of the 1983–1984 term, the result of 105 successful appointments.

In view of what is minimally required of a Supreme Court nominee, it is hardly astonishing that many of them have come to the bench with no previous judicial experience. Among the 102 Justices who had served on the Court by mid-1984, only 22 had had ten or more years of experience on any tribunal–federal or state–and 42 had had no judicial experience at all. Yet as Table 2 indicates, many of the most illustrious members of the Court were judicially inexperienced. Among them were 8 of the 15 Chief Justices*: John Marshall, Roger B. Taney, Salmon P. Chase, Morrison R. Waite, Melville W. Fuller, Charles Evans Hughes, Harlan F. Stone, and Earl Warren; and such outstanding Associate Justices as Joseph Story, Samuel F. Miller, Joseph P. Bradley, Louis D. Brandeis, Felix Frankfurter, Robert H. Jackson, and Lewis F. Powell, Jr.

In a learned essay calling for selection of Supreme Court Justices "wholly on the basis of functional fitness," Justice Frankfurter keenly argued that judicial experience, political affiliation, and geographic, racial, and religious considerations should not play a significant role in the selection of jurists.[1] He contended that a Supreme Court jurist should be at once philosopher, historian, and prophet–to which Justice Brennan, in a conversation with this writer, proposed to add "and a person of inordinate patience." Justice Frankfurter viewed their task as requiring "poetic sensibilities" and "the gift of imagination," as exhorting them to

> pierce the curtain of the future . . . give shape and visage to mysteries still in the womb of time. . . . [the job thus demands] antennae registering feeling and judgment beyond logical, let alone quantitative proof. . . . One is entitled to say without qualification that the correlation between prior judicial

* Hughes and Stone are included in the list because neither had had judicial experience at the time of his appointment as Associate Justice. Hughes served in the latter capacity from 1910 to 1916, and then returned as Chief Justice from 1930 to 1941. Stone was promoted from his Associate Justice position in 1941; he had been an Associate Justice since 1925 and would serve as Chief Justice until 1946.

> experience and fitness for the Supreme Court is zero. The significance of the greatest among the Justices who had such experience, Holmes and Cardozo, derived not from that judicial experience but from the fact that they were Holmes and Cardozo. They were thinkers, and more particularly, legal philosophers.[2]

As supporting witness, Frankfurter was fond of calling on Judge Learned Hand, the author of one of the most incisively thoughtful statements on the subject:

> I venture to believe that it is as important to a judge called upon to pass on a question of constitutional law, to have a bowing acquaintance with Acton and Maitland, with Thucydides, Gibbon, and Carlyle, with Homer, Dante, Shakespeare, and Milton, with Machiavelli, Montaigne, and Rabelais, with Plato, Bacon, Hume, and Kant as with books that have been specifically written on the subject. For in such matters everything turns upon the spirit in which he approaches the question before him. The words he must construe are empty vessels into which he can pour nearly everything he will. Men do not gather figs of thistles, nor supply institutions from judges whose outlook is limited by parish or class. They must be aware that there are before them more than verbal problems; more than final solutions cast in generalizations of universal applicability. They must be aware of the changing social tensions in every society which make it an organism; which demand new schemata of adaptation; which will disrupt it, if rigidly confined.[3]

What a pity that a man of Hand's intellect and pen never became a member of the Supreme Court—he would have graced it from every point of view. Alas, he was always either deemed too old or in the wrong political party! Taft blocked his potential nomination on several occasions and Frankfurter's "overkill" advocacy evidently deprived Hand of his last chance under F.D.R. in 1942.[4]

Yet the matter of judicial experience, although periodically ignored or downgraded by some Presidents, rarely lies dormant long—indeed, it has been present in almost exactly one half of all Presidential nominations to the Supreme Court to date. To Franklin D. Roosevelt judicial experience was of little importance; to Dwight Eisenhower it was crucial: after his initial appointment of

TABLE 2

Prior Judicial Experience of U.S. Supreme Court Justices and Their Subsequent Service

JUSTICE	YEAR NOMI-NATED**	NUMBER OF YEARS OF PRIOR JUDICIAL EXPERIENCE			YEARS OF SERVICE ON SUPREME COURT
		FEDERAL	STATE	TOTAL	
Jay*	1789	0	2	2	6
J. Rutledge*†	1789 and 1795*	0	6	6	2‡
Cushing	1789	0	29	29	21
Wilson	1789	0	0	0	9
Blair	1789	0	11	11	7
Iredell	1790	0	½	½	9
T. Johnson	1791	0	1½	1½	2
Paterson	1793	0	0	0	13½
S. Chase	1796	0	8	8	15
Ellsworth*	1796	0	5	5	4
Washington	1798	0	0	0	31
Moore	1799	0	1	1	5
J. Marshall*	1801	0	0	0	34½
W. Johnson	1804	0	6	6	30
Livingston	1806	0	0	0	16
Todd	1807	0	6	6	20
Duval	1811	0	6	6	24
Story	1811	0	0	0	34
Thompson	1823	0	16	16	20
Trimble	1826	9	2	11	2
McLean	1829	0	6	6	32
Baldwin	1830	0	0	0	14
Wayne	1835	0	5	5	32
Taney*	1836	0	0	0	28
Barbour	1836	6	2	8	5
Catron	1837	0	10	10	28
McKinley	1837	0	0	0	15
Daniel	1841	4	0	0	19
Nelson	1845	0	22	22	27
Woodbury	1845	0	6	6	6
Grier	1846	0	13	13	23
Curtis	1851	0	0	0	6
Campbell	1853	0	0	0	8
Clifford	1858	0	0	0	23
Swayne	1862	0	0	0	19

TABLE 2 (*continued*)

JUSTICE	YEAR NOMINATED**	NUMBER OF YEARS OF PRIOR JUDICIAL EXPERIENCE			YEARS OF SERVICE ON SUPREME COURT
		FEDERAL	STATE	TOTAL	
Miller	1862	0	0	0	28
Davis	1862	0	14	14	15
Field	1863	0	6	6	34¾
S. P. Chase*	1864	0	0	0	8½
Strong	1870	0	11	11	10¾
Bradley	1870	0	0	0	22
Hunt	1872	0	8	8	9
Waite*	1874	0	0	0	14
Harlan I	1877	0	1	1	34
Woods	1880	12	0	12	6½
Matthews	1881	0	4	4	8
Gray	1881	0	18	18	21
Blatchford	1882	15	0	15	11
L. Q. C. Lamar	1888	0	0	0	5
Fuller*	1888	0	0	0	22
Brewer	1889	5	14	19	20
Brown	1890	16	0	16	16
Shiras	1892	0	0	0	11
H. E. Jackson	1893	7	0	7	2½
E. D. White*	1894 and 1910*	0	1½	1½	27
Peckham	1895	0	9	9	14
McKenna	1898	5	0	5	27
Holmes	1902	0	20	20	30
Day	1903	4	3	7	19
Moody	1906	0	0	0	4
Lurton	1909	16	10	26	4½
Hughes*§	1910 and 1930*	0	0	0	17
Van Devanter	1910	7	1	8	27
J. R. Lamar	1910	0	2	2	5
Pitney	1912	0	11	11	10
McReynolds	1914	0	0	0	27
Brandeis	1916	0	0	0	23
Clarke	1916	2	0	2	6
Taft*	1921	8	5	13	9
Sutherland	1922	0	0	0	16
Butler	1922	0	0	0	17
Sanford	1923	14	0	14	7
Stone*§	1925 and 1941*	0	0	0	21

TABLE 2 (*continued*)

JUSTICE	YEAR NOMINATED**	NUMBER OF YEARS OF PRIOR JUDICIAL EXPERIENCE			YEARS OF SERVICE ON SUPREME COURT
		FEDERAL	STATE	TOTAL	
Roberts	1930	0	0	0	15
Cardozo	1932	0	18	18	6
Black	1937	0	1½	1½	34
Reed	1937	0	0	0	19
Frankfurter	1939	0	0	0	23
Douglas	1939	0	0	0	36½
Murphy	1940	0	7	7	9
Byrnes	1941	0	0	0	1
R. H. Jackson	1941	0	0	0	13
W. B. Rutledge	1943	4	0	4	6½
Burton	1945	0	0	0	13
Vinson*	1946	5	0	5	7
Clark	1949	0	0	0	18
Minton	1949	8	0	8	7
Warren*	1953	0	0	0	16
Harlan II	1955	1	0	1	16
Brennan	1956	0	7	7	
Whittaker	1957	3	0	3	5
Stewart	1958	4	0	4	22¾
B. R. White	1962	0	0	0	
Goldberg	1962	0	0	0	2¾
Fortas	1965	0	0	0	3½
T. Marshall	1967	3¾	0	3¾	
Burger*	1969	13	0	13	
Blackmun	1970	11	0	11	
Powell	1971	0	0	0	
Rehnquist	1971	0	0	0	
Stevens	1975	5	0	5	
O'Connor	1981	0	6½	6½	

* Indicates Chief Justice and date of his appointment or promotion.
† Rutledge's nomination was rejected by the Senate in December 1795, but he had served as Chief Justice under a recess appointment for four months.
‡ Actually Rutledge never served as Associate Justice, although he did perform circuit duty before his resignation in 1791.
§ Indicates no judicial experience when appointed as *Associate* Justice.
** Year nominated may be earlier than the year in which the appointee took the judicial oath—e.g., Cushing and Blair, who were nominated in 1789 but did not take the oath until 1790.

Earl Warren as Chief Justice, Eisenhower insisted that future nominees have judicial background, no matter how limited. Of the nine men who served on the Court as a result of F.D.R.'s appointments (or promotion to Chief Justice in the instance of Harlan F. Stone), six had had no judicial experience when they ascended the bench: Chief Justice Stone and Associate Justices Stanley F. Reed, Felix Frankfurter, William O. Douglas, James F. Byrnes, and Robert H. Jackson. Of the three with experience, Wiley B. Rutledge had served on the Court of Appeals for the District of Columbia for four years and Hugo L. Black and Frank Murphy on state tribunals for one and one-half and seven years, respectively. Harry Truman had a mixed record: of his four appointees, Harold H. Burton and Tom C. Clark had no judicial experience at all, but Fred M. Vinson and Sherman Minton had seen five and eight years, respectively, of service on lower federal courts. The four men Eisenhower appointed following Warren—Associate Justices John M. Harlan II, William J. Brennan, Jr., Charles E. Whittaker, and Potter Stewart—all had had judicial experience, although the total number of such years for the four was but fifteen. Neither Associate Justices Byron R. White nor Arthur J. Goldberg, appointed by John Kennedy, nor Abe Fortas, appointed by Lyndon Johnson, had served below the Supreme Court, although L.B.J.'s last successful appointee, Thurgood Marshall, had been a federal appellate judge for three and one-half years. Of President Nixon's four selections, Chief Justice Warren E. Burger and Associate Justice Harry A. Blackmun had served on lower federal tribunals for thirteen and eleven years, respectively, but Associate Justices Lewis F. Powell, Jr., and William H. Rehnquist had served on no court. Although their service on tribunals below was quite brief, both Justices Stevens and O'Connor, appointed by Presidents Ford and Reagan, respectively, had judicial experience. Thirteen appointees with no judicial background were sent to the Court by the eight most recent Presidents; but with the exception of one or two, all possessed at least some qualifying attributes: broad experience in the public sector, strong personality and strength of character, capacity for hard work, political *savoir faire,* a modicum of intellectualism, and verbal as well as written articulateness. To raise judicial experience to the level of either an express or implied *requirement* would render a distinct disservice to the Supreme Court.[5]

Fortunately, Congress has hardly been of one mind on the necessity or even the desirability of judicial experience as a prerequisite for appointment to the Court. Rarely does a session of Congress go by that does not see proposed legislation embodying such a requirement, usually specifying from five to ten years of prior service. In the Ninety-fifth Congress (1977–1979) some fifteen such bills were sponsored by members on both sides of the aisle in both houses. But they all failed to be enacted, as had thirteen such bills in the Eighty-ninth Congress (1965–1967). A majority of the members of Congress–two thirds of whom are lawyers!–continue to agree that judicial experience is *not* essential. Clearly, they recognize that the Supreme Court is not a trial court in the sense of the federal district courts and that it does not deal with a particular constituency as do the federal district courts and, to a considerably lesser degree, the federal courts of appeal. Further, experience gained in the lower courts may be of little significance in the Supreme Court, as their procedural and jurisdictional frameworks are really quite different. The private litigation at common law so prevalent in the lower courts is practically absent at the bar of today's Supreme Court, which is almost exclusively occupied with questions of public law.

Returning again to Felix Frankfurter and Learned Hand, today's business of the Supreme Court is what Judge Hand categorized as the "application of rather fundamental aspirations," what he styled "moods" that are embodied in constitutional provisions, such as the due process clauses of the Fifth and Fourteenth amendments. Evidently these clauses were deliberately designed, in Justice Frankfurter's words, "not to be precise and positive directions for rules of action." According to him:

> The judicial process in applying them involves a judgment on the processes of government. The Court sits in judgment, that is, on the views of the direct representatives of the people in meeting the needs of society, on the views of Presidents and Governors, and by their construction of the will of the legisla-

tures the Court breathes life, feeble or strong, into the inert pages of the Constitution and the statute books.[6]

Indeed, this is a function calling for a combination of philosopher, historian, and prophet—but it also calls for other vital attributes that enter into the judicial process.

A glance at the personnel of the 1980–1981 Court will perhaps serve to underscore that judicial experience is not necessarily vital to a Supreme Court jurist. Of the nine men—Chief Justice Burger and Justices Brennan, Stewart, B. R. White, T. Marshall, Blackmun, Powell, Rehnquist, and Stevens—who commenced that term of Court, only six could point to judicial experience on lower courts, and in four instances it was for but a period averaging five years.

Yet *all* of the members of that Court had come to the high tribunal with considerable experience in *public* life, frequently of an administrative-executive nature. In order of seniority of service on the bench: Justice William J. Brennan, Jr., an army colonel in World War II, had practiced law for fifteen years and had served for seven years on three state courts in New Jersey, including the State Supreme Court, before he was appointed in 1956. Justice Potter Stewart, who saw three years of service overseas during World War II, had practiced law for more than a decade, had been a member of the City Council of Cincinnati, and had served on the U.S. Court of Appeals for the Sixth Circuit for four years when he was appointed in 1958. Justice Byron R. White, Rhodes scholar and All-American football star, had been Chief Justice Vinson's law clerk, had practiced law for fourteen years, and was Deputy Attorney General of the United States when John Kennedy sent him to the Court in 1962 at age forty-four. Justice Thurgood Marshall—the first black to reach the highest court and a nationally known civil rights leader—had practiced law for three decades, much of it constitutional law at the bar of the Supreme Court, and had served for three and three-quarter years on the U.S. Court of Appeals for the Second Circuit. When he was appointed in 1967 to the Supreme Court, he held the position of U.S. Solicitor General. Chief Justice Warren E. Burger, appointed in 1969, had practiced law for twenty-three years, had been politically active in his native Minnesota, and for three years had held the post of Assistant Attorney General, heading the Civil Division, before becoming a federal jurist in 1956. With thirteen years on the U.S. Court of Appeals for the District of Columbia, he had had the most extensive judicial background. Justice Harry A. Blackmun, appointed to the Court in 1970, had a record similar to that of his fellow Minnesotan Burger, having practiced law in a Minneapolis firm for sixteen years, and had served as General Counsel for the Mayo Clinic and Rochester, Minnesota, for seven years when in 1959 he was named to the U.S. Court of Appeals for the Eighth Circuit. Justice Lewis F. Powell, Jr., appointed to the Court late in 1971, had a long and distinguished record as a legal practitioner and civic leader in Virginia–including the chairmanship of the Richmond public school board in the late 1950s and, later, the Virginia State Board of Education–and he had been President of the A.B.A. Justice William H. Rehnquist had clerked for Justice Robert H. Jackson, had practiced law and been active in Arizona politics for many years, and was serving as Assistant Attorney General of the United States, in charge of the office of Legal Counsel, at the time of his elevation to the Court in December 1971. And John Paul Stevens, the sole Ford appointee, had clerked for Justice Wiley B. Rutledge, and had practiced private law, specializing in antitrust litigation, when he was sent to the U.S. Court of Appeals for the Seventh Circuit, five years antecedent to coming to the Supreme Court in 1975.

If for the sake of argument one were to grant the necessity of *judicial* experience as a requirement for all Supreme Court nominees, the rich nonjudicial backgrounds of the individuals just described would not compensate for their lack of actual experience on lower benches. But almost all Supreme Court jurists have had extensive *legal* experience. Moreover, all of the 102 who actually served on the Court, with the sole exception of Justice George Shiras, Jr. (1892–1903), had engaged in at least some public service at various levels of government or had actively participated in political enterprises. Nevertheless, unlike the jurists of France, for example, who are trained and schooled as jurists, a great many

TABLE 3

Occupations of Supreme Court Designees at Time of Appointment†*

Federal Officeholder in Executive Branch	22
Judge of State Court	22
Judge of Inferior Federal Court	21
Private Practice of Law	18
U.S. Senator	8
U.S. Representative	4
State Governor	3
Professor of Law	3
Associate Justice of U.S. Supreme Court‡	2
Justice of the Permanent Court of International Justice	1

* Many of the appointees had held a variety of federal or state offices, or even both, prior to their selection.
† In general the appointments from state office are clustered at the beginning of the Court's existence; those from federal office are more recent.
‡ Justice E. D. White and H. F. Stone, who were *promoted* to the Chief Justiceship in 1910 and 1941, respectively, while sitting as Associate Justices.

American jurists have no judicial background. And in the considered judgment of a majority of the members of the bar as well as most nonlegally trained students and observers of the Court, it is not a vital prerequisite to a successful judicial career. Table 3 indicates the occupations (at the time of appointment) of those (using the full figure of 105 here) who have served on the Supreme Court.

Discounting rare individual exceptions, the caliber of the Supreme Court has been universally high. No other part of the American government can readily match its general record of competence and achievement. Yet there is nothing particularly astonishing about the essentially upper-middle-class "establishment" components that by and large have tended to characterize the members of the Court. A fusing of the background characteristics of the 102 individuals who have sat on the Court thus produces the following profile:

NATIVE-BORN (there have been but six exceptions, the last two being the England-born George Sutherland and Austrian-born Felix Frankfurter); WHITE (the first nonwhite,

> Thurgood Marshall, was appointed in 1967); MAN (there was no woman on the Court until President Reagan's appointment of Sandra Day O'Connor in 1981);[7] GENERALLY PROTESTANT (six Roman Catholic and five Jewish Justices); FIFTY TO FIFTY-FIVE years of age at the time of appointment; FIRST-BORN (fifty-six);[8] ANGLO-SAXON ETHNIC STOCK (all except fifteen); UPPER-MIDDLE TO HIGH SOCIAL STATUS: REARED IN A NONRURAL BUT NOT NECESSARILY URBAN ENVIRONMENT; MEMBER OF A CIVIC-MINDED, POLITICALLY ACTIVE, ECONOMICALLY COMFORTABLE FAMILY; B.A. AND LL.B. OR J.D. DEGREES (usually, although not always,[9] from prestigious institutions); SERVICE IN PUBLIC OFFICE; from POPULOUS STATES (see Table 4).

Present-day egalitarian trends may well operate to alter that profile somewhat: assuredly, a "woman's seat" and a "black seat" are political certainties, conceivably in multiples. Yet a dramatic alteration of the other major components of the depicted profile is not likely. With the indicated exceptions, the described composite is not only more or less self-operating, but most members of the American body politic would not welcome any drastic change in it. Notwithstanding the frequent attacks on the Supreme Court as an institution, its personnel has generally been held in high esteem by the average citizen.

The religious factor is based on the notion of a "Roman Catholic seat" and a "Jewish seat" on the Supreme Court. A development of dubious communal wisdom, the concept of religious-group representation has become one of the facts of American political and judicial life (see Table 5)—although it has been less of an emotional problem in the courts than in the makeup of election slates in minority-conscious cities, such as New York, for example, and it has become far less of a problem *cum* consideration than race or gender.

Six men have occupied the "Roman Catholic seat" to date: Chief Justice Roger B. Taney (Jackson, 1836); and Associate Justices Edward D. White (Cleveland, 1894—he was promoted to

TABLE 4

The Thirty-one States from Which the 105 Supreme Court Appointments Were Made

State		State	
New York	15	Iowa	2
Ohio	9	Louisiana	2
Massachusetts	8	Michigan	2
Virginia	7	Minnesota	2
Pennsylvania	6	North Carolina	2
Tennessee	6	Colorado	1
Kentucky	5	Indiana	1
Illinois	4	Kansas	1
Maryland	4	Maine	1
New Jersey	4	Mississippi	1
Alabama	3	Missouri	1
California	3	New Hampshire	1
Connecticut	3	Texas	1
Georgia	3	Utah	1
South Carolina	3	Wyoming	1
Arizona	2		105

TABLE 5

Acknowledged Religion of the 102 Individual Justices of the Supreme Court (at time of appointment)

Religion	
Episcopalian	27
Unspecified Protestant	25
Presbyterian	17
Roman Catholic	6
Unitarian	6
Baptist	5
Jewish	5
Methodist	4
Congregationalist	3
Disciples of Christ	2
Lutheran	1
Quaker	1
	102

Chief Justice by Taft, 1910), Joseph McKenna (McKinley, 1898), Pierce Butler (Harding, 1922), Frank Murphy (F. D. Roosevelt, 1940), and William J. Brennan, Jr. (Eisenhower, 1956). With the exception of the seven years between Justice Frank Murphy's death in 1949 (when President Truman deliberately ignored the unwritten rule of the "reserved" seat and nominated Protestant Tom C. Clark to the vacancy created by Murphy's death) and the nomination of Justice William J. Brennan, Jr., in 1956, a Roman Catholic has been on the Supreme Court continually since White's appointment. In characteristically forthright manner, Truman (a good Baptist) had commented publicly when he broke the unwritten "religion seat" code: "I do not believe religions have anything to do with the Supreme Bench. If an individual has the qualifications, I do not care if he is a Protestant, Catholic or Jew."[10]

The "Jewish seat" was established in 1916 with the appointment of Louis D. Brandeis. That tradition was broken when in 1969 President Nixon successively nominated three Protestants (Haynsworth, Carswell, and Blackmun) to succeed Fortas. In 1971 Nixon had two opportunities to appoint a Jewish Justice, but he again nominated two more Protestants–William H. Rehnquist and Lewis F. Powell, Jr. Questioned on the continued "oversight" at one of his infrequent news conferences, Nixon gave the appropriately logical response: that merit rather than religion should and must govern[11]–a laudable aim provided it is indeed invoked. The five occupants of "the Jewish seat" to date have been: Louis D. Brandeis (Wilson, 1916), Benjamin N. Cardozo (Hoover, 1932), Felix Frankfurter (F. D. Roosevelt, 1939), Arthur J. Goldberg (Kennedy, 1962), and Abe Fortas (L. B. Johnson, 1965).

In June 1967 Lyndon B. Johnson designated Thurgood Marshall, the first black ever to be nominated to the Supreme Court. The President, leaving no doubt that the nominee's race was probably the major factor in his decision, told the country: "I believe it is the right thing to do, the right time to do it, the right man and the right place."[12] There is no doubt that there now exists a "black seat" on the bench that is, in effect, far more secure than a "Catholic seat" or a "Jewish seat." That is unquestionably also true of a "woman's seat," to all intents and purposes established with President Reagan's dramatic appointment of Judge Sandra Day O'Connor of Arizona in September 1981 as the first woman Justice of the Supreme Court of the United States.

Political and ideological compatibility often go hand in hand in influencing Presidential choices for the Supreme Court. Among the points a President is almost certain to consider are the following: (1) whether his choice will render him more popular among influential interest groups; (2) whether the nominee has been a loyal member of the President's party; (3) whether the nominee favors Presidential programs and policies; (4) whether the nominee is acceptable (or at least not "personally obnoxious") to the home-state Senators; (5) whether the nominee's judicial record, if any, meets the Presidential criteria of constitutional construction; (6) whether the President is indebted to the nominee for past political services; and (7) whether he feels "good" or "comfortable" about his choice.

It is an unwritten law of the judicial nominating process that the President will not normally select an individual from the ranks of the political opposition. To lessen charges of Court politicizing, however, this rule is purposely relaxed now and then—but only within "political reason"—which seems to have meant roughly to the tune of six percent of all appointments to district and appellate tribunals and an on-its-face-surprising fifteen percent to the Supreme Court. In at least thirteen instances, the appointee to the Supreme Court, including two to the post of Chief Justice, came from a political party other than that of the President: Whig President John Tyler appointed a Democrat, Samuel Nelson, and Republican Presidents Abraham Lincoln, Benjamin Harrison, William Howard Taft, Warren G. Harding, Herbert Hoover, Dwight D. Eisenhower, and Richard M. Nixon appointed nine Democrats—Taft alone three! The nine Justices and their nominators were Stephen J. Field (Lincoln); Howell E. Jackson (Benjamin Harrison); Horace H. Lurton, Edward D. White (promoted to Chief Justice), and Joseph R. Lamar (Taft); Pierce Butler (Harding); William J. Brennan, Jr. (Eisenhower); and Lewis F.

TABLE 6

Avowed Political Affiliation of the 105 Supreme Court Justices (at time of selection)

Federalists	13
Whig	1
Democrats	49*
Republicans	41
Independent	1
	105

* Includes the four Democrat-Republican Presidents (Jefferson, Madison, Monroe, and J. Q. Adams).

Powell, Jr. (Nixon). And Democratic Presidents Woodrow Wilson, Franklin D. Roosevelt, and Harry S Truman appointed three Republicans: Louis D. Brandeis (Wilson), Harlan F. Stone (promoted to Chief Justice by F.D.R.), and Harold H. Burton (Truman). To this list some would add F.D.R.'s selection of Felix Frankfurter, who labeled himself an Independent.

There will always be some crossing of party lines, particularly at the lower court levels, to maintain at least the appearance of judicial nonpartisanship and to placate the opposition, but the practice may be safely viewed as the exception rather than the rule (as Table 6 and the following statistics indicate). Many a President has been told by his political advisers to stay on his side of the fence, where surely there are just as many qualified and deserving lawyers as on the other side. "Think Republican," Republican National Chairman Rogers C. B. Morton urged President Nixon at the latter's first opportunity to fill seats on the Supreme Court.[13] As Table 7 amply demonstrates, Morton's sentiments are not confined to his political party! If the percentage of "other party" *Supreme Court* appointees has been markedly higher than that of the lower federal courts, it is because the President recognizes that what matters more than anything else, certainly more than a nominee's *nominal* political adherence, is the ideological compatibility of the candidate—what Theodore Roosevelt referred to as the nominee's "real politics."

TABLE 7

Percentages of Federal Judicial Appointments Adhering to the Same Political Party as the President, 1888–1984

PRESIDENT	PARTY	PERCENTAGE
Cleveland	Democrat	97.3
Harrison	Republican	87.9
McKinley	Republican	95.7
T. Roosevelt	Republican	95.8
Taft	Republican	82.2
Wilson	Democrat	98.6
Harding	Republican	97.7
Coolidge	Republican	94.1
Hoover	Republican	85.7
F. D. Roosevelt	Democrat	96.4
Truman	Democrat	93.1
Eisenhower	Republican	95.1
Kennedy	Democrat	90.9
L. B. Johnson	Democrat	95.2
Nixon	Republican	93.7
Ford	Republican	81.2
Carter	Democrat	94.8
Reagan	Republican	98.1*

* As of September 1984.

Whatever the merits of the other criteria attending Presidential motivations in appointments may be, what must be of overriding concern to any nominator is his perception of the candidate's *real* politics. The Chief Executive's crucial predictive judgment concerns itself with the nominee's likely future voting pattern on the bench, based on his or her past stance and commitment on matters of public policy insofar as they are reliably discernible. All Presidents have tried, thus, to pack the bench to a greater or lesser extent. They will indubitably continue to do so!

In the public eye Court-packing has been most closely associated with Franklin D. Roosevelt. Having had not a single opportunity to fill a Court vacancy in his first term (1933–1937) and seeing his domestic programs consistently battered by the Court, the frustrated President attempted to get his way all at once. His Court-packing bill, however, died a deserved death in the Senate.

It is not surprising that Court-packing and the name of President F. D. Roosevelt have become synonymous. Yet even such popular heroes as Jefferson, Jackson, and Lincoln followed similar courses of action in the face of what they considered "judicial intransigence and defiance." Their approach was not so radical as Roosevelt's, but they very likely would have been sympathetic to his efforts. George Washington, although broadly regarded as far removed from "politics," insisted that his nominees to the Court meet a veritable smorgasbord of specific qualifications.[14] In fact, every President who has made nominations to the Supreme Court has been guilty of Court-packing in some measure. It is entirely understandable that a President will choose individuals he hopes will share his own philosophy of government and politics, at least to the extent of giving him a sympathetic hearing. Theodore Roosevelt, for example, in discussing the potential candidacy of Horace H. Lurton with Henry Cabot Lodge, put the issue well:

> [T]he nominal politics of the man has nothing to do with his actions on the bench. His real politics are all important. . . . He is right on the Negro question; he is right on the power of the federal government; he is right on the Insular business; he is right about corporations; he is right about labor. On every question that would come before the bench, he has so far shown himself to be in much closer touch with the policies in which you and I believe than even White [Associate Justice Edward D. White] because he has been right about corporations where White has been wrong.[15]

Lodge concurred in substance, but he replied that he could see no reason "why Republicans cannot be found who hold those opinions as well as Democrats."[16] Consequently, he strongly urged the candidacy of a Republican; T.R. then duly nominated one: William H. Moody, his Attorney General.

Thus, concern with a nominee's *real* politics is a fundamental issue–and examples abound. It prompted Republican Taft to give half of his six appointments to kindred souls who were Democrats; Republican Nixon to appoint Democrat Powell; Democrat

Roosevelt to promote Republican Stone; and Democrat Truman to appoint Republican Burton. Yet there is no guarantee that what a President perceives as *real* politics will not fade into a mirage. Hence Charles Warren, eminent chronicler of the Court, observed entirely realistically that "nothing is more striking in the history of the Court than the manner in which the hopes of those who expected a judge to follow the political views of the President appointing him are disappointed."[17] Few have felt the truth of that statement more keenly than Teddy Roosevelt did with Oliver Wendell Holmes, Jr., whose early "anti-administration" opinions in antitrust cases (notably in *Northern Securities* v. *United States*)[18] were entirely unexpected. A bare 5:4 majority in that case did uphold the government's order under the Sherman Antitrust Act dissolving the Northern Securities Company, a brainchild of E. H. Harriman and J. J. Hill—the rich and powerful owners of competing railroads who had organized the company to secure a terminal line into Chicago. Roosevelt had won that important litigation, but he was furious about his recent appointee's "anti-antitrust" vote in the case and stormed: "I could carve out of a banana a Judge with more backbone than that!"[19] Holmes reportedly merely smiled when told the President's remark, made a *sotto voce* reference to "shallow intellects," and noted his intention to "call the shots as I see them in terms of the legal and constitutional setting." Later, during T.R.'s second term of office (1905–1909), Holmes expressed his sentiments to a labor leader at a White House dinner with characteristic directness: "What you want is favor, not justice. But when I am on my job, I don't give a damn what you or Mr. Roosevelt want."[20]

James Madison was similarly chagrined with his appointment of Justice Joseph Story, having refused to heed his political mentor, Thomas Jefferson. The Sage of Monticello had warned him that Story was an inveterate Tory who would become a rabid supporter of Chief Justice Marshall—and he was right: Story not only instantly joined Marshall's approach to constitutional adjudication and interpretation, he even out-Marshalled Marshall in his nationalism! Perhaps even more chagrin was felt by Woodrow Wilson when the first of his three Supreme Court appointees, his Attorney General, James C. McReynolds, proved himself quickly to be the antithesis of almost everything for which his nominator stood and in which he believed.

More recently, Harry Truman observed that "packing the Supreme Court simply can't be done . . . I've tried and it won't work. . . . Whenever you put a man on the Supreme Court he ceases to be your friend. I'm sure of that."[21] Future Presidents may well be advised to heed the admonition of Zechariah Chafee, Jr., Harvard's famed expert on the judicial process, who contended that to forecast the behavior of a future jurist it is wiser to consider the books in his library than the list of clients in his office.

There is indeed a considerable element of unpredictability in the judicial appointing process. To the often-heard "Does a person become any different when he puts on a gown?" Justice Frankfurter's sharp retort was always, "If he is any good, he does!" At least to some extent, F.F. assuredly did! In the tellingly colorful prose of Alexander M. Bickel, "You shoot an arrow into a far-distant future when you appoint a Justice and not the man himself can tell you what he will think about some of the problems that he will face."[22] And late in 1969, reflecting upon his sixteen years as Chief Justice of the United States, Earl Warren pointed out that he, for one, did not "see how a man could be on the Court and not change his views substantially over a period of years . . . for change you must if you are to do your duty on the Supreme Court."[23] It is a duty that in many ways represents the most hallowed in the governmental process of the United States.

Who the 102 individuals to sit on the Court were; why they were appointed (and why some were not); who chose them; how they performed (and/or how they were perceived to have performed) is the concern of the balance of this book.

5

The *First* Forty Years: From George Washington to John Quincy Adams 1789-1829

George Washington, whom the experts on the Presidency (see Appendix B, *infra*) continue to regard as second only to Lincoln in terms of greatness in stature and accomplishment[1] among our Chief Executives, made few mistakes during his eight years in office. Both judicious and secure in his pursuit of excellence, he knew what he wanted and readily admitted to staffing both the judicial and the executive branches with reliable, cautious, conservative adherents to the Federalist cause. It was his opportunity to nominate fourteen putative members to the Supreme Court, then a judicial body of unknown practical power. Only ten of these fourteen served, however: twelve were confirmed; one (John Rutledge, as Chief Justice) was rejected; one (Paterson) was withdrawn (although resubmitted successfully later); and two (Robert H. Harrison and William Cushing, as Chief Justice) refused to serve after their confirmation. Whether one uses the figure fourteen, thirteen, twelve, or ten,[2] Washington's number of appointment opportunities constitutes a record to this day—one hardly likely to be overcome. (In second place stands F.D.R.'s record of nine successful appointments.)

In choosing his candidates, Washington, probably more than any other President, not only had a clear set of criteria for Court candidacy, but adhered to them predictably and religiously: (1)

support and advocacy of the Constitution; (2) distinguished service in the Revolution; (3) active participation in the political life of state or nation; (4) prior judicial experience on lower tribunals; (5) either a "favorable reputation with his fellows" or personal ties with Washington himself; (6) geographic "suitability." Of these criteria, evidently the most important to him was advocacy of the principles of the Constitution–the more outspoken the better. Perhaps more than many of his contemporaries he recognized the potential strength and influence of the judicial branch, keenly sensing the role it would be called on to play in spelling out constitutional basics and penumbras. In letters of commission to his initial six nominees to the first Supreme Court in 1789, he wrote: "The Judicial System is the chief Pillar upon which our national Government must rest."[3] That Pillar needed strong men–proponents of the Federalist philosophy of government. Indeed, seven of those the President sent to the bench had been participants in the Constitutional Convention of 1787. He knew most, if not all, of his appointees intimately.

John Jay of New York–lawyer, jurist, diplomat, soldier, political leader–at forty-four years of age was Washington's first appointment and his choice for Chief Justice. All but unique among the Founding Fathers, he claimed a line of ancestry of entirely non-British stock–his forebears were French Huguenot refugees to England. Jay, whom Washington had known since the first Continental Congress and with whom he had worked closely and corresponded for well over two decades, had not been in Philadelphia during the summer of 1787. Yet he had contributed to *The Federalist Papers,* had been influential in Hamilton's cliff-hanger struggle to secure New York's ratification of the Constitution, and, while President of the Continental Congress in 1778–1779, had staunchly defended the General's military conduct and authority when George Washington was under heavy political attack. The President's choice was a true-blue loyalist.

Another among the first President's original choices, however, had been a key figure at the Convention, John Rutledge of South Carolina–a former governor of that state and a judge of its Chancery Court. As Chairman of the Committee on Detail, which composed the first draft of the Constitution, he was regarded as one of the central personalities behind the creation of a *United* States of America. In fact, Washington referred to Rutledge rather extravagantly, and quite *in*correctly, as the individual who "wrote the Constitution."[4] He had seriously considered appointing Rutledge as the first Chief Justice—which is what Rutledge and his supporters had really craved—but opted for Jay because he wanted to honor the key state of New York, whose ratification of the Constitution had proved so decisive. Rutledge, at age fifty-two, was confirmed as Associate Justice in 1791, but he had stepped down from the bench before the Court actually convened to assume the Chief Justiceship of South Carolina. When Jay resigned as Chief Justice in 1795 to become governor of New York, Washington again chose Rutledge, this time for the center chair, yet the Senate now rejected the nomination because of Rutledge's pronounced opposition to the Jay Treaty. Rutledge did, however, serve in the post of Chief Justice on a recess appointment, presiding over the August 1795 term of the Court, until the Senate turned thumbs down on him by a 10:14 vote on December 15, 1795—the *only* Justice on record among the fifteen who functioned in such a recess capacity who was not subsequently confirmed.

Pennsylvania's James Wilson, a signer of the Declaration of Independence, was also a key member of the Convention. One of the outstanding lawyer-scholars of his time—he would become the fledgling Republic's first law professor (University of Pennsylvania) and was one of the few Founding Fathers to propound "a general theory of government and law"[5]—Wilson was greatly instrumental in strengthening the role of the judicial branch and was widely regarded as the Father of the judicial article of the Constitution. He had fought successfully for a judiciary independent of both the states and of the national legislative and executive branches. He had argued in favor of the establishment of lower ("inferior") federal courts, advocated judicial appointment by the President, and had fortuitously convinced his fellow delegates that judicial independence would be impaired if the President—at the request of Congress—were able to remove Justices from the bench (a proposal that a good many future Presidents would have loved to have had available!). At the ratifying convention of his home state, Wilson was among those most influential in obtaining its consent to the U.S. Constitution, and he was the architect of Pennsylvania's Constitution of 1790. He not only proposed his own nomination to President Washington in writing, but he expressed a preference for the Chief Justiceship. Yet it was Jay, of course, who was named Chief Justice, and the President, who was initially torn between Wilson and the latter's fellow Pennsylvanian, Chief Justice Thomas McKean, chose the forty-seven-year-old Wilson as an Associate Justice. It would prove to be a fortunate decision, indeed, for McKean later became a rabid states' rights advocate who rejected the power of judicial review by the federal courts, the U.S. Supreme Court in particular.

John Blair of Virginia, at fifty-seven the second-oldest member of this first Supreme Court, had also been a participant at the Convention, although he had figured much less prominently than Wilson. But Blair had shown himself an excellent team player when, subordinating his own strong personal preferences, he had cast his lot with Washington and Madison to carry the Virginia delegation and the Convention for the establishment of the electoral college, just as the Convention seemed hopelessly deadlocked over the method of selecting the President. Ultimately Blair, Washington, and Madison were the only members of the Old Dominion delegation to vote for the Constitution in its entirety.

William Cushing, Chief Justice of the Supreme Judicial Court of Massachusetts, completed the group of five chosen for the Court in 1789. At fifty-seven plus (a few months older than Blair), he was the oldest appointee. Although he had not attended the Constitutional Convention, he had been active in the cause of the Constitution, having initially persuaded Massachusetts to send delegates to Philadelphia. In 1788 he had served as Vice-President of his state's ratifying convention, emerging as its most dominating single figure. While sitting as an Associate Justice of the Supreme Court, he became Washington's second choice (after John Rutledge had been rejected) for Chief Justice to succeed Jay in 1795. The Senate confirmed him; but Cushing, who was now sixty-four years old, pleaded advanced age and ill health–he was also disinclined to take on what he viewed as the Chief's "additional burdens." Thus, he rejected the post and opted for continued service as Associate Justice until his death fourteen years later.

The last of the original six justices was James Iredell, former Attorney General of North Carolina, appointed in 1790, one year later than the group of five. He was the youngest member of the first Court at thirty-eight. Although he had not been a Convention participant, he had been an influential proponent of ratification; very likely it was because of his massive public "educational" campaign that North Carolina approved the Constitution. Actually, Iredell was Washington's second choice for the position: he had first nominated, and the Senate had confirmed, his close personal friend and former private military secretary during the Revolutionary War, Robert Hanson Harrison. But Harrison was chosen Chancellor of Maryland just a few days after his confirmation to the Court, which he had reluctantly accepted and then almost immediately declined, accurately citing ill health. He decided to accept the state post—notwithstanding Washington and Hamilton's warmly urgent pleas to decline it. Iredell, however, would prove to be a source of considerable satisfaction to Washington during his service on the high bench—so much so that the President seriously considered his promotion to Chief Justice when Cushing stepped aside.

Washington's pattern of seeking men with Convention participation or support continued with his remaining four successful appointments. In 1791 he chose Thomas Johnson of Maryland, fifty-nine, a former governor of that state and a lower federal judge at the time of appointment. There was no doubt as to Johnson's adherence to Federalist principles. He had been a delegate to the Constitutional Convention and had faithfully supported the finished document. Reluctant to accept appointment to the Court because of his aversion to the rigors of circuit-riding, Johnson saw his fears realized when he began to serve, and he resigned in less than two years' time. His replacement was William Paterson, the forty-eight-year-old Chancellor of New Jersey and former state Attorney General and U.S. Senator. A strong Federalist "with such consistency as possible to a small-state man,"[6] Paterson had been one of the foremost leaders of the Constitutional Convention, offering the "small state" plan or New Jersey Plan, for equal representation of all states in the national legislature. One of his most significant services to the new Union was his work–second only to Oliver Ellsworth's–on behalf of the Judiciary Act of 1789, which implies the judicial review that was so vital to Washington's visualization of a strong federal judicial system. Paterson's nomination was initially withdrawn by Washington because the former's term in the U.S. Senate had still four days to run, but he was readily confirmed on resubmittal.

A signer of the Declaration of Independence and a hero of the Revolution, Chief Justice Samuel Chase of Maryland, fifty-five, was the President's initial choice to fill the vacancy caused by the Senate's rejection of John Rutledge as Chief Justice in December 1795, yet wisely he refrained from designating the acid-tongued, outspoken Chase. Instead he named him to the Associate's seat vacated by Blair in January 1796, which had not yet been filled. Washington had been widely cautioned about Chase's character and temperament, but the President knew him well and eventually decided that his service to the causes of independence warranted his appointment. Chase had opposed the adoption of the Constitution on grounds that were rather nebulous, and he had voted against its adoption at the Maryland ratifying convention. Subsequently, however, he had seen the light, "recognized" the merits of the Constitution, and had become a zealous, vocal backer of the Union. Once on the high bench, Chase immediately began to make a specialty of attacking Republicans and rendered himself thoroughly obnoxious to them: in 1796 he predicted that under Jefferson "our republican institution will sink into a mobocracy, the worst of all possible governments";[7] and he charged Jefferson, both before and after his election as President, with "seditious attacks on the principles of the Constitution." For these attacks the House of Representatives impeached Chase on grounds of "high crimes and misdemeanors" by a vote of 72:32 in March 1804. Fortunately for the cause of judicial independence and the principles of separation of powers, when the Senate voted on the charges brought by the House on March 1, 1805, enough Republicans joined the Federalists to acquit the colorful figure by a four-vote margin.[8] It was just as well that Washington did not live to see the controversies that surrounded his but mildly contrite appointee—he would have been chagrined and embarrassed.

In 1796, one year before the end of his second term, Washington made his last appointment: Oliver Ellsworth of Connecticut, fifty-one, a staunch Federalist, state jurist, federal legislator, diplomat, and the principal author of the Judiciary Act of 1789. Like the other Washington appointees, Ellsworth was an influential spokesman in behalf of Union and had been a delegate to the Philadelphia Convention. He had also been particularly effective in bringing about Connecticut's ratification of the Constitution. During the Philadelphia debates he emerged as an early and articulate exponent of the Supreme Court's inherent power of judicial review, which he, like Washington, saw as an essential constitutional check on potential legislative excesses. Yet Ellsworth remained at the helm for only a brief time. Notwithstanding grave inherent questions of the propriety and constitutionality of assigning nonjudicial functions to a sitting jurist, John Adams had appointed him envoy to France early in 1799. While still in France late in 1800 Ellsworth resigned because of ill health—thus setting the stage for the appointment of John Marshall by the lame-duck John Adams.

In addition to insisting on strong Federalist credentials, Washington searched for men who had rendered service during the Revolution and, if possible, men who had been active in the affairs of their home states and communities. Seven of his successful appointees had been delegates to the Constitutional Convention, the exceptions being John Jay, William Cushing, and James Iredell. But Jay, in addition to having written the New York Constitution of 1777, had been a member of the Second Continental Congress and had been appointed "chief foreign relations officer" of the Confederacy. Cushing had served as Chief Justice of Massachusetts during the difficult and crucial period of 1777–1789. Iredell had served North Carolina—as Attorney General, as a member of the Council of State, and as a Superior Court judge. Six of the President's choices—John Jay, Oliver Ellsworth, Samuel Chase,

William Paterson, Thomas Johnson, and John Rutledge–had been members of the Continental Congress at various times. Samuel Chase, William Paterson, and James Wilson were signers of the Declaration of Independence. And, to the President's particular delight, several of the ten had experienced active involvement in the field during the Revolutionary struggles. For example, Paterson had served as an officer in a company of Minute Men, and Cushing, indomitably energetic, had ridden circuit and held court in Massachusetts during the entire Revolutionary era. The President was perhaps proudest of all of Thomas Johnson: in 1777 when General Washington was literally struggling to keep his army on its feet, Governor Johnson of Maryland had recruited a force of 1800 men and personally led them to Washington's camp. Indeed, for three successive terms as governor, Johnson displayed an uncanny ability to supply food, arms, and supplies as well as men to the embattled Continental Army.

Yet Washington sought still other attributes in his candidates–among them previous judicial experience–and with the exception of Wilson and Paterson all came to the Court with such background. In fact, his eight other appointees had sixty-three years of collective judicial experience. Four had served on the Supreme Court of their respective states (Jay, Ellsworth, Samuel Chase, and Cushing); the remaining four had been jurists on other high state courts: Iredell on the Superior Court of North Carolina; John Rutledge on the South Carolina Court of Chancery; Johnson as Chief Judge of the General Court of Maryland; and Blair on both the General Court and the High Court of Chancery of Virginia. As for Paterson and Wilson, the "mitigating circumstances" were clearly acceptable: Paterson was a coauthor of the federal Judiciary Act of 1789 and while governor of New Jersey had codified its laws and updated the rules of practice and procedure in its courts. Wilson, one of the country's most widely acclaimed legal scholars, and a superb practitioner at the bar, had emerged as an expert on the judiciary in the Constitutional Convention.

Geography must also be noted as one of the elements that strongly influenced Washington's appointments. He regarded it as extremely important in the light of his constant endeavor to be President of *all* the states of the fledgling nation, and he repeatedly stated his desire to see each "section" of the land "represented" on the Supreme Court. On several occasions Washington "rewarded" a strategic state. For example, in commenting on Iredell's appointment, the President frankly stated: "he is of a State of some importance in the Union that has given no character to a federal office."[9] And perhaps the decisive consideration in his appointment of Jay rather than John Rutledge as Chief Justice was that Jay hailed from New York, a critical state that had so narrowly and recently ratified the Constitution. Rutledge, Wilson, and Jay had been Washington's three "finalists" for the post. The President eliminated Wilson because of what he regarded as a lack of "appropriate" administrative and political experience, leaving the New Yorker and the South Carolinian as contenders. Since Washington himself, Secretary of State Thomas Jefferson, and Attorney General Edmund Jennings Randolph were all Virginians, Washington determined that yet another top federal office occupied by a Southerner would be unwise. Hence Rutledge had to settle for an Associate Justiceship, from which he resigned seventeen months later.

Washington died too soon to see the full on-the-bench record of his ten Federalist appointees, but he would have been well pleased with their performances. Practically no anti-Federalist decisions were rendered by them or their Federalist successors; and none of them wrote what could be called an anti-Federalist dissenting opinion. It was a pity that the first President could not witness the momentous decisions of the Court under the firm guidance of the towering John Marshall, who by his opinions and decisions as Chief Justice did so much to bring to fruition Washington's dreams for a strong Republic.

John Adams was of considerably less stature than Washington; but the second President did what he could to follow what was indeed a "tough act." History and most historians have been kind to Adams, even ranking him as a "near great" President (see Appendix B, *infra*). Overshadowed by the talented, shrewd, and ambitious Hamilton and by the memories of Washington's Administration, he proved to be a weak leader and poor administrator, often taking the easy way out. Yet he managed to keep a shaky peace with France despite Hamilton's hawkishness and plotting.

John Adams appointed but three men to the Court (there were four if one counts the Senate-confirmed reappointment of John Jay as Chief Justice late in 1800, which Jay declined): Bushrod Washington, Alfred Moore, and John Marshall. His criteria for nomination are identifiable but considerably less numerous than Washington's. The preeminent requirement was that candidates be of strong Federalist persuasion. Thus, George Washington's nephew, Bushrod, although only thirty-six years old at the time of his selection, had amply proved his Federalist loyalty during his career in the Virginia House of Delegates; Moore, forty-five, had had extensive judicial as well as executive experience in his native North Carolina and was widely regarded as one of the most gifted and persuasive Federalist lawyers in the states; and Virginian John Marshall in general personified the Federalist creed.

As with his predecessor, a potential appointee's home state was of genuine importance to Adams. There had been no "Virginia seat" on the Court since Justice John Blair's resignation in January 1796, and John Adams, determined to avoid a potentially explosive situation, offered to John Marshall the post caused by James Wilson's death in 1798. Yet Marshall declined to serve, pleading financial exigencies. The President now turned to Bushrod Washington, who had studied law under James Wilson, the man whose seat he would now take on the high bench. And when James Iredell of North Carolina died in 1799, Adams selected that state's Alfred Moore.

On the other hand, Adams did not insist that his nominees have previous judicial experience; in fact, neither Washington nor Marshall had. In Adams's eyes public service was more important, and all of his appointees fit that criterion well: Washington had served as a state legislator; Moore had been North Carolina's Attorney General and a judge of its Supreme Court; and Marshall had been Congressman, Cabinet officer, soldier, and diplomat. In sum, whereas President Washington followed a well-publicized set of six criteria in his quest to staff the Court, his successor contented himself with four: Federalist loyalty, appropriate geographic base, public service, and a good reputation.

John Adams's great achievement was his appointment of John Marshall. No one has had a more profound impact on Court and Constitution than the crafty, hedonistic, and brilliant Virginian. No wonder that the 1970 poll of sixty-five experts on constitutional law, ranking all Supreme Court Justices from 1789 to 1969 (see Ch. 1, *supra,* and Appendix A, *infra*), was *unanimous* in categorizing Marshall as "great," the sole Justice to receive such recognition. Ironically, Marshall had played second fiddle to John Jay, Adams's initial selection for the Chief Justiceship vacated by Oliver Ellsworth in December 1800. But Jay, whom Adams had not consulted before forwarding his name to the Senate, declined to serve, although his commission of appointment had been duly delivered, signed by Adams and his Secretary of State, John Marshall! Jay cited reasons of health; more accurately, he declined because—like a good many other colleagues on the bench—he loathed circuit-riding and quite prophetically doubted that Congress would act reasonably soon to relieve the Justices of that fatiguing and often unpleasant chore. Further, he felt that the young Court lacked "energy, weight, and dignity."[10] Adams's associates now urged him to return to a man frequently mentioned as worthy of Supreme Court status, Samuel Sitgreaves of Pennsylvania—especially since no Pennsylvanian was then on the Court. But Adams demurred—and he did so even more firmly when they suggested two prominent candidates of the Hamiltonian faction of the Federalist party: General Charles C. Pinckney of South Carolina, who had declined an appointment offered by Washington in 1791, and sitting Associate Justice William Paterson of New Jersey. Adams wanted his own man, one of whose loyalties he could be absolutely certain, especially because he had now lost the election of 1800 and "that Radical" Jefferson was about to succeed him. On January 20, 1801, with but minimal consultation and practically no fanfare, John Adams sent to the Senate the name of his forty-five-year-old Secretary of State, John Marshall, Virginia lawyer and Thomas Jefferson's distant cousin and avowed political enemy, to whom Jefferson liked to refer as "that gloomy malignity."[11]

The Senate, although still Federalist, was not pleased with its fellow partisan's nomination. Most of its leaders would have preferred William Paterson, despite his link with the party's Hamiltonian wing. Indeed, there is considerable evidence that they stalled for at least a week in the hope that Adams could be persuaded to substitute Paterson after all. But Adams, now a lame duck and no longer subject to the kind of political strictures that might otherwise have caused him to waiver, remained firm. The Senate—recognizing John Marshall's ability and the danger of a low-ranking "spite" nomination should it reject Marshall (or the vista of leaving the vacancy for the eager incoming Jeffersonians)—yielded and voted confirmation on January 27, 1801. No Federalist could possibly have had any cause for regret: Marshall's record on the Court proved to be blue-ribbon Federalism in every respect. Moreover, he would serve the Court and his country longer (thirty-four and one-half years) than any other member of the Supreme Court—except Justice Stephen J. Field (1863–1897) and, the longevity champion to date, Justice William O. Douglas (1939–1975)—and he did so with an excellence and a distinction that deserve to be categorized as *sui generis*. In 1826 John Adams could proudly and justly say: "My gift of John Marshall to the people of the United States was the proudest act of my life. There is no act of my life on which I reflect with more pleasure. I have given to my country a Judge equal to a Hale, a Holt, or a Mansfield."[12]

In John Jay's view the young Supreme Court was an "inauspicious" body, characterized by little work, dissatisfied personnel, and a lack of popular esteem and understanding. Jay so thoroughly disliked his job as first Chief Justice that he not only spent one year of his brief tenure (less than six) in England on a diplomatic mission, he also twice ran for governor of New York. On the second try he won that post and happily resigned the Court; he later (1800) declined, although Senate-confirmed, to succeed Oliver Ellsworth as Chief Justice. He was "convinced that under a [judicial] system so defective [the Supreme Court] would not obtain the energy, weight, . . . dignity . . . public confidence and respect which as a last resort of the justice of the nation, it should possess."[13] Ellsworth, too, had few regrets as he left his post for a diplomatic mission in France. John Marshall's helmsmanship brought about a change in the Court's posture and position that was as far-reaching as it was dramatic. Completely dominating his Court–what few dissents there were came almost solely from William Johnson, a Jefferson appointee–Marshall delivered the opinion for the Court in 519 out of a total of 1215 cases between 1801 and 1835, and he wrote thirty-six of the sixty-two decisions involving constitutional questions.[14] It is simply beyond dispute that he, more than any other individual in the history of the Court, determined the developing character of America's federal constitutional system. It was Marshall who raised the Court from its lowly if not discredited position to a level of equality with the executive and the legislative branches–perhaps even to one of dominance during the heyday of his Chief Justiceship.

John Marshall called his constitutional interpretations as he saw them, always adhering to the following creed: ". . . It is a constitution we are expounding . . . intended to endure for ages to come and, consequently to be adapted to the various crises of human affairs."[15] Yet he hastened to add that "judicial power, as contradistinguished from the power of the laws, has no existence. Courts are the mere instruments of the law, and can will nothing."[16]

Thus "willing nothing," Marshall handed down four of the most momentous decisions in the nation's history: (1) *Marbury* v. *Madison* (1803)[17]–judicial review, supremacy of the U.S. Constitution; (2) *McCulloch* v. *Maryland* (1819)[18]–implied powers of Congress, reaffirmation of the supremacy of the Constitution, federal immunity from involuntary state taxation, federal government held to derive its power directly from the people rather than from the states; (3) *Dartmouth College* v. *Woodward* (1819)[19]–inviolability of contracts; and (4) *Gibbons* v. *Ogden* (1824)[20]–plenary federal authority over interstate and foreign commerce. In Justice Cardozo's words: "Marshall gave to the constitution of the United States the impress of his own mind; and the form of our constitutional law is what it is, because he moulded it while it was still plastic and malleable in the fire of his own intense convictions."[21] Truly, the Marshall Court led the federal government and gave it the means to develop and work. Lord Bryce, close student of the American democracy, and Britain's Ambassador to the United States from 1907 to 1913, spoke of Marshall's decisions as "never having been surpassed and rarely equaled by the most famous jurists of modern Europe or of ancient Rome."[22] Under Marshall's guidance the Federalist dreams of a powerful nation found articulation and sanction. The Federalists gave way to the Democrat-Republicans at the century's turn, but the broad outlines of the Federalist philosophy were secure. The many years of Jeffersonianism, whatever its success at the nonjudicial policy-making level proved to be, did not reverse the Federalist doctrines of the Marshall Court. Indeed the six men appointed by Jefferson, Madison, and Monroe—all loyal Democrat-Republicans—entered nary a dissent to the key Federalist rulings of Marshall's Court.

Yet Jefferson's arrival on the canvas of government and politics represented a major departure from the *Weltanschauung* of the administrations of his predecessors. Not entirely comfortable as Chief Executive, the stately Virginian was above all a great leader of the legislature, a superb congressional party chief and party organizer. He would have been an ideal British Prime Minister, then as well as now. Jefferson has been ranked as "great" by the Presidential historians; yet the man himself had doubts about his accomplishments in that office, and he did not wish to see his Presidency memorialized on his gravestone in the cemetery at Monticello. "And not a word more," read his instructions asking that the following accomplishments be chiseled into simple stone: "Here was buried Thomas Jefferson, Author of the Declaration of American Independence, of the Statute of Virginia for Religious Freedom, and Father of the University of Virginia."

Jefferson's first opportunity to appoint a Supreme Court Justice came in 1804 when Associate Justice Alfred Moore resigned—after barely five years on the bench—because of ill health. The President, eager to designate only solid Democrat-Republicans, made it clear that any candidate would have to meet at least two criteria: loyalty to the Jeffersonian cause and "appropriate geographical provenance." There was no question about the first; only true-blue Democrat-Republicans were considered. As for the second, because both the Second and Sixth circuits were not "represented" on the Court, the nominee had to come from New York, South Carolina, or Georgia. There was no dearth of worthy candidates and Jefferson looked to several highly qualified and faithful-to-the-cause South Carolina attorneys. His choice devolved on a young lawyer, the barely thirty-two-year-old William Johnson, who had already been a judge of the South Carolina Supreme Court. Johnson was the only Democrat-Republican member of the Court to stand up to John Marshall on occasion. He also stood up to Jefferson, thus demonstrating early the spirit of independence that has so often characterized members of the Supreme Court.

On Justice Paterson's death in 1806, President Jefferson's second appointment went to forty-nine-year-old Henry B. Livingston of New York. He had been very much in the running at the time of William Johnson's appointment; Jefferson had long been attracted by Livingston's consistent loyalty to Democrat-Republicanism, his proved legal scholarship, and his effective public needling of the Federalists. Moreover, along with Aaron Burr, George Clinton, and his cousins Edward and Robert R. Livingston, Henry Livingston was a part of the New York political faction that had joined Jefferson's supporters from Virginia to form the Virginia-New York Alliance, so important in Jefferson's election. Not quite in Johnson's class as a jurisprudential figure, Livingston nonetheless would prove himself to be an able, thoughtful, delightfully humorous, and learned member of the Court during his sixteen years there.

Jefferson would have had to content himself with two appointments only, had not Congress created a seventh seat on the Supreme Court in 1807. The mounting population and resultant escalating judicial business in Kentucky, Ohio, and Tennessee dictated the creation of the additional post and the new Seventh Circuit. Ever conscious of the need to mend political fences, Jefferson now adopted the unique strategy of officially requesting each member of Congress to suggest to him two individuals for the vacancy, indicating first and second choices. Delighted to be thus involved, Congress caucused repeatedly, debating the relative merits of three men: John Boyle and James Hughes, both of Kentucky, and U.S. Representative George W. Campbell of Tennessee, ultimately asking Jefferson to designate Mr. Campbell. But the President demurred—he had serious doubts, and appropriately so, as to the constitutionality of appointing a sitting member of the legislative branch to an office created during his incumbency, and he was also less than enthusiastic about Campbell's expertise as a lawyer. Still wishing to abide by his determination to select someone entirely congenial to Congress, he chose Thomas Todd of Kentucky, who, alone among the names advanced by Congress, was listed as either the first or the second choice of each of the ten members of Congress from the three states of the new circuit.

Todd—who was forty-two years old and serving as Chief Justice of the Court of Appeals of Kentucky at the time of his appointment—established but a modestly distinguished record on the Court, writing only a few opinions. The choice of Todd was in considerable measure a testimonial to the importance Jefferson attached to the geographic suitability of a Supreme Court nominee. His three appointees came from different circuits, each circuit having a valid claim to "representation" in Jefferson's eyes.

Jefferson was also greatly concerned with his candidates' record of public service, preferably judicial service. Lawyer William Johnson had six years of judicial experience and long legislative service, capped by the Speakership of the House of Representatives of South Carolina; Henry Livingston had served three times in the New York State Assembly and was a hard-working member of the New York Supreme Court; and Todd had served both as a member and as Chief Justice of the Kentucky Court of Appeals.

Jefferson's fervent hope that his three appointments would serve to break the Marshallian-Federalist stranglehold on the course of Supreme Court decisions was not realized, although Johnson—a concerned humanitarian—provided a measure of success for him. Johnson, along with Story and John Marshall, the only truly outstanding Justice until the Taney Court period (Taney succeeded Marshall in 1836 and served until 1864), displayed considerable intellectual independence while on the Court and, disdaining Marshall's bossy displeasure, insisted on writing a good number of separate opinions. Yet the major thrust of his jurisprudence was the enhancement of national power, particularly in foreign and interstate commerce and in treaty matters. Livingston and Todd, despite a joint total of almost four decades on the bench, went along with Marshall with all but complete docility. Todd, for one, during whose career 644 cases were decided by the Court, wrote exactly fourteen opinions. His sole dissent was his first written opinion as a Justice—a five-line comment penned in the 1810 term.[23] No wonder that Jefferson, now back at his cherished Monticello and in the process of establishing his beloved University of Virginia, would in 1820 refer to the Court (on which then still served all of his three appointees) as "a subtle corps of sappers and miners" consisting of "a crafty chief judge" and "lazy or timid associates."[24]

James Madison, who succeeded Jefferson to the Presidency in 1809, did not find the office congenial. The "Father of the Constitution," a first-rate statesman and diplomat, and a superb intellect, Madison neither liked the political process nor was he adept in it. He proved the maxim that great statesmen are by no means great—or even good—politicians. He was essentially uncomfortable in the Presidency and proved to be indecisive and inept in the very area he had been deemed an expert: foreign affairs. Moreover, he failed where Jefferson had been so strong: in his relationship with and ability to manage Congress. But he did give the country Joseph Story—second only to John Marshall in influence and power on the high bench in the first third of the nineteenth century and one of the truly great Justices to grace the Supreme Court.

It was midway in Madison's first term that two vacancies occurred on the Court. The last two surviving Washington appointees, Justices William Cushing and Samuel Chase, had died in the fall of 1810 and mid-1811, respectively. Jefferson's party looked forward to their replacements with great expectations, for here was the first chance to turn the Federalist majority on the bench into a minority. All knowing eyes were on the President, who was bombarded with advice from many Democrat-Republican quarters—most notably from Jefferson. Publicly espousing the two cardinal

Jeffersonian criteria of party loyalty and geography, Madison began his search soon after Cushing's death, but it would not end until November 1811. To fill Cushing's seat, Madison first turned to Jefferson's able Attorney General (from 1801 to 1804) Levi Lincoln of Massachusetts, whose dedication to Democrat-Republicanism was beyond question and for whom Jefferson strongly lobbied. Madison had been alerted that the candidate might well decline for reasons of age or health–he was sixty-two and plagued by very poor eyesight–but Jefferson continued to press for the nomination, and in October 1810 the President asked Lincoln to accept it. Late in November Lincoln responded negatively; yet Madison chose to disregard the refusal and formally nominated him on January 2, 1811. The Senate confirmed him with enthusiasm on the following day and sent his commission to him forthwith. But Lincoln, now in effect facing blindness, felt he had to persist in his decision–much as he would have relished becoming a thorn in Marshall's side.

Madison waited a month, then nominated another proved and prominent New England Democrat-Republican leader, Alexander Wolcott of Connecticut. An attorney of little distinction, Wolcott had long served as U.S. Collector of Customs, making himself obnoxious to the Federalists through what they regarded as his extreme partisanship both in and out of office. As mentioned earlier, the Senate rejected him decisively 9:24. Within ten days the President had selected another candidate–another Democrat-Republican but one who had begun to show a measure of political independence–his Minister to Russia, John Quincy Adams. The latter was then eminently acceptable to both political parties, and the Senate confirmed him unanimously as soon as the nomination reached it. But to Madison's consternation–he sensed a future political rival–Adams declined the appointment, pleading insufficient legal acumen and quite frankly acknowledging too much political ambition. Madison now resolved to sit back and wait–it was not until seven months later, in mid-November 1811, that he sent to the Senate the controversial name of Joseph Story of Massachusetts, passing over Jefferson's hard-pushed candidacy of his former Postmaster General, Gideon Granger of Connecticut.

What finally prompted the President's selection of Story is unclear, although Story's uncle, Isaac Story, was a long-time friend of Madison's. What is clear is that Jefferson and almost the entire Democrat-Republican leadership opposed the just-turned thirty-two-year-old legal whiz—a nineteen-year-old Harvard graduate in 1798—a personal friend of John Marshall who had given every indication of leaning toward Federalism. He also had refused to support Jefferson's controversial Embargo Act of 1807. All this bothered Madison considerably less than Jefferson—indeed the President was much more inclined to look sympathetically at some aspects of Federalist policy than was Jefferson, although Jefferson himself was a pronouncedly more adamant anti-Federalist out of office than he was in office. It is often easier to be a dogmatic critic than a dogmatic fashioner of policy! Story's nomination sent Jefferson into a rage. He pronounced him a "pseudo-Republican," a "political chameleon," an "independent political schemer."[25] Jefferson particularly feared Story's admiration for the Chief Justice personally and for his propertarian views. He would see some of his worst fears confirmed shortly.

The Senate was not especially enchanted with the Story nomination either; yet its members were ready to end the impasse that had caused the vacancy of one Supreme Court seat for more than a year and another for several months. The country, too, had tired of what looked like an appointment charade, and there was general relief when the Senate quickly and without a record roll call confirmed the controversial young New Englander on November 18, 1811, three days after Madison had sent his name over. At a mere thirty-two, he would be the youngest appointee to attain the Court (William Johnson having been a month and a half older when he preceded Story in 1804).[26]

Story's nomination was to be one of the most fortuitous appointments in the history of the country. Both in terms of intellectual leadership and jurisprudential commitment, he proved himself to be an outstanding Justice. Standing with Marshall for almost a quarter of a century and continuing for another decade after Marshall's death until his own in 1845, Story was perhaps even more determined than Marshall to further the national posture in the face of mounting storm signals to the Union. To be sure, Story was neither a democrat nor a confirmed majoritarian and, thus, proved to be the intellectual antithesis of the Democrat-Republican creed. Yet the role this great common-law jurist played in the stabilization of the Republic and in its growth and security was second only to Marshall's. He left lasting monuments to constitutionalism, nationalism, and legal scholarship with: his famed lectures at the Harvard School of Law, his cosponsorship with Chancellor James Kent of New York of the American equity system, his work on copyrights and patents, and his elucidation of property, trust, partnership, insurance, commercial, and maritime law. His *Commentaries on the Constitution of the United States,* published in 1833, remains an indispensable work in the study of constitutional law and history.

On the same day the Senate confirmed Joseph Story it also approved the nomination of fifty-eight-year-old Gabriel Duval of Maryland, a faithful Democrat-Republican, to fill the vacancy caused by the death of his fellow Marylander Samuel Chase. Of less stature and surrounded by infinitely less controversy than Story, Duval nonetheless proved to be a competent if unexciting jurist, fulfilling Madison's expectations both on grounds of political compatibility and legal acumen. He had served with distinction on his state's highest court for six years and in 1802 had become Comptroller of the Treasury in the Jefferson and, subsequently, Madison administrations. Looking every inch the legendary jurist, he spent more than twenty-three workmanlike, quiet years on the bench, resigning at eighty-two, almost totally deaf.

During the six remaining years of his Presidency, Madison had no further opportunities to make a Supreme Court appointment. It commenced what remains by far the longest no-vacancy stretch in the history of the Court: twelve years! In fact, no vacancy arose until 1823 when Justice Henry Livingston died after sixteen years of service—enabling James Monroe to make his one and only appointment. Monroe, a President of above-average ability and performance, encountered difficulties with Congress similar to those encountered by his friend and colleague Madison. But he was a better administrator, and he knew how to pick excellent associates, especially in the foreign policy field. Monroe was a good Democrat-Republican, but he was even less committed to party doctrine than was Madison, and it was widely doubted that he would be more than casually concerned with a nominee's party loyalty. Yet when his opportunity to select one came at last in 1823, he turned to someone with whom he felt comfortable both politically and personally, Smith Thompson, his fifty-five-year-old Secretary of the Navy. Fortuitously, Thompson also hailed from New York, the deceased Livingston's circuit. Moreover, he met the other criteria Monroe had determined on for any Supreme Court nominee: personal integrity, judicial or other high public-service experience, and active party service.

Monroe deliberated awhile before nominating Thompson—there were other attractive names to consider. Among these was Senator Martin Van Buren of New York, a loyal Democrat-Republican with excellent professional and political credentials and considerable bipartisan support, including that of Secretary of State John Quincy Adams. Two others were the prominent New York State jurists Ambrose Spencer and James Kent. The latter, widely regarded as second in ability only to the great John Marshall, was an avowed Federalist, but one known as a champion of states' rights because of his stance in a series of decisions culminating in the famed Steamboat Monopoly Case of *Gibbons* v. *Ogden* (1824),[27] which would spell out the federal government's plenary power over interstate commerce. Yet the President neither trusted Van Buren's political ambitions nor regarded Spencer or Kent as sufficiently reliable politically. Thompson was Monroe's choice because he met the President's criteria and because Monroe liked, respected, and admired him. Thompson had had an extensive career in public service: as a member of the New York Constitutional Convention of 1801, as a New York State legislator, and as an Associate Justice (twelve years) and then Chief Justice (four years) of the New York State Supreme Court. He had studied law under James Kent, whose law practice he had taken over, and he was widely regarded as an excellent legal technician.

After hesitating awhile, Thompson accepted the Court nomination in December 1823 and was quickly confirmed by a generally admiring Senate. His twenty years on the high tribunal constituted a diligent and unspectacular but above-average performance. Thompson occasionally stood up to John Marshall determinedly, especially during the last seven or eight years of Marshall's tenure, but, like practically all who served under the persuasive Chief Justice, more often than not he succumbed to his spell, notwithstanding generic political differences.

In 1825 John Quincy Adams became President as a result of a bitterly contested four-way race between himself, William H. Crawford, General Andrew Jackson, and Henry Clay–all nationalist Democrat-Republicans. When no one attained the necessary constitutional majority in the electoral college vote (Jackson had received the highest number of electoral votes, ninety-nine, and John Quincy Adams, eighty-four), the election was thrown into the House of Representatives. There, on the first ballot taken in January 1825, Adams won by a margin of one state with three decisive states' votes allegedly delivered by Clay–who had come in fourth–in return for Adams's promise to appoint him as Secretary of State. (He did.) It proved to be a Pyrrhic victory, for Adams's tenure as President was essentially frustrating and unfulfilled–notwithstanding his high "average" ranking by the Presidential historians. The distinguished public servant of three decades who had been such a brilliant diplomat and courageous legislator–and who would again serve his country as a member of the House of Representatives after his Presidency–had little taste for day-to-day Presidential politics. Moreover, he faced a divided party and a divided legislature and proved himself incapable of effective party leadership, which inescapably influenced the decision-making processes.

John Quincy Adams had two chances to make Supreme Court appointments and he succeeded in but one of these. To fill the vacancy created by Justice Thomas Todd's death in February 1826, Adams nominated Todd's fellow Kentuckian, Robert Trimble, then U.S. District Court Judge for Kentucky (the first Supreme Court appointee with previous federal judicial experience). Indeed, before his death Todd had indicated to his colleagues his devout hope that Trimble, his long-time friend and ex-associate, would be chosen to succeed him. Although Judge Trimble had an accurate reputation for furthering the cause of Federalism and was widely viewed as an ideological Marshallian–having frequently opted for upholding federal over states' rights–John Quincy Adams was confident that Trimble's Democrat-Republican political label would facilitate his confirmation. The President himself regarded Trimble as amply meeting the criteria he believed to be of significance for elevation to the Court: the "right" geographic location, appropriate judicial experience, a scholarly background in constitutional law, and *real* politics acceptable to both major political camps in the Senate. Adams's prognosis proved correct, but Trimble's confirmation by a vote of 27:5 did not come until after a month-long acrimonious struggle. He had incurred the displeasure of a number of Senators–including that of John Rowan of his own home state of Kentucky–because of his repeated and articulate insistence on the supremacy of federal over state power while he served on the lower federal bench.

Yet death came to the new Justice barely two years after his confirmation. In line with his criteria for nominees, John Quincy Adams first offered the post to Charles Hammond, neighboring Ohio's most distinguished lawyer (Ohio, Kentucky, and Tennessee being in the same judicial circuit). Hammond declined the honor, preferring to remain in private practice. The President next turned to his ally of the political wars of 1824, the colorful Henry Clay of Kentucky, who also declined, still having bigger stakes in mind. But Clay, supported by Chief Justice Marshall, recommended that Adams nominate another able lawyer, a well-known Whig statesman, former Senator John J. Crittenden of Kentucky. Adams, now a lame-duck President, sent Crittenden's name to the Senate late in December 1828. Yet victorious Andrew Jackson's Democratic supporters in that body were not about to award the Supreme Court plum to a Clay Whig, and by a vote of 23:17 "postponed" the nomination in February 1829, thus consigning it to oblivion. It was the end of an era. Within less than a month Jackson would assume the reins of office, and his influence on the Court and its personnel would prove to be second only to George Washington's in its impact on the young nation's history.

6

The *Next* Forty Years:

From Andrew Jackson to Andrew Johnson 1829-1869

Andrew Jackson and his disciples were destined to dominate the political system of the United States until the onset of the Civil War and the accession of Abraham Lincoln. Whatever one's views of Jackson's theory and practice of egalitarianism, Old Hickory was unquestionably a great popular hero, a superb leader, and a stunning political practitioner. Pragmatic and assertive, he was not averse to challenging even John Marshall's citadel to the point of outright defiance, as he did in a celebrated Georgia missionary case. In *Worcester* v. *Georgia* (1832),[1] Marshall upheld the landed rights of the Cherokee Indians against sundry hanky-panky by the state of Georgia and certain of its citizens by ruling that the jurisdiction of the federal government in Cherokee Territory was exclusive. Georgia's reaction was predictably hostile, as was that of states' rights champion Jackson, who allegedly said: "Well, John Marshall has made his decision, now let him enforce it."[2] In fact, Jackson probably did not make that statement; but he assuredly did not stop Georgia from defying the Court's decision. His attitude toward the controversy made it clear that he would not hesitate to take on the Court if he thought its actions violated the separation of powers. On the other hand, he stopped short of claiming an inherent prerogative to defy or disregard judicial decisions. Jackson wished to make clear that he was dedicated to coequality. In his veto message of the proposed rechartering of the Bank of the United States in 1832 he wrote: "The authority of the Supreme Court must not . . . be permitted to control the Congress or the Executive when acting in their *legislative* capacities but to have only such influence as the force of their reasoning may deserve."[3] Yet "his" Court (he succeeded in making six appointments, more than any other President except Washington, Taft, and F.D.R.) would by no means be universally submissive to the attempts that Jackson and his successors made to keep it in line. Indeed, the Taney Court—however pleasing the course of its decisions would be to the Democrats—was hardly a supine Presidential instrument. Roger Brooke Taney, a faithful friend and political ally of Jackson, was the President's choice to succeed John Marshall. Under Taney's assertive, sophisticated leadership, the Court maintained its base of power and, although it unquestionably became states' rights and anticorporation in orientation, it continued to nurture and secure the Marshall creed of judicial sovereignty—the now well-established role of the Court as the final arbiter of constitutional questions. It is a pity that the Taney Court has not only been widely misunderstood but even maligned. It is simply too facile a rationalization exclusively to use the tragic *Dred Scott* decision of 1857,[4] which came in the waning years of Taney's Chief Justiceship, as a basis for that misunderstanding.

President Jackson's criteria for Supreme Court candidacy represented at least some departure from those of his six predecessors—if for no other reason than he rendered them less explicit. Yet he held to the traditional considerations of geography, public service, and political loyalty, making it clear that political loyalty would have primacy in his decisions. He was determined to reward the party faithful; if that meant extending his much-vaunted "spoils system" to include nominees to the highest judicial body in the land, so be it. Ironically, Jackson's first selection, Postmaster General John McLean, was hardly a party faithful, yet the appointment was clearly intended to serve political purposes.

The Senate's deliberate refusal to approve John Quincy Adams's nomination of John J. Crittenden to replace the recently deceased Justice Trimble presented Jackson with a Supreme Court vacancy at the very outset of his Presidency. He was delighted to oblige, but his choice of the forty-three-year-old McLean, a native of Ohio and one-time judge of the Ohio Supreme Court (from the same judicial circuit as Trimble), was dictated by the contemporary partisan politics concerning personalities as well as the range and degree of federal authority that reflected the intraparty struggle among the Democrats. An ambitious aspirant to high office, McLean had been Postmaster General since the days of the Monroe Administration. He had given the impression of being friendly to both the John Quincy Adams and Jackson forces during the election of 1828, cultivating many prominent Jacksonians without unduly antagonizing the Adams wing. Jackson, who had kept McLean on in his former post, did not really trust him; indeed, he felt actively threatened by McLean's foot dragging in patronage matters, especially when the latter resisted his requests to replace Adams supporters with Jackson loyalists in the postal service. Yet Jackson also realized that McLean was immensely popular in the West and he feared the consequences of a public clash so early in his incumbency. Thus, when McLean promised not to pursue his political ambitions while a member of the Court, Jackson tendered him the nomination–although not without some misgivings. The Van Buren forces in the Administration were delighted to see the man they considered an adversary safely shelved, for McLean had been a member of the Calhoun faction in the government.

To no one's great astonishment, McLean did not hold to his promise.[5] While *on* the bench he became a Presidential candidate four times: in 1832 as an Anti-Mason; in 1836 as an Independent; in 1842 as both a Whig and a Free-Soiler; and in 1856 as a Republican (he had officially joined the Republican party). No doctrinaire he![6] But McLean served on the Court for thirty-two years–one of the longest tenures on record–having remained there until his death in 1861–unpredictable and independent to the end.

There was no doubt whatever of the political loyalty of Jackson's next selection for the Court. When in 1829 Bushrod Washington died, also after thirty-one years of service, the President turned to Henry Baldwin, aged fifty, a popular Pennsylvania Congressman. Long an aggressive and enthusiastic supporter, Baldwin had been instrumental in bringing Pennsylvania into the Jacksonian fold in the election of 1828. The President, alive to Baldwin's services, had rewarded him immediately after the election by nominating him to the Cabinet post of Secretary of the Treasury. But that nomination was blocked in the Senate by Vice-President John Calhoun, chiefly because of Baldwin's avowed championship of a high-tariff policy that was anathema to Calhoun and his supporters. The Calhoun forces then attempted to scuttle Baldwin's nomination to the Court too, but they succeeded only in delaying it for two days. On January 6, 1830, the Senate approved him by a vote of 41:2, the sole dissenters being the two Senators from South Carolina, Calhoun's home state, Robert Y. Hayne and William Smith. The latter had just declined nomination for the Washington vacancy on the Court because he wanted to stay in the Senate to "defend federal rights against nationalization." Jackson would give Smith another chance to mount the Court after his defeat for reelection to the Senate in 1834, when Justice Duval resigned in 1835, but Smith again declined.[7] By choosing a Pennsylvanian rather than a Virginian, Jackson in a sense "atoned" for John Adams's selection of a Virginian (Bushrod Washington) for the seat held by a Pennsylvanian (James Wilson) in 1798–although that was not a major consideration in the selection. Loyalist that he was, Baldwin, too, would vote "wrong" on the Court on a number of crucial issues championed by Jackson. He even committed the unpardonable sin of siding with the "pro-Bank" forces during Jackson's great struggle over rechartering the Bank of the United States. Still, Baldwin's "deviations" during his fourteen years on the Court were minor in the eyes of the Jacksonian Democrats in comparison to those of McLean and Jackson's next nominee, James M. Wayne.

After Baldwin's appointment in 1830, the Supreme Court's membership remained stable for five years–a relatively long period in view of the vagaries of age and health. During that time Jackson reorganized his Cabinet and began his assault on the Bank of the United States. Presumably party policy had now been clarified and, although Jackson could not eliminate all party factions, he had a firm grip on the majoritarian direction of his Democratic party. His remaining choices for the Court reflected even more of a commitment to party principles than did his first two selections. Nominees James M. Wayne, Rogert B. Taney, Philip P. Barbour, and John Catron had all evinced a close adherence to the Jacksonian creed and had rendered many services to the President. James Moore Wayne, forty-five, former Judge of the Supreme Court of Georgia, was one of those rare Southerners who was also a Unionist. In appointing Wayne to the seat of the recently deceased William Johnson of South Carolina, Jackson not only kept that judicial circuit's "representation" intact but placated the Whigs, who had feared the designation of an avowed states' righter from the South. Wayne was confirmed enthusiastically within two days and Jackson found himself widely praised for a "statesmanlike" appointment, notwithstanding Wayne's loyalist Democratic history. To Jackson's later dismay, Wayne would, in a significant number of cases, side with the nationalist rather than the states' rights side in decisions involving the interpretation of federal and judicial power.[8]

Within hours after Wayne had taken the judicial oath on January 14, 1835, the octogenarian Justice Gabriel Duval of Maryland resigned. The worst apprehensions of the Whigs and Calhounians were promptly confirmed when President Jackson nominated his close friend and loyal adviser and supporter, Roger Brooke Taney, to the seat. Taney, now fifty-eight, had successfully navigated the political shoals from the localism of Maryland politics to national prominence, having served as Chairman of the Jackson Central Committee of Maryland in 1828, as Jackson's Attorney General, and on a recess appointment as Secretary of the Treasury after the Cabinet reorganization of 1832. It was in the last post that Taney had incurred the undying enmity of the Whig-Calhounian political axis: he had fully approved of, and complied with, Jackson's order that all government deposits be removed from the Bank of the United States—the major controversy of the time. The enraged opposition struck back at Jackson and Taney by rejecting the latter's formal, post-recess appointment as Secretary of the Treasury, thus forcing him to resign.

Jackson vowed revenge and, in a letter to Taney that left little doubt that his political opponents had not heard the last of the matter, he wrote: "For the prompt and disinterested aid thus afforded me, at the risk of personal sacrifice which were then probable and which has now been realized, I feel that I owe you a debt of gratitude and regard which I have not the power to discharge. . . ."[9] Duval's resignation gave Jackson his first opportunity to discharge that debt of gratitude. The Senate thwarted him by "postponing" the nomination on the last day of its session–but not before it had voted to do away with the vacant seat entirely, a maneuver that failed of enactment, however, in the House of Representatives.

Enraged, Jackson refused to make another nomination and resolved to try Taney again. Fate played into his hands. On July 6, 1835, after thirty-four and one-half eventful years on the bench, Chief Justice John Marshall died in Philadelphia. Jackson now had two vacancies to fill! That one of them would go to Taney was a foregone conclusion. But the President bided his time; he appeared to be considering a host of candidates for both the Associate and the Chief Justice vacancies. All attention focused on his choice for Chief Justice of course. A strong possibility was the brilliant Justice Joseph Story; but Jackson was not about to promote the man whose record out-Marshalled Marshall. There was wide advocacy of Daniel Webster, but he too personified the old Federalist team. A good many urged the promotion of John McLean, yet he had already incurred the displeasure of the President and most Democrats by his iconoclastic behavior on the Court. Jackson kept his counsel until the end of December and then proposed Roger Brooke Taney of Maryland to succeed John Marshall of Virginia and Philip Pendleton Barbour of Virginia to succeed Gabriel Duval of Maryland. Even-Steven geographically–and, "Senate of the United States, here we go again"–Jackson might well have chuckled.

Philip Barbour, fifty-two years old when nominated, had himself been rumored in line for the Marshall vacancy. A strong states' rights advocate of the Southern school and a strict constitutional constructionist, he had nonetheless been a loyal Jacksonian on many key issues and a conciliating force in the divided party. He had seen many years of public service in his home state and in Congress, including the Speakership of the House of Representatives (1821–1823) and eight years on the Virginia and federal benches. "The pride of the democracy of Virginia" was as well qualified as he was popular. Yet because it was tied to Taney's confirmation, Senate approval of Barbour's appointment did not come until May 7, 1836, by a vote of 30:11. Barbour died after less than five years on the bench, but he served diligently and in a manner pleasing to his nominator.

"Judge Story thinks the Supreme Court is *gone,* and I think so, too," wrote Daniel Webster.[10] The remarkable Chief Justiceship of Taney would prove both men wrong indeed. But first Jackson's favorite nominee would have to run the gauntlet of a hostile and powerful group of Senators. For close to three months the battle raged in the upper house; when the vote finally came, it was not nearly so close as the bitter debates had led the country to believe. Taney won the nomination by a 14-vote margin, 29:15, opposed to the last by such powerful and influential Senate leaders as Calhoun, Clay, and Webster, who later would come to respect the superb performance of the man they had so ardently opposed. Taney, whom history and the experts have justly accorded the mark of judicial greatness, was resolved to enhance the role of the states as governmental and philosophical entities. But shrewd political tactician and skillful leader that he was, Taney knew how to exercise judicial self-restraint. Not a devotee of overt manifestations of power, he guided his Court along pathways of conciliation and compromise virtually devoid of dogmatism and ploys. Thus, not only were the Court's actions accepted by the majority of political leaders of the time, but its position as the logical, ultimate, and fair-minded arbiter of the Constitution was fully secured as well. Far from assaulting the Marshall-built fortress of judicial power, the Taney Court secured it and did so with all but general approbation.

Even the *Dred Scott* decision, monumental aberration though it was, could not destroy the institution that Taney and Marshall had fashioned. It is a pity that Taney is so often remembered by that case rather than by his supreme accomplishments in achieving governmental concord and constitutional understanding. For with *Dred Scott*, the Court, in an attempt to stem the oncoming tide of civil war, had in effect hastened the war. Ruling that no Negro could be a citizen; that the Negro was a "person of an inferior order"; that the Negro was a slave and, thus, his master's permanent property; that no Negro was a "portion of the American people"; and that the Missouri Compromise was unconstitutional, the decision has generally been regarded by most observers as one of the most disastrous, even *the* most disastrous, ever handed down by the Supreme Court. Its impact could not be lessened by Justice James M. Wayne's anxious explanation that "there had become such a difference of opinion that the peace and harmony of the country required the settlement of the slavery issues by judicial decision. . . . In our action we have only discharged our duty as a distinct and efficient department of the Government, as framers of the Constitution meant the judiciary to be. . . ."[11]

Nine opinions (seven in the majority and two in dissent) were written by members of the Court. One of the former, a separate concurrence, was authored by Andrew Jackson's last nominee—selected on Jackson's last day in office—his fellow Tennessean, Justice John Catron. Abetted by Justice Grier, Catron had informed President Buchanan of the thrust of the decision in advance, the major and best authenticated, although not the sole, such breach of secrecy on record.[12] Catron's nomination had not been Senate-confirmed until after Jackson had left office in March 1837; but Van Buren, whose Tennessee Presidential campaign Jackson had directed in 1836, readily allowed it to stand. Catron's nomination was very much in the nature of a repayment for faithful services rendered. The vacancy on the Court had fallen to Jackson as a result of a last-minute law that increased the number of Associate Justices of the Court from six to eight, thus creating a nine-member body. The two additional positions were earmarked for two newly created circuits in the West and the Southwest. Catron, Jackson's choice for the Western circuit, gladly accepted and readily won Senate approval 28:15. A long-time personal and political friend of the President's; a leading, highly visible Jacksonian Democrat; and a prosperous and respected member of Nashville's ruling elite, he had served with Jackson in the War of 1812 and had been a strong ally in the struggle against the forces of nullification later. He was also a strong projudiciary figure, having served as both Judge and Chief Justice of the Supreme Court of Tennessee, during which time his lucidly written opinions had created a favorable public climate on behalf of Jacksonian policies. Catron had been on Jackson's side in most of the major political disputes during his Presidency—a factor stressed heavily in a romantic journal allegedly written by Mrs. Catron, who apparently traveled from Tennessee to Washington to plead her husband's case with her warm friend "Andy" Jackson. Joseph Catron served for twenty-eight years, always striving to balance strong federal authority with potent states' rights. Yet his *Dred Scott* concurring opinion rendered him suspect, both philosophically and politically, in his adopted Union camp for the remainder of his career.

William Smith of Alabama was Jackson's choice for the other new position on the Court. Smith at one time had been a U.S. Senator from South Carolina and had cast one of the two opposition votes against Jackson's nomination of Henry Baldwin in 1830. But he was now a loyal Jacksonian, and the Senate confirmed him on March 8, 1837. He declined to serve, however, frankly citing what he regarded as the position's inadequate pay. Thus, the seat remained vacant for incoming President Van Buren's action.

Despite the fact that Jackson's criteria for appointments to the Court were less visible and less precise than those of the early Presidents, certain strands of policy were in evidence. Thus, in each of his eight nominations, the President followed the current strictures of geography: he made a point of representing each circuit, as had his predecessors. Of his choices only Taney and Baldwin lacked judicial experience. Both men had experienced long and distinguished public service, but apparently Jackson was not overridingly concerned with his candidates' record on that score. Political acceptability, on the other hand, was a major consideration. In short, Jackson had few equals as a politician.

Martin Van Buren, who had been Taney's colleague in Jackson's Cabinet, was a shrewd and effective political leader in his own right. He succeeded to the Presidency largely as a result of Jacksonian dictation. Jackson's Vice-President in his second term, he had been Secretary of State in the first, and he was the first governor of a state (New York) to attain the White House. Van Buren was, thus, superbly qualified for the Presidency—although the charismatic Jackson was difficult to succeed. Shrewd, able, and poised, Van Buren might have received a much higher rating as President had he not fallen heir to an economic depression—the Panic of 1837. That depression plus his pronounced opposition to the annexation of Texas and his refusal to give aid to the Canadian rebels, who in the fall of 1837 moved (unsuccessfully) to expel the British from North America, very likely cost him the reelection he deserved.

Van Buren inherited not only an enlarged Court but a practically new and relatively young one. His only two chances to appoint a Justice came almost literally on the first and last days of his Presidency, when William Smith (the Jackson appointee) refused to serve and when Justice Philip P. Barbour died. (Some credit him also with the Catron appointment but, as explained earlier, Catron had been nominated by Jackson and was confirmed on Van Buren's fourth day in office.) For his first appointment Van Buren selected another Alabaman, Senator John McKinley, fifty-seven, an experienced lawyer who in addition to meeting the required geographic criterion had impeccable political credentials. Although only a recent convert to Jacksonian Democracy, McKinley had established a record of unflagging support of its cause. Thus, during the nullification battle, McKinley had been an eloquent and conspicuous supporter of the Union. Moreover, he was highly regarded by Old Hickory himself. These factors alone would have been more than adequate rationale for his nomination but, in addition, McKinley had been one of Van Buren's key managers during the Presidential campaign of 1836 and was personally responsible for capturing Alabama's electoral votes. He would not disappoint his nominator during his fifteen years on the high bench.

On February 24, 1841, Justice Barbour died suddenly of a

coronary thrombosis; fate had permitted him not even a handful of years on the Court. For the vacancy the President's choice was Peter Vivian Daniel, fifty-seven, another Jacksonian, and a Van Buren loyalist. At the time Daniel was serving in his fifth year as U.S. District Judge in Virginia, having succeeded his fellow Virginian Barbour in that post. (It would be 130 years ere another Virginian, Lewis F. Powell, Jr., reached the Supreme Court!) Long an active and powerful member of the Richmond Junto, Virginia's ruling Democratic elite, he was a stormy petrel in the law, life, and politics of his day and generation (who had killed one John Seldon on the first shot in a duel). Daniel had served his state government as both a member of the lower house and as Lieutenant Governor. He had worked hard for Jackson in the abortive campaign of 1824 and in the ensuing campaigns as well, and during the Bank and nullification controversies he had stood with, and spoken for, the President. When Martin Van Buren was nominated, Daniel had continued his effective organizational labors in Van Buren's behalf. Later Daniel became one of his most effective advisers and supporters, although he did refuse the President's tender of the Attorney Generalship. Theirs was a close philosophical-political affinity on the issues of the day: both disliked banks in general, and U.S. banks in particular; both favored states' rights, but not nullification; and both backed an agrarian conception of government. Yet before Daniel was confirmed by the Senate he and Van Buren had some anxious moments. The President had but a few remaining days in office (he had lost the 1840 election to Whig William Henry Harrison), and he rushed Daniel's name to the Senate even before there was time to bury Barbour. The victorious Whigs, who were not amused, launched a series of tactical maneuvers to prevent the nomination from reaching the Senate floor. But because of their defective strategy, absenteeism, and crossed signals, the Whigs were ultimately outmaneuvered by the Democrats, who managed a bare quorum with most of the Whigs absent and forced a vote that carried 22:5. Daniel's record on the Court amply justified Van Buren's faith in him: it proved to be as nondeviationist as McLean's was the opposite.

From 1841 to 1845 the country saw the first of what would be two Whig interludes in the Presidency. General William Henry Harrison, the hero of the Battle of Tippecanoe of 1811, rode into the White House at the advanced age of sixty-eight on the strength of his personal popularity and his ability to avoid involvement in any controversy or to take a stand on any major issues. Harrison contracted pneumonia shortly after his inauguration (his two-hour-long address, still a record, was delivered on a freezing day mixed with rain and snow) and died after thirty-one days in the Presidency. His successor, John Tyler, was a generally unhappy President who lacked a personal political base and political support and who was in constant conflict and competition with the powerful Henry Clay and his followers. Rated "below average" by the experts, he nonetheless performed the significant service of proclaiming himself President rather than Acting President, a manifestation of the meaning of Presidential succession that has stood the test of time.

But also standing the test of time is Tyler's record of five Supreme Court nominations *rejected*—more than any other President in the history of the Court. During a four-month period of his incumbency (December 1843–April 1844) Justices Smith Thompson and Henry Baldwin died, and in attempting to fill their seats Tyler made a total of six nominations. Tyler's first nominee for the Thompson (New York) seat was a New York lawyer, John C. Spencer, a Whig who had held two Cabinet posts in the Tyler Administration. But he was an avowed political enemy of Henry Clay and his followers, and it was with more ease than the rejection vote of 21:26 indicates that the Clay faction succeeded in blocking Spencer. Next Tyler selected an able lawyer though again a potentially controversial nominee: Chancellor Reuben H. Walworth of New York, whom the Senate Whigs cordially disliked. Before the Senate could act, Justice Baldwin succumbed, leaving the second seat vacant. To Baldwin's Pennsylvania slot Tyler resolved to nominate James Buchanan, also of the Keystone State. When Buchanan declined the honor, Tyler chose a distinguished Philadelphia lawyer and legal scholar, Judge Edward King. It was now June, and the Whig Senators, thinking they had victory in their grasp in the forthcoming Presidential election, moved to "postpone" both the Walworth and King nominations by votes of 20:27 and 18:29, respectively. The angry and frustrated Tyler, in turn, renominated King in December; but the Senate would not act, and the President withdrew both nominations in January 1845.

Tyler was not through, however, especially after Jackson Democrat James K. Polk defeated the Clay Whigs in the Presidential race of 1844. Having pretty well broken with the Whigs, Tyler now selected Samuel Nelson, fifty-two, an able and dignified lawyer and long-time Justice and Chief Justice of the Supreme Court of New York who had been an elector for President Monroe in 1820. A clear writer and incisive scholar, Nelson was adept at commercial law, one of the most litigated areas of the day. This time Tyler hit pay dirt: within ten days, and with only scattered Whig opposition, Nelson won confirmation to the seat that had been vacant for fourteen months. By no means outstanding on the Court, he would nonetheless serve diligently and perceptively for almost three decades—generally in a manner anticipated by, and pleasing to, the Jacksonians.

Tyler had still one more chance: the Baldwin seat had remained unfilled, given a series of Senate "postponements." He nominated a well-known Philadelphia lawyer with supporters in both the Whig and Democratic camps, a one-time U.S. Attorney of proved legal acumen and political deftness, John Meredith Read. But it was now mid-February, and a weary Senate adjourned without acting on the nomination—thus handing Tyler his fifth failure. It was widely expected that the incoming President Polk would have more luck.

James Knox Polk, the underdog victor in 1844 over the aging but still powerful Henry Clay, is best remembered for his aggressive pursuit of America's Manifest Destiny to extend westward to the Pacific and southward to the Rio Grande, if not farther. His successes in that ambitious endeavor—the acquisition of California, the conquest of Oregon, and the securing of Texas—found wide-ranging support in the country. Forceful and a fine administrator and legislative leader, Polk was given to crafty and devious methods that frequently brought him major policy victories. Accordingly, history has been increasingly supportive of his overall record and achievements. Not surprisingly, the President-watcher experts have ranked him in the "near great" category, eighth in the overall standings.

Polk's Supreme Court nominees, however, were little more than mediocre. There were three: one was rejected, one lived but little more than five years after his appointment, and one served in routine fashion for a quarter of a century. Polk made his decisions based on now well-established criteria: demonstrated party loyalty, compatibility, and geographic suitability—although party loyalty was less important to him than it had been to his political lodestars, Andrew Jackson and Martin Van Buren.

Polk made his first nomination after six months in office: he was in no particular hurry and domestic appointments took a back seat to foreign policy matters. To the still-vacant seat of the deceased Justice Baldwin he nominated James Buchanan—to whom Tyler had offered the job in 1844. This time Buchanan appeared to want the position but asked for time to give his final answer. After pondering the matter for a couple of months, the politically ambitious Buchanan once again decided to reject the offer. In the interim Justice Story—second only to Marshall in distinction and accomplishments on the Court until that time—had announced his resignation as of the end of the term of Court. Worn out and disillusioned by what he viewed as the declining quality and influence of his beloved tribunal, Story proposed to devote full time to his Harvard Law School professorship; but in September 1845 he died, shortly before he was to leave the bench. He had served magnificently for almost thirty-four years. Thus, Polk had an additional opportunity to make a nomination. At this point he decided to forget the jinxed Baldwin vacancy for a while and to concentrate on Story's slot.

The President's choice for Story's "New England" seat on the Court was fifty-five-year-old Levi Woodbury, U.S. Senator from New Hampshire. Woodbury, a solid Democrat but a conservative one highly acceptable to the Whigs, was an eminently qualified public servant who had served in all three branches of government: legislative (as Senator), executive (as Governor of New

Hampshire, Secretary of the Navy under Jackson, and Secretary of the Treasury under Van Buren), and judicial (as a judge on New Hampshire's Supreme Court). Few men had come before the Senate with such extensive credentials; and his confirmation was so taken for granted that Polk gave him a recess appointment in September, which was confirmed as soon as the Senate reconvened the following January. A long-time supporter of the governmental and jurisprudential commitments of Chief Justice Taney, Woodbury embraced Taney's conviction that, rather than looking eternally to the British judicial system, the legal profession in the United States should develop an "American" legal system. But barely six years later death cut short his promising career.

Meanwhile Polk still had the old Baldwin vacancy to fill. Because Secretary of State Buchanan would not take the position, the President turned to a jurist on the lower Pennsylvania bench, George W. Woodward. Although a member of a distinguished family and a proved Democrat, Woodward had acquired a reputation as an extreme "American nativist" and was staunchly opposed by several Democratic Senators, among them Simon Cameron of his home state. Cameron's resolute opposition and the negative votes of five other Democrats along with a solid "no" vote by the Whigs resulted in Woodward's rejection 20:29 late in January 1846. The exasperated Polk let six months go by, and then *again* asked James Buchanan to take the job. Flattered and never one to be unduly decisive, the latter accepted–only to turn it down for the third time two months later! Next the President selected Robert Cooper Grier of Pennsylvania, the fifty-two-year-old President Judge of the Allegheny County (Pittsburgh) District Court.

It was now August 1846, and Henry Baldwin had been in his grave for twenty-eight months! It was about time to fill his seat, and the Senate responded by confirming Grier in less than a day. It was not a difficult task for the upper house, for Grier was a conservative Democrat and a cautious constitutionalist who was generally acceptable to all factions of the party. His long service on the bench proved to be predictably low key, and his performance was average. He loved being on the Supreme Court and resigned only when (having become a mental and physical wreck) he yielded to the combination of liberalized retirement provisions for Justices and the repeated entreaties of his colleagues—who at one stage sent a delegation headed by Mr. Justice Stephen J. Field to urge him to step down. Grier is probably best remembered for that episode and the ignoble role he played—with Justice Catron—in informing President-elect Buchanan of the thrust of the *Dred Scott* decision in advance of the Court's public announcement.

Polk's successor, General Zachary Taylor, was the third Whig President. Taylor was firm, forthright, and honest, but this professional soldier was ill qualified and ill prepared for the political process. He lived only sixteen months after his inauguration in March 1849 and was the second of four Presidents to date who made no appointments to the Supreme Court. His successor, Vice President Millard Fillmore (the last Whig President, who brought the first galvanized bathtub into the White House in 1851), worked hard and with considerable determination to preserve the endangered Union. He had but one chance to appoint a member of the Court, yet his choice was an excellent one: Benjamin R. Curtis. Three other attempts to fill a later vacancy were frustrated by the Senate.

Fillmore's initial opportunity came in the fall of 1851 when Justice Levi Woodbury died. The President gave much thought to a successor, for he was genuinely concerned about mounting attacks on the Court because of what abolitionists termed its pro-Southern stance in the slavery and fugitive slave issues. Accordingly, he wanted to find a man who had not only strength of character and the potential for judicial presence but also an understanding of contemporary history and politics. Moreover, he specified that the nominee had to be a Whig, a comparatively young man, and a New Englander.

All these criteria he found in Benjamin Robbins Curtis of Massachusetts, who came not only highly recommended but enthusiastically backed by the still enormously influential Daniel Webster (although Webster's first choice had been Rufus Choate, who declined to be considered). A renowned, skilled commercial lawyer—the *Massachusetts Law Quarterly* referred to the forty-one-year-old Curtis as "the *first* lawyer of America"[13]—Curtis was a follower of the legal philosophy of Marshall and Story. Yet he had never campaigned for Court membership. While he was being considered for the position, he continued to let his constitutional shots fall where they might, including support of the constitutionality of the hated and embattled Fugitive Slave Act of 1850. That he personally might have been opposed to the Act was not at issue: at issue was his posture in constitutional interpretation and application, a role that did not permit the intrusion of personal-political or result-oriented rulings. His belief that the majority of the Court had permitted political expediency to govern in the *Dred Scott* decision—for which he had written one of the two dissenting opinions—was one of the main factors that prompted him to resign after the decision had been rendered early in 1857. Justice Curtis, whose confirmation had been delayed by leading abolitionists in the Senate for the then inordinately long period of more than two months, thus served barely six years on the Court. But he left a lasting mark, having displayed careful judgment and judicial independence. He did this not only in his dissent in *Dred Scott,* but also in a series of crucial opinions dealing with the nature of the federal power over interstate and foreign commerce, of which the most significant was his pronouncement of a proper concurrent state power to legislate in the absence of federal action.[14] Fillmore could be proud indeed of his one appointment.

In the summer of 1852 Justice John McKinley died after fifteen colorless years on the bench—during which time, because of illness, he was as much absent as he was present. Fillmore attempted to fill the vacancy with dispatch not only because he was eager to see a full bench—one with additional Whig sympathizers—but because the Presidential election of 1852 did not look very promising either for his candidacy or for a Whig victory. He was a good prophet: neither was he selected (General Winfield Scott became the candidate) nor did his party win (the Democrats won under Franklin Pierce). Fillmore's first choice to succeed the late Alabaman was Edward A. Bradford of Louisiana, a well-known, able lawyer from the same circuit. The Senate, however, was about to adjourn, and it was in no mood to expedite a Fillmore nomination. When it reconvened after Pierce's victory, Fillmore named a U.S. Senator: George E. Badger of North Carolina. A conservative Whig who was not readily identifiable as either proslavery or antislavery, Badger was nonetheless a clearly identifiable Whig who had served as Secretary of the Navy in the Harrison and Tyler cabinets. The Democratic majority in the Senate was not about to deprive the victorious incoming President of the choice of his own man, even though rejecting one of its own members would be little short of political sacrilege. Senator Badger, however, saw his nomination permanently "postponed" by one vote, 25:26. Finally, the lame-duck Fillmore turned back to Louisiana and to another well-known attorney, William C. Micou–law partner of U.S. Senator-elect Judah P. Benjamin, to whom Fillmore had offered the Court post, but who preferred to go to the Senate. (Had Benjamin accepted Fillmore's offer, he would have been the first Jewish Supreme Court Justice. Now there would be none until Wilson's appointment of Brandeis in 1916.) Predictably, the Senate refused to act on Micou's nomination, and the McKinley seat remained vacant for the incoming Franklin Pierce to fill.

The only incumbent President to date to be resolutely denied a second crack at the Presidency by his own political party, Franklin Pierce–New Hampshire's sole contribution to the Presidency–was a tragic figure both personally and politically. A man of mediocre talents at most, he did his best–which was simply not good enough to fend off the approaching Civil War. He had the misfortune of presiding over the assault on the Missouri Compromise in favor of the ill-starred Kansas-Nebraska Act of 1854. Designed to apply the doctrine of "popular sovereignty" to questions of the extension of slavery to the territories, it was largely the creation of Pierce's potential rival, the powerful Senator Stephen A. Douglas of Illinois. Pierce's often pathetic efforts to "do right" by both North and South brought about more rather than less alienation; and his party leadership role was tenuous throughout his term. No wonder, then, that he is ranked close to, or at, the bottom of the scale among our Presidents.

Yet the sole Supreme Court appointment he made proved to be an excellent one: John Archibald Campbell of Alabama, whose name he sent to the Senate shortly after his inauguration in 1853. A highly visible, brilliant young lawyer, the forty-one-year-old Campbell was respected nationwide as an expert in both civil and common law and was noted for his uncanny ability as an advocate in trial courts. Although he had no judicial experience, he had served two terms in the legislature of his state and twice had been tendered nominations (which he declined) to the Alabama Supreme Court. A strong advocate of states' rights and a "strict constructionist," Campbell nonetheless opposed secession, yet favored improving the lot of the slaves. He, thus, received support from practically all sides of the political spectrum. In what probably still stands as a unique action, the entire incumbent membership of the Court wrote to Pierce in behalf of Campbell and deputized Associate Justices Catron and Curtis to deliver the supportive letters to the President personally.[15] It is, thus, understandable that Pierce did not seriously consider anyone else for the nomination and that the Senate confirmed Campbell promptly. Campbell served the Court nobly and gave high promise of a distinguished career thereon. But in 1861—although personally opposed to secession *and* the war—he felt duty bound to resign and join the Confederate cause, spending much of the ensuing four years as Assistant Secretary of War for the Confederate States of America.

Franklin Pierce was followed by Pennsylvania's James Buchanan, who had passed up at least three formally tendered opportunities to serve on the Supreme Court in favor of pursuing the Presidency. At last attaining it in 1857 at the age of sixty-five, he was destined to be plagued by a divided, disloyal Cabinet and by a hostile, negative Congress that refused to act on any of his many desperate proposals designed to stem the tide of war. Unlike his activist successor, Abraham Lincoln, Buchanan disdained a strong show of Presidential force: if Congress would not provide the tools of authority, he would not forge them himself. No wonder, then, that Buchanan—who is now ranked even below Pierce by the experts—would greet Lincoln on Inauguration Day in 1861 with these pathetic words: "My dear sir, if you are as happy in entering the White House as I shall feel on returning to Wheatland [his house in Lancaster, Pennsylvania], you are a happy man, indeed."[16]

Buchanan had two opportunities to make Supreme Court nominations, but he succeeded with only his first, Nathan Clifford of Maine, still the sole appointment from that state. The vacancy was caused by the dramatic resignation of Justice Benjamin R. Curtis of Massachusetts, following the *Dred Scott* decision in 1857. Although what he regarded as inadequate remuneration also played a role in his withdrawal from the high bench, Curtis acted chiefly because he felt that the Court had become an instrument for personal and political aggrandizement and that under Chief Justice Taney it could not be expected to be restored to its former high station of judicial and public esteem. The country was startled and troubled by Curtis's resignation and anxiously looked to Buchanan for his replacement nomination. The President, after initially wavering on the geographic consideration, determined to remain within the First Circuit and considered a number of New Englanders. Yet he felt more comfortable personally and politically with Nathan Clifford, an old political ally, with whom he had served in President Polk's Cabinet when Clifford was Attorney General. Democrat Clifford, then fifty-four years old, was an able lawyer and legal scholar who had also been a successful representative in both the Maine and U.S. lower houses.

But his political posture was a complicated one—one that combined an apology, even a defense, of slavery with a record of firm support of Jacksonian egalitarianism. It was hardly astonishing that his nomination would run into bitter opposition from abolitionist and allied forces in the Senate, where a five-week-long battle ensued, marked by acrimonious debate. Only the closing of Democratic party ranks plus the absence of two of his most prominent Northern opponents, Senators Charles Sumner of Massachusetts and Simon Cameron of Pennsylvania, and a last-minute change of mind by Democratic Senator Philip Allen of Rhode Island, brought about Clifford's confirmation by a 3-vote margin, 26:23, on January 12, 1858. Until he died twenty-three years later, Clifford served on the Court competently and diligently but without particular distinction—although he wrote more opinions for the Court than any of his colleagues and more than any preceding Justice, with the single exception of John Marshall.

President Buchanan's second chance to make a nomination came when Justice Peter V. Daniel died on May 30, 1860, after more than nineteen years on the Court. A hard worker, he had written 185 opinions during his tenure, and he proved to be "his" Court's leading dissenter. Although the jockeying for Presidential nominations was already in full swing and Buchanan wanted no part of another term, he still had a number of months in office, and his Democratic colleagues looked to him for an acceptable appointment. Understandably the South desired someone from its own region. Daniel was a Virginian, and the high tribunal was now evenly divided between four Southerners and four Northerners. Just as understandably the North sought to gain the balance of power over the proslavery forces on the Court. Characteristically, Buchanan moved slowly. There is some evidence that, still dreaming of maintaining peace, he considered a number of moderate Southerners for the post, including Chief Justice William J. Robertson of Virginia's Court of Appeals, but he eventually decided against them. He then toyed with the idea of leaving the post vacant for his successor to fill, especially since the next term of Court would not commence until December 1860–after the election. At last the President hit on what he viewed as a viable compromise: he would send up a fellow Pennsylvanian, Jeremiah S. Black, a good Democrat acceptable to the South but not a Southerner, a strong Union man but not an abolitionist. Black, an able and knowledgeable lawyer, was well known in public circles: he had had extensive judicial and executive experience–as Justice and Chief Justice of the Pennsylvania Supreme Court and as U.S. Attorney General–and at the time of his nomination he was Secretary of State. Buchanan's plan might well have worked at an earlier stage, but now it was too late. The date was February 5, 1861–less than a month before Lincoln's succession; the embittered loser to Lincoln in the 1860 Presidential campaign, Stephen A. Douglas, was opposed to Black. A good many Southern Senators had already left their seats as a result of secession, and the victorious Republicans certainly were not going to lend a helping hand to fill a vacancy that Mr. Lincoln would presumably be delighted to attend to shortly. Still the confirmation vote was close, indeed—Black lost by only one vote, 25:26. Although he briefly considered submitting yet another candidate, Buchanan decided to stop. The path was clear for President Lincoln.

If earlier evaluations had often placed Abraham Lincoln second to George Washington in stature, historians now consistently accord him the top rank among his fellow Chief Executives. Lincoln, the personification and the symbol of the Union, more than any other person was responsible for its ultimate preservation; and, in attaining that goal, he demonstrated qualities of personal and political leadership that have become almost legend. He was not instinctively tough or heavy-handed, but he could be both when necessary: not even the letter of the Constitution was spared to the ideal of Union.

Lincoln had five chances to appoint Supreme Court Justices during little more than four years in office. He visualized the Court as a partner in the nation's preservation—not an easily realized vision, for the Court was at best a toss-up in terms of its stance on Lincoln's policies. The Court did, however, support the President in the crucial decisions dealing with his wartime policies, notwithstanding the battle between Lincoln and Chief Justice Taney concerning the constitutionality of the Presidential suspension of the writ of *habeas corpus*—so excitingly dramatized in the case of *Ex parte Merryman* in 1861.[17] John Merryman, a militant Maryland secessionist, had been imprisoned by Union forces. Taney issued a writ of *habeas corpus,* which Merryman's custodian, General George Cadwalader, ignored in view of Lincoln's action. Taney, unsuccessful in bringing Cadwalader into Court, wrote a brilliant opinion rejecting Lincoln's asserted right and arguing for exclusive congressional control over suspension. He sent a copy to the President, who disdained the ruling, denying any illegal or unconstitutional action, but Lincoln later ordered Merryman released and turned over to civilian authorities. (He was indicted for treason, but the case against him was ultimately dropped.) The very inconclusiveness of that struggle enunciated the principled posture of the two protagonists. Just before his death in 1954, Justice Robert H. Jackson would comment: "Had Mr. Lincoln scrupulously observed the Taney policy, I do not know whether we would have had any liberty, and had the Chief Justice adopted Mr. Lincoln's philosophy as the philosophy of law, I again do not know whether we would have had any liberty."[18]

The Civil War dominated all aspects of Lincoln's Presidency. Clearly, then, the effect a proposed Court member might have on the conduct of the war was of paramount importance to him. All other considerations were secondary. Even so, he regarded as desirable and perhaps even essential geographic suitability, political loyalty, and payment of political debts. He assigned lesser importance to judicial background. Almost immediately on taking office Lincoln had been presented with three vacancies on the Court: the still unfilled seat of the deceased Justice Daniel; that of Justice McLean, who had died in April 1861 after thirty-two years of service; and that of Justice Campbell, who had resigned that April to join the forces of the Confederacy. Yet the President's probably inexcusable delay in making any appointments for almost a year seriously imperiled the Court's ability to function effectively, especially since Justice Catron and Chief Justice Taney were ill for much of 1861. At this early stage of the war, however, Lincoln was determined to appoint to federal posts only those whose views on slavery and the war were not suspect—who would not alienate the Border States and the upper South, which Lincoln hoped to induce to return to the Union quickly.

Noah H. Swayne, an eminent fifty-seven-year-old Ohio lawyer, was Lincoln's first nominee and met all of the President's criteria. Swayne's antislavery convictions (he had freed his slaves and moved North from Virginia), his loyalty to the Union, and his solidly conservative Republicanism rendered him eminently acceptable on political grounds. Yet his Southern heritage was certain to count in his favor in the Border States. From Lincoln's point of view Swayne was the ideal candidate: a born Southerner, yet an abolitionist and a strict Quaker—whose pacifist religion might be a healing influence during a time of civil strife. Swayne's excellent ties with the financial and business community, whose support was crucial to the Northern war effort, also influenced Lincoln; further, replacing McLean with a fellow Ohioan would repay the huge debt Lincoln owed Ohio Republicans for their vital third-ballot support at the Republican party's National Convention in 1860. Easily Senate-confirmed (38:1), Swayne amply lived up to his nominator's expectations, yet his work on the Court during his tenure of close to two decades deserves but an average performance rating.

Lincoln's second appointment was intimately linked with the politics of judicial redistricting then alive on Capitol Hill. With the admission of new states into the Union, the existing judicial circuits had become increasingly large and unwieldy in terms of work loads, particularly because individual members of the Court were still being called on for occasional circuit-riding. As more territories of the South and the West became formal components of the United States, Congress resolved to readjust the physical boundaries of the existing circuits. To that end the five old Southern circuits were reduced to three; Indiana was moved to the Ohio circuit; Illinois was grouped in the Eighth Circuit with Michigan and Wisconsin; and a new trans-Mississippi circuit, the Ninth, was created, including Minnesota, Iowa, Kansas, and Missouri. This boundary game effectively removed from consideration two active candidates for the Daniel vacancy, Republican Senator Orville H. Browning of Illinois and Caleb B. Smith of Indiana, Lincoln's Secretary of the Interior. Lincoln then turned his attention to Samuel Freeman Miller of Iowa, at forty-six probably the outstanding trans-Mississippi lawyer of the time.

The President did not really know Miller—in fact, at this point he relied heavily on the recommendations of others. A native Kentuckian with a medical as well as a law degree, Miller had left the South because of his opposition to slavery. He was a loyal Republican with impeccable political and professional credentials, and he was from the right geographic region. All these factors were brought to Lincoln's attention by one of the most vigorous nomination drives in the history of the Court. Numerous insistent voices chorused Miller's qualifications; the President heard not only from western governors, the Iowa Attorney General, and the Iowa Supreme Court, but also from prominent figures in the world of law and politics throughout the country, capped by a petition from Congress containing the names of 129 of 140 members of the House and all but 4 Senators! Lincoln gladly forwarded Miller's name to an eager Senate, which confirmed it unanimously within half an hour on July 16, 1862. Scholarly, skillful, and creative, Miller justified Lincoln's and his supporters' faith during twenty-eight productive years. He was to become one of the outstanding Justices to grace the bench, recognized as such with a "near great" rating by the Court experts. It is a pity that his labors are so often exclusively characterized by his contentious 5:4 majority opinion in the *Slaughterhouse Cases* of 1873.[19] There he held, in interpreting the privileges and immunities clause of the Fourteenth Amendment, that there is a "citizenship of the United States and a citizenship of a state, which are distinct from each other," thus turning aside for many a decade the warm contention that the basic freedoms in the Bill of Rights cannot be encroached on by state governments, just as they cannot by the federal government.

With the new circuit now staffed and given the wartime contraction of the Southern circuits, Lincoln was free to fill Campbell's seat without feeling any obligations toward the latter's native Alabama. In fact, the President could now select someone from his own state to "represent" the Eighth Circuit. The three most likely and assertive ones were the aforementioned Senator Browning, Judge Thomas Drummond of the U.S. District Court, and Judge David Davis of the Illinois Circuit Court. The race soon narrowed to Browning and Davis. Both men were as well qualified as Drummond, but they were closer to Lincoln and their political supporters were more powerful. Lincoln bided his time, however. For a while he considered solving the dilemma by appointing Davis to a Cabinet post and sending Browning to the Court, but Davis made it clear that he would have none of such an arrangement. Ultimately, the President was aided by a cooling among Browning's fellow Republican Senators, who accused their colleague of appeasing secessionist elements in Illinois, and by the attacks made on Browning by the influential Illinois publisher, Joseph Medill. To the relief and delight of Davis's allies, who had incessantly reminded the President of their candidate's staunch services on behalf of the Republican party and its leader, Lincoln turned to Davis in December of 1862.

Davis and Lincoln had been close personal and political friends for many years. Recognizing Lincoln's ability and promise, Davis had worked hard to see him elected to the U.S. Senate in 1858. At the 1860 Convention, it was Davis who was instrumental in marshaling the crucial Illinois Republican forces behind Lincoln. And as Lincoln's campaign manager Davis had worked tirelessly. Clearly, the President was greatly indebted to his nominee. Yet Davis was also eminently qualified. From the appropriate geographic area, he had extensive legal and judicial experience, including fourteen years on the Illinois bench; he was politically wise and shrewd; he was a loyal Republican and philosophical Lincolnian; even his age–forty-seven–was ideal. He was quickly confirmed with near unanimity and, at least during Lincoln's lifetime, supported Lincoln's constitutional interpretations. Intriguingly, it was Davis who, scarcely a year after the President's death, wrote the *Ex parte Milligan* opinion,[20] in which a unanimous Supreme Court, containing all five Lincoln appointees, held unlawful the military commission authorized by the President to operate judicially in areas where civil courts were open and functioning.

In March 1863, with the enthusiastic backing of Abraham Lincoln, Congress created a Tenth Circuit consisting of California and Oregon, to which Nevada was later added, allegedly because of the anticipated increase in Court business in the West. The increase in the number of Justices from nine to ten suited Lincoln's purposes admirably: his fourth Court appointee would bring at least some security to the prospects of a favorable judicial stance in the enormously significant Civil War litigation now on the Court's docket. It was widely expected that the President would nominate someone from the new circuit–someone familiar with its needs and problems, but also someone who could be counted on strongly and vocally to back the cause of Union. Lincoln found his man in the camp of the Democrats–Stephen J. Field of California, easily the most distinguished jurist in the Pacific States. In addition, he was enthusiastically backed by California's powerful Governor, Leland Stanford. Although Field had been a Buchanan Democrat as recently as 1860, Lincoln correctly perceived his *real* politics to be akin to his own. Nonetheless, the appointment represented the first *bona fide* instance of a Presidential crossing of major party lines to fill a Supreme Court vacancy. The forty-six-year-old Field, who was graduated first in his class at Williams College in 1837, had served as both an Associate Justice and Chief Justice on the Supreme Court of California. Following stints in the California State Assembly and in successful private practice, he had played a crucial role in keeping the state loyal to the Union and had often eloquently espoused the Union's cause in public. Moreover, he was the brother of David Dudley Field, the prominent abolitionist, who had become a trusted adviser to Lincoln after playing a key part in Lincoln's nomination for the Presidency. The President nominated Field on March 7, 1863, and the Senate confirmed him unanimously three days later. It was the same day on which the Union blockade of the South (initiated by Lincoln in 1861) was upheld by the Supreme Court in the *Prize Cases,*[21] in a cliff-hanger vote (5:4).

Stephen Field served the Court for close to thirty-four and three-quarters years, second-longest to date. He did not disappoint Lincoln during the two years that remained to the President, but the development of Field's jurisprudence once the Civil War was over might have caused Lincoln a good many second thoughts. Although the Court experts have justly rated Field "near great" rather than "great," the Californian's role and influence on the bench were far-reaching and often decisive. Strong-willed; a superb linguist; a pithy, analytical stylist; a prolific author of key opinions; creative; intellectual; result-oriented; and a classical property-rights advocate, Stephen Field became the Court's personification of *laissez-faire* economics.

On October 12, 1864, Chief Justice Taney died at the age of eighty-seven, having served for almost three decades. Alone, tired, and disillusioned, he succumbed not realizing how much he had meant to his government and his people. He and John Marshall had presided over the Court for almost sixty-five years! Who could now replace him? From the outset Abraham Lincoln's former Secretary of the Treasury, fifty-six-year-old Salmon Portland Chase of Ohio, was a major contender for Taney's seat. Insanely ambitious and conniving, Chase, who had been governor of Ohio as well as U.S. Senator, was unquestionably able; but Lincoln had never liked or trusted him and was not comfortable with him. Hence, although certainly not ruling Chase out, Lincoln stalled in filling the vacant chair—undoubtedly in the hope of finding someone more in line with his expectations of character and personality. Among the other men he considered were sitting Associate Justices James M. Wayne and Noah H. Swayne and, to a lesser extent, Associate Justice David Davis; Secretary of War Edwin M. Stanton; Secretary of State William H. Seward; Secretary of the Treasury W. P. Fessenden; former Attorney General Edward Bates; former Secretary of the Interior Caleb B. Smith (a perpetual candidate); and former Postmaster General Montgomery Blair, plus a host of distinguished lawyers throughout the land, notably William Strong of Pennsylvania and William M. Evarts of New York.

Had Lincoln been able to select whom he really wanted and deemed most personally deserving as well as promising, he would have chosen Montgomery Blair, whose candidacy was ardently embraced and furthered by Secretary of State Seward and Secretary of the Navy Gideon Welles. Blair, a noted attorney from St. Louis with extensive public and private experience in government and at the bar, was a political moderate with long-time family roots in the original Free Soil contingent of the Republican party and a bitter foe of Chase. Bright, scholarly, and humane, he was among eminent counsel who had argued on the losing side in *Dred Scott.* The President knew Blair well and was keenly aware of his devotion to principle and courage. Yet he was not convinced that Blair possessed sufficient strength, leadership, or ability to unify disparate groups within the party. Lincoln quite correctly and dispassionately recognized that Chase did have all of these qualifications. Moreover, the President had not the slightest doubt of Chase's dedication to the Union cause. Still, deeply troubled and concerned, Lincoln delayed his decision for eight weeks, during which time he carefully weighed his step—a period well described by such perceptive chroniclers as Carl Sandburg and David M. Silver.[22]

The President finally concluded that in the interest of national unity and security the nod would have to go to Chase. If only Chase were not so politically ambitious! He had spent much of his time in the Lincoln Cabinet scheming for personal political gain; he was ruthless, stubborn, self-seeking, perhaps even malicious; and Lincoln was convinced that even as Chief Justice, Chase would remain an active candidate for the Presidency. He had sought the Republican candidacy in both 1856 and 1860 (and while on the bench in 1868 would seek the candidacy for *both* parties). But three overriding reasons finally prompted the President to send Chase's name to the Senate: first, he had no doubt that Chase's policy views on the war and future Reconstruction were sound and reliable; second, if anyone could heal the widening breach in the Republican party, it would be Chase, even from the high bench; third, Chase held an important I.O.U.: although he had been Lincoln's rival for the Presidency in 1860 and had even angled for it in 1864, he had campaigned hard and effectively for Lincoln's election. Without even referring Chase's name to committee, the Senate confirmed its ex-colleague on the same day the nomination reached it.

Lincoln's shrewd evaluations of the new Chief Justice proved to be generally correct: Chase's political ambitions were, of course, never stilled by his new post. Yet he voted "Lincoln" on all war and related issues during Lincoln's lifetime and, although yielding on some issues, he stood up to Congress on a good many others during Reconstruction. On the other hand, Lincoln would have been as displeased as Congress was with Chase's 1870 opinion for a 4:3 Court that–employing tortured constitutional reasoning–struck down the Legal Tender Act of 1862,[23] which had made greenbacks legal tender in payments of debts. One other Lincoln appointee, Stephen J. Field, joined the Chase-led majority–which saw both a due process violation and a contract violation in the "fiat money." (But within fifteen months the other "Lincoln men" who had dissented from the first decision–Swayne, Miller, and Davis–would join two Grant appointees to overrule it in the *Sec-*

ond Legal Tender Cases.)[24] In retrospect Chase's greatest contribution probably was his superbly skilful and shrewd handling of Andrew Johnson's impeachment trial by a hostile Senate. The assertive, no-nonsense leadership he exercised as the presiding officer during the proceedings in the upper chamber was nothing less than brilliant; it may well have saved the institution of the Presidency itself.

It was Andrew Johnson's misfortune to fall heir to an office for which he was only marginally qualified, temperamentally ill suited, and politically out of step (although a Union Democrat, he never became a Republican after joining the Lincoln ticket). He entered the Presidency at a moment in history that called for a combination of Washington, Jefferson, Jackson, and Lincoln. He was not made of such stuff. With a kind of stubborn courage, he often needessly inflamed a powerful Republican Congress that *a priori* was not too kindly disposed toward him. The ultimate result was his impeachment on February 24, 1868, by a House vote of 128:47. Charged with eleven largely spurious articles of impeachment, centering on his summary removal of Edwin M. Stanton, his disloyal Secretary of War, he went on trial in the Senate on March 30. In late May the President escaped conviction by one vote on Article Eleven—a catchall provision through which the House managers hoped to obtain the necessary Senate votes to convict Johnson—and thereby effectively on the entire charge, the tally of 35:19 falling just one short of the constitutionally required two-thirds majority. He was saved by the courageous "nay" votes of seven Republican Senators who, as John F. Kennedy wrote nine decades later in his *Profiles in Courage,*[25] "looked down into [their] open grave[s]" and committed political suicide by casting their ballots with the Democratic minority in favor of Andrew Johnson's acquittal.

President Johnson's one opportunity to appoint a member of the Supreme Court came on the death of Justice Catron on May 30, 1865. Vacillating for almost a year, Johnson finally chose Attorney General Henry Stanbery, an Ohio Republican of considerable legal skill and a well-liked public figure. But it is doubtful that the Senate would have approved God himself had he been nominated by Andrew Johnson. Not only did it fail to act on the Stanbery nomination, it also passed a bill that abolished the Catron seat, reducing the Court's membership from ten to nine. An added proviso stipulated that after the next vacancy the Court be further reduced to eight members. This maneuver, it was hoped, would accomplish two things: first, it would block further Johnson nominations; second, it would increase the voice of the presumably "safe" Lincoln appointees. The Radical Republicans' scheme was indeed crowned with success: Johnson never had another crack at a nomination, for when Justice James M. Wayne died in 1867, after more than three decades on the Court, the vacancy was statutorily abolished. On the other hand, the presumably "safe" Court certainly did not prove to be a supine servant of Radical Republican construction or Reconstruction, as it demonstrated in a series of postwar decisions that ran counter to Radical pleasure.[26] Yet its repeated dodging of major questions of constitutionality concerning the Reconstruction Acts[27] between 1867 and 1869 was proof positive that the Court did not wish to embark on a major struggle with Congress over the delicate and emotion-charged issues of Reconstruction.

7

The Balance of the Nineteenth Century:

From Ulysses S. Grant to William McKinley 1869-1901

As President of the United States, General Ulysses S. Grant, the North's Civil War hero, has been rated all but universally as a failure by the experts. Grant was one of those strange paradoxes in American history: a leader enthusiastically backed by the people in the face of a visibly disgraceful performance in office. Not only was he unanimously nominated twice by the Republican party on the first ballot, not only was he easily elected in 1868 with a large popular majority, and not only was he reelected with an even larger majority in 1872, but he almost broke the two-term tradition in 1876, leading all other Republican nominees through the first thirty-five convention ballots! Ignorant about, and bored by, the political process; prejudiced, undignified, vacillating, and naïve; conducting government through a bevy of cronies who betrayed his confidence, he presided over two Administrations wracked by scandal and corruption. Yet the four Supreme Court members Grant appointed proved to be generally able and in two instances even superior individuals.

Grant may have been bored by government and politics, yet he carefully heeded the entreaties of prominent Republican leaders at his side, led by Ebenezer Rockwood Hoar, his first Attorney General. They made clear to the President the need to pack the Court with Republican loyalists; consequently, he resolved at the outset that a safe Republican record would be a basic requirement for nomination, to which he added geographic suitability. Other qualifications appeared not to matter; no discernible pattern of selection can be found in the eight nominations* Grant forwarded to the Senate. Thus, it is hardly astonishing that all except one of his appointees (Ward Hunt) would vote contrary to the heart of the libertarian legislation growing out of the three Civil War amendments that Grant presumably favored.

To the re-created ninth seat on the Court—a "gift" to Grant by Congress—the President nominated his Attorney General, the popular—although not in the Senate—outspoken, and independent Ebenezer R. Hoar. Hoar was superbly qualified, but after seven weeks of debate and delay the Senate rejected him 24:33 on February 3, 1870. The majority was furious with Hoar for his refusal to back their strictly partisan suggestions for lower-court nominees, his active labors on behalf of a merit civil service system for the federal government, and his opposition to Andrew Johnson's impeachment.

While the Senate was still arguing over Hoar, Grant was presented with a second opening: the aged and ill Robert C. Grier at last yielded to his colleagues' urgent pleas—they had sent the youngish Justice Stephen J. Field to do their dirty work—and resigned in early 1870, after more than twenty-three years on the Court. Grant thought he might be able to strike a compromise with the Senate's opponents to the still-pending Hoar nomination by acceding to a petition signed by a large majority of both the Senate and the House in favor of Lincoln's Secretary of War, the impetuous Edwin M. Stanton. Grant was not happy with this nomination, but he felt reasonably certain that it would help Hoar's cause in obtaining the other vacancy. He was quite wrong: although the Senate eagerly approved Stanton by a vote of 46:11 on December 20, one day after it officially received his name, it refused to budge on Hoar. Ironically, four days later the fifty-four-

* One of the reasons that the President had so many opportunities to make nominations was that Congress had restored the Court's membership to nine within a month after the maligned Johnson's return to Tennessee. Only four of Grant's eight nominees, however, ultimately served on the Court.

year-old Stanton succumbed to a coronary thrombosis—and the President still had two seats to fill!

Grant now acted quickly. Four days after Hoar's rejection, he sent to the Senate two nominations: for the Grier seat, William Strong of Pennsylvania, and for the "new" ninth, Joseph P. Bradley of New Jersey. Strong, whom Grant had actually wanted to nominate instead of Stanton, was a distinguished and experienced state jurist who had been very much in the running for the Chief Justiceship of the United States in 1864. Enthusiastically backed by Hoar, by many prominent Pennsylvanians of both major political parties, and by incumbent members of the Court, the sixty-two-year-old Strong was easily confirmed by the Senate within ten days, the nine opposition votes coming chiefly from Southerners who felt their region should have received the nod.

Things did not go so smoothly for the scholarly, thoughtful Bradley, five years Strong's junior. Also backed by Hoar, and certainly Grant's most highly qualified appointee, he had been initially recommended for the post by Justice Grier himself—even though Grier was a Democrat and Bradley a Republican. Before he was finally confirmed six weeks later by a vote of 46:9, Bradley came under heavy fire from Eastern "hard money" interests who quite correctly regarded him as dedicated to a "soft money" economic philosophy. Yet Bradley had excellent business connections and, although he had no previous judicial experience, he had practiced a variety of law for many years, obtaining considerable prominence as one of the foremost railroad attorneys in the nation. He would not disappoint the conservative business community during his more than two decades on the bench, nor would he let Grant and the Republicans down in the legal tender controversy. And as a member of the Electoral Count Commission in the disputed Presidential Election of 1876 he cast the decisive 8:7 ballot in the cases of each of twenty disputed electoral votes, thereby awarding the election to Republican Rutherford B. Hayes over Democrat Samuel J. Tilden.[1]

Assuredly, Bradley was Grant's most fortuitous appointment in terms of ability and party loyalty. But he was not a happy choice in terms of advancing civil rights legislation—as exemplified by his votes in such crucial decisions as those attacking the Enforcement Acts of 1870–1871[2] and the Civil Rights Acts of 1871 and 1875.[3] Indeed, he wrote the opinion striking down the latter by ruling that Congress could not use the Fourteenth Amendment enforcement clause to prevent discrimination by private persons—not even in such privately owned public accommodations as hotels, theaters, buses, and trains. Nonetheless, Bradley's overall performance, characterized by judicial ingenuity, craftsmanship, lucidity, and eloquence, was of such caliber as to earn him a "near great" ranking by the Court's leading contemporary observers. Together with Associate Justices Miller, Field, and Harlan I he provided the intellectual leadership present on the high bench in the latter decades of the nineteenth century.

When Justice Samuel Nelson resigned in November 1872 after almost three decades of dedicated and able service, President Grant designated a fellow New Yorker, Ward Hunt, to replace him. Then sixty-two, Hunt came to the Court with a wealth of legislative and judicial experience and the added attraction of having been one of the organizers of the Republican party in 1856—although he had begun his career as a Jacksonian Democrat and had been elected as such to state and municipal offices. But he had become disenchanted with the Democratic party's national posture in post-Jackson days and, through the Free-Soil movement, had eagerly embraced the fledgling Republicans—on whose ticket he successfully ran for a seat on the New York Supreme Court. Backed by the influential Hoar and the entire New York congressional delegation as well as the state's and nation's business community, Hunt was an ideal candidate from Grant's point of view. Within a week he was decisively confirmed, 53:11. Hunt proved to be at once the most judicially loyal and least effective of Grant's appointees during his relatively brief tenure of nine years on the Court.

On May 8, 1873, after but eight and a half years in his post, Chief Justice Salmon P. Chase died, still harboring ambitions for the elusive Presidency. Grant, now in his second term, turned the process of his last appointment into somewhat of a comic opera, offering the Chief Justiceship to no fewer than *seven* individuals!

When he began his quest for Chase's replacement, Grant was quite aware that at least two of the sitting Associate Justices—Samuel F. Miller and Joseph P. Bradley—were interested in being promoted and, further, that they were eminently capable of performing the job. Yet he ruled them out immediately: it was his way of keeping the peace and harmony on the Court, and perhaps on that score he had reasoned wisely. He then began to consider other possibilities, and after six months of dawdling finally offered the post to the shrewd, outspoken Senator Roscoe Conkling of New York, his close friend, policy confidant, and political supporter. The youthful Conkling, to his credit, declined at once: he was neither interested in the position nor was he sufficiently qualified for it in terms of judicial experience—a fact he acknowledged candidly.

It was now November and Grant, realizing that he had to take some action, turned to his Attorney General, George H. Williams of Oregon, an honest but only marginally capable individual. Williams's nomination ran into immediate flak from the bar, press, and public—who all quite rightly deemed him to be lacking in stature—but Grant persisted in pushing the fifty-year-old lawyer until the Judiciary Committee approved his nomination. The full Senate, however, demurred, and the President withdrew Williams's name early in January 1874 at the nominee's own request. Almost as if to sass the Senate, Grant now came up with the name of his good friend, seventy-four-year-old Caleb Cushing. Unquestionably highly qualified, possessed of a superb mind, Cushing, in addition to being far too old for the position, had made many enemies in and out of public life by virtue of his chameleonic political record: he had been a Whig, a Tyler Whig, a Democrat, a Johnson Constitutional Conservative, and he now was a Republican! The opposition was widespread and rampant, focusing not only on Cushing's shifting political persuasions, but on an exchange of controversial letters that had once taken place between him and Jefferson Davis. Grant was not long in withdrawing his nomination. He then offered the Chief Justiceship to three others, Senator Timothy P. Howe (Wisconsin), Senator Oliver P. Morton (Indiana), and Secretary of State Hamilton Fish—but he did not formally nominate any one of them; he seemed to enjoy the suspense. Finally, recognizing that the time for experimenting and game playing was over, he yielded to continuing clamor from the Midwest and settled on another Ohioan, the rather undistinguished, noncontroversial, quietly efficient, well-liked Morrison Remick Waite.

The Senate confirmed him 63:0 on January 21, 1874, two days after he was nominated, and, now more than eight months after Chase's death, the Court had its first Justice ever to be confirmed by a unanimous, formal roll call. The fifty-eight-year-old attorney had been recommended to the President at the very outset of his quest for a successor to Chase. Grant had, in fact, known Waite when the latter served, with others, as Counsel before the Geneva Arbitration Commission of 1871 that considered the *Alabama* claims and deposits. An expert in real estate and titles, Waite was not too well known beyond Ohio; he had no judicial experience; and he had never argued a case in the U.S. Supreme Court. But he was respected as hardworking, able, and conscientious, a citizen of great integrity and considerable expertise in constitutional law. Widely called His Accidency because of his seventh-fiddle nomination and described by Justice Field as a "man that would never have been thought of for the position by any person except President Grant . . . an experiment which no President has a right to make with our Court,"[4] Waite nonetheless developed into an effective and tactful leader of a difficult and contentious Court. He deservedly earned the "near great" rating accorded him in the light of history by most Court observers.

Yet if Grant had expected Waite to lead the way in the liberal interpretation of the Civil War amendments, he was badly mistaken. The new Chief Justice, like Bradley and Strong, gave a restrictive rather than liberal construction to the amendments, particularly to the Fourteenth Amendment, whose "due process of law" and "privileges and immunities" clauses became the special targets of illiberal reading. Thus, Waite, echoing the devastating *Slaughterhouse Cases*[5] of three years earlier, wrote in 1876 that the Fourteenth Amendment "adds nothing to the rights of one citizen as against another. It simply gives an additional guarantee against any encroachment by the States upon the fundamental rights which belong to every citizen as a member of society."[6] On the other hand, Waite wrote the majority opinion in the famed *Granger Cases* of 1877,[7] which wrought a revolution in constitutional law: Waite's opinion in the leading case of that group, *Munn* v. *Illinois,* recognized that the due process of law clause of the Fourteenth Amendment, although a barrier against illegal governmental assaults on property, did not forbid the exercise of governmental (here, state) police power to regulate those categories of business "affected with a public interest." He went on to point out that "when private property is affected with a public interest it ceases to be *juris privati* only," and he concluded with the often repeated admonition that for "protection against abuses by legislators, the people must resort to the polls, not the courts." Despite this landmark decision—for which he is best remembered—Waite's career on the Court was basically that of a constitutional and economic conservative.

Rutherford Birchard Hayes, the nation's nineteenth President, entered the White House under a cloud after his rather dubious victory in the so-called "Stolen Election of 1876." Yet there is no doubt that the three-time governor of Ohio and two-time member of Congress was an excellent President and that he richly merits the somewhat delayed recognition that Presidential historians now bestow in ranking him just below the "near greats." He was not a brilliant man, but he was strong, public spirited, perceptive, effective, and—so vital after the shadowy and shady Grant era—a bright symbol of rectitude, morality, and honesty. Despite the blot on his election, a Democratic Congress during most of his regime, and considerable backbiting and factionalism in his own party, he gave the country strong leadership; he restored to the Republican party much of the good will and faith that Grant's performance had wiped out. Unquestionably Hayes's most memorable and far-reaching executive move was his immediate recall of federal troops from the South. Thus fulfilling a campaign promise, he, in effect, wrote *finis* to both military and political Reconstruction. Conciliatory and sensitive, he strove mightily to "bind up the wounds."

During his four years at the helm, Hayes had three opportunities to make nominations to the Supreme Court. Two of these, John Marshall Harlan I and William B. Woods, he saw confirmed; the third, Stanley Matthews, nominated in the waning days of the Administration, was not acted on before Hayes left office, but President Garfield would successfully resubmit his name. If Woods, who died after little more than six years in office, was mediocre at best, Matthews was an excellent Justice and Harlan was among the most renowned to serve on the highest bench. Even if Hayes did not approve of all aspects of Harlan's jurisprudence or of his advanced libertarian opinions on the Bill of Rights and the Civil War amendments, he might well be proud of the ex-Kentucky slaveholder who had come aboard to fight for the Union cause. All of Hayes's nominations reflected, of course, his spirit of compromise and reconciliation. Thus, his choice of nominal Republicans, who were presumably moderate to conservative and broadly acceptable to the South, was hardly surprising. The geographic factor that had once figured so prominently appeared to be of little importance to Hayes; he did not hesitate to substitute Kentucky (Harlan I) for Illinois (Davis), and Georgia (Woods) for Pennsylvania (Strong). For his last nomination he did, however, stay with Ohio (Matthews) for Ohio (Swayne). The resignation of Justice David Davis—a graduate of Kenyon College, like Hayes and Matthews—prior to Hayes's assumption of the Presidency, provided him with an immediate vacancy to fill. In mid-October he proposed to the Senate the forty-four-year-old Harlan, a man to whom he was deeply indebted politically.

Harlan had been an indispensable ally to Hayes both during the Republican Convention and the election campaign of 1876. He had headed his state's delegation to the Convention, throwing Kentucky's votes to Hayes at a critical point in the balloting. During the campaign, he was largely responsible for important political work in the Border States. And he also served as a member of the Commission investigating Louisiana's disputed electoral returns in the 1876 election: his vote helped to adjudge the results in Hayes's favor. Yet it would be wrong to attribute Harlan's nomination solely to political considerations—indeed, at the time of his selection Harlan could have been looked on as both nonpartisan and bipartisan, a characterization not at all inconsistent with his political history. Both a Democrat and a Whig before the Civil War, he had been an unsuccessful Whig candidate for Congress in 1859 and a Presidential elector on the Bell-Everett Constitutional Union party ticket in 1860. A staunch defender of the Union, he reluctantly converted to Republicanism, yet initially opposed the Civil War amendments and supported General George B. McClellan rather than Lincoln for the White House in 1864. But he was directly responsible for rejuvenating Kentucky's Republican party; he ran twice for the governorship, although unsuccessfully; because he had been a firm Grant backer in 1868, his name was prominently mentioned as a Vice Presidential candidate on the Grant ticket in 1872. Harlan's ancestors were Southern slaveholders; but by now Harlan had not only become a firm devotee of the Civil War amendments, he had also begun to commit himself with consistency and eloquence—almost always in solo dissenting opinions—to the proposition that the Fourteenth applied or "incorporated" the Bill of Rights. More than any other public figure on the nineteenth-century Supreme Court Harlan would amply and poignantly demonstrate that commitment, though almost invariably in dissent.[8] It would not be until the heyday of the Warren Court that, chiefly owing to the efforts and persuasiveness of Justice Hugo L. Black, Harlan's dream of the "nationalization" of the Bill of Rights, its "incorporation" by "absorption," would become reality—over sustained, although not total, objections by his grandson.

An ideal choice for Hayes in terms of public service, ability, and political compromise, Harlan still ran into considerable bipartisan, biregional Senatorial opposition. But after a month-long delay he was confirmed. For thirty-four years John Marshall Harlan I would grace the tribunal he loved. Grandfather of the future Associate Justice (1955–1971), who proudly bore the same name—although not the same jurisprudence—John Marshall Harlan I became "the brilliant precursor in liberalism and dissent of Justice Holmes."[9] As long as conscience will govern men and women, they will remember his outcry in solitary dissent from the Court's 1896 opinion in *Plessy* v. *Ferguson,* which upheld the "separate but equal" doctrine: "Our Constitution is color-blind, and neither knows nor tolerates classes among citizens."[10]

Hayes's second nomination, designed to replace Justice William Strong, who had resigned in December 1880 after more than a decade and one-half of routine service, was fifty-six-year-old Judge William B. Woods of Georgia. Nominee Woods shared several characteristics with Harlan, but he would prove to be in a totally different class as a jurist. Like Harlan a confirmed Unionist who served with the Federal Army, he, too, had reluctantly become a Republican. An ex-resident of Ohio, he had moved to Alabama and then to Georgia, where he was serving as a U.S. Circuit Judge when Hayes selected him for the Supreme Court—the first Southerner to get the nod since the appointment of James A. Campbell in 1853. Although Woods—whose selection was recommended by Chief Justice Waite—had lingering and fond attachments to the North, his professional loyalties were to the South. Thus, he was precisely the kind of candidate Hayes sought to help bind bitter sectional wounds. Less visibly controversial in the Senate's eyes than Harlan, Woods was confirmed within five days by a solid 39:8 margin just before Christmas Eve.

An avowed one-term President, Hayes was already a lame duck when, in late January 1881, he nominated his Kenyon College classmate and fellow Union Army combatant, Stanley Matthews of Ohio, to fill the Court vacancy created by the retirement of the aged Justice Noah H. Swayne, who had given almost two decades of diligent service. Hayes might have been willing to wait for the incoming Garfield, but illness had thinned the ranks of the Court and, after all, Matthews was not only his good friend and political ally, but he was cast in the mold Hayes perceived as highly desirable in the pursuit of sectional peace and compromise. Like Harlan I and Woods, a political maverick, Matthews had supported Democrat Polk but also the politically versatile Salmon P. Chase. He was firmly opposed to slavery, yet he faithfully sought to enforce the Fugitive Slave Act in his capacity as U.S. Attorney for Ohio (Ohio was a frequent terminus of the Underground Railway). President Grant, apprised of Matthews's political *savoir faire* and his experience as a state legislator and Presidential elector, had appointed him to the sensitive and crucial post of counsel for the Republican faction arguing Hayes's case before the Electoral Count Commission of 1876–1877. Matthews had proved his mettle, persuasively arguing that the Commission and Congress should not "go behind the election returns," but should instead shun a probing of motives and accept the certified results by legally constituted state authorities. He had, thus, been of no small aid to his old friend, President Hayes!

What caused the two men untold difficulties, however, was Matthews's avowed association with corporate financial and railroad interests, both as a practicing attorney and as a U.S. Senator from Ohio. When the President nominated Matthews to the Court, he was serving as Midwestern Chief Counsel to financier Jay Gould. The Senate exploded in anger, its Committee on the Judiciary flatly refusing to report the nomination out for floor action. It was perhaps the first clear instance of concerted, patent opposition to a nominee on the grounds of economic affiliation. Matthews's nomination appeared to be understandably dead.

To the surprise of a good many, however, incoming President Garfield renominated Matthews almost immediately after taking the oath of office in March 1881. James Garfield had never really sought the Presidency; if there was ever in our Presidential history a dark-horse draft, it was that of the long-time Ohio Congressman and ex-General, whose selection was desired neither by those who nominated him nor by Garfield himself. A decent but gullible and weak man, Garfield was President for six months only. Four of these months were spent actively in office, the last two in a courageous but futile struggle for life against the bullet that a disappointed office seeker, Charles J. Guiteau, fired into the President as he was about to entrain for a Williams College reunion.

Why Garfield really nominated Matthews is not entirely clear, although considerable evidence points to the political and financial influence of Gould and his associates as well as Garfield's desire to heal party wounds. The clout of the Gould-led group might well explain the shift of Senatorial votes that resulted in Matthews's razor-thin confirmation, 24:23, after two months of acrimonious debate. The opposition, thus, barely fell short of preventing what the *New York Times* had characterized as one of Hayes's "most injudicious and objectionable acts" and "a sad and inexcusable error" on Garfield's part.[11] Yet the history of the Court proves that appointees often rise above associational and philosophical predispositions, and Stanley Matthews was one of those. Although he died less than eight years after he reached the Court, the only Justice to date (mid-1984) to have sat on the Court by dint of a one-vote margin of confirmation demonstrated an entirely open mind on such crucial questions as governmental regulation of the economy, of business as well as of labor. Far from establishing a slavish ideological attachment to a *laissez-faire* economy, he frequently joined other fair-minded independents on the bench, such as John Marshall Harlan I and Chief Justice Waite, in regulatory opinions that confounded prognosticators.

In 1881 on Garfield's death, Chester A. Arthur of New York came to the Presidency with almost everyone predicting doom and failure: his selection as Vice President had been steeped in political hacksmanship and spoilsmanship, nurtured by the nether Roscoe Conkling wing of New York's Republican party. His public career had been limited to the notoriety surrounding his removal from a New York Port customs office post by President Hayes; although his reputation as a shrewd attorney was widespread, he was much better known as a Conkling machine politician. No wonder the nation stood apprehensive, even horrified, in anticipation of his performance as Chief Executive! Yet in what was one of the most dramatic character reversals in the country's history, President Arthur not only turned his back on his spoilsmen-cronies, but he championed the great Pendleton Civil Service Reform Act of 1883—a monument to the principle of public office based on merit rather than patronage. Moreover, he gave proof of solid, intelligent administrative expertise, generally acquitting himself with aplomb. Historians accord him no more than an "average" rating, but that is much higher than he could have expected had he not altered his erstwhile approach to government and politics.

Arthur had three opportunities to nominate Justices for two vacancies, and the two men he would see appointed—Horace Gray and Samuel Blatchford—were admirably in line with his newfound regard for meritorious service. Arthur's first vacancy was a hold-over from his predecessor's term: the aged and ill Justice Nathan Clifford had died shortly after Guiteau's fatal attack on Garfield, and the slot had simply been left empty. Two months after assuming office, President Arthur nominated the fifty-three-year-old Horace Gray, a distinguished and experienced jurist with almost two decades of service on the Supreme Court of Massachusetts, including eight as Chief Justice. One of the youngest graduates in the history of Harvard College, Gray was an eminent legal scholar and historian whose selection was universally applauded. As a federalist Republican, with an acute appreciation of limited states' rights, Gray was a fiscal and economic conservative. Yet he would not be averse to siding with such Justices as Waite, Harlan I, and Matthews (his father-in-law, but only three years Gray's senior) in upholding selective government regulation of the economy. He fully lived up to Arthur's expectations and served diligently for more than twenty years, demonstrating an enormous capacity for research and writing.

Barely two months after Gray's appointment, Justice Ward Hunt, who had been ill for five of his nine years on the bench, resigned his post. It was widely expected that President Arthur would tender the nomination to Senator George F. Edmunds, a brilliant lawyer and influential public servant from Vermont (a state that to this day has never been "represented" on the Supreme Court). But to the consternation of most observers, Arthur had a "relapse" and offered the post to his one-time political mentor and boss, Senator Roscoe Conkling of New York (who, it will be remembered, had been tendered the Chief Justiceship by Grant in 1873 but, to general relief, had refused it). Conkling had pondered the matter for several days, during which time the press had a field day in lambasting nominator as well as nominee. This time, however, he accepted the proffered Associate Justiceship and, true to its tradition of never rejecting one of its own, the Senate, although only after a bitter floor fight, confirmed Conkling with a comfortable 39:12 margin on March 2, 1882. Yet to audible sighs of relief, Conkling, after having expressed his gratitude to his colleagues, formally declined five days later, after all, with the *New York Times* and the *Nation,* among others, suggesting sarcastically that he did so because there was not enough money in the post of Justice of the U.S. Supreme Court.

In thus paying homage to his political spoilsman and teacher, Arthur had only narrowly been spared a potentially disastrous appointment. The President now fortunately reverted to his merit principles and turned to Edmunds, who, however, declined for personal reasons. Arthur, thus, gave the nod to the well-qualified Samuel Blatchford of New York, a federal judge with fifteen years of experience, then serving on the U.S. Court of Appeals for the Second Circuit, and a specialist in admiralty law. Blatchford presented ideal legal, political, and geographic qualifications. Sixty-two years old and a moderate Republican, Blatchford had excellent connections to New York's business and political elite. He was a noncontroversial public figure who had amply proved his mettle in public service as well as having established a distinguished career in private law practice. Thus, Blatchford was quickly confirmed *viva voce* by the Senate. His career on the Court was in the mold of his colleague Gray. What he lacked of Gray's quickness, shrewdness, and astuteness, Blatchford—the author of a significant number of *Reports* and *Blatchford's Circuit Court Reports*—made up in productivity. He became one of the Court's most avid opinion writers, a veritable workhorse, during his eleven years of service. Well might Arthur be pleased with his two appointees, both in terms of performance and expectations. He had selected two professionally experienced moderate Republicans of judicial temperament and open-mindedness, and both would serve diligently and thoughtfully without rocking the ship of state.

Rather generously ranked "near great" by the experts (although they placed him at the lowest level in that category), Grover Cleveland of New York was both our twenty-second and twenty-fourth President, serving 1885–1889 and 1893–1897. He actually received a majority of the popular vote three times, for he also bested Benjamin Harrison by almost 100,000 votes in the election of 1888; but the vagaries of the Electoral College caused him to lose that election. The sole Democrat to serve between the Presidencies of

James Buchanan and Woodrow Wilson, Cleveland was an economic conservative of such intensity that Wilson had cause, if only half jokingly, to regard himself as the first President of the Democratic party since 1860.[12] Cleveland was a courageous, conscientious, and principled President, honest and incorruptible during a time in which graft, conspiracy, and corruption found favor at the highest levels. Energetic and pragmatic rather than imaginative or intellectual, he was essentially a nay-sayer, no matter how powerful and ardent the interest or the pleader. He did "what was right"—as he so often stated—and that even extended to his public acknowledgment during his election campaign of an illegitimate son, whose existence had given rise to the infamous 1884 campaign chant-slogan: "Ma! Ma! Where's my Pa? Gone to the White House, Ha! Ha! Ha!"

Cleveland was neither a social nor an economic reformer. His basically conservative economic-proprietarian philosophy was clearly reflected in the four appointments he made to the Court during his two terms as President. With the exception of a few of the judicial votes to be cast by his third appointee, Edward D. White,[13] Cleveland's choices lived up to his expectations amply. The President's criteria were easy to behold: a Democrat in good standing (no Democrat had been appointed since Stephen J. Field in 1863), an individual known to him personally, an economic-proprietarian of generally conservative bent, and a non-Populist from an appropriate geographic area.

Lucius Quintus Cincinnatus Lamar of Mississippi was, thus, the first Democrat to be selected in a quarter of a century. The President called on him in late 1887, following the death of Justice William B. Woods of Georgia after six and one-half years in office. There were other "firsts" that characterized the Lamar choice: whereas Woods was but a transplanted Ohioan who had fought with the Union, Lamar was a real Southerner—the first sent to the Court since Campbell's appointment by Pierce in 1853. He was also the first appointee with active service in the Confederate Army, and he was the first with a background of legislative and executive service in *both* the Union and the Confederate governments. The ex-General—who had surrendered at Appomattox as a Colonel—

had written the Mississippi Ordinance of Secession, had served in the Confederate Congress, and had been the Confederate envoy to Russia. Yet he had labored hard and successfully to facilitate adoption of the Compromise of 1877 by the South. Elected to the U.S. House of Representatives in 1872 and to the Senate in 1876, he became Cleveland's Secretary of Interior in 1885 and quickly won the President's admiration, confidence, and affection, particularly because of his integrity and sound judgment. A Democratic leader in his native Mississippi, he had earned universal respect as a gentleman and a scholar in the Southern tradition (at the University of Mississippi, he had taught mathematics, law, ethics, and metaphysics), as a brilliant orator, and as an honest, scrupulously fair man. He was Cleveland's first, and apparently only serious, choice for the vacancy despite his age—sixty-two—and Confederate affiliations. Led by angry Northern Republicans, the confirmation battle raged on for six weeks, finally ending with Lamar's approval by a four-vote margin, 32:28, on January 16, 1888, aided by the crossover of one Independent and two Western Republican Senators, including Leland Stanford of California, who feared a vote against Lamar would be interpreted as a ban against all Confederate veterans. In all, only six of the pro-Lamar votes came from North-of-the-Border states. Death came to him just five years later, following a series of strokes. Justice L. Q. C. Lamar's most notable opinion occurred early in his all-too-brief Court career when, in 1888, writing for his unanimous brethren, he held that "manufacture is transformation . . . while commerce is the buying and selling . . . and transportation of goods." That ruling in *Kidd* v. *Pearson*[14] preceded the Court's momentous decision in *United States* v. *E. C. Knight Co.* in 1895, differing between "manufacture" and "movement" in terms of the reach of congressional power over interstate commerce.[15]

Two months after Lamar's confirmation, Chief Justice Morrison R. Waite died after a stewardship of fourteen years. Cleveland, thus, became only the sixth President, and but the second Democrat, to confront the awesome responsibility of filling the highest judicial post in the nation. Waite, who had served ably and intelligently with a fine nose for compromise and conciliation, was conservative but not dogmatic, and he had effectively presided over an often seriously divided but enormously able Court. Who would the President select? Determined to adhere to his perceived and announced criteria, Cleveland moved cautiously but with considerable dispatch. He was offered a plethora of suggestions, including some self-serving ones by Associate Justice Field, who ardently aspired to the top post. But Cleveland, who did not want Field, was determined to consider only someone from the Midwest–preferably Illinois, a state not then "represented" on the high bench and the state with more litigation than any other except New York–who was a solid, active Democrat as well as someone with whom he could be comfortable both ideologically and personally. He considered the promotion of Associate Justice Miller, an Iowan, but that superb, influential jurist was seventy-two years old. He also pondered Kentucky's able barrister John G. Carlisle, but Kentucky was already "represented" by the great John Marshall Harlan I. His initial choice devolved upon a fifty-four-year-old distinguished Illinois lawyer, John Scholfield, strongly recommended by their close mutual friend, Melville Weston Fuller. Scholfield refused the honor, however. Cleveland now turned to the considerably less-than-eager Fuller himself, an active Illinois Democrat–he had attended four Democratic National Conventions–whose business connections made him acceptable to Republicans. Proclaimed by one Philadelphia newspaper as "the most obscure man ever nominated as Chief Justice"[16]–indeed, he did come to that post less well known than any other in the Center Chair's annals–the Maine-born Fuller possessed sundry "appointable" credentials. A Harvard Law graduate, well-to-do corporation lawyer, prominent Episcopal layman, from the "right" state (Illinois), and at fifty-five the "right" age, Fuller shared most of the President's generally conservative social, economic, and political ideas. He had given a number of indications that he would become even more conservative in his Darwinian commitments to sound money, free trade, states' rights, and absence of government "paternalism" in the economic sector.

Fuller's confirmation was delayed for two and one-half months, an uncommon hiatus owing almost entirely to the personal Senatorial vendetta by the Republican Chairman of the Senate Judiciary Committee, George F. Edmunds of Vermont. Edmunds—himself a putative candidate for a Supreme Court seat in Chester Arthur's Administration—claimed that Cleveland had promised the nomination to one of his constituents. But in the end Edmunds capitulated—faced with wholesale Republican defections (nine)—and Fuller was approved by a vote of 41:20 on July 20, 1888. During his twenty-two years as Chief Justice—the third longest tenure in that office to date—Fuller ran true to form: he presided over and was supported by a Court that became a veritable bastion of economic *laissez-faire,* espousing a policy of preserving *in extremis* the notion of "freedom of contract," which he and most of his associates found in the "vested rights" inherent in the "property" concept of the due process of law clauses of the Fifth and Fourteenth amendments. Indeed, the Fuller Court would go down in history as the incarnation of free enterprise, of the equation of *laissez-faire* with constitutionally protected rights. Fuller himself wrote few opinions, and few memorable phrases or quotations crept into those opinions. He was less interested in being a Justice *qua* jurist than he was in providing the Court with efficient administrative and organizational leadership. This he achieved with great success—he was simply a superb manager and executive—and he is generally regarded as one of the two or three best presiding officers in the Court's history. Yet in terms of his contributions to overall jurisprudence, the nonintellectual Fuller is quite justly ranked by the experts as little more than average, roughly on a par with his predecessor once removed, Salmon P. Chase.

Four months after Grover Cleveland returned to the Presidency in 1893, following the Harrison interregnum, the able and popular Justice Samuel Blatchford died after eleven years on the Court. It was Cleveland's third opportunity to make an appointment. This time, however, he had to make three nominations before he was able to fill the vacancy. According to his principle, Cleveland wanted to replace New Yorker Blatchford with another New Yorker. The state's astute and powerful Senator David B. Hill advanced numerous suggestions to the President. But Hill was a member of an anti-Cleveland patronage faction in New York's

Democratic party, at odds with the President on personnel matters, and the President refused to heed the Senator despite the latter's threats to invoke Senatorial courtesy. When Cleveland thus proposed William B. Hornblower, a conservative corporation lawyer and Cleveland loyalist, to the Senate at the end of the summer, Hill, although with some difficulty, rallied his colleagues and Hornblower went down to defeat 24:30 four months later. Not one to capitulate readily, Cleveland again ignored Hill's admonitions, and nominated another New Yorker of similar persuasions, Wheeler H. Peckham, that January. Following a month of debate, Hill's Senatorial-courtesy claims proved to be victorious again, this time by a nine-vote margin, 32:41. Angry and frustrated, the President, noting that he had no more "appropriate" New York names in reserve, determined to be satisfied with a draw: Hill's vetoes would stand, but there would be no more New Yorker nominations, at least not for the present vacancy.

Instead, and to the nation's surprise, Cleveland turned to the South and to the U.S. Senate, selecting its respected and popular Democratic Majority Leader, forty-eight-year-old Edward Douglass White of Louisiana. According to Cleveland's own account, provided to Bliss Perry–a distinguished Harvard professor of literature–he first thought of White as a serious candidate as a result of an encounter at a party at the home of Senator Thomas Francis Bayard, Jr. (D.-Del.). As the Saturday evening gathering adjourned, the President overheard Senator White asking his host if there were a Roman Catholic Church in the neighborhood; if so, he wanted to attend early mass on Sunday morning. "I made up my mind," Cleveland told Bliss, "that there was a man who was going to do what he thought was right; and when a vacancy came, I put him on the Supreme Court."[17] E. D. White, a product of Jesuit education, was the second Roman Catholic on the Court, the first to be appointed since Chief Justice Taney in 1836. His surprised but delighted colleagues confirmed him unanimously on February 19, 1894, the very same day his nomination came over from the White House.

Notwithstanding Cleveland's rather facile explanation, the designation of Senator White was partly an effort by the President to reingratiate himself with the Senate, but there were several other sound reasons for it: White came from a state previously neglected in Court appointments, he had supported Cleveland both in and out of the Senate, his brand of conservative economics appealed to Cleveland, and the President had a warm personal regard for the kind, self-effacing, civic-minded, devout bachelor. There have also been suggestions, recently increasingly disputed, that Cleveland wished to remove White—a staunch defender of Southern agrarian interests and states' rights—from the Senate because as the owner of a rich sugar plantation (on which he was born), White had ardently opposed any relaxation in the protective tariff legislation the President was then endeavoring to see enacted. If White's opposition was a motive, the President's gesture was in vain: although Congress did pass a new tariff bill, it was but a slight improvement over the previous one. And the man who led the battle against the President's tariff reform legislation was none other than Supreme Court Justice-Designate White, who remained in the Senate for several weeks following his confirmation! The portly 250-pound White was advanced to the Chief Justiceship in 1910 by the portly 300-pound President Taft, but Cleveland did not live to see the promotion. He would have been pleased with it, however, for although White did not "come through" on a number of issues, his record on the bench was close enough to the Cleveland philosophy to be "well within normal limits."

There had been yet another vacancy for Cleveland to fill, perhaps as unwelcome as it was unexpected: after having served for only two and one-half years Justice Howell E. Jackson of Tennessee died in August 1895. Because Cleveland had given the New York seat to the Deep South in the last appointment round, he was determined to try to return to New York for his nominee. Stubborn when he chose to be, the President moved to renominate the already rejected William B. Hornblower; but the latter had had his fill of internecine combat and refused Cleveland's offer. Wisely, the President now swallowed his pride and resolved to placate Senator Hill. He wrote him an exceedingly tactful letter of inquiry, concerning (of all people) the brother of the rejected Wheeler H. Peckham, the fifty-seven-year-old Rufus W. Peckham, in which he in effect asked Hill to approve the latter's candidacy. Cleveland closed his missive with the courteously stated hope that Hill might "find it consistent and agreeable to pave the way"[18] for the appointment. The placated New York Senator, although still vehemently opposed to Wheeler Peckham, voiced no objection to the nomination of brother Rufus, for Rufus had in no way been involved in the patronage squabbles between Hill and the President. His confirmation came promptly and easily.

Peckham, an able lawyer and public servant, enjoyed a varied career: private law practice for a quarter of a century, nine years as judge on the New York Supreme Court and the New York Court of Appeals, and seven years as District Attorney and corporation counsel for the state in Albany. His work had not received universal acclaim, but he was both shrewd and effective. Whatever his professional qualifications for the high bench, his avowed political philosophy was very much Clevelandesque Democratic: anti-Populist, antipaternalistic in government, economically and socially conservative. In fact, Peckham embraced a Social Darwinist approach that went considerably beyond that of his nominator, fitting in comfortably with the kindred views of such established *laissez-faire* specialists as Chief Justice Fuller and Associate Justice Brewer. The confidant of tycoons, such as James J. Hill, George F. Baker, Cornelius Vanderbilt, John D. Rockefeller, James Speyer, and Pierpont Morgan, he would not disappoint them during the fourteen years he served on the Supreme Court. Students of constitutional law and of the Fuller era remember Peckham best for his opinion for a bitterly split 5:4 Court in *Lochner* v. *New York* in 1905, where that bare majority declared unconstitutional New York's statute limiting hours of labor in bakeshops to sixty hours per week, or ten per day.[19] Invoking the age-old device of the *argumentum ad horrendum,* Peckham declared that laws such as New York's fatally violated "freedom of contract," the freedom of the employer and the employee to enter into whatever contracts they wished to make, free from governmental interference–a freedom he saw guaranteed absolutely by the due process of law clauses of the Constitution. Over withering dissenting opinions by Justices Harlan I and Holmes, with Holmes crying out "the Fourteenth Amendment does not enact Mr. Herbert Spencer's *Social Statics,*" Peckham conjured up horrid visions of the all-powerful, all-intrusive state if government were allowed thus to regulate contractual relationships. Vested property rights seemed indeed still secure!

William Henry Harrison's grandson, Benjamin, the "filling" of the "Cleveland Sandwich," a General in the Union Army, and an Indiana lawyer with service in Congress, is appropriately regarded as one of our lesser Presidents, but certainly not as a disastrous one–the historians having accorded him a low "average" ranking. An aloof and withdrawn aristocrat, an intellectual but generally devoid of much insight about government and politics, he was content to let the Republican party hierarchy dominate the affairs of state during his four years in office–although he was assuredly aware of what was going on. He was an economic conservative who, not without some misgivings, signed into law some potentially far-reaching regulatory legislation, such as the Sherman Antitrust Act of 1890. But he correctly guessed that the impact of such legislation lay in the future, notwithstanding the budding Populist movement. Honest about motives, reliable and conscientious, he made no secret of the kind of individual he wanted to send to the Court, and the four he appointed during his single term in office (1889–1893, between the two Cleveland terms) met his criteria readily: they were good Republicans (with the exception of Democratic family friend Howell E. Jackson), governmental and economic conservatives, experienced practicing lawyers and judges, and, if they were not from the same states as the jurists they replaced, they were at least from the same circuit or the same general geographic area. Like Cleveland, Harrison could be well pleased with the judicial performance of his nominees, although Henry B. Brown, his second nominee, occasionally proved more friendly to governmental regulation than his nominator might have wished. But as a group, both the Harrison and Cleveland Justices neatly followed Chief Justice Fuller's orchestration of freedom of contract, absence of governmental restraint on business activities, and the sanctity of property.

Harrison's first opportunity to make an appointment came with the death of Justice Stanley Matthews in March of 1889 after a remarkably impressive stint of eight years on the Court. It took the cautious President almost nine months to decide on a replacement. He considered some two-score individuals, all of whom he had thoroughly investigated, ultimately narrowing his choice to two friends, David Josiah Brewer of Kansas and Henry Billings Brown of Michigan. They were conservative ideological kinsmen; they both had fine records as state and federal lower court judges; they were both from the Midwest; they had been Yale classmates; they were both in their early fifties; they were both loyal Republicans; and they had both been recommended highly not only by their political allies, but, respectively, by sitting and future Supreme Court Justices Miller and Jackson. It was truly an *embarras de richesse* in Harrison's eyes, and he evidently resolved that he would send both to the high bench. But whom to name first? What apparently clinched the matter was a letter written by Brewer to Brown—conveniently brought to the President's attention by a mutual friend—in which Brewer, having become aware of Brown's candidacy as well as his own for the Matthews vacancy, self-effacingly expressed the hope that Brown rather than he would get the nod. Brewer expressed similar sentiments to a coterie of his friends who had begun to mount a letter-writing campaign to Harrison in his behalf. The President was so impressed with Brewer's apparent generosity that he opted for *him* (confirmation came speedily, 53:11), silently resolving to reserve any future vacancy for Brown. (Apparently, Brown, too, had written a letter of similar tone and sentiment to Brewer, but the President was unaware of it.)

Brewer was the nephew of the powerful, pyrotechnical Justice Stephen J. Field, whom he now not only joined on the Court but whose policies he embraced and furthered eagerly. Indeed, the aging Field now more or less relinquished his jurisprudential leadership to his nephew during the remaining eight years of their joint tenure on the bench. Born the son of a missionary in Izmir (Turkey), Brewer was jovial, witty, and intellectual. He had served fourteen years on the Supreme Court of Kansas and five on the U.S. Court of Appeals for the Eighth Circuit. Together with Justice Peckham, he became the leader of the ultraconservative economic *laissez-faire* advocates on the Court, not only smoothly fitting into the Fuller Court's approach to public policy, but going well beyond it in terms of judicial activism on behalf of vested property rights based on the "freedom of contract" doctrine. A diligent worker, Brewer wrote almost 600 opinions during his twenty-one years on the bench, only one-tenth of these in dissent. His philosophy could be summarized in excerpts from a famed commencement address he delivered to the June 1891 graduating class at Yale:

> . . . The demands of absolute and eternal justice forbid that any private property, legally acquired and legally held, should be spoliated or destroyed in the interests of public health, morals, or welfare without just compensation [which, of course, he wanted the judiciary rather than the legislature to determine]. . . . From the time in earliest records, when Eve took loving possession of even the forbidden apple, the idea of property and sacredness of the right of its possession has never departed from the race . . . [for] human experience . . . declares that the love of acquirement, mingled with the joy of possession, is the real stimulus to human activity.[20]

Brewer's labors assuredly merited the high "average" rating granted him by the Court's observers; President Harrison had every reason to be pleased with his nominee, even if he did not entirely agree with all of his ideas.

The President did not have to wait long to realize his hopes for a place for Brown. After twenty-eight years of distinguished service, Justice Samuel F. Miller died on October 14, 1890, thus giving Harrison his second appointment in little more than a year. For two months he went through the motions of considering other worthy candidates; but there was never any doubt that he would nominate the prominent, conservative admiralty lawyer from Detroit, who at the time of his selection was a judge of the U.S. District Court for Eastern Michigan. Earlier he had served as Federal Marshal and as Assistant U.S. Attorney in the same jurisdiction and as Judge of the Wayne County Circuit Court. He was confirmed without a record roll call in a matter of days. Blessed with a commendable judicial temperament, intelligent, expertly trained, hardworking, and pleasant, Brown became a worthy member of the Court. Deserving perhaps more than the "average" ranking accorded him, he demonstrated genuine independence while still generally adhering to the philosophy of economic conservatism of the day. Although he was on the Peckham-Brewer-Fuller majority side in the notorious 1905 *Lochner* decision striking down New York State's maximum-hour law for bakers,[21] he had been the author of the 1896 majority opinion—with Brewer and Peckham in dissent—upholding a maximum-hour law for miners in Utah.[22] Today he is best remembered for quite another opinion—*Plessy* v. *Ferguson,*[23] handed down in 1896, written for an 8:1 Court (with Harlan I alone in dissent): it enshrined the "separate but equal" racial doctrine in constitutional law for the next six decades.

Justice Joseph P. Bradley, who had served so ably and influentially on the Court for twenty-two years, died in January 1892. Harrison, determined that the crucial Third Circuit (Pennsylvania, New Jersey, and Delaware) continue to be represented on the high bench, resolved to find a Pennsylvanian—especially since that state had not been so represented since Justice Strong retired in 1880. (Bradley, of course, was from New Jersey, but Harrison had convinced himself that New Jersey had no desirable candidate to offer.) The resolve may have appeared easy to carry out, yet any Pennsylvanian of the President's choice would have to overcome the almost certain opposition of U.S. Senator Matthew Quay, that state's Republican "boss," who had been very instrumental in Harrison's election, but whose potent political machine was now at bitter odds with the President, largely over patronage issues. Quay also had his own candidate: J. H. Brown, an amiable, well-known attorney, eagerly backed by Pennsylvania's well-oiled Republican organization. Harrison, however, was not amused. Nor would he accept two other machine suggestions that would have received Quay's blessings: the aged Justice Edward Paxton and Justice Henry William, both of the Pennsylvania State Supreme Court, both of whom enjoyed extensive support from the legal fraternity as well as from local, state, and national figures.

Instead, the President turned to a relatively unknown Pittsburgh lawyer, sixty-year-old George Shiras, Jr. Shiras came highly recommended by Harrison's Secretary of State, James G. Blaine (who also happened to be the candidate's cousin). Respected and well liked by the Pennsylvania bar, Shiras was easygoing and amiable, and he readily received non-Quay political support. Although he was not at all well known outside Pennsylvania, he had established an influential clientele of railroad, banking, oil, coal, and iron and steel interests—the natural constituents of a lawyer from western Pennsylvania. Among them was Andrew Carnegie, who personally urged Harrison not to be dissuaded by Senator Quay and promised his own support to the candidate. By now convinced that he had found the man he wanted, Harrison nominated the energetic Shiras, whose moderately conservative social, political, and economic persuasions dovetailed neatly with his own. Confirmation took a while but, aided by Senate Democrats, Shiras ultimately won confirmation on July 26, 1892. He was the first and to date the only appointee to reach the Supreme Court without holding some type of public office or without actively participating in the political process. George Shiras's performance during eleven years on the bench was of average quality. He was workmanlike and predictably conservative, but not as inflexible as his colleagues Field, Fuller, Brewer, and Peckham on governmental regulatory questions. Yet he joined them far more often than not and could normally be counted aboard the *laissez-faire* bandwagon of the times.

President Harrison's fourth opportunity for an appointment, his last, came when he was a lame duck, having been defeated by Grover Cleveland in November 1892. Justice L. Q. C. Lamar died on January 23, 1893, with two months of the Harrison term still remaining. The President's choice was not only natural, but far easier than might have been expected under the circumstances, for available candidates acceptable to him *and* the Senate were hardly numerous. But then serving on the U.S. Court of Appeals for the Sixth Circuit was Howell E. Jackson of Tennessee—not from Lamar's Mississippi, but close enough. A former colleague of Harrison's in the Senate, the sixty-year-old Jackson was a moderate Democrat and a close family friend. Associate Justice Henry B.

Brown urged Harrison to make the appointment–just as Jackson had done for Brown's candidacy three years earlier. Indeed, Brown insisted that it was he who had clinched matters by "inducing the President"[24] to nominate Jackson, who, although opposing secession, had held office under the Confederacy. Despite a delay in committee, Jackson was easily confirmed in a ten-minute executive session two weeks after the nomination reached the Senate early in February 1893. But what gave every indication of a promising career on the Court was truncated by tuberculosis, which began to plague Jackson soon after he took his seat. He carried on ably and courageously and close to the end attempted–unsuccessfully–to save the federal income tax with his vote in the *Second Income Tax Case* in May 1895.[25] Yet three months later he died–after less than two and one-half years of service on the bench.

William McKinley of Canton, Ohio, had been comfortably reelected for a second term when he was fatally wounded on September 6, 1901, at the Pan-American Exposition in Buffalo by Leon F. Czolgosz–the third President to be assassinated in office. Before he became President he had been probably best known for the protective tariff bill he had authored while a seven-term member of the House of Representatives. McKinley's Presidential renown, however, is based largely on his leading the country "into the World," as he liked to put it, however reluctant he may have been initially and however he may have disapproved of war. Cheered on by his powerful political mentor, Marcus Alonzo ("Uncle Mark," or "Boss") Hanna, the business community, the press, Congress, and his party, McKinley took the Stars and Stripes to Cuba, Hawaii, Puerto Rico, the Philippines, and even China. A skillful political organizer and one of the ablest manipulators of Congress ever to sit in the White House, McKinley readily deserves the high "average" ranking bestowed on him by the historians of the Presidency. The dignified, yet warm and congenial, McKinley was a truly popular figure, responsive to, and at home with, the public at large, who trusted him and respected his leadership even when it seemed to be vacillating.

McKinley had but a single opportunity to name a Supreme Court Justice during his four and one-half years in office, his two predecessors having appointed eight members between 1887 and 1896! Yet his one selectee gave him, if not everyone else, particular pleasure: Joseph McKenna, fifty-four, a good friend and fellow legislator. McKenna had first entered national politics as a member of the U.S. House of Representatives from California. He served four consecutive terms; during the third term he became a member of the potent tax-writing Ways and Means Committee, chaired by then Congressman William McKinley. There McKenna faithfully supported the controversial McKinley Tariff and related social and economic measures. Generally regarded, and rightly so, as a distant and austere individual, McKenna nonetheless grew close to such prominent and influential Republican leaders as Theodore Roosevelt, Mark Hanna, William H. Taft, Speaker of the House Joseph G. "Czar" Cannon, and Senator Leland Stanford of California. It was on Stanford's recommendation in 1892 that Harrison had named McKenna to the Ninth U.S. Circuit Court of Appeals, where he provided five undistinguished or even incompetent years of service.

McKinley and McKenna had become good friends, and there was widespread speculation that McKenna would get the first vacancy on the Court. A party faithful, he could boast of a staunchly conservative record in Congress as well as on the bench; the roster of his political associates was indeed impressive; and his philosophy of government and politics resembled McKinley's. The President had hoped that the aged Justice Stephen J. Field, then in his thirty-fourth year on the bench, would gracefully retire with the Administration change, but Field made no such move and McKinley appointed McKenna as his Attorney General. One abortive, often-chronicled effort to persuade Field to leave the Court came early in 1897 when the brethren sent John Marshall Harlan I on the delicate and difficult errand. Harlan aroused the slumbering Field in the robing room and endeavored to set the stage for his mission by reminding the old man how he, Field, had successfully approached the then similarly conditioned Justice Grier in 1869. As Charles Evans Hughes described the incident years later, Field "listened, gradually became alert and finally, with his eyes blazing the old fire of youth, burst out: 'Yes! And a dirtier day's work I never did in my life.' "[26] So much for *that* effort to induce Field to retire!

But nine months later, Field, now in a state of marked physical and mental decline, was at last persuaded by his colleagues to step down from the seat he so treasured—secure in the knowledge of a highly influential, distinguished tenure spanning almost three and one-half decades (which stands second next to William O. Douglas's longevity record) and nine (!) Presidencies. McKinley quickly nominated McKenna—like Field a Californian—who had been a staunch Administration advocate of high tariffs, sound money, support of big business (without, however, being anti-labor *per se*), and economic *laissez-faire* (but not totally averse to some governmental regulation). Another factor that weighed in the President's decision was his nominee's religion: McKenna was a devout Roman Catholic who had once considered the priesthood. His selection, McKinley hoped, would serve to allay the broadly held belief that he was partial to the American Protective Organization, a contemporary anti-Catholic association. The nomination was delayed for five weeks, in part because of the vocal opposition of antitrust and antirailroad interests, in part because of religious bigotry, and in part because of allegations by members of both bar and bench that McKenna's record on the lower federal court was mediocre, if not downright incompetent. But on January 21, 1898, he was confirmed without a formal roll call vote, the third Roman Catholic to reach the Court.

McKenna served for almost twenty-seven years; his record ran generally true to expectations both in terms of his jurisprudence and his average performance as a jurist. He proved, however, to be more flexible in the economic sector than might have been predicted—of which McKinley would very likely have approved. Although readily classifiable as politically conservative, neither McKinley nor Joseph McKenna was wedded to rigid doctrine. Nor was McKinley's Vice President, T.R., whom fate thrust into the Presidency less than three years later.

8

Into the Twentieth Century: From Theodore Roosevelt to Herbert Hoover 1901-1933

The youthful ex-governor of New York, who had reluctantly yielded to the entreaties of old-guard Republicans to accept the Vice Presidency under McKinley in 1900, suddenly found himself President in 1901. Unlike those among his predecessors fate had unexpectedly advanced to that post, Theodore Roosevelt had little apprehension, let alone feelings of dismay or uncertainty. Supremely confident and a born leader, T.R. was a soldier-of-fortune and man-about-society who went on to become a true man of the people. His public literally adored him and were willing to forgive him almost anything. And there were some things to forgive!

Roosevelt threw himself into national leadership with a vengeance. Determined to give life and expression to the progressive movement, the "liberal nationalism" he embraced, he pursued with the zeal of a crusader his vision of a better, more egalitarian nation. He coined the "stewardship theory" of the Presidency, which means that the President can do anything the Constitution or a congressional act does not proscribe. In his words, it was the President's "duty to do anything that the needs of the nation demanded unless such action was forbidden by the Constitution or by the Laws. I acted for the public welfare, I acted for the common well-being of all our people."[1] The "All-American-Boy President" by no means succeeded in all he set out to do. But the overall record of this courageous showman-activist has generally earned him the second-highest "near great" ranking by the historians—just below Andrew Jackson, thus according him the number seven spot among the Presidents. Some would rank him still higher.

Theodore Roosevelt was determined to fill any vacancies on what he viewed as a "conservative and hidebound" Supreme Court only with those individuals who would reflect his progressive political views—particularly in such areas as labor (pro), corporations and trusts (anti), improved race relations (pro), and regulatory power of the national government (pro). To share his philosophy of government and politics would, thus, become his single dominant criterion for nomination. As he wrote to fellow Republican leader and confidant Senator Henry Cabot Lodge of Massachusetts: "I should hold myself as guilty of an irreparable wrong to the nation if I should put [on the Court] any man who was not absolutely sane and sound on the great national policies for which we stand in public life."[2] Yet T.R. always insisted—at least publicly—that a jurist's "views on progressive social philosophies are entirely second in importance to his possession of a high and fine character."[3] In view of his emphasis on ideological kinship and character, it is hardly astonishing that he considered the geography principle of no moment. If his choice for a vacancy happened to reside in the "appropriate" state or circuit, fine; if not, fine too: "I have grown to feel, most emphatically," he wrote to Lodge, "that the Supreme Court is a matter of too great importance to me to pay heed to where a man comes from."[4] Consequently, Roosevelt sent two citizens of Massachusetts to the Court within four years, becoming the first President to go on public record with a policy of downgrading geography.

Roosevelt appointed three Justices to the Court, among them the judicial philosopher of the age, Oliver Wendell Holmes, Jr. In his choice of Holmes and the others—William H. Moody and William R. Day—the President faithfully adhered to his announced criteria of philosophical compatibility, good character, and competence. Indeed, if Day clearly left the progressive reservation on many issues, Holmes and Moody would not. Yet Roosevelt was happy only with Moody, who was forced to resign less than four years after his appointment because of ill health. Holmes, especially during his early years on the Court, was "a bitter disappointment" to the President, "not because of any one decision but because of his general attitude."[5] Yet his antagonism actually stemmed chiefly from Holmes's "anti-antitrust" vote in the *Northern Securities Case* of 1904, prompting T.R.'s aforementioned famed "banana . . . backbone" explosion.[6]

President McKinley had been aware of Justice Horace Gray's failing health; for some time he had pondered a replacement for the able and hardworking jurist from Massachusetts. But Gray held on to life and bench until September 1902—one year after McKinley's murder. Roosevelt knew that his predecessor had intended to nominate Alfred Hemenway, a leading Boston attorney, in Gray's place, but he did not feel bound by McKinley's plans and had begun actively to scout about for other candidates even before Gray's death. Among those who caught T.R.'s eye was the renowned Oliver Wendell Holmes, Jr., Chief Justice of the Supreme Court of Massachusetts. A Boston Brahmin, author, editor, and Harvard faculty member, Holmes had served on the Massachusetts court for twenty years, three as Chief Justice. It was the same post Gray had held when President Arthur appointed him to the Supreme Court. That Holmes was from Gray's state and former judicial station meant little to Roosevelt; his concern lay in the *real* politics of registered-Republican Holmes. As he did so often, T.R. turned for advice to Holmes's fellow Bostonian, Henry Cabot Lodge, to whom he addressed a lengthy letter of inquiry. What were the candidate's views on antitrust legislation? On corporations? On labor? What of his philosophy on the evolving American scene of "liberal nationalism"? And what of a recent address given by Holmes on the centenary of John Marshall's appointment as Chief Justice in which Holmes had praised Marshall's role as "an independent political statesman" rather than that of "a great jurist"?

There were of course no doubts in T.R.'s mind concerning Holmes's exceptional legal and intellectual qualifications for the post: his wit, articulateness, learning, and verve. The President, a physical-culture addict himself, admired the sixty-one-year-old, thrice seriously wounded Civil War veteran's energy, his amazing physical prowess, his sterling character, his judicial expertise, his sophistication. But he wanted to be reassured on Holmes's *real* as opposed to his *nominal* politics. Senator Lodge's response provided that reassurance: Holmes was universally considered "a constructive statesman," a "broad-minded constitutionalist," a man blessed with "broad humanity of feeling." In addition he possessed "sympathy for the class" from which he had drawn so many clients while practicing law in Boston. He seemed right on antitrust issues and right on race. T.R. was particularly pleased to note a Holmes dissent in a labor law case, *Plant* v. *Woods,* written while Holmes was Chief Justice of Massachusetts. It was entirely lawful, he wrote there, "for a body of workmen to try by combination to get more than they are now getting, although they do it at the expense of their fellows, and to that end strengthen their union by the boycott and the strike."[7] On December 2, 1902, Roosevelt sent Holmes's name to the Senate; two days later the appointment was unanimously confirmed.

Justice Holmes graced the Court for thirty exciting years, retiring at almost ninety-one. He will forever remain one of the intellectual giants of the high bench, a man who left a lasting mark not only on jurisprudence but on American society. He is one of the few in American constitutional history who can lay claim to undisputed greatness; sixty-one of the sixty-five Blaustein and Mersky study (see Appendix A, *infra*) Court observers rated him "great," with only John Marshall and Louis Brandeis ahead of him, Brandeis by just one vote. In many ways the supreme scholar and philosopher, Holmes insisted on objective examination of the facts and forces that explain the life of the law and its direction; far from blinding him to the vagaries of life, his philosophical bent prompted a healthy pragmatism in his view of democratic society. His consistent deference to the legislative process—unless it cut into the vitals of the Bill of Rights—demonstrated a commitment to the democratic process that has become legendary. Essentially, Oliver Wendell Holmes was no democrat: he was a cynic and a skeptic who had little faith in reform movements (to him, "social reform worker types" were "the greatest bores in the world"). Although he fully respected the ideas and ideals of others, he was at heart an intellectual elitist who had no time for the unenlightened, let alone the foolish. But his questioning mind was thoroughly open and he believed in letting others have their say and their play.

Thus, at least as much as, and probably more than any other jurist to date, Holmes bowed to legislative judgment—even if he may well have disagreed with it and have disrespected the supporters of legislative judgment (he frequently did!); even if, as he more than once put it with characteristic bluntness, it made him "vomit." For this sturdy Yankee was fully persuaded that the people, speaking through their representatives, had a constitutional right to "make asses of themselves." As he once put it in an often-quoted statement to constitutional lawyer John W. Davis in connection with an interpretation of the Sherman Antitrust Act (which he regarded as one of the worst and certainly most poorly written pieces of federal legislation to be enacted during his lifetime): "Of course I know and every other sensible man knows, that the Sherman law is damned nonsense, but if my country wants to go to hell, I am here to help it."[8] Wisdom and constitutionality were not related; to Holmes and his many followers the Constitution required governmental obedience to its terms, not governmental wisdom.

Nor did Holmes confuse, in the words of one experienced Holmes observer, "his personal tastes and distastes with constitutional necessity."[9] One of his most frequently cited commentaries on that central point was made to his colleague Stone, who was then sixty-one years old: "Young man, about 75 years ago I learned that I was not God. And so, when the people . . . want to do something that I can't find anything in the Constitution expressly forbidding them to do, I say, whether I like it or not, 'Goddamit, let 'em do it.' "[10] He did find that the Constitution expressly forbade the invasion of fundamental civil liberties—especially freedom of expression. There he readily and resolutely invoked his power of judicial interposition.

To Holmes laws were made by men, not angels! And his abiding conviction that the transcendent obligation is to heed (what he styled) "the felt necessities of the time" was perhaps the foremost among the many facets that rendered him the judicio-intellectual leader of his Court and his time. Even in dissent–which is where he found himself more often than not on key contemporary issues–Holmes led. Indeed, it is as "the great dissenter" that he is best known, especially since the post-1937 Court turned so many of his classic dissenting opinions into majority opinions. Yet although Holmes is second to Douglas in total written opinions (975), the 72 dissenting opinions he penned–no matter how notable–rank him but eleventh in dissents to date.* The following excerpts from dissenting opinions in five milestone cases in constitutional law, spanning a generation, represent both literature and law.

The 1905 New York Bakeshop Case (in which the Court struck down 5:4 the state's attempt to limit hours of work in bakeries):

> The Fourteenth Amendment does not enact Mr. Herbert Spencer's *Social Statics*. . . . A constitution is not intended to embody a particular economic theory. . . . It is made for people of fundamentally differing views. . . .[11]

The 1918 Child Labor Case (in which the Court struck down 5:4 the federal government's attempt to regulate child labor):

> If there is any matter upon which civilized countries have agreed it is the evil of premature and excessive child labor. I should have thought that if we were to introduce our own moral conceptions where in my opinion they do not belong, this was preeminently a case for upholding the exercise of all its powers by the United States.[12]

The 1919 Pro-Soviet Pamphleteer Case (in which the Court upheld 7:2 the conviction of six self-styled "anarchist-Socialists" under the Espionage Act of 1917):

* Douglas is also the champion *dissent* writer; in second place (as of early 1984) stands Black, followed by Frankfurter, Harlan II, Brennan, and Harlan I. For convenient statistics through 1972, see Albert P. Blaustein and Roy M. Mersky, *The First Hundred Justices: Statistical Studies on the Supreme Court of the United States* (Hamden, Conn.: Shoe String Press [Archon Books], Inc., 1978).

> When men have realized that time has upset many fighting faiths, they may come to believe even more than they believe the very foundations of their own conduct that the ultimate good desired is better reached by free trade in ideas—that the best test of truth is the power of the thought to get itself accepted in the competition of the market, and that truth is the only ground upon which their wishes can be safely carried out. That at any rate is the theory of our Constitution. It is an experiment as all life is an experiment. Every year if not every day we have to wager our salvation upon some prophecy based upon imperfect knowledge. While that experiment is part of our system I think that we should be eternally vigilant against attempts to check the expression of opinions that we loathe and believe to be fraught with death, unless they so imminently threaten immediate interference with the lawful and pressing purposes of the law that an immediate check is required to save the country.[13]

The 1925 New York Criminal Syndicalism Case (in which the Court 6:2 upheld Benjamin Gitlow's conviction for violating the 1902 Criminal Anarchy Act by publishing a "Left Wing Manifesto"):

> It is said that this manifesto was more than a theory, that it was an incitement. Every idea is an incitement. It offers itself for belief and if believed it is acted on unless some other belief outweighs it or some failure of energy stifles the movement at its birth. The only difference between the expression of opinion and an incitement in the narrower sense is the speaker's enthusiasm for the result. Eloquence may set fire to reason. . . . If in the long run the beliefs expressed in proletarian dictatorship are destined to be accepted by the dominant forces of the community, the only meaning of free speech is that they should be given their chance and have their way.[14]

The 1928 Wiretapping Case (in which the Court held 5:4 that wiretapping did not constitute a violation of the Fourth Amendment guarantees against unreasonable searches and seizures):

> Wiretapping is dirty business. . . . The Government ought not to use evidence obtained, and only obtainable, by a criminal act. . . . It is desirable that criminals should be detected and

> to that end all available evidence should be used. It is also desirable that the Government should not itself foster and pay for other crimes. . . . We have to choose, and for my part I think it a less evil that some criminals should escape than that the Government should play an ignoble part.[15]

Theodore Roosevelt had every reason to praise Oliver Wendell Holmes, Jr.; instead, he peevishly carped about the work of this preeminent American jurist. Indeed, far from opposing him, Holmes furthered and articulated Roosevelt's ideas through his presence on the Court—even if he did consider the President a "shallow intellect."

If Roosevelt had any reason to be disappointed or even to feel betrayed by an appointee, it was by virtue of the record established on the Court by his next choice, fifty-three-year-old William Rufus Day of Ohio. Initially, Day pleased T.R. mightily; he cast his vote in support of the government's position in the aforementioned celebrated *Northern Securities Case*. But then he let the President down, opposing such vital federal programs as legislation designed to regulate hours and wages of labor. Thus, he wrote the majority opinion, with Holmes in dissent, that struck down the Child Labor Law of 1916.[16] Moreover, he usually opposed assertive executive policy actions. Day had not been Roosevelt's first choice (that was William Howard Taft), but his selection was entirely in line with the President's stated objectives and requirements.

In the summer of 1902 Justice George Shiras, Jr., of Pennsylvania told the President that he intended to retire early in the next year. He had served ably but unspectacularly for a decade. T.R., meeting with two firm rebuffs from Taft, then governor of the Philippine Islands, sought the latter's advice as well as that of other prominent Republican leaders such as Mark Hanna, Elihu Root, and Nelson Aldrich. Ohioan Hanna knew Day well from their association during the McKinley Administration, when the latter had served as both Assistant Secretary of State and Secretary of State; and Taft had served with Day on the "Learned Sixth"—the U.S. Court of Appeals for the Sixth Circuit—to which McKinley had appointed him in 1899. Day had demonstrated his

Republican fealty by working for Benjamin Harrison's election; ultimately, he had become one of President McKinley's favorite legal, personal, and political advisers. As Assistant Secretary of the Navy, T.R. himself had worked closely with him. There had been ample opportunity to ascertain Day's *real* politics, and the President, if he could not have Taft, would be glad to have Day. He was confirmed quickly without a roll call on February 23, 1903.

Roosevelt's third and last opportunity to make a Supreme Court appointment came when Justice Henry B. Brown of Michigan announced that he would retire at the end of the 1905–1906 term. T.R. first focused on the man Brown recommended, former Attorney General Philander C. Knox, now a U.S. Senator. But Knox declined, viewing the Court as "a political dead end." The President, without any real hope, again offered the vacancy to Taft, now home from the Philippines and serving in his Cabinet as Secretary of War. But Taft was gunning for higher stakes. Roosevelt next proffered it to his trusted Secretary of State and political ally, Elihu H. Root, who declined, preferring to remain in active politics. Shortly thereafter Roosevelt called in Attorney General Moody, went over a list of possible candidates with him, suddenly stopped, grinned, and asked him: "Is it possible that you do not know whom I am to appoint to this position? You, and you only, are the man."[17]

Massachusetts-born and educated at Andover and Harvard, William Henry Moody had entered on the stage of national politics during the McKinley Administration, serving seven years in the U.S. House of Representatives. Previously he had established himself as a leading member of the Essex County bar, gaining national prominence in 1893 as one of the Commonwealth's prosecuting attorneys in the celebrated Lizzy Borden trial. Resembling Theodore Roosevelt in looks as well as actions, Moody became friendly with him during the President's stint as Assistant Secretary of the Navy under McKinley. In May 1902 Roosevelt had brought Moody into his own Cabinet as Secretary of the Navy (the two men held identical views on the significance of naval power), an office in which Moody displayed exceptional administrative and organizational talents. When Philander Knox, the incumbent Attorney General, moved to the Senate in 1904, the President switched Moody to that position, one for which he was tailor-made. A trial lawyer par excellence, Moody launched assaults on the beef, sugar-refining, and oil trusts, although not always successfully. He also entered the thick of the railroad-rate controversy with relish. In his early fifties he was at the apex of his career and politically and socially close to Root, Taft, and Lodge as well as Roosevelt—here was a "natural" for the Court. T.R.—although he did anticipate serious criticism on the score—was not about to be stopped from selecting Moody, even though he would be the second Massachusetts appointee to the high bench in barely four years. Happily and eagerly he forwarded the nomination, which was confirmed without delay *viva voce* in mid-December 1906. Moody did not disappoint the President, who frequently voiced satisfaction with his friend's work on the bench; it has received high marks despite its brevity. Today Moody is probably best remembered for his learned and lucid opinion for the Court in *Twining* v. *New Jersey* (1908)—though it would be overruled six decades later—in which he held that the Fifth Amendment's privilege against self-incrimination was not as such binding on the states via the Fourteenth Amendment's due process of law clause.[18]

Although he was elected to, and embarked on, the Presidency as Roosevelt's handpicked protégé, William Howard Taft's conception of the office differed dramatically from his predecessor's in style as well as substance. Far from regarding it as an assertive "stewardcy," as had T.R., the bulky Ohioan—the only man in American history to date to serve as *both* President and Chief Justice—viewed the role of President as a "passive" or "supervisory" one. As he made clear in *Our Chief Magistrate and His Powers,* a work based on lectures delivered at Columbia University in 1915, he was wholly dedicated to the proposition that the Chief Executive is bound by a literal interpretation of the Constitution; that there exists no "undefined residuum of power which he can exercise"; that not only respect but deference is due Congress.[19] Yet Taft, the executive humilitarian and literalist, would be a driving judicial activist. He was happier and far more effective on the Court than in the White House. To him the Chief Justiceship was the realization of the dream of a lifetime; the Presidency, although an honor, was but a job to be done. Predictably, the President watchers have ranked him just "average." Court observers, however, have ranked him "near great" for his work there as "Chief."

In a number of ways Taft endeavored to continue the Roosevelt program of progressivism, of "liberal nationalism." Thus, although less sympathetic to conservation than T.R., he successfully battled exploiters and speculators in coal and oil, and he instituted twice as many antitrust suits, winning more than his political mentor, the legendary "trust buster." Even so, Taft was far more conservative than T.R., cautious, and at home with the G.O.P.'s conservative leadership. Often surprisingly indecisive, he found it easy to temporize and equivocate in a host of policy matters, although he stood firm against military involvement abroad. He was astonishingly inept politically—yet the burden of following the Teddy Roosevelt act would have weighed heavily on almost any successor. He frankly acknowledged that his administration was ". . . very humdrum, uninteresting . . . [which] does not attract the attention or enthusiasm of anybody."[20]

In his single term Taft appointed six Justices to the Court, including one Chief Justice—up to that time more than any President since George Washington. And in view of his often successful "pushing" for kindred souls during the years of his Chief Justiceship (1921–1930), it might be claimed that he was responsible for the placement of even more Supreme Court Justices. Taft chose his jurists with great care and with little concern for their nominal political affiliations (Lurton, White, and Lamar were Democrats, although all three were Southern conservatives), yet their performance on the bench was spotty in terms of his expectations. But he was philosophical about his choices; they met his criteria: all were men of integrity; all were personally known to him; all except Hughes had had judicial experience. But most important, he had carefully considered their *real* politics—he wanted no "liberals" of the stamp of Learned Hand, Louis Brandeis, or Benjamin Cardozo, potential candidates he regarded as "destroyers of the Constitution."[21] If some of his Justices were occasionally unpredictable, well, that was the price to be paid for the separation of powers in which he so strongly believed.

Taft's first opportunity to nominate a member of the Court came with the death of Justice Rufus W. Peckham in October 1909. Peckham, a firm apostle of *laissez-faire* capitalism, had served for fourteen years as a pillar of the Field-Brewer-Fuller approach to constitutional interpretation. Taft wanted someone in a rather different mold, and he knew exactly who: his close friend, Professor Horace H. Lurton of the Vanderbilt University School of Law, for eight years his fellow judge on the "Learned Sixth." Earlier, in 1906, T.R. had wanted to appoint Lurton but had been dissuaded by fellow Republican Henry Cabot Lodge because Lurton was a Tennessee Democrat. To Taft that was a *non sequitur;* he and Lurton were philosophical, political, and personal kinsmen. The President had long known and respected the legal talents of the Confederate Army veteran who had seen more than a quarter of a century of judicial service–sixteen years on the federal bench and ten on the state bench. Hence, he resolved to appoint Lurton despite the latter's age (sixty-five) and despite Taft's avowal of a youth movement on the bench following a pronouncement that members of the Court who held on to their jobs in the face of advanced age were "near senility." "There was nothing," commented a jubilant Taft after Lurton's prompt, routine confirmation, "that I had so much at heart in my whole administration as Lurton's appointment."[22] Lurton died only four and a half years later. He had had little time to establish a record, let alone leave an imprint; what little of it there was pointed to a cautious, competent jurist steeped in judicial self-restraint.

In late March 1910, just a few months after Lurton's confirmation, Justice David J. Brewer died after more than twenty years of influential, doctrinaire service on the Court. It had earned Brewer the respect, if not the admiration, of students of constitutional law everywhere. If Brewer was not the equal of his Court-colleague and uncle, Stephen J. Field, the contemporary high priest of judicial activism on behalf of *laissez-faire* capitalism, he had carried the family ideological banner proudly and effectively. His departure from the scene enabled Taft to make his second and, as time would prove, his most important appointment: Charles Evans Hughes, governor of New York, who was then a youthful and vigorous forty-eight and a bright new star in the Republican constellation. Taft had been afraid of him as a potential rival in 1908; now he frankly regarded Hughes as clear Presidential timber—stronger, indeed, than himself or Teddy Roosevelt. When he learned that Hughes seemed prepared, indeed, eager to leave the political scene, Taft quickly turned to him. Because he had some doubt as to Hughes's willingness to accept, Taft dangled the Chief Justiceship before him in a celebrated letter:

> The Chief Justiceship is soon likely to be vacant and I should never regard the [until now] established practice of never promoting Associate Justices as one to be followed.[23]

But the President added an equally celebrated postscript:

> Don't misunderstand me as to the Chief Justiceship. I mean if that office were now open, I should offer it to you and it is *probable* that if it were to become vacant during my term, I should promote you to it; *but, of course, conditions change,* so that it would not be right for me to say by way of promise what I would do in the future. Nor, on the other hand, would I have you think that your declination now would prevent my offering you the higher position, *should conditions remain as they are.*[24]

Hughes, fully conscious of the meaning of these ambiguities, acquiesced with grace and generosity. Those "conditions" would indeed "change" within a matter of months—with the coveted plum going to Edward D. White, not Hughes. And Hughes would resign from the bench in 1916 to run for the Presidency after all, almost but not quite winning it!—only to return as Chief Justice in 1930 to succeed Taft, who had reached the post he so desperately craved after White's death in 1921.

Only a few days after his designation Charles Evans Hughes sailed through the Senate *viva voce* with nary a ripple. He was a child prodigy who entered college at fourteen, earned a Phi Beta Kappa key as a junior at Brown University, and was graduated at twenty-two from Columbia Law School, where he attained highest honors. As a youthful and brilliant lawyer he soon earned the universal respect of the profession; in addition to practicing law, he also taught it, and ultimately embarked on a governmental career as a legislative counsel, culminating in the governorship of New York. But Hughes's ambitions for the highest office of all were initially blocked by Teddy Roosevelt, whose early plans had centered on Taft—not Hughes, whom he disliked. After his narrow 1916 defeat Hughes ceased his quest for the Presidency and returned to the law and governmental service, ultimately becoming Secretary of State as well as a judge of the World Court.

Hughes's six years as Associate Justice were marked by carefully drafted, frequent opinions. He was a superb communicator, an elegant writer. A happy blend of conservatism and liberalism, he embraced a protective approach vis-à-vis both economic-proprietarian rights and civil rights and liberties. Thus, he could say no to many pre-1937 attempts by the federal government to broaden the reach of the interstate commerce power, yet champion political dissent in often beautiful and persuasive language:

> The greater the importance of safeguarding the community from incitements to the overthrow of our institutions by force and violence, the more imperative is the need to preserve inviolate the constitutional rights of free speech, free press, and free assembly in order to maintain the opportunity for free political discussion, to the end that government may be responsive to the will of the people and that changes, if desired, may be obtained by peaceful means. Therein lies the security of the Republic, the very foundation of constitutional government.[25]

During his brief Associate Justiceship Hughes wrote more opinions for the Court (151) than any other contemporary on-the-bench jurist; in them he almost invariably spoke for a unanimous Court. In fact, in only nine of these cases were there dissents—in only three of them by more than one Justice. (Hughes also wrote 32 dissenting opinions himself.) The days of his Chief Justiceship, however (to be discussed in Ch. 8 and Ch. 9), would prove to be dramatically different.

Hughes's confirmation came on May 2, 1910; on July 4, Chief

Justice Fuller died, having been the faithful steward of economic *laissez-faire* for twenty-two years—an era marked by a jurisprudence never again to return. The general expectation by insiders was that Taft would promote Hughes—his letter to Hughes being a well-known secret. Holmes, for example, wrote his friend Sir Frederick Pollock of his conviction that the post would go to Hughes rather than to himself.[26] The press also confidently predicted his elevation. But the President bided his time, during which a "boomlet" developed for Justice John Marshall Harlan I. Taft, however, contemptuously dismissed such a possibility: "I'll do no such damned thing. I won't make the position of Chief Justice a blue ribbon for the final years of any member of the Court. I want someone who will coordinate the activities of the Court and who has a reasonable expectation of serving ten or twenty years on the bench."[27] The President's confidential aides, such as Archie Butts, continued to urge him to appoint Hughes, but it now became evident that Taft was steering away from him. He asked Attorney General George W. Wickersham to poll the sitting members of the Court for their preference, which proved to be E. D. White. Teddy Roosevelt got into the act by informing Taft of his intense dislike of Hughes, "that upstart." And the more the President pondered Hughes's forty-eight years and excellent health, the less convinced he became that he should promote him—after all, it was *the* post Taft wanted for himself.

On December 12, 1910, having waited more than seven months to make up his mind, Free Mason, Unitarian Taft nominated devout Roman Catholic Edward Douglass White to the Chief Justiceship—the first sitting jurist to be promoted to that post in the history of the Court. "White, Not Hughes, for Chief Justice," proclaimed the headline in the *New York Times*[28] to what was popular acclaim, notwithstanding Speaker of the House "Uncle Joe" Cannon, who cracked: "If Taft were Pope, he'd want to appoint some Protestants to the College of Cardinals."[29] The ascertainable reasons for the appointment were multiple: Taft considered White, then in his seventeenth year on the Court, to be the ablest administrator on the high bench; he knew that White was popular among his colleagues; and the conservative White's *real* politics had proved eminently compatible with his own. Yet assuredly Taft was also motivated by his own all-consuming ambition to attain the Chief Justiceship himself some day, and soon. He literally grieved aloud when he signed White's commission: "There is nothing I would have loved more than being Chief Justice of the United States . . . I cannot help seeing irony in the fact that I, who desired that office so much should now be signing the commission of another man. . . . It seems strange that the one place in the government which I would have liked to fill myself I am forced to give to another."[30] Indeed! But White (who had been confirmed unanimously by the Senate in less than an hour) was now in his sixty-sixth year–hardly of the youthful strain Taft had publicly promised but had, in fact, produced to date only in the person of Hughes. Given the age of the new Chief Justice and some of the good fortune that had blessed the paths of the Taft family for some time, might not a future President on White's death, resignation, or retirement select a candidate so uniquely qualified and experienced–so "pregnant" a candidate–as William Howard Taft? It proved to be a superbly educated guess: White died conveniently in May of 1921–adamantly having refused increasing pressure to retire–and President Harding selected his fellow Ohioan to fill the post. Had White succumbed during the Wilson era (1913–1921), it is highly unlikely that Taft–who loathed Wilson and was not precisely loved in return–would ever have realized his cherished dream.

During his decade on the Court as Chief Justice, Edward Douglass White had continued the cautiously independent and evaluative approach to the law that characterized his lengthy service as an Associate Justice. He had earned the respect and affection of his colleagues as well as Court experts who have ranked him, perhaps somewhat generously, as "near great." Although by background and persuasion an ideological conservative suspicious of the exercise of large-scale governmental power, he proved to be far from doctrinaire and, when he deemed it constitutionally justifiable, would back broad exercise of federal power, albeit selectively. Thus, he authored opinions on the Adamson Act of 1916, which upheld the federal statute providing for an eight-hour day for railroad labor, and on the Importation of Impure Tea Act of

1897, which backed legislation sanctioning generous delegation of legislative power for the purpose of establishing standards to the executive branch. He also voted to uphold the federal income tax statute of 1894. On the other hand, he sided with Holmes in the *Northern Securities Case;* was the author of the Court's "rule of reason," which held that the Sherman Antitrust Act forbade only those combinations or contracts in restraint that were "unreasonable"; and voted with those who struck down the federal child labor law of 1916.[31] Congenial and flexible—although somewhat deficient as a "manager"—he proved himself to be a capable leader of the Court and sufficiently pleasing to his nominator. If he was not of the stature of the great Chief Justices, such as Marshall, Taney, Hughes, Stone, and Warren, he deserves to be ranked with a second group that includes Taft and Waite.

White's promotion left his own Associate Justiceship to be filled. This time Taft turned to his own party, selecting the urbane Willis Van Devanter of Wyoming, a fifty-one-year-old Judge of the U.S. Court of Appeals for the Eighth Circuit. As a young man, the erstwhile Midwesterner had gone to Wyoming, where he befriended the Republican territorial governor—U.S. Senator—Francis E. Warren, becoming his indispensable ally and helpmate. An uncommonly able draftsman and administrator, he had supervised the revision of the territorial statutes and had served in various local and state legislative posts as well as Chief Justice of the Supreme Court of Wyoming. His reputation as a progressive during his stint in the U.S. Department of the Interior, where he served as an attorney specializing in matters involving public lands and Indian affairs, had been a real factor in his appointment to the Circuit Court by T.R. Roosevelt; but it soon became evident that his long-time association with powerful Western business combines had left him strongly conservative in terms of constitutional interpretation. Taft was well aware of that fact, yet he wanted to please restive elements in the Republican party. He was also seeking a candidate from the Midwest or the West, and he was generally comfortable with Van Devanter. The two men became close personal allies on the high bench—Taft regarded him as his favorite colleague—notwithstanding Van Devanter's far more pronounced intellectual conservatism. He is best known in his twenty-seven years on the Court for his senior membership in the anti-New Deal group, the "Four Horsemen" (the other three being Justices James C. McReynolds, George Sutherland, and Pierce Butler); for being the tail to his colleague Sutherland's intellectual kite; and for writing fewer opinions not only than any other Justice who served with him, but also than any Justice appointed between 1853 and 1943. He barely averaged three a year during his last decade on the Court—only one in two years, none in one; and in his entire career on the high bench he penned only four dissenting and one concurring opinion! Although he apparently made significant oral contributions in the Justices' conferences and, with Taft, was co-author of the seminal "Judges Bill" of 1925, the dearth of his opinions and his doctrinaire rigidity prompted the Court experts to rate Justice Willis Van Devanter a "failure"—arguably much too harsh a judgment.

President Taft's fifth appointment (his fourth in little more than a year—how some future Presidents would envy him!) also went to the Senate on December 12, 1910, and, like Van Devanter, was quickly confirmed by it without audible dissent. The vacancy, created by Justice William Henry Moody's widely regretted resignation after not quite four years on the Court—because of incapacitating acute rheumatism—went to Joseph Rucker Lamar, like White and Lurton a Southern Democrat, a plantation-born veteran of bar and bench. Moody hailed from Massachusetts, but in Holmes that state and circuit had more than distinguished representation; in any event, geography did not figure large in Taft's appointment criteria. A member of the same family as ex-Supreme Court Justice L. Q. C. Lamar, the fifty-three-year-old renowned and popular Georgia lawyer and legal historian had served on his state's Supreme Court; had been a state legislator for two terms; and was being actively considered for an appointment to the U.S. Commerce Court when the President decided to send him to the top tribunal instead.

Although Taft was not so close personally to Lamar as he had been to Lurton, the former readily met the President's essential criteria. His judicial and legislative record had manifested the conservatism and ideological bent with which Taft was comfortable; his real politics were eminently acceptable. For example, the two men saw eye-to-eye on the protective tariff question, which was of great moment to the President. Moreover, Lamar's selection would strengthen Taft with such influential Southern political leaders as Democratic Senators Augustus O. Bacon of Georgia and Joseph W. Bailey of Texas; close Presidential advisers, such as Archie Butt and George W. Wickersham, also urged Lamar's choice insistently. His confirmation came within three days and without any audible dissent. Although he gave Taft no reason to regret his action, Lamar's record of five years on the Court was as insignificant as it was undistinguished.

Taft's sixth and last opportunity to people the Court came with the death of John Marshall Harlan I on October 14, 1911. The Hayes-appointed Kentuckian had served brilliantly for thirty-four years; his labors in behalf of a broad national interpretation and application of the Bill of Rights–its "incorporation" via Section 1 of the Fourteenth Amendment–and the Civil War amendments laid the groundwork for many of the libertarian decisions of the mid-twentieth century. Mahlon Pitney of New Jersey–Taft would name him to the Harlan seat after a hiatus of some four months–was cast in a different mold.

Initially, the President had looked west of the Mississippi for Harlan's replacement, seriously considering Judge William Hook of Kansas (Eighth U.S. Circuit Court of Appeals), whom he had also pondered for the White-promotion vacancy, and his Secretary of Commerce and Labor, Charles Nagel of Missouri. But Hook had rendered himself *persona non grata* with the country's black citizens in a 1911 ruling upholding Oklahoma's "Jim Crow" statute,[32] and Nagel had become increasingly unpopular with labor, particularly because of his liberal stance on immigration. Taft now looked to the East and to New Jersey, a state from which no Justice had come since Joseph P. Bradley more than four decades earlier. But more important in Taft's mind as well as in those of his political strategists was that New Jersey could become a battleground between Taft's supporters and those of Theodore Roosevelt, whose "return" Presidential candidacy was now clearly emerging. Whether or not the selection of Pitney was decisive, New Jersey's Republican delegation did cast its votes for Taft in the National Convention of 1912.

But political implications of his nomination aside, Mahlon Pitney was appealing to Taft for other reasons: the "right" age at fifty-four, he had amassed eleven years of judicial experience (a key factor in Taft's eyes) while serving on various New Jersey courts; he had been a U.S. Congressman for two terms; and he had served as Republican Floor Leader and President of the New Jersey Senate. Pitney's record on the state bench showed a general commitment close to Taft's own, but Taft had nagging doubts about his approach to governmental regulation. Liberals and labor forces, however, had more than nagging doubts: they questioned Pitney's entire philosophy of government and politics and so mounted a major campaign against him. Although it succeeded in delaying confirmation for almost a month, the Senate finally approved him 50:26. Pitney's undistinguished decade of the Court, marked by increasingly reactionary votes–especially as the leader of the Court's antilabor faction–soon began to displease his nominator. Later, as Chief Justice, Taft publicly pronounced Pitney to be a "weak member" of the Court to whom he could "not assign cases."[33]

Woodrow Wilson, according to most, although not all, historical experts, is outranked among American Presidents only by Abraham Lincoln, George Washington, and Franklin Roosevelt. Wilson came to the office with the strongest of intellectual as well as executive and administrative qualifications: a Ph.D. in political science, lawyer, college and university professor, president of Princeton, governor of New Jersey; he had few peers, if any, in the theory and practice of the processes of government and politics. Despite these high qualifications and his general success, Wilson experienced an unprecedented measure of pain and anguish in his country's rejection of the League of Nations and the Treaty of Versailles–to which his questionable tactics vis-à-vis the U.S. Senate contributed significantly. To him that defeat was the end of his life as well as his dream.

Victor in 1912 only because of the fatal Taft/Roosevelt split and but narrowly triumphant over Hughes in 1916, Wilson personified the New Freedom's quest for social and economic justice. In many ways he built on the heritage of political reformers, such as William Jennings Bryan and Theodore Roosevelt, and he eagerly sought the advice of practical idealists, such as Louis Brandeis, whom he would send to the Court in 1916. Aristocratic, highly moral, Calvinistic, he preached rectitude—France's Georges Clemenceau once commented that "talking to Wilson is like talking to Jesus Christ"[34]—yet he understood and learned well the Presidential role. Until the tragedy of the League of Nations felled him, he was a powerful, driving political and intellectual leader. Indeed, he was a simply superb politician, until he forgot or ignored the necessity to compromise.

Largely because of the avalanche of appointments that had fallen to Taft, Wilson had but three opportunities to appoint men to the Court during his eight years in office. One of those appointments went to Louis D. Brandeis, a giant among the occupants of the Court; another to John H. Clarke, a noble and sensitive spirit; another, unfortunately, to James C. McReynolds, who would come to be universally, and justifiably, regarded as a total on-bench failure.

Woodrow Wilson's appointment criteria were neither novel nor precious. Like his two immediate predecessors he was more concerned with a candidate's *real* rather than nominal politics—hence, Brandeis's registration as a Republican in Massachusetts was of no moment to him. Broadly, he required a liberal-progressive public policy and, especially, a dedication to trust busting. Also, like Taft and Roosevelt before him, he paid little attention to geography: if it was a factor at all, it appeared only in McReynolds's appointment. Again like the two earlier Presidents, Wilson tended to favor individuals he knew personally or professionally. The one noticeable difference from the criteria of Taft and Roosevelt lay in his disregard for judicial experience. McReynolds and Brandeis had no judicial background, and Clarke had but two years. It is fair to conclude that the absence of such experience had no bearing on the collective performance of Wilson's nominees: they served as they did because of their cosmos and their commitments—not because of presence or absence of judicial experience.

When in the summer of 1914 Horace H. Lurton died after little more than four and one-half years on the Court, Wilson moved rapidly to make his first nomination. It fell to James Clark McReynolds, his fifty-two-year-old Attorney General—like Lurton from Tennessee (although born in Kentucky)—who had attended the Law School of the University of Virginia, ultimately entering government service. He evinced an early interest in trust busting, receiving national attention in 1907 when, as Assistant Attorney General under Philander Knox in T.R.'s Presidency, he did yeoman duty in his handling of the tobacco trust. Later, when the Taft Administration—in which he served in the same post (on two separate occasions)—took actions that McReynolds regarded as unduly compromising, he publicly resigned twice and finally turned his back on the Republican party. These events established his image as a fighter of trusts and big business. In due course McReynolds joined the Wilson forces and actively campaigned for Wilson's election. Ultimately, he was appointed Attorney General as a Democrat.

As Attorney General, McReynolds continued his trust-busting activities, although with some aberrations. Still, Wilson was satisfied that his man would stand up to what he liked to refer to as the "Mr. Bigs," no matter what post they held and regardless of McReynolds's personal motivations—which, as has been suggested, were grounded in his fundamental agrarianism as well as in his dislike and distrust of "bigness" generally. So Wilson sent his Attorney General of a year and one-half's tempestuous service to the Court, perhaps with a tinge of doubt but with sufficient confidence in his progressivism. History would prove him utterly wrong—for McReynolds, continuing to manifest his violent temper and abrasive nature on the bench, not only became a member of the anti-New Deal Four Horsemen, he turned into their loudest, most cantankerous, sarcastic, aggressive, intemperate, and reactionary representative. There have been suggestions, in increasing number of late, that Wilson was aware of McReynolds's inherent reactionist jurisprudence, but that he was nonetheless willing to appoint him to the Court to get him out of the Cabinet and out of his political hair, while seemingly demonstrating appreciation for services rendered. In the judgment of such a wise observer as Wilson's Secretary of the Navy, Josephus Daniels, the President, refusing to scuttle his faith in McReynolds and still convinced that he was a progressive at heart, resolved gracefully to "kick him upstairs."[35] If he was impossible to live with, Wilson rationalized, that did not mean that he was not politically progressive. And McReynolds, strongly backed by the Democratic party, was confirmed 44:6 ten days after his nomination reached the Senate in mid-August 1914—just one Democrat (James K. Vardaman of Mississippi) and five Progressive Republicans voting nay.

James Clark McReynolds's record and antics during his ensuing twenty-seven years on the Court are legion. Politically and jurisprudentially, the lifelong bachelor, a confirmed misogynist, came to embrace a philosophy of reaction to progress second to none, and in his personal demeanor on the bench was a disgrace to the Court. Manifesting blatant anti-Semitism, McReynolds refused to speak to Brandeis (the first Jew to sit on the Court) for three years following Brandeis's appointment. He was only somewhat less obnoxious in his behavior to the gentle Benjamin Cardozo, during whose swearing-in ceremony he pointedly read a newspaper, muttering "another one." In 1922 McReynolds refused to accompany the Court to Philadelphia on a ceremonial occasion because, as he wrote to the exasperated Chief Justice Taft: "As you know, I am not always to be found when there is a Hebrew abroad. Therefore, my 'inability' to attend must not surprise you."[36] And because McReynolds would not sit next to Brandeis (where he then belonged on the basis of seniority) for the Court's annual picture-taking session in 1924, Taft decided that no Court picture would be taken at all that year.[37] Nor would McReynolds sign the customary dedicatory letter sent routinely to all Court members on their retirement when that time came for Brandeis in 1939; nor would he attend Frankfurter's robing ceremonies ("My God, another Jew on the Court!") earlier in 1939.

McReynolds also disliked Harlan Stone and his jurisprudence and carped about almost every opinion Stone wrote. When, on one occasion, Stone observed to McReynolds that a particular attorney's brief had been ". . . the dullest argument" he had ever heard, McReynolds, in typically abrasive and tactless fashion, replied, "The only thing duller I can think of is to hear you read one of your opinions."[38] Another one of his targets was the gentle John Hessin Clarke, whose voting record on the bench equally displeased him, especially because he had thought of Clarke as one of his "protégés." Although McReynolds's enmity was not decisive in Clarke's resignation from the Court in 1922, it clearly contributed to his resolve to leave. "McReynolds," he wrote to Woodrow Wilson, "as you know, is the most reactionary judge on the Court. There were many other things which had better not be set down in black and white. . . ."[39] And ex-President Taft not only considered McReynolds weak, he regarded him as a selfish, prejudiced, bigoted person "and one who seems to delight in making others uncomfortable. . . ."[40]

Justice McReynolds's bigoted personality became evident quickly: he would not accept Jews, "drinkers," blacks, women, "smokers," married or engaged individuals as law clerks; and according to Justice Douglas he once asked a black Supreme Court barber, "Tell me, where is this nigger university in Washington?"[41] Douglas named a card game after McReynolds, which he entitled "son of a bitch." McReynolds's performance on the Court was, of course, a bitter disappointment to Wilson. Not only did he shock the President almost at once by his vote against the constitutionality of a Kansas law outlawing yellow dog contracts,[42] he would *never* side with Wilson on any significant issue involving governmental regulatory activity. (On the other hand, Brandeis rarely, Clarke never, cast an "anti-Wilson" vote.) Unlike his Court colleagues Sutherland and Van Devanter, McReynolds made no distinction between areas of public law–such as legislative power and Presidential authority in domestic and foreign policy decision making–and those of the Court's role in guarding civil rights and liberties. His on-bench votes evinced no compassion or understanding, whatsoever, for the travails of underdogs. In the latter area, even his sour colleague-in-arms, Pierce Butler, would now and then join an opinion upholding a beleaguered individual.[43] Certainly, James Clark McReynolds deservedly earned the all but unanimous condemnation of the Court experts, who have rated him at the top of their brief list of failures.

Wilson's next appointment, Louis Dembitz Brandeis, was designated "great" by all but three of the sixty-five experts in the Blaustein and Mersky 1970 study. The Brandeis confirmation battle still ranks as the most bitter and most intensely fought in the history of the Court, and the delay of more than four months after Wilson submitted Brandeis's name to the Senate on January 28, 1916, is still a record.

The President's selection of the famed Boston attorney, "The People's Lawyer," had come on Justice Joseph R. Lamar's death earlier that January. Wilson had known and admired Brandeis for a good many years. As a youth of nineteen he had entered Harvard Law School directly from the Annen-Realschule in Dresden, Germany, graduating two years later at the head of his class. As a partner in the distinguished Boston law firm of Warren and Brandeis, he had amassed a fortune and toward the end of the century—with the encouragement of his partners—had begun to involve himself in public affairs, soon becoming a renowned legal champion of the redress of economic and political inequities. At the Supreme Court bar he was a familiar figure, always arguing eloquently and persuasively. His authorship of what became known as the "Brandeis Brief," which he first introduced in 1908 in *Muller* v. *Oregon,*[44] wrought a substantive and procedural revolution in the judicial process. In the *Muller Case,* the Fuller Court—to universal surprise, given its record on attempted governmental regulation of hours and working conditions—unanimously upheld Oregon's 1903 statute forbidding the employment of women in "mechanical establishments," factories, and laundries for more than ten hours per day. There is general agreement, however, that had it not been for the "Brandeis Brief," the Oregon law would have been declared unconstitutional as a violation of due process of law. Brandeis's innovative tactic was to submit a brief to the Court that disposed of the constitutional issues and precedents in two pages but devoted more than a hundred pages to statistical data on hours of labor, health, morals, and factory legislation abroad—all emphasizing the special status of women. (One cannot help wonder whether such an emphasis would be utilized or sanctioned in the 1980s!)

But, as Wilson knew, Brandeis was far from a radical. He was deeply dedicated to his country and wanted to do all he could to attain a greater measure of democracy, of social justice, of egalitarianism. Yet notwithstanding his detractors in many segments of the business community, he was emphatically not "anti-business" or even "anti–big business"; he was no enemy of capitalism, of free enterprise, of profits. Indeed, during his tenure of more than two decades, in which he wrote a myriad of opinions, Brandeis never *authored* an opinion in favor of the government in an antitrust case. Nonetheless, he was acutely conscious of maldistribution of power, reward, and opportunity, and he dedicated his life to a rectification of that condition–on as well as off the Court. Although Brandeis had been no stranger to President Wilson, the two men had not worked together until the Presidential campaign of 1912, when Brandeis's advice to the candidate was largely instrumental in shaping the Democratic position on social and economic matters. Brandeis became Wilson's close friend, adviser, and collaborator, and the President was determined to have him aboard during his Administration. When the Attorney Generalship, to which he had intended to appoint Brandeis, fell through because of the volatile opposition of the Boston bar, Wilson vowed to himself that another even more important spot would be found for Brandeis.

Recognizing the furor that a Brandeis nomination to the Court would cause, the President moved with extreme caution when the time came. Fearing the consequences of early disclosure, he had consulted only one Senator before announcing the nomination: Robert M. La Follette, the influential Wisconsin progressive, whose small but vital band of supporters in the Senate were needed. La Follette was delighted and assured the President of his backing, adding that it was about time that a Progressive got on "that Court." When Wilson's gleeful announcement came in January 1916, all hell broke loose in the financial, legal, and political communities, where many powerful elements had long fought and feared him as a "radical." The opposition was directed largely at

Brandeis's social and economic record and at his "sociological jurisprudence." But there is no question that much of the anti-Brandeis campaign was anti-Semitic in origin. Among the leaders of the large number of well-known members of the organized bar who mounted the professional opposition were its president, Elihu Root, and ex-Attorney General George W. Wickersham and William Howard Taft.

Taft was no anti-Semite—quite the contrary!—but he loathed Brandeis for the nominee's role six years earlier in unearthing an embarrassing sleight-of-hand that he and Wickersham had executed in behalf of an accused Taft Cabinet member, Secretary of the Interior Richard A. Ballinger. But above all, Taft wanted the vacancy for himself! How he could have deluded himself into believing that Wilson would even consider him is difficult to comprehend; they had been outspoken enemies for some time. Suffice it to say that Taft craved the position so much that he was given to fantasies. In any event he was livid and wrote to one of his aides that the nomination represented "one of the deepest wounds" that he had sustained "as an American and a lover of the Constitution and a believer in progressive conservatism . . . [that] when you consider . . . that men were pressing me for the place, *es ist zum lachen* [it is ridiculous]."[45]

The confirmation battle raged against a background of some of the ugliest charges ever leveled against a distinguished public servant. It was finally terminated on June 1, 1916, by a 47:22 affirmative vote (the Judiciary Committee having reported the nomination favorably 10:8). Of those voting "aye," forty-four were cast by the forty-five Democratic Senators present and voting. The three lonely Republican votes in favor were those of Robert M. La Follette, George W. Norris of Nebraska, and Miles Poindexter of Washington. The Wisconsin statesman had kept his promise to Wilson. Twenty-one of the twenty-two negative votes came from the other Republican Senators then present and voting, including such illustrious and influential men as Henry A. du Pont of Delaware, Henry Cabot Lodge of Massachusetts, George Sutherland of Utah (soon to be a colleague of the appointee), Warren G. Harding of Ohio (the next President of the United States), and Albert

B. Fall of New Mexico. The lone negative vote cast by a Democrat was that of Francis G. Newland of Nevada, who regarded Brandeis as lacking in "judicial temperament." Twenty-seven Senators, including the powerful William E. Borah of Idaho, did not vote: of them, twelve Republicans were paired against confirmation and ten Democrats and two Republicans were paired in favor; three were absent (and not recorded or paired: one Democrat and two Republicans). The President and his supporters were jubilant.

Until he retired at eighty-three in 1939, Justice Brandeis kept the Wilsonian faith, serving with diligence and conviction. He and Holmes, despite their different background and, indeed, political philosophy, constituted a veritable team–although frequently for different reasons. "Justices Holmes and Brandeis dissenting" became a hallmark for some of the most famous libertarian opinions of the fifteen and one-half years they served together.[46] It is a pity that Wilson did not live to hear Brandeis at his most eloquent: in a concurring opinion concerning civil liberties–joined by Holmes–he wrote: "Those who won our independence by revolution were not cowards. They did not fear political change. They did not exalt order at the cost of liberty. . . . Fear of serious injury cannot alone justify suppression of free speech and assembly. Men feared witches and burnt women. It is the function of free speech to free men from the bondage of irrational fears. . . ."[47]

Nine days after Brandeis had been confirmed, Associate Justice Charles Evans Hughes resigned to run for the Presidency, which gave Wilson his third and last opportunity to make a Supreme Court nomination. Six months later he proposed another liberal, a progressive of Wilsonian bent with a solid antitrust record, fifty-nine-year-old John Hessin Clarke of Ohio. Clarke, an old friend and associate of the new Secretary of War, Newton D. Baker, was then in his fourth year of service as a U.S. District Judge for Ohio, a post to which he had been appointed by Wilson on Baker's recommendation. Now Clarke's supporter again interceded with the President on his friend's behalf; so did Brandeis. Wilson carefully studied Clarke's record off as well as on the bench. Not entirely satisfied, he asked Baker to travel to Ohio to discuss matters with the judge, especially the antitrust question. Baker's report pleased Wilson, who was now convinced that Clarke "could be depended upon for a liberal and enlightened interpretation of the law."[48] In July the President sent Clarke's name to the Senate, which confirmed the nomination unanimously ten days later despite the opposition of ex-President Taft, a fellow Ohioan.

Clarke's brief tenure (six years) on the bench was solidly Wilsonian: progressive on social and economic matters and liberal on civil rights and liberties. His votes did not stray from his nominator's reservation. Indeed, Clarke's philosophy was considerably to the left of Wilson and Brandeis (and much closer to the position of the man who ultimately succeeded Brandeis, William O. Douglas). Thus, Clarke was the sole dissenter in the Court's veto of the 1922 child-labor tax law.[49] A committed and conscientious Justice, nevertheless, he was unhappy on the Court. His resignation in 1922, purportedly to enable him to devote full time to the causes of peace, was caused by at least two factors: first, he grew increasingly disillusioned with what he regarded as the Court's failure to embrace a genuinely liberal approach to public policy; second, the McReynolds antics and hostilities were anathema to the gentle Clarke, who was unwilling to ignore them and unable to cope with them. Ironically, the vacancy he created by resigning would be filled by the putative intellectual leader of the "Four Horsemen," George Sutherland, who utterly rejected Clarke's philosophy.

The election of 1920 brought to the Presidency the man who has been universally regarded as the post's crassest failure to date, Warren Gamaliel Harding of Marion, Ohio. There is no doubt that he was patently unqualified to serve as President: his scandal-ridden Administration was a disaster. And Harding was pathetically conscious of his deficiencies. "My God," he told editor William Allen White, "This is a hell of a job. . . . My God-damn friends, White, they're the ones that keep me walking the floors nights. . . . This White House is a prison. I can't get away from the men who dog my footsteps. I am in jail."[50] And in a moment of introspection he admitted to President Nicholas Murray Butler of Columbia University: "I am not fit for this office and should never have been here."[51] That Harding was not really "a bad man . . . [but] just a slob"[52] did not alter the fundamental truth of Harding's and history's conclusion: he was an individual who should never have allowed himself to be chosen by the cynical "Ohio gang" and his Senate colleagues in that "smoke-filled room" in Chicago in mid-1920.

Yet Harding's public embrace of a "return to normalcy" had widespread popular support. Indeed, the "Presidential-looking" former U.S. Senator was far from an unpopular figure in those brief two and a half years before his still somewhat clouded death in August 1923–but the accelerating evidence of financial and personal scandals penetrating his Administration could hardly be ignored. Although some of the worst, such as the Teapot Dome scandal (which involved his Departments of the Interior, Justice, and the Navy), did not break until after his demise, they could not fail to characterize his Presidency perpetually. True, he had some outstanding public servants in his Administration–such as Secretary of State Charles Evans Hughes, to whom he happily delegated plenary authority–but such public servants were too few. Far too many betrayed Harding's rather childish faith and took advantage of his penchant for seeing and hearing no evil, which he extended to his own private behavior.

Harding appointed four men to the Supreme Court during his short tenure as President, two of whom, William Howard Taft and George Sutherland, have generally been accorded high ratings. Of the other two, Edward T. Sanford is usually rated mediocre, and Pierce Butler, a failure. Each of these four met Harding's general criteria for candidacy–which, in fact, were those of his designee for Chief Justice, William Howard Taft: thus their *real* politics were "right"; they were all experienced public figures; they were all conservative, property-minded, business-oriented attorneys. On the bench they ran true to form and with rare exceptions* voted together.

Taft's influence over Harding in Court appointments is a unique

* One of the exceptions was Taft and Sanford's recognition of governmental regulatory authority when, together with Holmes, they unsuccessfully attempted to sustain the 1918 District of Columbia minimum-wage law for women and children.[53]

illustration of a sitting jurist's potential clout. After virtually appointing himself—with divine assistance—Chief Justice in 1921, Taft made himself instantly available to Harding as an adviser on nominations—and not only judicial nominations. Taft's *modus operandi* was very simple: once a vacancy presented itself, he would literally bombard the President with firm recommendations and casual suggestions. True, he was not notably successful in winning his first choices, but he tellingly "used his influence to defeat selection of an 'off horse,' such as . . . Cardozo of New York. . . ."[54] Taft was determined to block the nomination of anyone who might side with that "dangerous twosome," Holmes and Brandeis. "As long as things continue as they are, and I am able to answer in my place," he announced, "I must stay on the Court in order to prevent the Bolsheviki from getting control. . . ."![55] On the other hand, he enthusiastically backed the Sutherland and Butler candidacies and did nothing to stop Sanford's, for he was satisfied that all three were sound economic conservatives with proved antagonism toward contemporary "liberal progressive elements." To Taft, "[i]dentity of outlook was absolutely essential";[56] everything else was secondary.

On June 29, William Howard Taft had finally become Chief Justice, affirmed with only four no votes on the very same day the nomination reached the Senate. Yet the position that he regarded "next to my wife and children . . . the nearest thing to my heart in life"[57] did not fall into his lap without considerable maneuvering. Months before Harding's inauguration he had started to lobby. He had organized a campaign staff and, to dispel any notions Harding might have of appointing him to an Associate Justiceship, he had written the President-elect a note emphasizing that his interest "lay solely in the post of Chief Justice."[58] But now Taft had to bide his time: Chief Justice White had agreed to hold on until a Republican President succeeded Wilson, thus paving the way for Taft. And hold on he did—half blind and half deaf, White spurned the retirement pension for which he was eligible, serving until he died in harness on May 19, 1921. The country expected an instant announcement, *the* announcement, from President Harding. But the President procrastinated, hoping for the rumored impending resignation of Associate Justice Clarke to reward his intimate political adviser, ex-Senator George Sutherland. Almost beside himself with anxiety, the now sixty-three-year-old Taft pulled out all the stops and through intermediaries succeeded in convincing the President that no additional vacancy would occur—short of another death. Finally Harding concurred and acquiesced to the magisterial Taft, who exulted: "I love judges and I love courts. They are my ideals on earth of what we shall meet afterward in Heaven under a just God."[59] The greatest aspiration of his life had been fulfilled at last!

William Howard Taft served in his beloved center chair until acute circulatory ailments, resulting in a series of crippling strokes, necessitated his grief-stricken resignation on February 3, 1930, and caused his death one month later. His dedication to, and affection for, the Court were almost without parallel. Few worked as hard in the post as he did; thus, during his membership, he wrote almost twenty percent of the Court's opinions. William Allen White would describe Taft as serving on the Supreme Court like "one of the high gods of the world, a smiling Buddha, placid, wise, gentle, sweet."[60] Taft worshipped the institution and its functions; its personnel had become "his," even if Holmes, Brandeis, and Stone—all of whom respected and liked the "Big Chief"—would more often than not dissent from what had become a comfortable Taft majority. Demonstrably, Chief Justice Taft provided administrative and technical leadership second to none. His orchestration of consensus, of "massing" the Court into a majority, was often spectacular. He proved to be a superb judicial leader and architect, even in the face of a seriously divided, aged, backlog-ridden, contentious Court. And his sponsorship of, and successful lobbying for, the famous "Judges Bill" of 1925[61] stands as a milestone in the Court's ability to function with discretion, dispatch, and efficiency. Yet the Court experts have not rated Taft "great"—and appropriately so. Neither his intellectual stance nor his applied jurisprudence was in a class with Chief Justices voted "greats": like his predecessors John Marshall and Roger Taney, nor like his successors Charles Evan Hughes, Harlan F. Stone, and Earl Warren. Instead, he has deservedly been placed in the "near great" group, which also contains his predecessors Morrison R. Waite and Edward D. White.

On September 4, 1922, Justice John Hessin Clarke withdrew from the Court—bored, disenchanted, and disillusioned. On the following morning Harding nominated to the post sixty-year-old George Sutherland of Utah, and the Senate confirmed him that very same day—a speed record still extant in the appointment process. Seldom in the history of the Court has a successor-candidate been so universally obvious: a close personal and political ally to the President, Sutherland was also enthusiastically backed by Taft, who had written to the nominee: "I look forward to having you on the bench with me. I know, as you do, that the President intends to put you there."[62] Sutherland was the first and to date (mid-1984) the only Supreme Court Justice from Utah and one of the very few of foreign birth (England) to reach the high tribunal.

Sutherland came to the Court with a wealth of legal and governmental experience: a leading expert in constitutional law and an active member of the Utah bar and the Supreme Court bar for many years, he had served in the Utah Senate, the U.S. House of Representatives, and the U.S. Senate. His friendship with Harding began when the two served together in the upper house, the association culminating in the role of brain-truster to the President. He could have had any position in the Harding Administration he desired, but he preferred to accept spot and trouble-shooting assignments in Washington and abroad for the President in anticipation of a vacancy on the Court.

Once he attained the Court, George Sutherland demonstrated that the evaluation of his supporters had been entirely correct: he not only proved himself the conservative everyone knew him to be, but he soon became the lucid and articulate spokesperson for the Court's solid Darwin-Spencer wing (also peopled by his colleagues Van Devanter, McReynolds, and Butler). The intellectual whom his biographer characterized aptly as "A Man Against the State"[63] spent sixteen years on the Court as the personification of those against whom Holmes had railed in his anguished *Lochner* dissent: "The Fourteenth Amendment does not enact Mr. Herbert Spencer's *Social Statics.*"[64] Yet to Sutherland—far more than to his fellow "Four Horsemen"–the Fourteenth Amendment meant "keep-your-hands-off-government" in the traditional libertarian as well as the proprietarian sense. Thus, it was he who in 1932 wrote the 7:2 majority opinion in the landmark *Scottsboro Case, Powell* v. *Alabama,*[65] which became the bellwether in the gradually developing application of procedural safeguards in the Bill of Rights to the states by way of interpretation of the due process of law clause of the Fourteenth Amendment. His colleagues McReynolds and Butler dissented of course.

As the intellectual-philosophical leader of the "Four Horsemen" and their allies, Sutherland proved himself a worthy successor of the Field-Brewer-Peckham wing of the Fuller Court era. In the 1930s he became the scourge of the New Deal, heading a majority that struck down more than a dozen pieces of domestic legislation fundamental to the New Deal in 1935–1936.[66] Yet he was not blindly opposed to the exercise of governmental power, particularly in the realm of foreign relations. One of the most significant, indeed historical, opinions in support of Presidential authority, *United States* v. *Curtiss-Wright Export Corporation,*[67] was from his pen. It is only just that no matter how many of them disapproved of his social Darwinism and Spencerian economics, the Court experts have rated him "near great." Sutherland, tired and outvoted after the Hughes and Roberts switch and Van Devanter's retirement in the spring of 1937, left the bench voluntarily in 1938. He had more than fully lived up to Harding and Taft's expectations.

So did Harding's next appointment, Pierce Butler, fifty-six, the least gifted and in many ways arguably the most doctrinaire of the "Four Horsemen." The vacancy arose when Justice William Rufus Day, after almost two decades of vacillating performance on the Court, retired in October of 1922. It was the President's third opportunity in little more than a year to make an appointment. Taft, with Harding's blessing and the aid of his closest personal associate on the high bench, Willis Van Devanter, had already surveyed the field of prospective candidates, among them New York's Republican governor, Nathan Miller, who declined for financial reasons. Taft's first choice, John W. Davis, a leading member of the bar, former Solicitor General, Ambassador to the Court of Saint James—and future (1924) Democratic nominee for the Presidency—also declined for financial reasons. The Chief's second choice was Pierce Butler, like Davis a conservative Democrat. Taft readily persuaded the President that the Court had become "too Republican" in the public eye and that, consequently, the new appointee ought to be a "congenial" Democrat, whose real politics would readily meet the Harding-Taft requirements. In Butler, they did.

Butler was one of nine children of a devout Roman Catholic immigrant family who had settled on a Minnesota farm after the mid-nineteenth-century potato famine in Ireland. He was a self-taught, self-made millionaire lawyer who had made his fortune as the able counsel for several Western and Midwestern railroads—whose interests he faithfully endeavored to serve after he reached the high bench. A lifelong Cleveland Democrat, Butler preferred to practice politics behind the scene, usually as an adviser to Minnesota's governors, but in the courtroom he was a skilled and devastating trial lawyer. In his personal code he was sternly moralistic and inflexible; although he affected a sense of humor and could be a convivial companion, he was neither charming nor tolerant. Suspicious and disdainful of what he styled "kooks," "wishwashy patriots," "Bolsheviks," and "Germany-lovers," Butler—no friend of liberals or progressives—gained national recognition as a meddlesome member of the Board of Regents of the University of Minnesota: charging "unpatriotic behavior," "pro-Socialist attitudes," and "incompetence and insubordination," he was personally responsible for the cashiering of a political science professor, the nonrenewals of the contracts of a chemistry instructor and a rhetoric instructor, and the harassing of a senior economics professor.[68]

Taft did not approve of Butler's actions, but he did not consider them harmful either and, with Harding's backing, vigorously promoted his appointment. He personally led the public and private campaign for Butler, mapping strategy before and during the hearings of the Senate Judiciary Committee. Harding of course readily concurred: he found Butler's ultraconservatism entirely sympathetic; he deemed it prudent to appoint a "safe" Democrat who was also a member of a minority religion; and he found appealing the success story of the son of poor immigrant parents. Butler's candidacy ran into considerable opposition from the Senate, especially from the Progressives, led by Senator La Follette, who, in fact, initially succeeded in blocking the nomination from being taken up in a special session of Congress. Like other liberals and moderates, the Progressives had been antagonized by Butler's inflexible stance on economic-proprietarian matters and by his intolerance and dogmatism while he was a University of Minnesota Regent. In the regular session of Congress (to which Harding had resubmitted the nomination) the Senate, after a month's delay, finally approved Butler by a vote of 61:8, with the unusually large number of twenty-seven abstentions. The margin of the confirming vote belied the bitter and deep-seated opposition to him.

The fears of the Progressives proved as justified as did the hopes of Butler's backers: his record during seventeen years on the Court until his death in November 1939 was wholly and unswervingly in the Darwin-Spencer mold. Yet he was somewhat more sensitive than his companion-in-reaction, James McReynolds, to claims of procedural due process violations, going so far as to join Holmes, Brandeis, and Stone in dissenting from Taft's opinion for a 5:4 majority in the *Olmstead Case* (1928),[69] which upheld the use of evidence by wiretapping. But he was consistently intolerant even to mild libertarian claims in such vital areas as freedom of speech and press, where his reactionary reading of the Constitution was second only to McReynolds's. Rated a distinct "failure" by the experts, he hardly merits a kinder treatment than that historical evaluation has accorded him.

Harding's fourth and final opportunity to make an appointment to the Court resulted from the retirement of Justice Mahlon Pitney on the last day of 1922, after a decade of service characterized by vacillating judicial behavior and murkiness of style: one never quite knew what one's probings of a Pitney opinion would uncover. Since the President had received considerable political support from the South, the designation of a Southerner (but a Republican, because Democrat McReynolds was a Tennessean) would make good political sense. Taft readily agreed with Harding and—like a wine steward, always prepared—suggested such Southern Republican stalwarts as Henry Anderson of Virginia (a Harding acquaintance) and his own ex-Solicitor General, William Marshall Bullitt. He also proposed Judge Charles M. Hough of the Second U.S. Circuit Court of Appeals. But Hough seemed old at sixty-four; the other two appeared to have political liabilities. Attorney General Harry M. Daugherty, with Taft consenting, then suggested an oft-mentioned also-ran, U.S. Judge Edward T. Sanford of the Eastern District of Tennessee. Taft was not wild about Sanford, but he was aware of the virtue of the candidate's lengthy judicial experience on lower federal courts, which both Sutherland and Butler lacked entirely. Harding was satisfied, given Sanford's general popularity with Republican leaders, his apparent conservatism on the bench, and his support among some labor leaders, to whom Pitney had been anathema. Nominated in late January 1923, the fifty-eight-year-old native of Knoxville, Tennessee, an honor graduate from the Harvard Law School, was easily confirmed within a few days.

By and large, the last Harding appointee fulfilled his and Taft's expectations during seven colorless years on the bench. Usually he could be found with the "Chief" and the "Four Horsemen," but he was considerably more flexible than the latter group on some aspects of governmental regulation. For example, when it came to the enforcement of the antitrust laws, which he supported even more faithfully than old trust-buster Taft himself, he left the Spencer-Darwin reservation. On civil libertarian matters, too, the Sanford record betrays some mercurial behavior; at times, such as in an important 1929 naturalization case,[70] he joined Holmes and Brandeis in dissent; at others, such as in the landmark *Gitlow Case* (1925),[71] he left the two and sided with the state against the individual on a crucial free expression issue. Nevertheless, it is for his majority opinion in *Gitlow* that Justice Sanford is best remembered. Although he held against Benjamin Gitlow's specific plea of constitutional protection under the First and Fourteenth amendments, he penned a famous dictum that marked the beginning of the long process of "incorporation," of applying the provisions of the Bill of Rights to the several states: "We may and do assume," he wrote, "that freedom of speech and of the press . . . are among the fundamental personal rights and 'liberties' protected by the due process of law clause of the Fourteenth Amendment from impairment by the States [as well as by the federal government]."[72] It was a pronouncement that would prove of monumental significance as a judicial tool in the years to come. The next nominee to the Court, Harlan Fiske Stone, would avail himself of it with pioneering conviction and far-reaching determination.

Although the political and philosophical outlook of Calvin Coolidge was very much in line with that of the unfortunate man he succeeded, the one-time Massachusetts governor was a total opposite in personal demeanor, habit, and commitment from Warren Harding. Stern, dour, no man of profound, let alone controversial, ideas, Coolidge presented a facade of granite ("How can they tell?" asked Dorothy Parker when informed that Coolidge had died); he seemed unaware of the world about him ("Calvin slept more than any other President," noted Alice Roosevelt Longworth). Yet Coolidge knew what he was doing and why, and he was fully dedicated to the philosophy behind his famous slogan: "The business of the United States is business." Shy and retiring, yet stubborn and occasionally mercurial in temper, the hardworking, scrupulously honest, colorless, and moral President, known affectionately as "Silent Cal," was astonishingly popular. The times were tailor-made for his conservative businessman's approach to government. He was dedicated to running the country on a "sound, business-like, balanced-budget" basis; not only was he uninterested in foreign policy matters (he left these, like Harding, to Charles Evans Hughes and later to Frank B. Kellogg), he was positively annoyed by them. Normalcy and prosperity were to be America's passwords during Coolidge's time—although normalcy and prosperity apparently did not embrace farmers or laborers; the President regarded them as a collective nuisance, a thorn in the side of orderly, sound business practice. Yet the times obviously demanded more than the dedication to normalcy that Coolidge counseled. Social and economic turmoil lay just over the horizon and, given Coolidge's lack of foresight, his lack of interest in the world of ideas, and his nonassertive executive leadership, it is not surprising that the observers of the Presidency have ranked him "below average," between two earlier undistinguished leaders, Millard Fillmore and Franklin Pierce.

Yet Coolidge was to give his country one of its most renowned Justices in the person of his Attorney General, Harlan Fiske Stone—his sole appointee to the Court. Little could the President realize that his New Hampshire-born friend Stone, the presumably safe ex-corporation lawyer with excellent Republican credentials, would within a year join the Holmes and Brandeis dissenting duo, ultimately becoming such a devoted defender of the constitutionality of New Deal legislation—whatever he may have thought of its wisdom—that Franklin Roosevelt would promote him to the Chief Justiceship! To Coolidge, whose death in 1933 spared him witness of the last thirteen of his appointee's twenty-one years on the high bench, Stone's performance was a disappointment of only slightly less magnitude than such celebrated ones as Joseph Story's was to Madison, Oliver Wendell Holmes's was to Teddy Roosevelt, and James McReynolds's was to Wilson.

There is little doubt that the decision to send Stone to the Court was Coolidge's alone, although a good many contemporary public figures would later claim credit for it. Among them was the "Big Chief," who in a letter to his son Robert A. Taft stated pompously: "I rather forced the President into [Stone's] appointment";[73] and Nicholas Murray Butler (like Taft enamored of king making), who insisted that he had been largely responsible. Yet Stone later disputed both men, observing that he doubted that "the responsibility for my appointment weighs very heavily on either of them."[74] The record shows that although Coolidge did receive Taft's and Butler's advice (along with that of many others from Stone's legion of well-wishers), not only was the nomination his own choice, but it was an entirely natural one given Stone's qualifications and the two men's longstanding association.[75]

Stone's career in private as well as public life had been a distinguished one. After attending Amherst College (where Calvin Coolidge was a fellow student) and Columbia University Law School, he taught and practiced law for a quarter of a century, attaining the Deanship at Columbia in 1910. The Teapot Dome scandal became a national issue during his incumbency as Dean, and when Attorney General Harry M. Daugherty at last resigned in 1924, the President named Stone in his place. The appointment was received with general public acclaim as well as relief. Stone not only cleaned house in the Justice Department and in the administration generally, he aided considerably in Coolidge's successful campaign for a full term of his own later that year. When the octogenarian Justice Joseph McKenna (now practically senile) resigned in 1925 from the Court after twenty-seven years of at best mediocre performance, there were broad expectations that Coolidge would nominate another Californian, or at least a Westerner, to replace him. But the President was not concerned with geographic considerations: he wanted the man who had been his personal and political friend for three decades, who had been so helpful to him during the 1924 Presidential race, and who, above all, had proved himself to be a courageous, independent Attorney General. It was precisely because of these attributes that Stone was allegedly kicked upstairs, somewhat as McReynolds had been. The press had a field day conjecturing that Coolidge's move would bail him out with his many big business supporters, a number of whose enterprises had felt the sting of Stone investigations and threatened litigation. Prominent among his targets was the powerful Aluminum Trust, in which the influential Secretary of the Treasury, Andrew W. Mellon, had pronounced professional and personal interests. Yet at best the kicked-upstairs charge remains unproved; neither Stone himself nor Coolidge ever offered either comment or explanation on it.

Stone's nomination on January 5, 1925, met with all but universal approbation. But because he had incurred the enmity of the powerful Senator Burton K. Wheeler, a Montana Democrat of considerable influence, for refusing to drop a case brought against him (the Senator) by Attorney General Daugherty, his unanimous Judiciary Committee approval ran into trouble when it reached the Senate floor. Representations were made to both Coolidge and Stone that the nomination be withdrawn; when the President promptly made it clear that he would not even consider doing so, the Senate moved unanimously to recommit the candidacy to its Judiciary Committee. This move was followed by a "first" in the history of Supreme Court nominations: the personal appearance of a candidate before the Committee. Hostile Senators cross-examined Stone mercilessly, yet he came through with flying colors in a performance marked by strength, dignity, and articulateness. The Committee recommended approval by voice vote, without dissent, and the Senate concurred on February 5 by an overwhelming vote, 71:6. Senator Wheeler himself abstained, as did his Montana colleague Walsh, who had carried much of the burden of the anti-Stone case. Among the six who voted against approval was the redoubtable George W. Norris of Nebraska, who was convinced that Stone was a "tool of the House of Morgan." Sixteen years later, on the occasion of Stone's promotion to Chief Justice, Norris rose on the Senate floor, warmly applauded the elevation, and publicly confessed both error and regret for his earlier opposition.

Harlan Fiske Stone's sixteen years as Associate Justice and five years as Chief Justice earned him the nation's respect and gratitude and the accolade of "greatness" by the Court's observers. Because he was so frequently in dissent together with Holmes and Brandeis, and, later, Holmes's replacement, Cardozo, he is generally labeled as a liberal. But more than that, he was a fiercely independent, tolerant, courageous spirit whose creed combined a basic faith in the dignity and worth of the individual with a firm belief in the right and capacity of the people to govern themselves. His jurisprudential hallmark became a famed admonition and embrace of judicial self-restraint: his dissenting opinion in *United States* v. *Butler* (1936),[76] in which six members of the Court declared unconstitutional the New Deal's Agricultural Adjustment Act of 1933. Joined by Brandeis and Cardozo, Stone wrote: "The only check upon our own exercise of power is our own sense of self restraint. . . . Courts are not the only agency of government that must be assumed to have capacity to govern." He lived that creed until the end of his life, restating it dramatically from the bench on April 22, 1946—moments before he lapsed into unconsciousness, fatally stricken with a cerebral thrombosis: "It is not the function of this Court to disregard the will of Congress in the exercise of its constitutional power."[77]

Ironically, these last words were uttered by Stone in dissent from an opinion that upheld (5:3) an alien conscientious objector's right to qualify for citizenship—ironically because it was Stone who had for so long fought for the very right he here disavowed. But he felt compelled to cast his vote as he did because Congress had earlier reenacted the precise language of the naturalization laws here at issue, which Stone had opposed as "tortured constructions," unwise and undemocratic but not unconstitutional. To him this congressional reaffirmation of legislative intent demanded judicial self-restraint, no matter what one's personal views. Yet it was in the realm of civil rights and liberties that Stone made his other, and possibly his most important, contribution: his commitment to the letter and spirit of the libertarian provisions of the Constitution demanded that there be a judicial posture recognizing a "preferred position" in America's constitutional structure for the cultural freedoms guaranteed in the First Amendment: speech, press, worship, and assembly and all other crucial personal and political guarantees. Unlike enactments in the economic-proprietarian sphere, therefore, governmental action infringing on those "preferred freedoms" would have to be presumed invalid. As he put it in 1938, members of the Court had a duty to subject to "more exacting judicial scrutiny" any and all legislation "which restricts the political processes which can ordinarily be expected to bring about repeal of undesirable legislation" and which reflect "prejudices against discrete and insular minorities."[78]

Stone's happiest and most influential days on the Court were those as Associate Justice, not as Chief Justice. He was wholly dedicated, hardworking, and respected in both posts, but he lacked the executive capacity, the tactical decisiveness, and marshaling ability of a Taft or Hughes. Allowing himself to be drawn into too much petty detail and bickering, into too many endless Conference squabbles, he could hardly be regarded as an effective Chief. Nonetheless, his intellectual acumen, his perception of constitutional fundamentals, his eloquence and articulateness all combined to rank him among the great jurists.

Herbert Clark Hoover, the man who succeeded Coolidge in 1929, was a highly qualified, capable public servant. But despite every good intention, he was a failure as President. If the experts have bestowed on him a rating of "average" rather than "below average" or even "failure," it is very likely because they considered the "Great Engineer" abused, for the realities of his record were grim indeed. From West Branch, Iowa, Hoover had been a brilliant engineer and management expert, a masterful War Food Administrator, and a highly successful Secretary of Commerce under Harding and Coolidge. Yet he was simply incapable of coping with either the political process or, surprisingly, with the social and economic problems of his day. An apostle of "rugged individualism" and *laissez-faire* economics—a nineteenth-century man—he, too, was uncomfortable with the multiple demands of multiple interest groups and was pathologically opposed to strong federal action. After the stockmarket crash of October 1929, he had the inexorably bad luck to be saddled with the Great Depression. His experience theoretically qualified him to deal with the Depression but, sadly, his attempts to check it were belated, ineffectual, and unconvincing. Moreover, he consistently made little of this catastrophe, bridled at criticism, and was practically incapable of admitting to error. And his few halting attempts at establishing viable public relations in a time of crisis were disastrous. At the end, still pleading that "prosperity is just around the corner," he had begun to stoop to name-calling, categorizing his political detractors in a manner that ill befitted his position and character—notwithstanding some recent efforts at reconstructionist interpretations. In sum, Hoover provided little or no effective leadership. Nonetheless, years later he reemerged as a respected *éminence grise* of the governmental process under Presidents Truman and Eisenhower, especially with regard to institutional reorganization.[79]

Hoover appointed three outstanding individuals to the Supreme Court: Charles Evans Hughes, a Chief Justice with few peers; Benjamin N. Cardozo, one of the greatest men of the Court; and Owen J. Roberts, an able and conscientious jurist. Even John J. Parker, his so unfairly rejected nominee, was a jurist of outstanding credentials who unquestionably would have left a commendable record as a member of the Court. Indeed, other than an insistence on demonstrated merit, Hoover's criteria for selection are more difficult to ascertain than those of most other Presidents. He did favor prior judicial experience, which all of his appointees save Roberts possessed in considerable measure. He was, of course, concerned with real politics and, with the exception of Cardozo, the records of his candidates represented the kind of Republican moderate-to-progressive, conservative business orientation with which he was comfortable. He respected their upper-middle-class or upper-class educational and social backgrounds and their public mindedness. Geography and religion became an issue only in the case of Cardozo.

Because Hoover lived to a ripe ninety years, he not only witnessed the performances of his three appointees, all of whom he survived by a wide margin of time, but he also witnessed the metamorphosis of the Court in 1937. It is not clear how Hoover really felt about the change, but it *is* known that he, having learned some of the bitter lessons of the realities of government and politics under stress, regarded it as inevitable and probably necessary. Cardozo, of course, had never been his kind of jurist, although he ultimately came to pronounce Cardozo's appointment as the proudest act of his career. Hughes and Roberts, however, had established a record before the 1937 switch with which Hoover certainly could live.

The President's initial opportunity came with the resignation of the fatally ill Chief Justice Taft on February 3, 1939. On Taft's bedside table lay a touching message from his eight colleagues, beginning: "We call you Chief Justice still, for we cannot quickly give up the title by which we have known you for all these later years and which you have made so dear to us."[80] Within five hours after having received Taft's resignation, President Hoover—who had paid the dying Taft a bedside visit—named Charles Evans Hughes to replace him—with Taft's advance blessing and to the surprise of many observers, including the press, which had confidently expected the elevation of Stone. Actually, already in late January—given Taft's obvious terminal illness—Attorney General William D. Mitchell had sought the assistance of Justices Van

Devanter and Butler to ascertain that Hughes, who seemed somewhat hesitant, was available. On receiving their assurance, Hoover, in the presence of Under Secretary of State (then Acting Secretary) Joseph P. Cotton, telephoned Hughes from the State Department to offer the post. Hoover feared—and some hoped—that Hughes, now sixty-eight, happy and comfortable in private life, would be reluctant to accept; but the elder statesman readily assented.[81] There is considerable evidence that Stone himself (as well as the press) was convinced that he was in the running for the Chief Justiceship. His failure to be named caused as much of a public eyebrow-raising as had Taft's own choice of Edward D. White rather than Hughes twenty years earlier. And it is entirely possible that Hoover would have been almost as comfortable with the naming of Stone, a very close personal friend. (The Stones and Hoovers took Sunday evening suppers together for many years, and Hoover and Stone met daily at 7:30 A.M. on the White House lawn for a game of medicine ball.) Although he never admitted it in so many words, it is fair to conclude that, in fact, the President preferred Hughes's jurisprudential politics to Stone's and that the clamor of the Taft wing on behalf of Hughes probably proved to be rationalizing and decisive.[82] In any event the latter was Hoover's demonstrable first choice, notwithstanding repeated allegations to the contrary.[83]

Quite in contrast to his smooth confirmation as President Taft's nominee to the Associate Justiceship in 1910, Hughes now ran into considerable flak. His nominator, of course, was in deep trouble with Congress—where he would soon be faced with a Democratic majority—and some of the antagonism rubbed off on Hughes. But it was less a case of antinominator than antinominee: Charles Evans Hughes had, after all, voluntarily relinquished the Court for the active world of politics—why should he now be granted a return trip, and the top spot to boot? Moreover, Hughes had the misfortune of encountering opposition from both Republicans and Democrats in the Senate—albeit for different reasons. Conservative Southerners opposed him because they viewed him as too "city-bred," too record-prone to support national versus states' rights when the chips were down. The coalition of Republican-Progressive-Democratic liberals, centered on the Midwest and personified by such influential legislators as Idaho's Borah, Nebraska's Norris, Montana's Wheeler, and Wisconsin's La Follette, were unhappy with Hughes because of the erstwhile corporate law specialist's affinity for America's business and financial elite. "No man in public life," declared Senator Norris, "so exemplifies the influence of powerful combinations in the political and financial world as does Mr. Hughes."[84] In the end, however, supported by Democratic Senators Robert F. Wagner and Royal S. Copeland of New York (Hughes's home state), the bitterly contested nomination was approved on February 13, 1930, by a vote of 52:26, with eighteen Senators abstaining.

That Hughes, an impressive and stately figure, was superbly qualified to serve at the helm of the Court he knew so well was self-evident. Energetic, tough, and decisive, the near-septuagenarian firmly grasped the reins of leadership. An overwhelming choice as one of the great members of the Court, Hughes ranks at the pinnacle of achievement, perhaps second only to Marshall in administrative acumen and intellectual leadership and in a class with Taney, Stone, and Warren in jurisprudential impact. As a presiding officer he was as impressive as John Marshall himself. "To see Hughes preside," noted Felix Frankfurter repeatedly, "was like witnessing Toscanini lead an orchestra."[85] And his ability to be realistic, to blend conservation of basic principles with a recognition of the need for change, enabled him to enhance consensus on fundamental issues. His beautifully articulated embrace of the essence of fundamental liberty was often crucial to its enhancement—perhaps even survival—in troubled moments. A leader and a doer, he was a realist at home in the world of ideas as well as in practical politics. In that role he consciously came to face the need for the all-important change in direction of the Court over which he presided in 1937, stimulated by the *Realpolitik* of the times. Charles Evans Hughes was a giant among men.

In March 1930, barely one month after Hughes had replaced Taft, Justice Edward T. Sanford died unexpectedly, behind him seven years of average but not unimportant Court service. Although Hoover was not genuinely concerned with geography, he initially looked to the South for a replacement for the late Tennessee jurist. His choice devolved on a well-known and well-liked North Carolina Republican, Judge John J. Parker of the U.S. Court of Appeals for the Fourth Circuit. His rejection (see Ch. 3, *supra*) by the narrow vote of 39:41 is now all but universally regarded not only as unfair and regrettable but as a blunder. It was the last Senatorial veto of a Supreme Court nominee until the aborted promotion of Abe Fortas to Chief Justice and the Haynsworth and Carswell rejections four decades later.

The failure to win confirmation for Judge Parker resulted in President Hoover's selection of Owen J. Roberts, a fifty-five-year-old Pennsylvania Republican from a to-the-manner-born Philadelphia family. As the federal government's special prosecutor in the Teapot Dome oil scandals, he had achieved national recognition and praise; he had also served well as a Special U.S. Deputy Attorney General during World War I in connection with espionage and sabotage cases, and in the Justice Department of Pennsylvania. A judicious and modest person but an able and strong advocate, he was an eagerly sought out practitioner of the law, especially in the corporate field, where he was close to the then very powerful Pennsylvania Railroad. His nomination was broadly applauded—support came from all parts of the political spectrum. Conservatives looked to his long-standing business connections and liberals to his demonstrated humanitarian concerns. Thus, he commanded the vocal support of such key anti-Parker Republican Senators as Arthur Vandenberg (Michigan) and Charles L. McNary (Oregon) as well as of perpetual Republican mavericks Borah, La Follette, and Norris. Roberts was confirmed by acclamation literally one minute after the Judiciary Committee, with its unanimous endorsement, sent the nomination to the floor of the Senate on May 21, 1930.

Yet Justice Roberts would lastingly please neither political wing. There was an almost terpsichorean quality about this benign, conscientious jurist who established a probably difficult-to-equal record of inconsistency in his voting on the bench. Beginning his Court career of fifteen years as a "centrist" or "neutralist" with certain articulated liberal policy notions, he soon rather steadfastly embraced the "Four Horsemen" approach to governmental functions and powers—with important exceptions.[86] Yet it was Roberts who, along with Hughes, executed the 1937 switch that changed the course of constitutional law in our time. The Chief Justice had probably been prepared to effect that switch considerably earlier, but for reasons of strategy and maximum unity preferred to wait until Roberts would join him. Yet having been so instrumental in the change, Roberts began to revert to his former posture once the last of the Four Horsemen, James McReynolds, had retired in 1941. In many ways a sympathetic and noble citizen, Roberts tended to vacillate jurisprudentially, making evaluation difficult. Although he was considerably more able than "average," the rating usually accorded him by Court observers, Justice Roberts's performance makes any other categorization difficult to sustain. His resignation in 1945 was based largely on his disenchantment with what he regarded as wholesale deviations from established legal precedents by the Stone, or "Roosevelt," Court. If that was indeed the case, Roberts had had a hand in facilitating that policy.

On January 15, 1932, Oliver Wendell Holmes, Jr., now almost ninety-one but still alert and cheerful, bowed to old age and precarious health and resigned. More than three decades of an incredibly productive and towering judicial career thus came to an end. How to replace the "judicial philosopher of the age"? Hoover, striking out on his own, let it be known that he would like to see a "non-controversial western Republican" as the Old Yankee's successor. But almost at once the Chairman of the Senate's Judiciary Committee, George W. Norris, made it plain to the President that he and his fellow committeemen, largely Democrats and Progressive Republicans, would insist on a judicial statesman in the progressive Holmes mold. Others were rather more specific: the entire faculty of the Law School of the University of Chicago urged Hoover to nominate Benjamin Nathan Cardozo, Chief Judge of the New York Court of Appeals—a man widely regarded as one of America's most brilliant jurists, one who might already have been on the U.S. Supreme Court had it not been for Taft's sustained opposition to him during the 1920s. The Deans of the prestigious schools of law of Harvard, Yale, and Columbia universities joined in a similar strongly worded plea. Labor as well as business leaders, liberals as well as conservatives, advocates of judicial self-restraint as well as judicial activists, all participated in a uniquely unified appeal on behalf of a candidate to the Court—so strong an impression had Cardozo made, so splendid a record had he achieved during his eighteen years as Associate Judge and Chief Judge on New York's highest tribunal, then concededly the country's busiest and most distinguished appellate state court.

The President could hardly have been unaware of the clamor for Cardozo's nomination. The now sixty-two-year-old Sephardic Jew from New York had not only made his mark as a jurist, but his stylistically beautiful and scholarly publications, such as the still-seminal *The Nature of the Judicial Process,*[87] had won him universal praise. His lucid, cogent opinions, his realistic approach to law and democratic society, his love of his land and its Constitution stamped him as Holmes's logical successor. But Hoover continued to demur; he really did not want to appoint anyone, no matter how superbly and uniquely qualified he might be, from a state that already had two eminent "representatives" (Hughes—he had sent him there himself—and Stone) and whose religion (Jewish) was not only already "represented" on the Court (Brandeis), but would assuredly cause McReynolds to act up again. (It did.) No, Herbert Hoover would look elsewhere, even though Stone had told him he would be willing to resign so that the nation might have Cardozo.[88]

Now, however, the powerful Chairman of the Senate Foreign Relations Committee, Republican William E. Borah of Idaho, whose support Hoover needed on other fronts, got into the act and loudly and repeatedly called for Cardozo's designation. No particular friend of Easterners, especially New Yorkers, Borah, like Norris and other wise legislators similarly placed, recognized Cardozo's rare merit. Twenty-four hours before Hoover had indicated he would announce his candidate publicly he called for Borah. In an often-told, dramatic confrontation between two proud men, the President, after discussing the vacancy generally, suddenly handed Borah a list on which he had ranked those individuals he was considering for the nomination in descending order of preference. The name at the bottom was that of Benjamin N. Cardozo. Borah glanced at it and replied: "Your list is all right, but you handed it to me upside down." Hoover protested that, first, there was the geographical question to be considered and, second, he had to take "religious or sectarian repercussions" into account. Senator Borah sharply retorted that "Cardozo belongs as much to Idaho as to New York" and that "geography should no more bar the judge than the presence of two Virginians–John Blair and Bushrod Washington–should have kept President Adams from naming John Marshall to be Chief Justice." And, he added sternly, "anyone who raises the question of race [*sic*] is unfit to advise you concerning so important a matter."[89] Hoover at last bowed to what he now regarded as the inevitable. His memoirs simply state: ". . . On February 15, 1932 . . . I nominated Chief Justice Benjamin N. Cardozo of the New York Court of Appeals, a Democrat. The appointment met with Senate approval."[90] Indeed, it did, instantly and unanimously and without discussion or roll call when the nomination reached the floor of the Senate a few days later. In finally appointing Cardozo, commented Zechariah Chafee, Jr., Hoover "ignored geography and made history."[91] Cardozo's brothers on the Court were delighted: "Hope you come soon," Stone wrote Cardozo on the very day of his official nomination. "We have been saving up some interesting cases for you."[92] Accurately, the *New York Times* commented that "seldom, if ever, in the history of the Court has an appointment been so universally commended."[93]

Whatever President Hoover might have thought of that statement, it did not of course surprise him that Cardozo would continue in the Holmes tradition. Thus, unlike the other two later Hoover appointees, Hughes and Roberts, Cardozo at once joined the Brandeis and Stone wing of the Court, working with them in the minority for five years until the 1937 upheaval brought the other two Justices over. Although fate allowed him little more than six years on the high bench, he is eminently deserving of the recognition of greatness bestowed on him. Those six years were among the most emotion-charged and contentious in the Court's history, and Cardozo more than did his part in recording the history of that period with his more than 100 opinions, written with the pen of legal scholar and philosopher as well as of poet and teacher. No Justice in the annals of constitutional law and history ever rendered a more enduring contribution in so brief a span of years! Thus, it was he who so lucidly and carefully spoke for the Court in 1937 in upholding the several key provisions of the landmark Social Security Act of 1935.[94] And it was he who authored the most significant basic decision ever pronounced by the Court on behalf of the application of the federal Bill of Rights to the several states, the celebrated "incorporation" case of *Palko* v. *Connecticut.*[95] There, for a unanimous Court save for the dissent (without opinion) by Justice Butler, Cardozo identified certain rights "so rooted in the traditions and conscience of our people as to be ranked as fundamental," so clearly constituting "the matrix, the indispensable condition, of nearly every other form of freedom" (such as freedom of speech, the press, worship, assembly, and petition) that, unlike certain others, they were also protected against state infringement by virtue of the language of the Fourteenth Amendment.[96] The all but total application, absorption, or incorporation that has taken place since *Palko* is a tribute to Cardozo's jurisprudential pioneering in this fundamental aspect of democratic society.

Cardozo's friend and fellow judicial stylist and craftsman, Learned Hand, movingly eulogized the gentle spirit shortly after his untimely death, concluding:

> In this America of ours when the passion for publicity is a disease, and where swarms of foolish, tawdry moths dash with rapture into its consuming fire, it was a rare good fortune that brought to such eminence a man so reserved, so unassuming, so retiring, so gracious to high and low, and so serene. He is gone, and while the west is still lighted with his radiance, it is well for us to pause and take count of our own coarser selves. He had a lesson to teach us if we care to stop and learn; a lesson at variance of most that we practice, and much that we profess.[97]

And Felix Frankfurter, who inherited the Cardozo seat, justly observed that the man, whose opinions reflected not the "friction and passion of their day, but the abiding spirit of the Constitution," ranks "second only to Holmes in making of the judicial process a blend of continuity and creativeness."[98] Unlike Holmes, Cardozo lived to see, however briefly, the realization of at least some of his labors.

9

The Court Alters Course:

F.D.R. and Truman

1933-1953

In the depth of the worst economic and psychological depression in the history of the United States, a remarkable man was swept into office. Franklin Delano Roosevelt was the leader people needed, not only because of his training, background, and understanding, but also because of his optimism and his confident resolve to lead the nation out of a desperate situation that might well have doomed it. Far from turning the country over to the "Communists and Socialists," as was so often charged, he orchestrated a New Deal that in effect preserved the American system of enlightened free enterprise.

The antithesis of his predecessor, Herbert Hoover, Roosevelt was a man of action: tough, forceful, and decisive, he got things done. And by and large his countrymen approved of his action, electing him to the Presidency four times despite sustained and bitter attacks against him from powerful and influential critics, notable among them the press. Of course, as even his most ardent admirers admit, F.D.R. was a fox as well as a lion. He was not above deviousness, the dishonest rationale he advanced for the Court-packing bill of 1937 being a case in point. Yet he was an inspiring and successful leader; he gave to the American people ideals, confidence, and hope. "The only thing we have to fear is fear itself," he reassured them during the blackest days of the Depression: 13 million were unemployed, 9100 banks were closed, and government was at a standstill. "This nation asks for action, and action now," he stated in setting forth a program of drastic action: the Congress had literally begged the President to lead, and he responded in full measure. In the ensuing "Hundred Days" F.D.R. swamped Congress with nearly a score of carefully spelled-out legislative messages—tough, basic recommendations designed to bring about economic recovery and, simultaneously, reform. The legislative branch concurred eagerly; desperate, it was ready to improvise and even to experiment. The recovery was gradual, but in the process one of the nation's most gifted leaders would forge a coalition of support that would carry him to an unprecedented reelection victory in 1936, with 60.8 percent of the popular vote—a record until 1964, when Lyndon Baines Johnson (an early and ardent New Deal supporter) bested the master by three-tenths of one percentage point. By any count and any standard, Franklin Delano Roosevelt was a truly great leader, one who fully deserves his continuing ranking of third on the scale of our great Presidents, just below Lincoln and Washington.

Roosevelt was no radical, far from it. Yet he chafed under a governmental stand-off that, notwithstanding his overwhelming mandates in 1932 and 1936, saw the Supreme Court, now popularly dubbed the "Nine Old Men," say no to most New Deal legislation. The Court, usually by 6:3 or 5:4 votes, made mincemeat out of the measures that the President and his Congress had so ardently desired and enacted. True, he could usually count on support from Justices Brandeis, Stone, and Cardozo, who, in addition to being personally sympathetic to most New Deal measures at hand, practiced judicial restraint in the best tradition of the separation of powers. But the "Four Horsemen" (Justices Van Devanter, McReynolds, Sutherland, and Butler)—those direct descendants of Darwin and Spencer—were totally antagonistic to the New Deal, and they could usually count on support in their antagonism from Justice Roberts and Chief Justice Hughes.

When Roosevelt entered his second term he had made not a

single appointment to the Supreme Court! Little wonder he was convinced the fates were conspiring against him. Death and retirement seemed to have taken a holiday.

It was at this point that F.D.R., his patience thoroughly spent and his frustrations at their peak, resolved to effect radical Court reform: on February 5, 1937, he sent to the Hill a sweeping piece of legislation designed to reorganize the federal judiciary in general and the Supreme Court in particular.[1] The measure would grant the President authority to appoint an additional jurist for each federal judge who, having served ten years or more, failed to retire within six months after reaching his seventieth birthday. The additional judge would be assigned to the same court on which the reluctant septuagenarian was serving. A ceiling of fifty such additional judges (for the entire federal judicial system) was provided for in the bill—with the maximum size of the Supreme Court pegged at fifteen. Had the bill become law, F.D.R. would have been able to appoint six "additional" Justices to the Court to serve with the "Nine Old Men." Their ages at that point ranged from Brandeis's eighty-one to Roberts's sixty-two, but each of the Four Horsemen and the Chief Justice were conveniently above seventy, with Butler the youngest at seventy-one and Van Devanter the oldest at seventy-eight. Unfortunately, Roosevelt's message accompanying his scheme was devious and dishonest: as the main motivation for the bill it alleged that the Court was overburdened because of "insufficient personnel" and the physical disabilities of the jurists; it went on to charge that it was the conservatism bred of old age that caused so many of the Court's attitudinal difficulties. The real reason for the President's action was of course obvious to everyone: the Court's continuing vetoes over much-desired New Deal legislation.

The President's message grievously offended Justice Brandeis, the Court's most liberal and most pro-New Deal member, who suggested to Chief Justice Hughes that he (Hughes) publicly deny the Presidential charge. Hughes promptly did so in a letter to the influential Senator Burton K. Wheeler (D.-Mont.). His statistics were irrefutable; the Court was readily in command of its docket. Whatever the weight of the Brandeis and Hughes refutation of

F.D.R.'s charge, the ill-conceived plan for judicial reorganization hopelessly split the Democratic majority in the Senate; caused a storm of protest from bench and bar; and created an uproar among both constitutional conservatives and liberals. The bill was doomed: on June 14 the Senate Judiciary Committee reported it to the floor with an adverse vote of 8:10; on July 20 the Senate recommitted it to the Committee for burial. The vote was 70:20.

At least two interrelated crucial events had taken place between the bill's submittal in February and the Senate's actions in June and July. First, the Court made three key decisions that effected the "switch-in-time-that-saved-nine." The first took place on March 29, 1937, when Hughes and Roberts moved over to the Brandeis-Stone-Cardozo bloc by sustaining 5:4 Washington state's minimum-wage law for women in *West Coast Hotel* v. *Parrish,*[2] with Chief Justice Hughes authoring the dramatic opinion. The second was the April 12 decision upholding, again in a 5:4 majority vote, written again by Hughes, one of the prize New Deal laws, the National Labor Relations Act of 1935 (the "Wagner Act").[3] The third clincher came on May 24, when two Cardozo opinions upheld as constitutional the old-age tax and benefits (5:4) and the unemployment provisions (7:2, only McReynolds and Butler dissenting here) of another major New Deal statute, the Social Security Act of 1935.[4] Well might F.D.R. and Congress be jubilant! No matter how insistently Hughes and Roberts would later deny that their switch to the liberal wing had been politically motivated, few students of the Court view their move as anything but a recognition of, and inevitable bowing to, the handwriting on the wall.

The second major event followed closely on the heels of the Court's upholding the Social Security Act. The oldest of the "Four Horsemen" in both point of service (twenty-seven years) and age (seventy-eight), Mr. Justice Willis Van Devanter, announced on May 18—in what was scarcely accidental timing, the Court-packing bill being before the Judiciary Committee—that he would retire from the Court on June 1, 1937. At last, more than four and one-half years after his election to the Presidency, Roosevelt had a Supreme Court vacancy to fill. The appointment went to loyal

New Deal supporter Senator Hugo Lafayette Black of Alabama. And there would be eight other appointments, falling short of George Washington's ultimate record by only one: Stanley F. Reed, Felix Frankfurter, William O. Douglas, Frank Murphy, James F. Byrnes, Harlan F. Stone (promoted to Chief Justice), Robert H. Jackson, and Wiley B. Rutledge. They were distinguished men by anyone's standards: of them, Black and Frankfurter have been generally ranked as "great" by the Court experts, and Douglas, Jackson, and Rutledge as "near great"—a record of professional approbation attained by no other President.

No mystery attends Roosevelt's motivations in selecting his Supreme Court nominees. There were three major criteria: (1) absolute loyalty to the principles of the New Deal, particularly to governmental regulatory authority; (2) firm adherence to a libertarian and egalitarian philosophy of government under law—at least as it was viewed contemporarily; and (3) (once it had become clear that war clouds would cover the New World as well as the Old) full support of F.D.R.'s war aims—which necessitated a generous interpretation of the extent of executive power. Of lesser importance were age and geography; nevertheless, he considered such factors with great care. With occasional differences, all of F.D.R.'s appointees lived up to his expectations during his lifetime: few Presidents had been rewarded with judicial performances so pleasing.

When Justice Van Devanter announced his retirement, the leading candidate for the vacancy was Joseph T. Robinson of Arkansas, the Democratic Majority Leader of the Senate. A faithful New Dealer who had supported every New Deal measure that F.D.R. had sent to Congress, the popular, hardworking Robinson had also been an early and key backer of the President's Court-reorganization bill. Everything pointed to his designation. F.D.R. had evidently promised him a Supreme Court seat, although not necessarily the first available one. But according to the then still high-riding Postmaster General and Democratic National Committee Chairman, James A. "Jim" Farley, Roosevelt had said that Robinson could count on being nominated.[5] And in an unusual move the Senate as a body endorsed the candidacy of its Democratic Leader. Yet F.D.R. had been forced to wait more than four years for that precious initial vacancy; now he would bide his time. He liked and was grateful to "Arkansas Joe"; still, there was just enough basic conservatism in Robinson's past to cast doubt on his reliability. Then fate intervened: on July 14, while leading the floor fight for the Court-packing bill, Senator Robinson suffered a fatal heart attack. Roosevelt at once instructed Homer S. Cummings, his Attorney General, to canvass the field of other "suitables," keeping in mind that the nominee had to be absolutely loyal to the New Deal program. By early August the search had narrowed to four loyal New Deal Democrats: U.S. Solicitor General Stanley F. Reed of Kentucky, Senator Sherman Minton of Indiana, Senator Hugo L. Black of Alabama, and Assistant Attorney General Robert H. Jackson of New York. All four would become Supreme Court Justices eventually; it was Black's turn now (although there are assertions–firmly denied by Justice Douglas, for one–that F.D.R. offered Minton first refusal). "Jesus Christ!" exclaimed White House Press Secretary Stephen Early when F.D.R. disclosed his choice to him late at night on August 11.[6] The President grinned–it had been a well-kept secret indeed. Earlier that evening he had summoned Black to his White House study, showed him the nomination form he had filled out in longhand himself, and chuckled, "Hugo, I'd like to write your name here." A happy Black nodded assent.[7]

Steve Early's reaction was understandable. At first glance there was precious little in the impoverished rural background of the then fifty-one-year-old Senator, the eighth (and last) child of a small-town rural merchant, to qualify him for the Supreme Court. True, he had had considerable experience as a lawyer among country sharecroppers, as a county solicitor, and as a police-court judge and prosecutor in Birmingham; he had read widely; and he had a lucid, profound mind. But was he *really* the best F.D.R. could do? The President of course knew precisely what he was doing: Black, now in his second term in the Senate, had not only demonstrated enthusiastic and outspoken support of the New Deal, but he had staunchly supported the Court-packing bill. Those two factors were decisive–but F.D.R. also happily noted that Black had a long and effective record of siding with "little people" and "underdogs" and that he was from a part of the country that he, F.D.R., wanted to see represented on the Court. He was also aware of Black's principled discipline and his astounding educational achievements. His nominee never finished high school, moving straight into the Birmingham Medical School for one year, finishing two years' full requirements in one. Black then switched to the law, studying for three years at the University of Alabama School of Law at Tuscaloosa–where he was so bored that he took an *entire* liberal arts curriculum concurrently (!), graduating with high honors in 1907.[8]

The nomination's announcement was met with approbation by most of Senator Black's colleagues and most New Deal spokesmen throughout the land. Yet it also evoked loud protests from both public and private sources. The intellectual and soft-spoken liberal was portrayed as being utterly unqualified by training, temperament, and constitutional dedication; as being blindly partisan; as being a radical rather than a liberal; as being, in fact, a phony liberal when it was revealed that he had been a member of the Ku Klux Klan (K.K.K.) in the 1920s. The press–no more a friend of the Senator's than of his President–roasted Black for "combined lack of training on the one hand and extreme partisanship on the other,"[9] with the *Chicago Tribune* declaring that the President had picked "the worst he could find."[10] But the Senate, although treated to the somewhat unaccustomed spectacle of a public debate on the merits of a sitting member, quickly confirmed its colleague (backed 13:4 in the Judiciary Committee) by a vote of 63:16 on August 17.[11]

When the verdict was in, Justice-designate and Mrs. Black sailed for a European vacation. In their absence, Ray Sprigle, a reporter on the *Pittsburgh Post-Gazette,* published a six-day series of articles repeating the known facts of Black's erstwhile K.K.K. membership. Although acknowledging written proof of Black's resignation from the Klan in 1925, Sprigle alleged that, in fact, Black–notwithstanding on-the-floor denials by such powerful non-Democratic colleagues as Senator W. E. Borah (R.-Idaho), for example–was still a member of the hooded organization, having been secretly elected to life membership in 1926. Black was besieged abroad by reporters, but he characteristically disdained any comment until he stepped before radio microphones on October 1 to make the eleven-minute statement that was heard by the largest radio audience ever, save for those who listened to Edward VIII's abdication:[12]

> My words and acts are a matter of public record. I believe that my record as a Senator refutes every implication of racial or religious intolerance. It shows that I was of that group of liberal Senators who have consistently fought for civil, economic and religious rights of all Americans, without regard to race or creed. . . . I did join the Klan. I later resigned. I never rejoined. I have never considered and I do not now consider the unsolicited card given to me shortly after my nomination to the Senate as a membership of any kind in the Ku Klux Klan. I never used it. I did not even keep it. Before becoming a Senator I dropped the Klan. I have had nothing whatever to do with it since that time. I abandoned it. . . .[13]

The public was generally sympathetic and persuaded of his sincerity. Again characteristically, Justice Black—whose personality Gerald T. Dunne has described as "steel wrapped in silk"[14]—said no more on the subject, refusing to discuss or reopen the matter during the remainder of his long life. "When this statement is ended," he had said, "my discussion of the question is closed." Three days after the broadcast he donned the robes of Associate Justice—"he need not buy but merely dye his robes" was a favorite contemporary cocktail quip.[15]

Thus began a remarkable Supreme Court tenure of more than thirty-four years. It was one marked by a distinction and an influence rare in the annals of the Court. How right the *Montgomery Advertiser* had been when it observed: "What a joke it would be on Hugo's impassioned detractors if he should now turn out to be a very great justice of the Supreme Court. Brandeis did it when every Substantial Citizen of the Republic felt that Wilson should have been impeached for appointing him. . . ."[16]

Few jurists have had the impact on law and society of Justice Hugo Lafayette Black. A constitutional literalist to whom every word in the document represented a command, he, nonetheless, used the language of the Constitution to propound a jurisprudence that has had a lasting effect on the development of American constitutional law. His contributions were towering. They stand as jurisprudential and intellectual landmarks in the evolving history of the land he loved so well.[17] In Paul Freund's view, Black was "without a doubt the most influential of the many strong figures" who sat on the Court during his thirty-four years of membership.[18] In that of Philip Kurland, only one other member, John Marshall, "left such a deep imprint on our basic document."[19] He fully met F.D.R.'s expectations, of course. But that was in the short run; the New Deal as such had spent its course by the end of the 1930s. In the long run Black's achievements encompass securing the central meaning of the Constitution and of the Bill of Rights. At the pinnacle of his legacy stands the now-all-but-complete nationalization of the Bill of Rights, its application to all of the states through the due process clause of the Fourteenth Amendment. In what was probably his most influential opinion in dissent, the *Adamson* case of 1947,[20] Hugo Black called for that nationalization, dramatically expanding and elaborating the Cardozo position in the 1937 *Palko Case*.[21] He lost by only one vote. But by constantly reiterating the theme of constitutional intent as he perceived it in the Fourteenth Amendment—"I cannot consider the Bill of Rights to be an outworn eighteenth-century 'strait jacket,' " he had thundered in *Adamson*—he coaxed the Court step by step to his side. By the late 1960s the Warren Court had, in effect, written into constitutional law its concurrence.[22]

It is generally agreed that the nationalization of the Bill of Rights was Black's most visible achievement; yet it is but one of many. Among those achievements were his leadership in propounding an "absolutist" theory of the First Amendment's freedom of expression guarantees,[23] a theory that contributed heavily to the Warren Court's liberal definition of obscenity and to its striking down of much of the "subversive activities" legislation of the McCarthy era; his assertive majority opinions defining the line of separation between Church and State; his tenacious, literal interpretation of the protective provisions of the Constitution in the administration of justice, including the specific provisions against coerced confessions, compulsory self-incrimination, double jeopardy, and those defining the conditions of trial by jury and the availability of counsel; his victory over Justice Frankfurter in the arena of "political questions" that legalized the egalitarian representation ("one man, one vote") concept now broadly taken for granted. Probably Black's most moving opinion was written for a unanimous Court in the celebrated case of *Gideon* v. *Wainwright* (1963),[24] which overruled a decision of more than two decades earlier from which he had vigorously dissented:[25] *Gideon* enshrined the principle that any criminal defendant in a state as well as a federal proceeding who is too poor to pay for a lawyer has a constitutional right to be assigned one gratis by the government. For Black the opinion represented the affirmation of another moving plea written twenty-three years earlier in the famed case of *Chambers* v. *Florida.* Still viewed as one of his most beautifully penned, it held for a unanimous Court that the confessions obtained by Florida authorities to condemn four black defendants to death were patently coerced and, therefore, a clear violation of due process of law. In the most celebrated passage, at the close of his opinion, Black wrote:

> Under our constitutional system courts stand against any winds that blow as havens or refuge for those who might otherwise suffer because they are helpless, weak, outnumbered, or because they are non-conforming victims of prejudice and public excitement. Due process of law, preserved for all by our Constitution, commands that no such practice as that disclosed by [the *Chambers* case record] shall send any accused to his death. No higher duty, no more solemn responsibility, rests upon this Court, than that of translating into living law and maintaining this constitutional shield deliberately planned and inscribed for the benefit of every human being to our Constitution–of whatever race, creed, or persuasion.[26]

One week after ill health compelled his retirement in September 1971 at eighty-five, Justice Black died. He had written almost 1000 opinions during his thirty-four years of exemplary service. "The law," as one of those who knew him best wrote, "has lost a kindly giant."[27] Friends who called at a funeral home in Washington before his burial in Arlington National Cemetery received a poignant parting gift—a copy of the Constitution. On a desk bearing a book for visitors' signatures was a pile of small paperbound copies of the document Black had so often referred to as "my legal bible"—a copy of which he always carried in his pocket. He would have approved.

F.D.R.'s second appointment opportunity came within six months of Black's when Justice George Sutherland, second of the "Four Horsemen" to retire, stepped down in January 1938. F.D.R.'s choice was no surprise: Stanley F. Reed, the Solicitor General, had been high on the list when F.D.R. nominated Black. He was approved without objection on January 25. Reed, with B.A. degrees from Kentucky Wesleyan College and Yale University, had trained in the law at the Sorbonne, and attended both Columbia University and the University of Virginia; but he was graduated from neither. Instead, he completed his legal studies by reading law in a Kentucky attorney's office; was admitted to his native Kentucky bar in 1910; and then practiced law in his hometown of Maysville. In the late 1920s he entered governmental service in response to President Hoover's successive invitations to serve as general counsel to the Federal Loan Board and the Reconstruction Finance Corporation. He then moved to the Attorney General's office as a special assistant, serving there until F.D.R., conscious of Reed's faithful New Deal adherence, named him Solicitor General in 1935. It was a crucial period for the New Deal and its legislation and the President needed an individual in the post who could be trusted to back the Administration fully. Given the composition of the Court, Reed won but few of the cases he argued before it until the 1937 switch occurred; but he always ardently supported New Deal principles, and his presentations were widely admired as thorough and logical.

In terms of his fundamental commitment to F.D.R.'s governmental philosophy, Reed was a logical choice. But he also was an attractive candidate because of his age (fifty-three); his state (the Border States were then not "represented" on the Court); his impressive legal reputation; his solid character and personal popularity; and his noncontroversial image.

Reed, who authored 231 opinions for the Court, plus 20 concurring and 88 dissenting ones during almost two decades of service, was the least glamorous and least mercurial of the Roosevelt Justices. He faithfully backed the President's program, but observers generally label him as being far more of a judicial conservative than a liberal on the bench–probably because, "opposed to government by judges," he moved more slowly and cautiously than his colleagues on the frontiers of constitutional change, and because he was reluctant to side with his more liberal associates in their escalating rulings that favored individuals vis-à-vis government. This was especially true in national security and criminal-justice cases, in which Reed usually fit into the law-and-order mold. Yet he solidly backed the Court's developing position on racial segregation: thus, in 1946, he wrote the opinion in *Morgan* v. *Virginia* that invalidated racial segregation in interstate buses[28] and, in 1944, the opinion in *Smith* v. *Allwright*[29] that struck down for an 8:1 Court the "White Primary" of the Texas Democratic party as an unconstitutional violation of the Fifteenth Amendment. Ironically, Chief Justice Stone had initially assigned the case to Justice Frankfurter but, given the emotional nature of the controversy, had yielded to Justice Jackson's plea that it be given to someone else–someone more amenable to the South than a Harvard-educated foreign-born Jew, and a none-too-loyal Democrat.[30]

Felix Frankfurter was the next personage to be selected for the Supreme Court. This, Franklin Roosevelt's third opportunity to appoint a Supreme Court Justice, came with the untimely death of the jurist and man Frankfurter revered, Benjamin N. Cardozo (whose seat had been formerly occupied by one of Frankfurter's foremost heroes, Oliver Wendell Holmes, Jr.). For almost a quarter of a century Frankfurter would serve with brilliance, dedication, and persuasiveness, almost–but not quite–equaling the performance of Hugo L. Black in lasting impact and influence. Black and Frankfurter were often in fundamental Court-role and jurisprudential disagreement but usually, albeit not always, with respect and appreciation. These two, who towered over a Court replete with probably more talent than any other in the tribunal's history, left a legacy for American constitutional law and jurisprudence that was not only profound but seminal.

F.D.R., who had known Frankfurter since his days as Assistant Secretary of the Navy, had fully intended to send him to the Court, and told him so. Yet on Cardozo's death the President informed his friend and adviser that he could not do so now, that he hoped to appoint him when and if Brandeis resigned, that he felt a genuine political obligation to choose someone from west of the Mississippi to counterbalance a bench now entirely made up of Easterners. He then asked Frankfurter—who assured F.D.R. that he "understood perfectly"—to prepare dossiers on prospective candidates from the desired area;[31] the latter included Dean Wiley B. Rutledge of the University of Iowa—destined to be appointed to the Court in 1943. Roosevelt made no secret of his stated geographic intentions, which, in turn, set into motion a veritable ground swell for Frankfurter, which was reminiscent of the events surrounding Hoover's nomination of Cardozo. Unlike Cardozo, however, F.F. actively promoted his own candidacy, with F.D.R.'s brain-trusters Benjamin Cohen and Thomas Corcoran serving as F.F.'s almost daily advocates with the President. The fifty-six-year-old Frankfurter was a brilliant scholar and teacher (he had taught for twenty-five years at the Harvard Law School); a superb lawyer; an effective, shrewd administrator; a connoisseur of personnel; a powerful advocate of the underdog; and a highly effective public servant with considerable experience in federal and state government. He had become a close Presidential adviser and confidant in the evolving New Deal; he had aided in the drafting of legislation; and he had recommended many able young appointees to the Roosevelt Administration—often derisively referred to as "Felix's Happy Hot Dogs" because of their alleged political coloration as well as their fealty to Frankfurter.

The pressure on F.D.R. to designate Professor Frankfurter became intense: his closest personal and political advisers, such as his Solicitor General, Robert H. Jackson; his Secretary of the Interior, Harold L. Ickes; his Man Friday, Harry Hopkins; his friend and political ally, Senator George Norris; and perhaps most persuasively, Justice Stone, all implored the President to place excellence over geography. Jackson scored points by urging F.D.R. to choose the peppery constitutional expert, if for no other reason than naming "someone who can interpret [the Constitution] with scholarship and with sufficient assurance to face Chief Justice Hughes in conference and hold his own in discussion."[32] The President yielded, announcing to his entourage that "there isn't anybody in the West . . . who is of sufficient stature."[33]

Frankfurter himself recorded that at 7:00 P.M. on January 4, 1939, while he was in his B.V.D.s, late to receive a dinner guest, the phone rang in his study, "and there was the ebullient, the exuberant, resilient, warmth-enveloping voice of the President of the United States [whom F.F. adored] 'Hello. How are you?' " Then, after asking about Frankfurter's wife, Marion (in 1919 the two had been married by then New York Court of Appeals Judge Benjamin N. Cardozo), F.D.R. told him not once, but several times: "You know, I told you I don't want to appoint you to the Supreme Court of the United States. . . . I mean it. . . . I can't. . . . I mean this. I mean this. I don't want to appoint you. . . . I just don't want to appoint you. . . . I told you I can't name you." Underwear-clad, and eager to go down to dinner–Marion calling repeatedly from downstairs, asking F.F. to "hurry up. You are always late!"–Frankfurter agreed again and again with his caller, becoming more and more exasperated. He was hardly prepared for the President's next words: "But wherever I turn, wherever I turn and to whomever I talk that matters to me, I am made to realize that you are the only person fit to succeed Holmes and Cardozo." Adding: "But unless you give me an insurmountable objection I'm going to send your name in for the Court tomorrow at twelve o'clock." The overwhelmed Frankfurter replied softly, "All I can say is that I wish my mother were alive."[34] Senate confirmation, by unanimous voice vote, came twelve days later, after some protracted opposition by Senator Pat McCarran (D.-Nev.), who tried to link the nominee with communism.

Senator McCarran need not have worried. Frankfurter was a

native of Vienna, but he loved his adopted country and its institutions as few men did. This longtime champion of the poor, the oppressed, the underdog, the persecuted had but one aim: to make America an even better place to live for an even greater number of people. A passionate believer in the democratic process with an abiding regard for the British concept of legislative supremacy, he would dedicate his twenty-three years on the Court to the proposition that the people should govern, but that it was up to their elected representatives in the legislature, not to the appointed judiciary, to make laws. Thus, Frankfurter became increasingly known as an articulate and persuasive advocate of judicial abnegation in favor of legislative action. "When in doubt, don't" became the Frankfurter maxim. So dedicated was he to the principle of judicial restraint that Fred Rodell referred to him sarcastically as "the Supreme Court's Emily Post."[35] Walton Hamilton characterized him as "weaving crochet patches of legalism on the fingers of the case."[36] Frankfurter's jurisprudential philosophy of course enabled him to back the New Deal's program to the hilt—enacted as it was by the people's duly chosen representatives. F.D.R. was pleased indeed. In social and economic legislation Frankfurter could, thus, predictably be found with the other Justices appointed by Roosevelt. But when it came to the interpretation of the Bill of Rights, he and Black and the other "libertarian activists" (especially Douglas, Murphy, and Wiley Rutledge) would often part company—for Frankfurter brought the same principled sense of judicial restraint to legislation concerning human rights as he did to legislation concerning economic-proprietarian issues. He could be a powerful spokesman on behalf of due process of law: as the author for the unanimous Court in *Rochin* v. *California* (1952),[37] he delivered a magnificent lecture to Los Angeles County police authorities on the requirements of procedural due process. He accorded the Fourth Amendment's safeguards against "unreasonable searches and seizures" a place second to none in the Bill of Rights—in fact, more so than did Black. Yet this champion of human freedom, who had fought so hard to save Sacco and Vanzetti, stood like Canute against his *personal* convictions when it came to his role as a jurist. Thus, notwithstanding his abhorrence of capital punishment, he could not bring himself to provide the necessary fifth vote to save Willie Francis, a teenage Louisiana black, from a second trip to the electric chair (the malfunctioning instrument had failed to do its grim job the first time).[38] Frankfurter felt bound by what he viewed as the commands of the Federalist division of powers—in spite of his outcry to Justice Burton, whose strong dissenting opinion he had seen: "I have to hold on to myself not to reach your result."[39] Yet extrajudicially,[40] he had used all of his considerable influence—unsuccessfully—in trying through powerful friends to persuade the governor to commute Willie's sentence.

Frankfurter's scrupulous adherence to his duty as a judge *qua* judge, despite his personal commitments, is perhaps even better illustrated by his most famous dissenting opinion in a civil liberties case. It came in 1943 when a 6:3 Court, overruling an earlier Frankfurter opinion,[41] declared unconstitutional a West Virginia statute that compelled school children to salute the flag as a daily exercise.[42] Frankfurter of course would not have voted for such a law had he been a legislator because it compelled saluting even by those, like the Jehovah's Witnesses, who regarded the act as paying homage to a graven image. But as a jurist he could not bring himself to join the majority opinion that the compulsory salute constituted an unconstitutional invasion of the free exercise of religion and freedom of expression guaranteed by Amendments One and Fourteen:

> One who belongs to the most vilified and persecuted minority in history is not likely to be insensible to the freedoms guaranteed by our Constitution. Were my purely personal attitude relevant I should whole-heartedly associate myself with the general libertarian view in the Court's opinion, representing as they do the thought and action of a lifetime. But as judges we are neither Jew, nor Gentile, neither Catholic nor agnostic. We owe equal attachment to the Constitution and are equally bound by our judicial obligations whether we derive our citizenship from the earliest or the latest immigrants to these shores. As a member of this Court I am not justified in writing my private notions of policy into the Constitution, no matter how deeply I may cherish them or how mischievous I may deem their disregard. . . .[43]

Frankfurter's conception of the judicial function is also illustrated well by his continuing battle, successful until the momentous 1962 *Baker* v. *Carr*[44] reapportionment-redistricting decision, against the Court's dealing with "political questions." In an impassioned sixty-eight-page dissenting opinion, joined by his colleague-ally-disciple, John Marshall Harlan II, he warned the Court that it was about to enter a "mathematical quagmire," that it must stay out of such "a political thicket." He further admonished the majority of six: "There is not under our Constitution a judicial remedy for every political mischief. In a democratic society like ours, relief must come through an aroused popular conscience that sears the conscience of the people's representatives."[45] But, asked his opponents tellingly, what happens when there are no electoral channels open to "sear" that conscience?

Felix Frankfurter died on February 22, 1965, ill health having dictated his retirement three years earlier at the age of eighty. A great jurist in defeat as well as victory, he left a major imprint on the American scene, documented in some 750 written opinions. In a memorial editorial the *New York Times* summed up eloquently: "As a philosopher and scholar of the law, a judicial craftsman, a master of prose style and a formative influence on a generation of American lawyers and public officials, Felix Frankfurter was a major shaper of the history of his age."[46] And dozens of newspapers ended their obituaries with the above-quoted sentences from his *Baker* v. *Carr* dissenting opinion.

Four weeks after President Roosevelt had nominated Frankfurter, Justice Louis D. Brandeis retired after twenty-three years on the Court. F.D.R. thus had his fourth vacancy in little more than three and one-half years. How matters had changed since those first frustrating, appointment-barren four and one-half years! The President still wanted a Westerner, and his youthful Chairman of the Securities and Exchange Commission (S.E.C.), William O. Douglas, born in Otter Tail County, Minnesota, and raised in Yakima, Washington, was a likely candidate. He was an F.D.R. favorite and an "insider," on whom the President had often called for speechwriting duties and advice. But Douglas had spent half of his forty years in New York (Columbia Law School), in New Haven, Connecticut (Yale Law School Faculty), and in Washington, D.C. (governmental service), and Roosevelt viewed him as two-thirds Easterner. He had publicly promised a "true Westerner"–with Wiley B. Rutledge, now on the lower federal bench, again being mentioned–and, besides, the Court *was* in his corner, although perhaps not by a comfortable margin. Thus, he took no immediate action. Yet pressure began to build from his close advisers and from Brandeis, strongly urging F.D.R. to nominate Douglas. The latter, after all, was personally as well as philosophically close to Brandeis on social, economic, political, and constitutional policy; he was an ardent and articulate New Dealer; he believed that the law had to be alive to the demands of the times; he had an outstanding legal mind; he was a proved expert in the intricacies of public finance and corporation problems. Further persuasion came with a press conference dramatically called by Senator William Borah of Idaho–now ranking member of the Senate Judiciary Committee–during which he "claimed" Douglas as "one of the West's finest and brightest sons."[47] F.D.R., now convinced–Douglas himself believed that it was Brandeis's insistent support that became ultimately decisive with the President[48]–summoned Douglas from the ninth hole on the Manor Country Club golf course, where he was playing with some S.E.C. associates. The date was Sunday, March 19, 1939, and the summons was for "straight away" to the Oval Office.

Douglas feared that the hearty "I have a new job for you, Bill . . . a mean job, a dirty job, a thankless job" greeting F.D.R. extended to him was the vacant chairmanship of the Federal Communications Commission. It was a post he did not want, especially because he had been offered the deanship at the Yale School of Law as of that June. "The job," the radiantly bemused President continued, is "a job you won't like . . . a job you'll detest. . . . This job is something like being in jail." Enjoying Douglas's bewilderment hugely, the President finally beamed broadly and concluded: "Tomorrow I am sending your name to the Senate as Louis Brandeis' successor."[49] Two weeks later, Douglas was confirmed promptly by a vote of 62:4–at forty the youngest appointee since Justice Joseph Story in 1811. Ironically, the four no votes, cast by Republican Senators Gerald P. Nye (North Dakota), Lynn J. Frazier (North Dakota), Clyde M. Reed (Kansas), and Henry Cabot Lodge, Jr. (Massachusetts), categorized Douglas as a "reactionary tool of Wall Street!"[50]

For thirty-six and one-half years—a record not likely soon, if ever, to be broken—the feisty, determined, outspoken judicial activist for liberal causes and underdog individuals remained a highly visible member of the Court, notwithstanding a pacemaker in his chest, a fourth wife fifty years his junior, and gradually increasing circulatory difficulties. With great reluctance he bowed to the inevitable and, felled by a crippling stroke, confined to a wheelchair, a mere shadow of his former rugged self, he retired late in 1975. He had authored 1306 opinions: majority (550), concurring (173), and dissenting (583), a total also hardly likely to be overturned readily. Like Chief Justice Taft, he hated to leave his beloved seat—and, in a pathetic, doomed move, attempted to have Chief Justice Burger place a tenth chair on the high bench to be occupied by retired Justice William O. Douglas. Death came in 1980.

Douglas, of whom it was said with considerable veracity that he endeavored to alter the Supreme Court building's frontal emblem-inscription from "Equal Justice Under Law" to "Justice at Any Cost," compiled a civil liberties record on the bench second to none: in close to 96 percent of all cases involving line-drawing between the rights of the individual and those of society, he sided with the former. The Douglas human rights posture, thus, would not be checked by the verbiage of the Constitution: if that document and its Bill of Rights did not provide the kind of protection for the individual Douglas deemed necessary to bring about equal justice under law as he perceived it, well, he would find it—as he did in his famed, highly controversial precedent-setting "privacy" discovery opinion in the *Connecticut Birth Control Case* of 1965, in "*penumbras,* formed by emanations from those guarantees of the Bill of Rights that help give them life and substance."[51] It was *the* opinion that became midwife to the rationale of the momentous *Abortion Cases* decision in 1973.[52] Another testimonial to his ingenuity—although unsuccessful—was his attempt to obtain standing-to-sue status for rivers, trees, and mountains![53] Often embattled off as well as on the Court, this colorful and brilliant scholar eloquently articulated his posture again and again—in cases at law as well as from the lecture podium, in books as well as journals, including *Playboy* magazine. As he put it on one occasion: "The American Government is premised on the theory that if the mind of man is to be free, his ideas, his beliefs, his ideology, his philosophy must be placed beyond the reach of government."[54] Although unquestionably doctrinaire, result oriented, and defiantly disdainful of judicial self-restraint, Douglas deserves the "near great" rating of the Court experts, just as did his jurisprudential opposites Field and Sutherland.

No hesitation, whatever, attended F.D.R.'s filling of his fifth vacancy. On November 16, 1939, Pierce Butler, one of the two remaining "Four Horsemen," died after seventeen years on the Court. On the same morning, the President informed Frank Murphy, his forty-six-year-old Attorney General, that he was his choice to succeed the New Deal's nemesis. Murphy at first demurred, feeling "utterly inadequate,"[55] but he ultimately accepted and was officially nominated on January 4, 1940. The Senate confirmed him a few days later. The tall, gaunt Murphy was in many ways a "natural" for the position. Like Butler, he was a Midwesterner and a good Irish Catholic of middle-class origin. Widely known as a crusading New Deal liberal, he had served in the 1920s as a U.S. Assistant Attorney and as a Detroit judge—a post he held until, successfully courting the support of the numerous Irish and black citizens, he was elected mayor of Detroit in 1929. During the Depression, which affected the Motor City severely, Murphy became a strong and articulate advocate of federal aid. After Roosevelt's election in 1932, for which he worked tirelessly, Murphy was chosen president of the Conference of Mayors and later was appointed governor of the Philippines by F.D.R. In 1936 Murphy gave up that post not only to aid the Presidential campaign but to run (successfully) for the governorship of Michigan, and thus aid the national ticket in securing a key industrial state.

Two years later Murphy lost his bid for reelection, and Roosevelt appointed him his Attorney General. The repeated suggestions that Murphy was later "kicked upstairs" to the Court from the Justice Department may well hold some truth, but F.D.R. might have appointed Murphy anyway, if perhaps not quite so soon. Murphy, not an interested or conscientious administrator, paid little heed to the *modus operandi* of his department; he placed heavy emphasis on antitrust litigation, neglecting such crucial areas as internal revenue; and, like many Attorneys General before and after him, he did not get along well with the powerful head of the F.B.I., J. Edgar Hoover. In view of Murphy's other qualifications, F.D.R. quite conceivably decided to expedite his promotion and to give the Attorney Generalship to the man who was supposed to get it in the first place, Solicitor General Robert H. Jackson. "Bob, I suppose you know that you're to come into this office." Murphy had told Jackson, "that I am here only temporarily."[56]

Frank Murphy was cut down by a fatal heart attack little more than nine years later. During that relatively brief period of time he established himself as not only 100 percent loyal to the New Deal, but as one of the Court's most advanced civil libertarians, outscoring all others in his generous support of individual rights and claims. He alone among the libertarian bloc of Black, Douglas, and Rutledge dissented (together with Justices Roberts and Jackson) from the 1944 landmark decision of *Korematsu* v. *United States* written by Black,[57] which upheld the wartime evacuation from the West Coast of more than 110,000 Japanese-Americans, of whom three-quarters were American-born citizens. In his emotion-charged opinion,[58] Murphy assailed the evacuation program as one that "goes over the 'very brink of constitutional power' and falls into the ugly abyss of racism." Pronouncing it a flagrant violation of due process of law, he angrily and sarcastically characterized the military order, here sanctioned by the Court, as "based upon an erroneous assumption of racial guilt" and justified upon "questionable racial and sociological grounds not ordinarily within the realm of expert military judgment. . . ." And once again it was Murphy who, with Rutledge by his side, wanted to strike down as unconstitutional the military trial and conviction of Japanese General Yamashita, Commanding General of the Japanese army group that had wrought such havoc in the Philippines. Black and Douglas were with the majority opinion by Chief Justice Stone in that 1946 decision,[59] but Murphy argued in defeat that the Court's failure to extend the guarantees of the Fifth and Sixth amendments to General Yamashita was crassly unconstitutional and would hinder the "reconciliation necessary to a peaceful world."[60]

Murphy would all but inevitably side with the underdog—were he an enemy alien, a rank offender at the bar of criminal justice, or a member of a beleaguered religious sect. In *Adamson* v. *California* (1947),[61] with Rutledge concurring, he articulated the doctrine that if the specific provisions of the Bill of Rights did not provide sufficient safeguard against abusive governmental action, "constitutional condemnation in terms of a lack of due process despite the absence of a specific provision in the Bill of Rights" would be warranted. To Black—the dean of civil libertarians—who also dissented in that landmark case (but for different reasons), the Murphy and Rutledge posture was an obvious invocation of natural law, which he regarded as an "incongruous excrescence on our Constitution."[62] Very likely because his concerns and productivity on the Court were essentially one-dimensional, no matter how noble and hortatory, Murphy was accorded, with considerable justice, only an "average" rating by the Court watchers. Yet he was a major influence in the spectrum that concerned him most—man's freedom and dignity.

The last of the "Four Horsemen," and probably the most tenacious and reactionary member, announced his retirement in 1941, lamenting that he had tried to protect the country, but that "any country that elects Roosevelt three times deserves no protection."[63] James Clark McReynolds had been on the Court for twenty-seven years, was nearing eighty, and simply decided that there was no point in staying on—F.D.R. heartily agreed! In 1946 McReynolds died as he had lived—alone and embittered. Yet that strange, unhappy, cantankerous, bigoted man's will revealed astonishingly that not only had he quietly adopted thirty-three young children victimized by the Nazi blitz in Europe, but he bequeathed the majority of his estate to local charities, including nearly $100,000 for the Children's Hospital in Washington, D.C., and the Salvation Army.[64] Most Court observers believed that the President would now turn to his Attorney General, but Bob Jackson had been in office scarcely a year, and Roosevelt felt he could not now spare him. Moreover, many of his most influential party leaders, including Senators Alben W. Barkley of Kentucky, Pat Harrison of Mississippi, and Carter Glass of Virginia, were pushing hard for F.D.R.'s political and personal ally, Senator James F. Byrnes of South Carolina, who had often and prominently been mentioned as a possible candidate and who held a barrelful of I.O.U.s for loyal Democratic party service. The President himself had mentioned the Court to Byrnes on sundry occasions but, because of Byrnes's role as an influential, articulate, and shrewd Administration stalwart in the Senate, he hesitated to move him—especially because he no longer had to worry about the Court's posture on his programs. Byrnes was unquestionably more conservative than any of the other members of the Court F.D.R. had appointed, but the President was not genuinely concerned on that score—the Court was now safely "pro-New Deal" and "pro-libertarian." What finally determined Byrnes's selection was his failure to receive the Vice Presidential nomination in the Democratic Convention of 1940. Byrnes, who himself had harbored Presidential ambitions, but had staunchly supported F.D.R. for a third term, was grievously disappointed. The President was eager to please his loyal lieutenant, and he responded to Senator Glass's entreaties: "Of course, I will appoint him. . . . He is just as much my friend as yours—I wanted him to be my running mate in 1940. . . . My only regret in appointing him is that I need him so much in the Senate."[65] And appoint him he did—but only after delaying for close to five months because of crucial pending legislation in the Senate. On June 12, 1941, Byrnes's colleagues proudly confirmed him unanimously and without reference to the Judiciary Committee. Wesley McCune, a chronicler of the Roosevelt Court, reported that F.D.R. remarked during Byrnes's swearing-in ceremony:

> . . . He wished he were Solomon and could halve Jimmy Byrnes, keeping one half in the Senate and the other half on the Court. At that moment, he was losing the smoothest, most effec-

tive worker he had ever had in the Senate, at the same time acquiring an unknown quantity for his Court.[66]

The sixty-two-year-old Byrnes—who would live on for another three decades, most of it in a variety of federal and state governmental posts—had a remarkable record of governmental experience. After brief executive and judicial service in his native South Carolina, he served seven terms in the U.S. House of Representatives and two in the Senate. He had first met F.D.R. when the latter was governor-elect of New York; the two men had formed a lasting political and personal alliance. Byrnes gave important support to Roosevelt in the 1932 Presidential election, and he went on to become one of his most trusted advisers. An invaluable leader in the Senate, he even backed the Court-packing bill. And the President could count on him fully in such vital legislation as selective service and lend-lease.

Jimmy Byrnes lasted for little more than a year on the Court: a man of action, a doer, and a planner, he was not comfortable as a jurist. Thus, in the fall of 1942, when Roosevelt asked him to step down to assume the post of "Assistant President for Economic Affairs," he readily assented—he was delighted to be able to return to the active political arena. With the possible exception of his authorship of a case propounding the right of free interstate travel,[67] he left no mark on the Court, whose observers have rated him a "failure"—a grossly unfair judgment in view of the brevity of his membership.

On June 2, 1941, ten days before the Byrnes confirmation, the great Charles Evans Hughes, in his eightieth year, advised F.D.R. of his intention to retire on July 1. He had served admirably for eleven difficult years. His declining health dictated an earlier withdrawal, yet he wanted to see a replacement for the McReynolds vacancy before creating a new one. Roosevelt, with five of his appointees on the high bench and the sixth one certain to be approved by the Senate, felt no pressure to nominate a successor quickly, especially as the Court was about to adjourn until October. But Hughes and his colleagues strongly implored F.D.R. not to delay, and the President acquiesced. For some time he had been pondering a successor to Hughes, and it was widely assumed that his choice lay between two eminent lawyers: Associate Justice Harlan F. Stone and Attorney General Robert H. Jackson.

F.D.R.'s heart was clearly with Jackson, a New Deal loyalist of long standing who had fought with him all the way. Moreover, he had more than once mentioned the Chief Justiceship to Jackson, who had made clear to his President that he wanted the position very much. Still, F.D.R. hesitated—being acutely aware that a professional ground swell was about to arise for Stone. He called Hughes to the White House to discuss his successor; the retiring Chief immediately volunteered that "Stone's record gave him first claim on the honor."[68] Hughes also approved Jackson's candidacy but stuck to his preference, based on Stone's judicial performance. Roosevelt later conferred with Justice Frankfurter and asked him point-blank which of the two men he would prefer as Chief Justice. Wishing F.D.R. had not asked that question, Frankfurter—never at a loss for words—replied:

> On personal grounds I'd prefer Bob. While I've known Stone longer and our relations are excellent and happy, I feel closer friendship with Bob. But from the national interest I am bound to say that there is no reason for preferring Bob to Stone—quite the contrary. Stone is senior and qualified professionally to be C.J. But for me the decisive consideration, considering the fact that Stone is qualified, is that Bob is of your personal and political family, as it were, while Stone is a Republican. . . . when war does come, the country should feel you are a national, the Nation's President, and not a partisan President. Few things would contribute as much to confidence in you as a national and not a partisan President than for you to name a Republican, who has the profession's confidence, as Chief Justice.[69]

The President did not commit himself, but Frankfurter was fairly confident that the choice would be Stone, and he so informed his fellow Associate Justice. A few days later F.D.R. discussed the matter with Jackson, explained the persuasiveness of Frankfurter's logic, and again assured his Attorney General that he would send him to the Court. Jackson concurred fully with Frankfurter and received the President's permission to advise Stone himself. Not many years later, after he had become a member of the Court, Jackson would write that the need for judicial leadership and the "desirability for a symbol of stability as well as progress" were evidently the reasons for the initially Coolidge-appointed Stone's elevation "in the interest of [the fostering of the] judiciary as an institution."[70]

A nationwide chorus of praise and acclaim greeted Stone's nomination on June 12, 1941. The press was ecstatic, the judiciary delighted, the intellectual community reassured, Congress happy. When the nomination officially reached the floor of the Senate on June 27, he was confirmed *viva voce* without a single objection.

Harlan Fiske Stone was almost sixty-nine when he succeeded Hughes in the center chair. He would live only for not quite five years, but—although those years proved far less satisfactory, less happy than his sixteen as Associate Justice—they did not deter the experts from ranking him as one of the great jurists on the highest bench. Yet he was clearly more comfortable in being a member of the team than in leading it. Not a first-rate administrator like Taft, not a skillful and disciplinary Court-master like Hughes, not a ruthless craftsman like Marshall, not so persuasive as Taney, not so innovative *cum* activist as Warren, Stone was reluctant to crack down and averse to do battle with warring factions, contributing to a marked divisiveness on the Court during his Chief Justiceship, led by the prolonged and nasty feud between Black and Jackson. Moreover, he really disdained the routine of administrative detail that he now found incumbent on him. Yet there were precious few who understood and followed the commands and restraints of the Constitution, who supported the essence of limited government, who enhanced the concept of popular government under law, who furthered respect for the Bill of Rights as fully as Stone did.

As he could not be groom Robert H. Jackson would be best man, and it was to no one's surprise that the forty-nine-year-old Attorney General was selected to fill the vacancy created by the Stone promotion. His appointment took a while longer to be approved than had been anticipated, chiefly because of the opposition of Senator Millard E. Tydings (D.-Md.), who was unhappy with Jackson ever since he had refused to prosecute columnist Drew Pearson for publishing an alleged libel against the powerful and proud legislator. But the Judiciary Committee unanimously approved Jackson after but a few minutes' deliberation, and the Senate confirmed him on July 11 with only Tydings dissenting.

Jackson was eminently qualified to serve on the Court. Although he had not had a single day of judicial experience and although his formal legal training had been meager indeed (he passed the New York bar exams without having graduated from law school), he achieved a reputation as a brilliant private and public lawyer in upstate New York, where he had built a lucrative practice and become active in Democratic politics. He attained early national exposure as a close ally of Roosevelt when the latter was governor of New York, and as an effective campaigner for him at the Democratic National Convention as well as during the election of 1932. Initially he refused to follow his friend and idol to Washington, but ultimately he yielded, accepting Roosevelt's appointment as General Counsel of the Bureau of Internal Revenue. A vigorous defender of and spokesman for the New Deal programs (including the Court-packing scheme), Jackson began a rapid climb through sundry posts, notably in the Department of Justice. Beginning as an Assistant Attorney General in the Antitrust Division, he succeeded to the Solicitor Generalship, where he did so well in his role as the "Government's Lawyer" that Justice Brandeis was moved to comment that "Jackson should be Solicitor General for life,"[71] and then to the Attorney Generalship. In his posts he combined hard work and expertise with persuasiveness, charm, and a superb, elegant command of English.

The Court historians have recognized Jackson's achievements as "near great." But his tenure was not an entirely happy one. He had really wanted to be Chief Justice; tragically his path was blocked in considerable measure by a doctrinal and personal feud with Hugo Black. Largely because of Jackson's strong feelings, some of their controversy was carried on in public–harming Jackson far more than Black and exacerbating Chief Justice Stone's problems in maintaining a harmonious Court. Jackson's acceptance of President Truman's request in 1945 to become the U.S. Chief

Prosecutor at the Nürnberg Nazi War Crimes Trials, and his subsequent absence from the Court for an entire term, compounded his difficulties with his colleagues—not to mention the business of the Court, which had to operate with eight Justices and the attendant all-too-present danger of 4:4 tie votes. Jackson was brilliant at Nürnberg, yet he returned from the trials a different man: the once libertarian judicial activist,[72] who had so often sided with Black, Douglas, Murphy, and Rutledge, had become profoundly cautious, a markedly narrow interpreter of the Bill of Rights. He now more often than not sided with the Frankfurter wing of the Court, which took a generally restrictive stand in matters affecting national security and state criminal-justice procedures.[73] This intriguing metamorphosis may well have resulted from his Nürnberg experiences—his firsthand perception of the melancholy events resulting in the destruction of the Weimar Republic and the rise of Nazism. It was his conclusive judgment that one of the major contributory factors was the failure of the Weimer government to crack down on radical dissenters and extremist groups—which is why he exhorted his colleagues in his famous *Terminiello* dissent in 1949 that they beware lest they "convert the constitutional Bill of Rights into a suicide pact."[74]

Yet he remained an apostle of judicial restraint in the economic-proprietarian sphere, supporting governmental authority to regulate and thus remaining true to his basic New Deal commitments. And even if there were no other justification for holding Jackson in high esteem as a jurist, his magnificent prose—second in beauty and clarity perhaps only to that of Cardozo—has earned him the nation's high regard and gratitude. Who could ever forget the haunting beauty of his phrases, such as those in his memorable opinion striking down the West Virginia flag salute in 1943? "Those who begin coercive elimination of dissent," he warned his countrymen, "soon find themselves exterminating dissenters. Compulsory unification of opinion achieves only the unanimity of the graveyard." And elaborating:

> If there is any fixed star in our constitutional constellation, it is that no official, high or petty, can prescribe what shall be orthodox in politics, nationalism, religion, or other matters of opinion

> or force citizens to confess by word or act their faith therein. . . . The very purpose of a Bill of Rights was to withdraw certain subjects from the vicissitudes of political controversy, to place them beyond the reach of majorities and officials and to establish them as legal principles to be applied by the Courts. One's right to life, liberty, and property, to free speech, a free press, freedom of worship and assembly, and other fundamental rights may not be submitted to vote; they depend on the outcome of no elections.[75]

On October 9, 1954, untimely death came to Robert Jackson. That May he had still participated in the Court's unanimously decided, momentous *Public School Desegregation Cases*.[76] In some ways he died a bitter and disappointed man—never having attained the coveted Court leadership—but he left a legacy as "America's Advocate."[77]

Roosevelt had now appointed eight Justices in less than four years. Barring unforeseeable illnesses or resignations, that certainly would be the end of the line. Yet in October 1942 came Justice Byrnes's resignation from the Court and the ninth vacancy! This time there was no obvious successor, no obvious political debt to be paid. Such major New Deal supporters as Black, Reed, Frankfurter, Douglas, Murphy, Jackson, and Byrnes had been sent to the Court; Francis Biddle, the able Attorney General, was not interested; others, widely mentioned, were from the East or South: Senator Alben W. Barkley, Solicitor General Charles Fahy, Judge John J. Parker of the U.S. Court of Appeals for the Fourth Circuit, and Dean Acheson. At last F.D.R. might indulge his desire to nominate someone from west of the Mississippi. There was no rush as far as he was concerned, and he asked Biddle to look around carefully for a likely candidate. The ultimate nominee, pressed on the Administration by Biddle as well as by such allies as Senator Norris and Justices Murphy and Douglas, was Wiley B. Rutledge. F.F. and Stone still pleaded for the venerable Learned Hand's elevation (F.F. with not uncharacteristic overkill). Twenty people, F.D.R. told Douglas, had told him in a single day to appoint Hand: "Twenty, and every one a messenger from Felix Frankfurter."[78] Particularly backed by the distinguished *Des Moines Register* and *Chicago Sun* journalist Irving Brant, Rutledge was a rather "marginal" Westerner, but with more claims to that region than Douglas had held. Judge of the United States Court of Appeals for the District of Columbia, Wiley Rutledge was the only Roosevelt appointee with federal judicial experience (four years) and one of only three with *any* judicial background–the other two being Black and Murphy. F.D.R. was not personally acquainted with Rutledge, although he had seriously considered appointing him to the 1938 Cardozo vacancy, which ultimately went to Frankfurter, and the 1939 Brandeis one, which went to Douglas. But after chatting with him at the White House, and being assured by Biddle that the candidate was a *bona fide* libertarian, an early and solid New Dealer who had ardently championed the Court-packing plan, and a judge whose opinions demonstrated a solid commitment to the Presidential philosophy, F.D.R. nominated him in February 1943. "Wiley," he quipped contentedly, "you have geography!"[79] Confirmation came readily without a formal roll call.

Born in Kentucky, brought up there and in North Carolina and Tennessee, schooled in Tennessee and Wisconsin, Rutledge had taught and worked in the public school systems of Colorado, Indiana, and New Mexico before becoming a loved and respected Professor of Law at the University of Colorado (his *alma mater*), Professor of Law and Dean at Washington University in St. Louis, and Dean at the University of Iowa's School of Law. In 1939 he was appointed to the federal bench. Once he attained it, Rutledge, who genuinely loved people of all walks of life, promptly demonstrated his firm libertarian colors. Indeed, his score in behalf of individual claims against alleged violations by government was higher than any of his colleagues' (followed closely by Murphy's). Thus, it was Rutledge who joined Murphy's attempted generous extensions of civil liberty safeguards *beyond* the Constitution's verbiage when he concurred in the latter's famed dissenting opinion in *Adamson* v. *California* in 1947:

> I agree that the specific guarantees of the Bill of Rights should be carried over intact into the first section of the Fourteenth Amendment. But I am not prepared to say that the latter is entirely and necessarily limited by the Bill of Rights. *Occasions may arise where a proceeding falls so far short of conforming*

to fundamental standards of procedure as to warrant constitutional condemnation in terms of lack of due process despite the absence of specific provisions in the Bill of Rights.[80]

During his scant six and one-half years on the bench Rutledge's scholarship, his mastery of the law, his articulate explication of difficult issues, and his prodigious workmanship combined to establish him as a jurist who well earned the "near great" rating that the Court experts bestowed on him. The years of Rutledge's tenure saw the Court at its libertarian apogee; after his death it would not return to a similar posture until the heyday of the Warren Court.

Rutledge left a proud record, highlighted by some celebrated dissenting opinions, such as those for *In re Yamashita* and *Everson* v. *Board of Education of Ewing Township*. The former decision upheld 7:2 Japanese General Tomoyuki Yamashita's summary military commission conviction for violating the rules of war. The latter sanctioned 5:4 state-subsidized transportation of parochial as well as public school students. Rutledge regarded these opinions as his best. Thus, he admonished the Stone-led majority in *Yamashita* that it "is not in our tradition for anyone to be charged with crime which is defined after his conduct, alleged to be criminal, has taken place; or in language not sufficient to inform him of the nature of the offense or to enable him to make defense. Mass guilt we do not impute to individuals. . . ."[81] And, in *Everson,* before appending Madison's "Memorial and Remonstrance Against Religious Assessment," Rutledge warned the Black-led majority: "Like St. Paul's freedom, religious liberty with a great price must be bought. And for those who exercise it most fully, by insisting upon religious education for their children mixed with secular, by the terms of our Constitution the price is greater than for others."[82] When "this gentle but courageous man," as Justice Black observed,[83] succumbed to a cerebral hemorrhage at the age of fifty-five while vacationing in Maine in September 1949, an era came to an end. Wiley Rutledge had been the last Roosevelt appointee: the three (Burton, Vinson, and Clark) President Truman would send to the Court between F.D.R.'s and Rutledge's death were of a different philosophical and jurisprudential stripe indeed; so would be Rutledge's replacement, Sherman Minton.

When asked how he had felt when Mrs. Roosevelt informed him that afternoon of April 12, 1945, in her White House study that he was now the President, Harry S Truman responded, "Did you ever have a load of hay fall on you?"[84] Defying all predictions, Truman went on to become an assertive, powerful, and successful leader—at least in foreign affairs. He played a significant part in forging post-World War II American foreign policy, notably with regard to the initial combat use of the atomic bomb, the Marshall Plan, "Point Four," the Greece-Turkey Truman Doctrine, the North Atlantic Treaty Organization, the Berlin Airlift, the Korean War. To the surprise of many observers, the President-watchers have accorded him a "near great" rating, just below Jackson, Theodore Roosevelt, and Polk and just above John Adams and Cleveland.

Given his miserable relations with Congress—and they were just that, whether it was controlled by his own or by the Republican party—and his generally low public image, that rating may appear to be on the generous side. Yet the plain, although hardly plain-spoken, forthright man from Missouri, who knew and appreciated history as few, if any, other executives did, gradually won the grudging admiration and even affection of many of his countrymen. By 1948 he had won enough support to capture the election—an astounding victory in the face of insurmountable odds and in defiance of all major pollsters—over the urbane and experienced Thomas E. Dewey. Truman's warmth, folksiness, and simplicity atoned for much of his public coarseness and the all-but-impossible task of following in the footsteps of Franklin D. Roosevelt. Yet he showed a keen awareness of his country's needs and a toughness about first constitutional principles—as evinced by his summary sacking of that ideal of the American Center and Right, General of the Army Douglas MacArthur, when the latter began to assume too much civilian and military authority. Harry Truman knew how to make the big decisions.

Unfortunately, he was also given to extravagant notions of loyalty that prompted him to make many a "crony" appointment—not excluding those he was enabled to make to the Supreme Court. There were four, and all were old buddies: Harold H. Burton, a fellow U.S. Senator (R.-Ohio) and member of the highly effective Truman War Investigation Committee, which had catapulted the then-Senator from Missouri to national approbation and prominence; Fred M. Vinson, longtime legislative and executive ally; Tom C. Clark, the President's Attorney General and confidant; and Sherman Minton, another former Senatorial colleague (D.-Ind.) and friend. With the possible exception of Clark, whose almost eighteen years of service on the Court have often been underestimated, it was a mediocre group. The Court experts, in fact, have rated Burton, Vinson, and Minton among the eight "failures" to sit on the Court (Clark they rated as average). No serious Court observer or student has challenged that assessment in Minton's case, but a good many have challenged the ratings of Burton and Vinson. No one familiar with the record, however, has ever regarded either of the latter as being entitled to anything higher than "below average" or at best "average." Truman's appointments may have been undistinguished, but they assuredly did not represent a departure from his criteria for the post: they had all held public office; they were his political, professional, and personal friends; he understood them; he liked them; he liked their politics. Loyal to a fault, he wanted to reward them, and he did. That he was given a public roasting in almost every instance bothered him not one whit. He had done what he deemed appropriate; so, as he wondrously always managed to do where others fretted and worried, he slept the peace of the confident! Occasionally his appointees failed to support him: in the famed *Steel Seizure Case* of 1952[85] Truman lost Burton and Clark's votes and, thus, the decision–which prompted a now-famed intemperate public outburst by the angry President.[86] His appointees, however, generaly sided with his views of government and Constitution, views that were strongly weighted in favor of governmental regulatory authority and internal security.

The first Truman appointment was fifty-seven-year-old Republican Senator from Ohio Harold Hitz Burton, who succeeded to the seat vacated in July 1945 by Justice Owen J. Roberts. Burton's selection, which was unanimously approved by his Senatorial colleagues, was undoubtedly strongly motivated by personal and political kinship, but it would be unjust to label it only that. True, Burton and Truman had often championed similar causes in the Senate, and Burton had served well and closely with Truman when the latter headed the highly successful Special Senate Committee to Investigate the National Defense Program (Truman War Investigation Committee) in the early 1940s. But there were other, less personal, reasons for the choice. Foremost among these was that in the interest of national unity he designate a Republican to replace Roberts, a G.O.P. member from neighboring Pennsylvania. Other Republicans on the President's "short list" were Under Secretary of War Robert Patterson—a former federal judge—and Senator Warren Austin of Vermont. Next was Chief Justice Stone's advance approval of Burton because of his legislative experience (which Stone judged would prove helpful in cases of statutory construction); Burton's judicious and judicial temperament; the assumption that Democratic Governor Frank Lausche of Ohio would name a Democrat to Burton's Senate seat (he did); and the faithful support Senator Burton had given the Democratic party on foreign policy and even on some domestic programs, such as Tennessee Valley Authority (T.V.A.) and agricultural subsidies, during his four years in the upper house. Interestingly, for the first time a woman may have been in serious contention: veteran U.S. Court of Appeals Judge (Sixth Circuit), New Deal Democrat Florence E. Allen of Ohio, whom F.D.R. had placed on the appellate tribunal in 1934.

Popular among his colleagues and a hard worker, although only occasionally eloquent of pen, Justice Burton spent thirteen years on the Court, characterized by a combination of uncertainty, deliberate caution, independence, and unpredictability. He was most comfortable with the views and approaches to public law of his colleagues Vinson, Jackson, Frankfurter, Reed, Minton, and Clark—rarely could he be found in the libertarian Black-Douglas-Murphy-Rutledge wing. Nonetheless, there were times when he would cross over, especially when he believed the state or federal government to be taking impermissible shortcuts with constitutionally guaranteed basic liberties—as in the grisly *Willie Francis* "double electrocution" case, for one[87]—and he demonstrated a generally tough view on the question of separation of Church and State.[88] But he was essentially a devotee of the self-restraint, "when-in-doubt-don't" school of jurisprudence, and he was far happier in the role of follower than leader.

When Harlan Fiske Stone's distinguished career on the bench suddenly came to an end on April 22, 1946, President Truman was confronted with the awesome responsibility of naming a new Chief Justice of the United States. It was a particularly difficult task at the time because of the personality clashes that had recently developed—especially the increasingly unpleasant feud between Justices Black and Jackson, with the latter publicly accusing the former of blocking his ascendancy to the top spot on the Court and alleging a serious conflict of interest involving a former law partner. Although Black remained silent, he was obviously both hurt and angry about the unwarranted attack on his judgment, integrity, and honor.[89] Truman quickly perceived that, for the sake of intra-Court comity, he simply could not promote any of the Court's sitting members, although he was fully alive to Jackson's strong claims to the Chief Justiceship. Moreover, he had consulted with former Chief Justice Hughes and former Associate Justice Roberts, both of whom strongly urged the President to select someone not then on the Court to maximize a successful restoration of peace and harmony.[90] Yet, characteristically decisive, Harry Truman did not hesitate long: he turned to one of the nation's most versatile and most experienced public servants, his good friend and Secretary of the Treasury Fred Moore Vinson, then fifty-six years of age, whom both Hughes and Roberts had specifically suggested as an excellent candidate.[91] Vinson seemed ideal for the position, given his demonstrated administrative and legislative leadership. But he did not succeed on the Court, and his tenure was an unhappy one.

In 1924, after three years as Commonwealth Attorney in Kentucky, Fred Vinson had come to Washington as a young congressman and soon began yeoman service in behalf of the New Deal. As an expert member of the tax-writing House Committee on Ways and Means during much of his fourteen years in the House of Representatives, he had helped to forge some of the most significant parts of the Roosevelt program—including the T.V.A., the Agricultural Adjustment Act, the Coal Act, and the National Industrial Recovery Act—and he was one of the principal architects of the Social Security Act of 1935. In late 1937 he accepted F.D.R.'s reward of a judgeship on the U.S. Circuit Court of Appeals for the District of Columbia, where he served for five years. But in the spring of 1943 he resigned to become Director of the Office of Economic Stabilization. After two years in that hot spot he served briefly as Federal Loan Administrator and Director of the Office of War Mobilization and Reconversion before moving to the Treasury under Truman. Vinson had been of invaluable aid and a trusted adviser to the new President during his difficult first year in office; Truman not only shared Vinson's political philosophy, but he admired his popularity, his relaxed friendliness, his delightful sense of humor, and his ability to listen to all sides of a question and to effect compromise. To the President, Vinson was *the* person "capable of unifying the . . . Court and thereby improving its public image,"[92] and he eagerly nominated his friend to be the thirteenth Chief Justice on June 7, 1946. Confirmation by the Senate was uncontested and came two weeks later.

Fred M. Vinson served as Chief Justice for little more than seven years, just two years longer than the brief Chief Justiceship of Harlan Stone. His tenure was not a fortunate one, either in his role as presiding officer or as jurist. It is unfair and inaccurate, however, to categorize him as a "failure" on the bench—as the Court's historians have done. True, he did not succeed in eradicating the in-fighting on his Court; but he at least managed to confine it to the tribunal's inner sanctum, with even the Jackson-Black feud disappearing from the public stage. True, he was an indifferent, even poor, opinion-writer; but on his side he usually had such master craftsmen of style and intellect as Frankfurter and Jackson. True, the percentage of the work output of his Court was exceptionally low; but it did wrestle with trouble areas, such as inherent Presidential power (*Steel Seizure Case* of 1952), "that crazy decision that has tied up the country," as an irate President Truman put it";[93] national security (*Dennis Top Eleven Communists Case* of 1951);[94] segregation in schools (*Texas and Oklahoma Segrega-*

tion Cases of 1950);[95] and segregation in housing (*Restrictive Covenant Cases* of 1948).[96] The Chief Justice wrote the controlling opinions in all except the *Steel Seizure Case,* where he authored the dissenting opinion (pro-seizure) for himself, Reed, and Minton. Yet overall, Vinson demonstrated an astonishing lack of leadership: the role of Chief Justice was simply beyond his ken. The Court's jurisprudential split was, if anything, exacerbated during his tenure—with more 5:4 opinions than in any other comparable period. Vinson died suddenly in September 1953, a disappointed and dissatisfied occupant of the center chair.

Justice Murphy's sudden death in July 1949 created the third Court vacancy during the Truman Administration. Although few were particularly surprised that the President would once more turn to a trusted friend and political ally—this time his forty-nine-year-old Attorney General for the past four years, Tom C. Clark of Texas—both Clark and Attorney General McGrath seemed to be. The first Lone Star State denizen to sit on the Court, the energetic Clark, a skilled advocate, was known as a favorite protégé of the powerful Democratic Senator from Texas, Tom Connally. He had spent over a decade and a half as government attorney on both the state and federal levels, including several years in a Dallas County Civil District Attorney's office (a post that did not entail the prosecution of criminal defendants); two years as head of the federal Justice Department's Antitrust Division; several months in a ticklish assignment in 1942 of overseeing the removal of Japanese-Americans from the Pacific Coast to inland relocation centers; and two years as Assistant Attorney General in charge of the Criminal Division, before succeeding Francis Biddle as Attorney General. Clark, an assertive, resourceful, and courageous Attorney General, became one of Truman's closest advisers on key domestic issues. Their association had its genesis in Clark's cooperation with the Truman War Investigation Committee, which found a powerful working ally in him. Moreover, in pre-Presidential-election 1944, Clark and Truman, who was then still a Senator, collaborated in an abortive attempt to substitute Speaker Sam Rayburn for Henry Wallace as F.D.R.'s running mate. (Ultimately the Vice Presidential candidate would be Harry Truman himself.)

Clark continued as a Truman loyalist throughout the middle and late 1940s and was an important campaigner for Truman in 1948. His selection represented recognition and reward for proved loyalty to President and party.

But it was far from a popular one, and the soft-spoken Clark's confirmation by a vote of 73:8 does not indicate some of the sustained opposition to his selection from much, but not all, of the press, members of the legal profession, Congressman, and other influential public figures. The opposition, emanating shrilly from both sides of the philo-political spectrum, was based in part on what was considered Truman and Clark's blatant cronyism and the latter's cashing in of political I.O.U.s; in part on what was viewed as the attorney general's antilibertarian posture, especially regarding procedural safeguards in criminal justice and toward minority groups—although the National Association for the Advancement of Colored People (N.A.A.C.P.) and the Anti-Defamation League (A.D.L.) of B'nai B'rith as well as the American Federation of Labor (A.F. of L.) defended him; in part because of what some regarded as Clark's marginal and authoritarian performance in the Justice Department; and, in considerable measure, on at least three scandals that had plagued his career. Those scandals related to alleged irregularities in his early Texas law practice days; his purported role in the unjustified paroling of Al Capone gangsters from a federal penitentiary; and Clark's allegedly improper behavior during what became known as the Pendergast Machine Kansas City Vote Fraud. But none of these charges, although raised again and investigated by committees of Congress before, during, and even after the confirmation hearings, were ever laid conclusively at Clark's doorstep.[97]

Prominently outspoken among those who sought to block the Clark nomination was ex-Secretary of the Interior Harold L. Ickes, who made no secret of his outrage: in a *New Republic* article, entitled "Tom Clark Should Say 'No Thanks,'" he contended that the President had shifted Clark to the Court—in what he characterized as "the worst appointment ever made"—to get rid of the weakest member of his Cabinet; that Truman was under no obligation, whatsoever, to this "second-rate political hack who has known what backs to slap and when"; that the Court "needs more in a man than a Mona Lisa smile and a simpering interest in the Girl Scouts." He concluded that "perhaps it was in keeping that the least able of Attorneys General of the United States should, as a result of raw political favoritism, become the least able of the members of the Supreme Court."[98] Clark's initial performance on the Court appeared to bear out, if not Ickes's worst fears, a good many of the doubts of his detractors. He seemed ill at ease on the high bench; he was more concerned with "going along" than with independence or innovation; he seemed to be overly concerned with Truman's expectations of his role; and he betrayed a tough stance on the rights of defendants in internal security cases. Yet before long this much-maligned appointee began to demonstrate a cautious, innovative, independent streak in the authorship of major opinions in the separation of powers and civil libertarian sectors, evincing a sophisticated command of constitutional construction.

Thus Clark's concurring opinion in the *Steel Seizure Case* of 1952,[99] in which he voted to disallow Truman's seizure of the struck steel mills, came closer than any of the other six opinions to the heart of the matter: he objected to executive usurpation of legislative authority in the presence of ascertainable congressional intent.[100] Truman was not amused; in fact, he was livid: calling Clark "[t]hat damn fool from Texas" and "my biggest mistake," he added, ". . . well, it isn't so much that he is a *bad* man. It's just that he is such a dumb son of a bitch. He's about the dumbest man I think I've ever run across."[101] Yet the deep friendship between the two men continued, their closeness apparently unaffected–suggesting that, perhaps, this condemnation was more the result of a sudden outburst than a reflection of a lifelong conviction. Clark's declarations of unconstitutionality for unanimous Courts, also in 1952, of the Oklahoma loyalty oath for teachers and state officials[102] and of New York's censorship of the film *The Miracle*[103] as well as his opinion for the Court in the momentous 1963 *Schempp* and *Murray* decisions that struck down state-mandated Bible reading and prayer in the public schools[104] demonstrated a genuine attachment to the principles of the First Amendment. And a host of Clark-authored landmark decisions in the 1960s, such as the application of the exclusionary rule to state criminal procedure in the famed case of *Mapp* v. *Ohio,*[105] proved that a security-conscious law-and-order devotee, too, knew how to uphold fundamental rights even in the contentious realm of accused criminals.

Justice Clark's almost eighteen years on the Court cast him into a role of a determined, if cautious, craftsman of the law who frequently became a "swing man" between the "liberal" and "conservative" blocs on the bench. Although he remained essentially true to his assertive strong governmental position, he was fully alive to the basic lines and limits inherent in constitutionalism and the nature of the judicial function. Thus, he developed and embraced three admirable principles as endemic to the judicial role as he perceived it: (1) that it was essential that Justices generally follow precedent; (2) that although a Court should overturn an "unsound" case, it should only be done in the presence of a *clear majority*—one that could articulate and support the doctrinal basis for the precedent's destruction and the establishment of its successor; and (3) that a Justice should do everything feasible to render and maintain the Court's doctrines with *absolute clarity.*[106] With the passing of the years many of his critics had second thoughts about Tom Clark and gladly acknowledged that here was not only the ablest of the four Truman appointees, but a jurist of far above-average capability and performance. Thus, William O. Douglas, an outspoken, tough, and sporadically nasty critic of his brethren, concluded in 1980 that whereas Truman Justices Vinson, Burton, and Minton had been "mediocre," indeed, Clark had evinced "the indispensable capacity to develop so that with the passage of time he grew in stature and expanded his dimensions."[107] The country, thus, deeply regretted Clark's self-imposed resignation at the close of the 1966–1967 term when L.B.J. appointed his mercurial son, Ramsay Clark, Attorney General of the United States.

If Justice Clark's record on the Court is proof of man's inherent ability to grcw remarkably in a position of high responsibility and authority, President Truman's fourth and last appointee, Sherman Minton, pointed to the converse—notwithstanding impressive formal education credentials (Indiana, where he was graduated *summa cum laude* as first in his class; Yale; and the Sorbonne). Despite the genuine affection of his colleagues, "Shay" Minton was essentially uncomfortable among high-powered judicial individualists. His seven-year stint on the Court has been universally and justly regarded as a failure. He had had eight years of experience on the U.S. Court of Appeals for the Seventh Circuit, but that body was devoid of such judicial powers as Black, Frankfurter, Douglas, Jackson, and Warren. Minton, who succeeded to the seat vacated by Justice Rutledge's untimely death in the early fall of 1949, was essentially temperamentally happiest as a practitioner of practical politics. It was in that role that he had first met Harry Truman in a historical accident of seating in the U.S. Senate following the Democratic landslide victory in the congressional elections of 1934: a new row of seats had to be installed for the Democrats in the rear of the chamber, and freshmen Senators Minton of Indiana and Truman of Missouri found themselves seated next to one another. They soon became fast friends. Minton quickly rose to the post of Democratic Whip, but he lost his bid for reelection six years later when Wendell Willkie swept Minton's home state of Indiana into the G.O.P. column. F.D.R. thereupon appointed Minton, who had been a loyal New Dealer, to a White House post as Administrative Assistant, a role Minton enjoyed enormously. But he readily moved into the Court of Appeals opening that Roosevelt offered him just a few months later. It was while he was serving there that, eight years later, he received a now well-known telephone call from President Truman: "Shay," the President said, "I'm naming you to the Supreme Court. What do you think of that?" Minton's reply was quick: "I think it's fine."[108] Loyal political and personal dedication was once again rewarded.

Some of Minton's ex-colleagues in the Senate did not think it was so "fine," however, and Republican Senators Homer Ferguson of Michigan and Forrest C. Donnell of Missouri requested that Judge Minton appear before the Senate Judiciary Committee to respond to questions. He declined the "invitation," noting that he would stand on his record as a judge and Senator. The Senate subsequently proceeded to vote on his confirmation, approving him 48:16. The ardent New Dealer continued to support strong governmental action during his few years on the Court, and Truman had no cause to regret his appointment on that score. But he left the President and many old colleagues of his New Deal Senate days on the civil libertarian front, where he immediately joined the so-called "conservative" wing of the Court, then consisting of Chief Justice Vinson and Associate Justices Reed, Burton, and, for a time, Clark. The likeable, witty, popular, tobacco-chewing[109] Minton did his share of work on the bench and contributed to the smoothing of internal conflicts, but he wrote no opinions of lasting significance. It is characteristic of the essentially humble Minton that he regarded his most important vote on the bench to be a silent one: the one he cast with the unanimous Justices in May 1954, joining Chief Justice Earl Warren's historic ruling that, free from any either dissenting or concurring opinions, declared compulsory segregation of public schools unconstitutional.[110]

10

The Warren Court:

From Ike to L.B.J. 1953-1969

General of the Army Dwight David Eisenhower was elected to the White House as a Republican, but he could just as easily have been elected on the Democratic ticket. After two decades of Democratic rule, "Had enough?" was the key slogan of Eisenhower's campaign in 1952. He was elected by a wide margin and, following one popular term in office, he was reelected by an ever wider margin—although the Democrats recaptured both houses of Congress. "Ike," the Nation's foremost war hero, the victorious Commander of the Allied Expeditionary Forces in Europe, could do almost no wrong in the public's eyes. Enormously likeable and even modest despite his towering successes, he was accorded a fatherlike image, which enabled him, for example, to settle the Korean War on terms for which the Democrats undoubtedly would have been roasted. To his eternal credit, he cast off any accouterments of militarism, and when in doubt about engaging the military, as in Indochina, he opted for noninvolvement. On the one occasion on which he was persuaded to resort to military force to uphold the Constitution, the Little Rock desegregation crisis in the fall of 1958, he sent troops with the utmost reluctance. That action, according to his principal adviser-assistant, Sherman Adams, represented "a Constitutional duty which was the most repugnant to him of all his acts in his eight years in the White House."[1]

It is conceivable that Eisenhower's reluctance to be tagged "military" or "strong" caused him seemingly to step into the background, to provide *sotto voce* leadership. He gave the clear impression of wanting Congress to do the leading, and certainly so in domestic matters. His public attitude was one of pointed deference to the legislative process, often, or so it appeared, totally out of proportion to need or wisdom. Moreover this superb and beloved wartime leader frequently seemed reluctant to provide decisive, "up-front" leadership, even when he could, and arguably should, have done so readily and with demonstrably assured public support. Thus, when Republican U.S. Senator Joseph R. McCarthy of Wisconsin sent out his divisive and dangerous attacks not only on individuals, but on the very fiber of constitutional government, Ike failed to engage in what many felt was a much-needed public battle with the demagogic legislator. Yet Ike refused to "get into the gutter with that man." And when the President had the golden opportunity to lend the prestige of his person and office to the 1954–1955 Supreme Court decisions concerning desegregation of the public schools, he demurred–in part because he believed that the Court had transgressed its proper constitutional parameters of power. In the eyes of many observers, it was not until the last two years of his Presidency, after the dismissal of Sherman Adams and the death of John Foster Dulles, that Dwight Eisenhower in effect abandoned his policy of "reign in order to 'rule' "–albeit within carefully defined limits.

There is, hence, little doubt that because of what was widely perceived as unfulfilled expectations, wasted potential, a "when in doubt, don't" approach to government and politics, the 1962 Schlesinger poll of presidential historians[2] ranked Eisenhower a very low "average," barely above "below average." When he was informed that he had thus been rated twentieth and Truman eighth, the walls of his study in his Gettysburg farm reverberated with some old-fashioned purple outbursts. Those who were close to him knew that Ike's "rating" was patently much too low in terms of his real accomplishments for his country. Yet the observer-experts of his two terms had at that time concluded that he simply merited no more for his Presidency, given what they viewed broadly as his failure to provide the kind of leadership that he had demonstrated so successfully in uniform.

More than two decades of post-Presidency research and re-evaluation of Dwight D. Eisenhower–aided by the presence of the Eisenhower Library in Abilene, Kansas, and the availability of his papers–have proved the Ike-positivists indubitably correct. What has emerged as the appropriate *tableau* of Ike's *modi operandi* is his characteristic resolve to delegate a considerable measure of authority to associates and subordinates, while retaining full control and responsibility by expecting resolute accountability from the grantees of that delegation. In the apt title of one of the most influential scholars of the approbative revisionist judgment on Ike-the-President, Professor Fred I. Greenstein of Princeton University (who had twice voted for his opponent, Adlai E. Stevenson), Eisenhower practiced a "Hidden Hand Presidency,"[3] featuring much delegation, but reserving full final decisional judgmental power for himself. Concluding the latter to be the proper interpretation, the President watchers have now "jumped" Eisenhower from the ranks of the "average" to those approaching the "near greats." Thus, the most recent authoritative appraisal, conducted and published in 1982–1983 by Pennsylvania State University Professor of History Robert K. Murray, with a sample of 1997 historians, of whom 970 responded, placed Ike eleventh–three below Truman and one below Lyndon Johnson.[4]

No matter how one may judge his Presidency, Eisenhower deserves a hearty "well done" for all save one of the five Supreme Court appointments he was enabled to make between 1953 and 1958. For he sent to the Court a great Chief Justice (Earl Warren); a truly distinguished "jurists' jurist" (John Marshall Harlan II); a sensitive, assertive humanist (William J. Brennan, Jr.); and an able, independent legal craftsman (Potter Stewart). His one failure was the selection of Charles E. Whittaker, whom history has placed near the bottom in terms of Court performance. He has the rare distinction of being the only modern Supreme Court Justice publicly to criticize not only the Court's sitting members, but the institution itself. He stepped down from the bench after only five years. Ike's self-recorded set of criteria for nomination comprised:

(1) character and ability that could command the "respect, pride, and confidence of the populace";[5] (2) a basic philosophy of moderate progressivism, common sense, high ideals, the "absence of extreme views";[6] (3) after the Warren appointment, which would become Ike's most acute disappointment, prior judicial service, in the belief that such service would "provide an inkling of his philosophy";[7] (4) geographic balance; (5) religious balance; (6) an upper age limit of sixty-two, unless, as Ike put it, "other qualifications were unusually impressive";[8] and (7) a thorough F.B.I. check of the candidate *and* the approval of the American Bar Association (A.B.A.).[9]

On September 8, 1953, only eight months after Eisenhower had assumed office, Chief Justice Vinson died unexpectedly, evoking one of Felix Frankfurter's nastiest cracks on record: "This is the first indication I have ever had that there is a God."[10] It was Ike's first opportunity to act on a vacancy and the appointment he made would revolutionize American constitutional law (which is not precisely what he had in mind). As he chronicled it himself in his autobiography, initially he gave "serious thought" to appointing John Foster Dulles; but his Secretary of State declined, stating that as long as the President was happy with his performance in that post, he had no interest in any other.[11] Although Ike never expressly said so, it is now clear that there were other front-runners. Thomas E. Dewey of New York probably could have had the post, but he took himself out of the running; the evidence is inconclusive whether it was actually offered to him. Chief Judge John J. Parker of the U.S. Court of Appeals for the Fourth Circuit, who had been so unfortunately blocked by the Senate in 1930, was briefly in the running. Considered but fairly quickly rejected were suggestions to promote sitting Justices Jackson or Burton. The distinguished Chief Justice of New Jersey, Arthur T. Vanderbilt, a Republican in the Eisenhower-Dewey mold, and probably the nation's foremost judicial administrator, was also a frequently mentioned candidate. Indeed, there is some evidence that he thought he had the President's verbal promise of an appointment. His health was not good, however, and, in any event, Ike agreed with Attorney General Herbert Brownell that the political verities clearly mandated a preference for Governor Earl Warren of California, another strong contender. Perhaps there would be more than one vacancy to fill; Vanderbilt would be given every consideration. In the President's own words:

> A few months prior to the death of Chief Justice Vinson, I had talked to Gov. Earl Warren of California about his basic philosophy and been quite pleased that his views seemed to reflect high ideals and a great deal of common sense. During this conversation I told the Governor that I was considering the possibility of appointing him to the Supreme Court and I was definitely inclined to do so if, in the future, a vacancy should occur. However, neither he nor I was thinking of the special post of Chief Justice nor was I definitely committed to any appointment.[12]

Now, on Vinson's death, Ike's attention centered increasingly on Warren—although, according to Justice Douglas, for one, Ike did not like Warren personally.[13] But recognizing that his own contacts with the Californian had been sketchy, he asked Brownell to fly out to the Coast to find out more about the Governor's "record of attainments as a lawyer, as district attorney and as Attorney General of California." Ike wanted "the conclusions of a qualified lawyer on the matter."[14] Herbert Brownell was indeed that; he was also a shrewd political practitioner who had been Dewey's campaign manager on numerous occasions, had served as Chairman of the Republican National Committee, and had been a key figure in securing General Eisenhower's assent to the Republican nomination for President in 1952. Brownell was well aware of a political debt to be paid. For it had been Warren—whether or not he realized that his own candidacy for the Presidency in 1952 was probably doomed—who was primarily responsible for swinging all but eight of California's seventy-member delegation at the Nominating Convention to Eisenhower rather than to Senator Robert A. Taft at a particularly crucial stage in the jockeying involving the seating of certain contested Southern delegations.

Ike and Brownell as well as the President's closest other political advisers were also agreed that Warren's experience, leadership qualities, and administrative expertise constituted precisely the kind of medicine the badly faction-rent Vinson Court needed. Moreover, they were pleased to note that Warren had fought the 1937 Court-packing bill; favored state jurisdiction over offshore oil lands; and had backed the Court's anti–steel seizure decision in 1952. They were convinced that here was, as the politically savvy Brownell put it more than once (and it was an assessment Eisenhower shared), a *bona fide* "middle-of-the-road" or "moderate" Republican.[15] There may have been one other factor involved: Warren, the unprecedented three-term governor of California, although a loyal Republican, had long been a thorn in the side of the partisan California Republican leadership (which included Vice President Richard M. Nixon and Senate Majority Leader William F. Knowland) because of his confirmed progressivism, his independence, and his link to the Democrats, many of whom had consistently supported him. Ambitious and influential political figures (such as Nixon and Knowland) would be delighted to see Warren removed from California politics, for they realized that his position at the home polls was well-nigh impregnable. According to Douglas, Nixon and Knowland went to see Ike and asked him to "get Warren out of California," even if it meant giving him the Chief Justiceship.[16] Knowland's liberal U.S. Senate colleague from California, Thomas H. Kuchel, and his Administrative Assistant, James Gleason, vigorously denied that Knowland had a hand in that nefarious scheme, but suggested that "Nixon would be capable of anything."[17] He was!

Initially, Ike had offered Warren at least two cabinet posts—Secretary of Labor and Secretary of Interior—but Warren had declined, indicating that he would, however, be honored to be considered for "that other post" that the President had discussed with him some time earlier. Warren did finally, reluctantly, agree to accept the Solicitor Generalship in August 1953, and he prepared to move to Washington in early September just a few days before sudden death came to Vinson. But it was clear that Warren regarded the high Justice Department post merely as a stepping stone to the one to which he so ardently aspired. If there was no other way of removing Warren from the California scene, well, the state's

Republican orthodoxy was willing even to pay the price of his elevation to the Chief Justiceship of the United States.

Earl Warren seemed eminently qualified on all counts to serve as Chief Justice of the Supreme Court. Born in 1891 of Norwegian immigrant parents, he had capped his undergraduate days at the University of California at Berkeley with a bachelor of law and a doctor of jurisprudence degree. After practicing law for a brief time, he joined the infantry during World War I, ultimately attaining the rank of captain. On his return from the army he clerked for the California legislature, became Deputy City Attorney of Sacramento for a year, Deputy District Attorney of Alameda County for five years, then for fourteen years its District Attorney. His superb record in the difficult last post enabled him to cross-file on the Republican, Democratic, and Progressive party tickets for Attorney General of California in 1938, and, portending the future, he won all three! Warren logically progressed to the governorship, first being elected in 1942, then reelected in 1946 and 1950, inevitably with bipartisan and multipartisan support. He was Dewey's running mate in the Presidential election of 1948, and had it not been for Eisenhower's overwhelming national popularity, Earl Warren might have moved into the White House in 1952.

Instead, he happily found himself nominated for the Chief Justiceship on September 30, 1953, amid widespread public acclaim and approval. Three days earlier Herbert Brownell had tracked the candidate down on a deer-hunting holiday on Santa Rosa Island off Santa Barbara and reinterviewed him at some length on the mainland. After reporting to Ike, the latter instructed Brownell to telephone Warren and tender the appointment. Because Congress was not in session, Eisenhower gave Warren a recess appointment, fully anticipating more or less automatic confirmation on Congress's return in January 1954. Yet he had not reckoned with the diehard, perverse opposition of Republican Senator William Langer of North Dakota, a senior member of the Senate's Judiciary Committee, who had then begun his prolonged six-year campaign of opposing any and all nominees to the Court until someone from his home state (which had never been so honored) received an appointment. (He went to his grave in 1959, his hopes still unrealized–as they are to this day, mid-1984.) For two months Langer and a few conservative Southern Democrats, who joined in an attack on what they called Warren's "left wing," "ultraliberal" views, prevented a vote on the confirmation. It did not come until March 1, 1954, but when it did come it was unanimous.

Ironically, in the apt observation of one of Warren's law clerk-biographers, "neither Brownell nor Eisenhower sensed Warren's instinctive Progressivism. Warren was appointed as something he was not: an Eisenhower Republican."[18] And had the Senate been able to predict the ultimate course of the Warren Court–indeed, by his own assertions, had the President been able to look into the future–the confirmation would either never have been made or might have been denied then and there. But Warren's record as a prosecutor showed some tough law-and-order crusading; what is more, he was the man who had so strongly and successfully urged evacuation of the 110,000 Japanese-Americans from their California homes and land in 1942. Those were hardly the marks of a "muddle-headed liberal"! Yet though the bombshell of *Brown* v. *Board of Education of Topeka*[19] lay just two months in his post-confirmation future, the new Chief Justice moved cautiously at first, demonstrating the kind of gradualism and deliberateness that had characterized his approach to every new position he had held to date. Thus, notwithstanding the prolegomena to, and the imminence of, *Brown* and his decisive leadership therein, Warren did not immediately manifest the libertarian activism that would eventually result in all-out assaults on the Court, accompanied by the distribution of "Impeach Earl Warren" bumper stickers and Warren Impeachment Kits.

If any doubts at all remained after his *Brown* opinion, two years later–by mid-1956–it had become crystal clear that, as Chief Justice of the United States, Earl Warren was in the process of providing leadership for a libertarian activist approach to public law and personal rights that went far beyond the Eisenhower brand of progressive Republicanism. To Eisenhower the new Warren represented all but a betrayal of older beliefs and understandings, and his recognition of the man's judicial independence, which he regarded as judicial "legislating," was bitter and frustrating. But the Chief Justice, usually with Justices Black and Douglas (and later Brennan) by his side, wrought a constitutional revolution in the application of the Bill of Rights to the states; in the generous interpretation of specific provisions of criminal-justice safeguards for the individual ("Yes, but was it fair?" was a standard question he would put to prosecutors); in the application and interpretation of the Civil War amendments; in rendering any executive or legislative classification by race and nationality or alienage "suspect," and by gender close to, but not quite so; in the liberalization of the right to foreign travel, to vote, the right to run for office, and the right to fair representation, to "one person, one vote"; to an elevated commitment to freedom of expression; and in many other sectors of the freedom of the individual. Of course Earl Warren did not do this alone; the seeds were already there. But it was he who provided the leadership on the Court; he whose assertive views of the judicial role and vision of constitutional fulfillment made the judicial revolution that he was determined to achieve possible—even if that meant letting a personal sense of right and wrong *determine* the outcome of cases, supporting the result with any convenient—and not necessarily logically articulated—result; he whose knowledge of men and administrative *savior faire* succeeded in "massing" the Court for the "big decisions," with results second only to those achieved in different constitutional areas by John Marshall; he whose dedication to the ideals of equal justice under law gave hope to the downtrodden; he whose insistence that for democratic society to succeed, its people must have ready access to their government, including the judiciary.

Earl Warren was not a great lawyer in the mold of a Taney or a Hughes; not a great legal scholar in the tradition of a Brandeis or a Frankfurter; not a supreme stylist like Cardozo or Jackson; not a judicial philosopher like Holmes or Black; not a resourceful, efficient administrator like Taft or Warren Earl Burger, his successor. But he was the Chief Justice par excellence—second in institutional-leadership greatness only to John Marshall himself in the eyes of most impartial students of the Court as well as the Warren Court's legion of critics. Like Marshall he understood and utilized the tools of pervasive and persuasive power leadership available to him; he knew how to bring men together, how to set a tone, and how to fashion a mood. He was a wise man and a warm, kind human being. He was his Court, *the* Court.

It is a pity that some of the momentous Constitution-revolutionizing opinions Earl Warren wrote were not delivered with more clarity and explicitness, with more close legal reasoning, more historical proof—a pity because the public he loved and whom he served so conscientiously would have been better able to understand him. Yet in G. Edward White's frank avowal, the ethical values he found underlying the Constitution were seminal. Warren believed that vindication of the basic ethical imperatives of the Constitution was more significant than doctrinal consistency.[20] Still his leadership created more milestones in constitutional adjudication and interpretation than any other Chief Justiceship save Marshall's. Among the many decisions Warren himself wrote, five stand out: (1) *Brown* v. *Board of Education of Topeka* (1954) was his supreme achievement. His unanimous Court declared compulsory segregation by race in the public schools to be an unconstitutional violation of the Fourteenth Amendment's guarantees for the equal protection of the laws.[21] Of this decision, which wrought a veritable sociopolitical revolution, John P. Frank, a close Court observer and once clerk to Justice Black, wrote: "Of his individual contributions, history will have enough to say; but it will never need to say more than that he wrote the school-segregation opinion."[22] (2) *Watkins* v. *United States* (1975), in which the Court held 6:1 that "the vice of vagueness" so prevalent in the conduct of congressional investigating committees (particularly the House Committee on Un-American Activities) was a derogation of the due process of law clause of the Fifth Amendment.[23] The Chief Justice's rambling opinion constituted virtually a lecture to Congress on fundamental constitutional law. (3) *Reynolds* v. *Sims* (1964), where the Court ruled 6:3—in what was arguably a highly dubious interpretation of the Fourteenth Amendment—that both houses of a state legislature must be apportioned on a "one person, one vote" basis, with the Chief Justice holding that "legislators represent people, not trees or acres. Legislators are elected by voters, not farms or cities or economic interest."[24] Warren regarded his Court's work in redistricting and reapportionment of even greater importance than that of desegregation! (4) *Miranda* v. *Arizona* (1966), in which the Court held 5:4 that the confession of a person in custody cannot be used against that person unless he or she has been provided with a series of six specific and protective rules against self-incrimination.[25] The highly prescriptive nature of this opinion brought down the wrath of many an objective legal scholar as well as that of law-enforcement officers and laymen. (5) *Powell* v. *McCormack* (1969), Chief Justice Warren's valedictory opinion before turning over the center seat to U.S. Court of Appeals Judge Warren Earl Burger—who had disagreed with the outgoing Chief in this case. Here, Warren ruled for his 8:1 Court that the U.S. House of Representatives had improperly excluded the errant Adam Clayton Powell as a member in 1967 because—whatever else he might have done—he did meet the requirements of the Constitution as to age, citizenship, and residence.[26] It was characteristic and fitting that Warren's last opinion before his retirement was another lecture on constitutional law to Congress, specifically on separation of powers and checks and balances; that it was for an almost unanimous Court; and that it dealt with an issue most earlier Courts would have declined to hear on the ground that the issue constituted a "political question," into which "thicket" judicial bodies should not venture—the argument Felix Frankfurter had so warmly, albeit unsuccessfully, pressed on colleagues and country in *Baker* v. *Carr*,[27] the "parent" of *Reynolds* v. *Sims*.[28]

Among other key decisions rendered by the Court under Earl Warren's sixteen years at its helm were, for example, such far-reaching and contentious rulings as that of *Engel* v. *Vitale* (1962), written by Hugo L. Black for a 6:1 Court, ruling unconstitutional—on grounds of separation of Church and State—the daily recitation of state-prepared and prescribed prayers in public schools;[29] that of *New York Times Co.* v. *Sullivan* (1964), written by William J. Brennan for a unanimous Court, vastly extending freedom of the press by holding that a public official could not collect on a defamatory falsehood relating to official conduct unless he or she could prove that it was made with "actual malice"[30]; and of course a Warren source of pride, the Black-authored 9:0 *Gideon* v. *Wainright* (1963) landmark that nationalized the Sixth Amendment's guarantee to counsel in criminal cases.[31]

With Warren's departure an era had truly ended. But he left, in the words of the poet Archibald MacLeish, having "restored the future," having "enabled us to raise our heads and to begin."[32]

On October 9, 1954, Justice Robert H. Jackson, who had served brilliantly and controversially for thirteen years, suffered a fatal heart attack while en route to the Court. He had been initially stricken in March but had left the hospital on May 17, 1954, to join his colleagues in the announcement of the unanimously decided *Brown* v. *Board of Education of Topeka.*[33] President Eisenhower moved at once to fill the vacancy. His close advisers Dewey and Brownell could have had the nomination but, as before, neither was interested; thus, he turned to a "Dewey-Brownell man," a distinguished New York attorney and judge, John Marshall Harlan II. Named for his grandfather, who had himself been named for John Marshall, the second Harlan ideally fitted the Eisenhower criteria for Supreme Court service: he was a lifelong, solid Republican, but he had always kept a low political profile and was widely regarded as nonpartisan; he was well known, well established, and of unquestioned integrity; he was of proved legal acumen. Eisenhower had appointed Harlan to the U.S. Circuit Court of Appeals earlier that year; at fifty-five he was of the right age; although a native of Chicago, he had long lived in New York, Jackson's state. Moreover, the reserved but engaging legal scholar, who had practiced law versatilely for twenty-five years with one of New York City's most prestigious firms, was widely regarded as a progressive conservative in the Eisenhower mold. Ike, thus, happily nominated him to the Court early that November, fully expecting swift confirmation, especially as he had received the enthusiastic support of the A.B.A.'s Committee on Judiciary.

Yet the nomination ran into trouble. It had first gone to the Senate as a recess appointment early in November but, in a special session of Congress later that month, the Senate refused to take action. When the legislators returned for the regular session in January 1955, not only Senator Langer, who continued his now-predictable opposition to all non-North Dakotan nominees to the Court, but a bevy of largely Southern Democrats attacked the Harlan nomination, contending that he was "ultra-liberal," hostile to the South, dedicated to reforming the Constitution by "judicial fiat." Nothing, of course, could have been further from fact, especially in the light of Harlan's subsequent record of judicial restraint and cautious judicial craftsmanship, which must later have given some of his critics considerable pause. His detractors, however, managed to prevent confirmation until March 16, when it came 71:11.

If Warren fell far short of reaching Ike's expectations, Harlan's record on the Court more than amply fulfilled them. Harlan, committedly open-minded, probably gave his nominator some anxious moments during his first two years, when he more often than not joined the Court's libertarian wing in national security cases—even writing the Court's opinion in *Yates* v. *United States,*[34] which backed the right to advocate the *theoretical* overthrow of the government by force and violence as opposed to advocating direct action. But as of 1957 Harlan left that wing to find his niche with Frankfurter, Clark, and the other incoming Eisenhower appointees in a generally conservative, abstemious, restraint-oriented judicial approach. Indeed, it was Frankfurter who became Harlan's mentor and idol on the bench, and it was Harlan who assumed the role of Court leader and spokesperson of judicial restraint after Frankfurter's retirement in 1962. In stark contrast to the judicial posture of his grandfather, the second Harlan, thus, spent the balance of his total of sixteen years on the bench in arguing for a limited judicial role in political and social issues and for the strict separation of state and federal responsibilities. Like the first Harlan, often finding himself in the role of dissenter (he cast an average of more than sixty dissents annually between 1963 and 1967), his lucid, clearly and intelligently penned, precedent-invoking opinions, which explained and exhorted his philosophy of the judicial role in the governmental process, earned him wide recognition as an intellectual leader of the Court.

John Marshall Harlan's grandfather had earned his recognition as a great Justice largely because of his tenacious, pioneering, libertarian activism on an ultraconservative Court. The grandson was accorded the well-earned rank of "near great"–by the same Court experts who bestowed on his revered grandfather the top category–for consistently, and often persuasively, resisting the tempting use of the judicial function as the innovator and prescriber of social and political reform. He never tired of exhorting his colleagues as well as his fellow citizens that the only viable role for the Court is a limited one, that it should stay out of the "political thicket" at all costs, that it should eschew the dismantling of federalism, and that, as he put it so memorably in dissenting from the contentious *Reynolds* v. *Sims* (1964) 6:3 Warren opinion extending the "one person, one vote" rule to both houses of state legislatures:

> *The Constitution is not a panacea for every blot upon the public welfare; nor should this Court, ordained as a judicial body, be thought of as a general haven for reform movements.* This Constitution is an instrument of government, fundamental to which is the premise that in a diffusion of governmental authority lies the greatest promise that this Nation will realize for all its citizens. This Court, limited in function in accordance with that premise, does not serve its high purpose when it exceeds its authority, even to satisfy justified impatience with the slow workings of the political process.[35]

Yet although Harlan's philosophy of judicial restraint caused him often to disagree with the majority of the activist Warren Court, notably on issues such as reapportionment-redistricting, criminal justice, and the range of congressional authority over state elections, he would not stand for governmental shortcuts in the name of law and order. Thus, practices such as wiretapping and eavesdropping, illegal invasions of human privacy, incursions on freedom of expression and association, and racial segregation met his determined opposition. How intensely proud he was of his grandfather's lone dissenting opinion in *Plessy* v. *Ferguson* (1896)![36] On his death in 1971 one of his former law clerks, Paul M. Bator of the Harvard School of Law, praised Harlan's abiding faithfulness to law "in the largest sense–the sense that makes democracy possible." He was, recalled Professor Bator, "one of those rare public men" for whom the democratic faith meant "fidelity to the whole law, every day and not every other day, fidelity not only to those rules which define other people's power but also those which limited his own."[37]

In October 1956 Justice Sherman Minton resigned after only seven years on the Court. Ike moved quickly to fill his third vacancy–it was close to the Presidential elections and an able nominee would hardly hurt his chances for reelection. The President publicly insisted that his candidate would have to have at least three specific qualifications: relative youth, judicial experience, and excellent standing with his state bar as well as the A.B.A. The candidate advanced by the influential Chief Justice of New Jersey, Arthur T. Vanderbilt (long a potential nominee himself but now no longer in good health), appeared to possess these qualifications and more. He was Vanderbilt's longtime protégé, friend, and colleague on the New Jersey Supreme Court, William J. Brennan, Jr.–then but fifty years of age, a *magna cum laude* graduate of the University of Pennsylvania who became a scholarship student at the Harvard Law School. Justice Vanderbilt had pushed Brennan's candidacy for some time, but he was not alone in voicing support for the able and vigorous New Jersey jurist–the second of eight children of Irish immigrants–who had won admiration for his clear, thoughtful, and moderately liberal opinions on the state bench and for his expertise as a private lawyer specializing in labor litigation. Although Vanderbilt's statement to Ike that Brennan "possessed the finest 'judicial mind' that he had known"[38] may well have been overly enthusiastic, there was no doubt of Brennan's outstanding qualifications. Attorney General Brownell, White House Appointments Secretary Bernard Shanley–an old friend from New Jersey boyhood days whom Brennan believed to be primarily responsible for his ultimate nomination–the A.B.A., the New Jersey Bar Association, the American Judicature Society, and numerous prominent individuals and private groups, including the Holy Name Society and other Roman Catholic organizations, rallied around him. The President easily concurred in the encomiums and in the political wisdom of designating, especially in an election year, a Democrat who also happened to be a Roman Catholic. It might well avoid a "return home" to the Democratic nominee by the Eisenhower Democrats of 1952, buttressing the nonpolitical or bipartisan atmosphere in which Ike felt most comfortable. Moreover, there had been no one of Brennan's religious faith on the bench since Justice Murphy's death in 1949; why not "restore" the time-honored Roman Catholic seat on the Court? The metropolitan East would be pleased indeed! In fine, here was a still youthful, highly qualified, experienced jurist with broad political appeal and nationwide backing. Ike gave Justice-Designate Brennan a recess appointment that October, which he formalized on Congress's return in January 1957. "I never saw a man say 'yes' so fast when the President asked him to take the job," recalled Ike's Press Secretary, James B. Haggerty.[39] Brennan's confirmation, like Harlan's, was delayed. Predictably, there was the Langer opposition, but there was also that of Senator Joseph R. McCarthy—of whom the nominee had been openly critical in the past. McCarthy, however, now long beyond his days of heady power and influence, was able to do no more than to cast the lone audible no when the informal voice vote came in March.

Professor Frankfurter had always admonished his students not to be unduly swayed by professorial advocacy, that their guiding motto should be "think for yourself." Years later, when he served with one of those students—William Brennan—Frankfurter asked whimsically whether it was really necessary for Brennan to have taken his former teacher's admonition so literally. Indeed, Justice Brennan struck out on his own, with a creativity and diligence that won him a "near great" rating by the Court's observers. But the President who sent him to the Court was only slightly less irked by, and disenchanted with, Brennan's evolving record than with Earl Warren's (whose opinions Brennan joined in most instances). When Eisenhower was asked later if he had made any mistakes while he had been President, he replied: "Yes, two, and they are both sitting on the Supreme Court."[40] "Both" referred to Warren and Brennan.

By inclination less of a judicial activist than Warren at the outset and given to more careful, more communicatively reasoned expression, Brennan became a predictable member of the Court's libertarian wing. His abiding dedication to the freedoms of the First Amendment, notably those of speech and press, soon saw him assigned some of the leading libertarian opinions of the Warren Court era. Thus, he authored the tribunal's significant and unanimous judgment in the *New York Times Libel Case of 1964*,[41] which established that a public official to recover damages for a publication criticizing his official conduct would have to show "actual malice" on the part of its publisher. Extolling the "uninhibited, robust, and wide-open" nature of debate on public issues, Brennan held that "libel can claim no talismanic immunity from constitutional limitations," that it must be "measured by standards that satisfy the First Amendment."

Justice Brennan, now (late 1984) about to enter his twenty-eighth year on the Court, has continued to champion a generously expansive interpretation of the Bill of Rights and the Civil War amendments. In many ways he became the heir apparent to Justice Douglas's jurisprudence and his votes, especially after the latter's retirement from the bench in 1975. Together with Justice Thurgood Marshall, Brennan, thus, evolved into the leading libertarian activist on the Burger Court. In that role he has continued to be the tribunal's foremost expert on, for example, the vexatious line between freedom of artistic expression and proscribable obscenity[42] (predictably finding himself among the minority of four who dissented from the contentious 1973 decisions that accorded generous leeway to the states in judging what is obscene.)[43]

Probably the most devout member of the Court, Brennan, in his principled and consistent championing of the free exercise of religion and an absolute separation of Church and State became the high tribunal's leading antiestablishmentarian. Thus, his seventy-page concurring opinion in *Abington School District* v. *Schempp* and *Murray* v. *Curlett* (1963),[44] which held unconstitutional state-mandated Bible reading and the Lord's Prayer in public schools, and his impassioned dissenting opinions in such accommodationist holdings as *Roemer* v. *Maryland Public Works Board* (1976)[45] and *Tilton* v. *Richardson* (1971),[46] represent his creed that under our Constitution the State must resolutely stay out of the Church and the Church must resolutely stay out of the State.

Even more prominently, and equally consistently–but with considerably more resort to judicial policy-making, to judicial legislating–Justice Brennan would become watchdog and advocate on the egalitarian front, particularly in matters of race and gender. Joined all but always by Justice Thurgood Marshall and usually, although not always, by Justices B. R. White and Blackmun, he would more often than not succeed in finding a fifth vote to provide victory for claims of invidious discrimination, even to the extent of embracing racial quotas–giving rise to allegations of support of "reverse discrimination." Ergo, he marshaled Justice Powell's vote and his authorship of that part of the famed *Bakke* (1978) opinion sanctioning "affirmative action" by constitutionalizing resort to considerations of race as a "plus" in educational admissions.[47] In 1979, in what may well be the most clear-cut case of judicial legislating on behalf of remedial/compensatory race-conscious policies, he spoke for a five-member majority–this time gaining Justice Stewart's support–that, in the face of precise and express statutory language and patent congressional intent *to the contrary,* sanctioned racial quotas in employment, overridingly on the basis of what he frankly termed the "spirit" rather than the "letter" of Title VII of the Civil Rights Act of 1964.[48]

Perhaps, however, Justice Brennan will be best remembered for his precedent-shattering opinion for a 6:2 Court in *Baker* v. *Carr* in 1962.[49] There, over lengthy, bitter dissenting opinions by Frankfurter and Harlan, Brennan, joined by Warren, Black, Douglas, Clark, and Stewart, held that aggrieved individuals had a constitutionally guaranteed right to come to the judicial branch to scrutinize alleged discriminatory legislative apportionment by the states. The decision, which set into motion a revolution in electoral districting, was a fitting tribute to the judicial resourcefulness and perseverance of its self-effacing yet determined author–who, time and again, warned that "the interest of the government is not that it shall win a case, but that Justice shall be done!"[50]

In February 1957 Justice Stanley F. Reed retired after more

than nineteen years on the Court—although he would continue to serve in senior status on the lower federal bench until the age of ninety-one in 1975! (He died five years later, the longest-lived individual ever to have been a Justice of the Supreme Court.) Ike's fourth appointment went to a rags-to-riches figure who, on the basis of background and experience, gave every promise of becoming an outstanding Justice. But he did not: *au contraire,* Charles Evans Whittaker was a major disappointment on the bench, deservedly, and all but unanimously, rated as a "failure" by the Court experts. He found the pressures of the high tribunal's docket overwhelming; he was uncomfortable with the jurisprudence and personality of some of his colleagues (Douglas in particular), and, in the face of his general distaste for and anguish in his new role, his health began to deteriorate. In April 1962 he retired as "disabled," according to the Court's records. In fact, he was approaching or indeed had suffered a nervous breakdown—the reason for which, according to the acerbic Douglas, was "Whittaker changed his mind so often."[51] He had served a mere five years.

That the President had selected him, however, was entirely comprehensible, for he met all of Eisenhower's criteria: like Kentucky's Reed he came from a mid-central state (Missouri); his age (fifty-six) was appropriate; he had made a record as one of the outstanding corporate trial lawyers of the region; he was a conservative Republican, yet he had made a genuine effort to appear nonpartisan in his private and public legal career; he had the enthusiastic backing of bench and bar as well as of the G.O.P.'s political leadership; and he had previous judicial experience on lower federal benches. Moreover, both Ike and Attorney General Brownell were impressed with the success story of the President's fellow Kansan who, while going to law school in the evenings, had worked as an office boy in one of Kansas City's most prestigious corporate law firms, a firm in which he ultimately had become a senior partner. He had first come to the Administration's attention in 1954 when a vacancy occurred on the U.S. District Court for Kansas. Ike's brother Arthur, a Kansas City banker, was a close friend of Whittaker's; and Roy Roberts, influential Republican publisher of the *Kansas City Star,* plus Kansas's two Republican Senators, Harry Darby and Frank Carlson, had all pushed hard for Whittaker, who was given the District Court Judgeship forthwith. Two years later he was promoted to the U.S. Court of Appeals for the Eighth Circuit, whence, after less than a year, and on Arthur Eisenhower[52] and Herbert Brownell's strong recommendations, he was promoted to the Supreme Court. He was readily confirmed without a formal roll call in March 1957.

Whittaker's posture on the Court was conservative and fully in line with the President's expectations. But he never found satisfaction, let alone enjoyment, in his brief tenure and the eight majority opinions he authored were of no genuine consequence. In fact, he managed to average little more than one a year—thus breaking Justice Van Devanter's modern record of barely three annually. Three years after his "disabled" retirement in 1962, he requested to be relieved from that status and formally resigned to return to the world of private enterprise with General Motors. Only then were his health, spirit, and *joie de vivre* restored.

Ike's fifth, and last, Court appointment was cut from an entirely different cloth in terms of his posture vis-à-vis the judicial function. Potter Stewart had not only been brought up in comfortable circumstances, but his father, James Garfield Stewart, had served as Mayor of Cincinnati for nine years and as a Justice of the Supreme Court of Ohio for twelve. The Stewarts had long been prominently active in Ohio Republican politics as part of the political retinue of Senator Robert A. Taft—for whose Presidential aspirations young Potter campaigned assiduously in the late 1940s. In mid-1952, however, while serving as Vice Mayor of Cincinnati, he transferred his allegiance to Eisenhower. He was convinced that Ike could win, and he was, in fact, more comfortable with Eisenhower's political stance than he was with Taft's. Still, he kept his ties with Ohio's conservative Republican organization, in which the state's junior U.S. Senator, John Bricker, played a key role. It was Bricker who had first brought the likeable and well-educated (Hotchkiss School, Yale University, Cambridge University, and Yale Law School) Stewart to Ike's attention by suggesting him for a vacancy on the U.S. Court of Appeals for the Fifth Circuit in

1954. Impressed with his background and credentials, which included service as a naval officer during World War II and a partnership in one of New York City's best law firms, the President appointed the then only thirty-nine-year-old attorney to that court. Four years later came the call to the Supreme Court.

During his brief tenure on the Court of Appeals, Potter Stewart quickly came to the attention of the legal fraternity through his carefully crafted, lucid opinions, his engaging style, and his independent jurisprudence. He demonstrated a healthy respect for judicial restraint, yet he also indicated strong attachment to such libertarian commitments as freedom of expression and desegregation. His colleagues valued his understanding of the judicial role; and not surprisingly his name was prominently mentioned for promotion to the Supreme Court as early as the Reed vacancy in 1957. But he had to wait for another year and one-half until his fellow Ohioan, Justice Harold H. Burton, retired from the Court early in October 1958. Ike then gave the brilliant young jurist a recess appointment to the Supreme Court.

Not everyone, however, was enchanted. Not at all enchanted was the Southern Democratic establishment in the Senate that, quite correctly, assumed that Stewart would become a "sure vote" on behalf of claims of racial amelioration. His record on the lower bench had given every indication of such behavior. A confirmation battle on Congress's return in January was assured. Spearheading it was the distinguished and powerful leader of the Southern bloc, Senator Richard B. Russell of Georgia, who charged that the Stewart nomination was "a part of a deliberate policy by the Department of Justice to perpetuate some recent decisions of the Court in segregation rulings, which decisions were partly based on *amicus curiae* briefs submitted by the Department of Justice."[53] He and his colleagues made clear that the opposition was not against the nominee himself, that, as Senator James O. Eastland of Mississippi put it, he was "an able lawyer . . . a man of integrity . . . very conscientious . . . an improvement over what we now have on the supreme bench,"[54] but that his stance on civil rights was objectionable, that it was symbolic of what Eastland viewed as the "fundamentally wrong" trend on the Court.[55] Stewart had made no secret of his commitment to the 1954 *Desegregation Cases* decision when, during his confirmation hearings before the Senate Judiciary Committee, he noted: "I would not like you to vote for me on the assumption . . . that I am dedicated to the cause of overturning that decision. Because, I am not."[56] The Committee subsequently approved him 12:3, Democratic Senators Eastland, Olin D. Johnston of South Carolina, and John L. McClellan of Arkansas casting the nays. Two of their Southern colleagues, Estes Kefauver of Tennessee and Sam J. Ervin, Jr., of North Carolina, voted to report the nomination to the Senate floor; the latter, however, would ultimately oppose confirmation itself. For four months and one day opponents then delayed the Stewart confirmation vote. When at last it came on May 5, 1959, the tally was 70:17, with the entire senatorial delegations from Alabama, Arkansas, Georgia, Louisiana, Mississippi, North Carolina, South Carolina, and Virginia, and Senator Spessard L. Holland of Florida, voting no.[57]

Justice Stewart lived up fully to the expectations of President Eisenhower *and* the Southern Senators. He charted a generally progressive-conservative or moderately liberal course, depending on one's perception. During the heyday of the Warren Court, he was more often than not found on the cautious, conservative, or "centrist" side, especially in matters concerning law and order and reapportionment and redistricting. But his stance on racial and sexual discrimination, and, in particular, on the First and Fourteenth amendments' guarantees of freedom of expression, found him only slightly less proindividual or progroup than his most advanced libertarian activist contemporaries, such as Douglas, Brennan, and Marshall. Thus, although yielding to no one in his devotion to the tenets of federalism, Stewart brooked no equivocation with egalitarian constitutional guarantees and commands. And some of his well-known opinions in the constitutional "disaster area" of obscenity testify to his generous approach to freedom of speech and press as well as privacy. Hence, his exasperated, concurring observation in *Jacobellis* v. *Ohio* (1964) (involving the movie *Les Amants*) that, under the First and Fourteenth amendments, criminal laws in this area are *faute de mieux* limited to hard-core pornography–which, he went on to say, he could characterize only with "I know it when I see it."[58] He had hardly assumed his seat on the bench in 1958 when he gave notice of his opposition to censorship of any kind by writing the Court's unanimous opinion that struck down the New York Board of Regents' proscription of the film version of D. H. Lawrence's *Lady Chatterley's Lover,* warning that the advocacy of ideas was not subject to censorship; that by doing so the state had "struck at the very heart of constitutionally protected liberty."[59] At the same time, however, Stewart was not about to be a party to a policy that, in his view, transformed the Bill of Rights "into a suicide pact"–as Justice Jackson had warned so eloquently in *Terminiello*[60]–a commitment to law enforcement that might well mean giving the benefit of the doubt to government rather than individual. Consequently, it was natural for Stewart to line up with like-minded Justices Clark, Harlan, and White in the realm of criminal procedure in dissenting from such celebrated and contentious 5:4 rulings as those in *Escobedo* v. *Illinois*[61] and *Miranda* v. *Arizona.*[62]

Stewart, high in President Nixon's esteem, was being seriously considered for promotion to Chief Justice on Earl Warren's ultimate retirement in 1969–and he might very well have been nominated. But in a long talk with the President in the Oval Office, he asked Nixon to remove him from the list of possibilities, believing strongly that the interests of the tribunal warranted an appointment from outside its membership, and that promotion from within was delicate and difficult and had not worked well for the Court in the on-the-record instances of White and Stone. In a *post facto* comment to the Associated Press, following Warren E. Burger's nomination as Chief Justice, however, Stewart observed that he might not have taken himself out of the running, after all, had Abe Fortas resigned earlier.[63] After Warren and Fortas's departure from the bench, followed two years later by those of Black and Harlan, Stewart and Byron R. White turned into the "swing men" on what had by then become the Burger Court. It was a role admirably suited for the cautious, judicious, fair-minded student of judicial power, whom the Court historians have adjudged to merit a high "average" ranking. It was the "swing man" role he comfortably continued until he issued the surprise announcement of his retirement at the end of the 1980–1981 term of Court, having served twenty-three years. At sixty-six, he was one of the younger Justices on the bench and in excellent health; but, as he told the press conference in which he informed the country that he had decided to step down: "I'm a firm believer that it's better to go too soon than stay too long."[64] In a gracious letter notifying his colleagues of his decision he observed: "This is not a time to try to say what these years as a member of the Court have meant to me. Probably you know. Let me only thank each of you for your friendship and your help."[65]

Although Stewart would not have won a prize for being the hardest worker on the Court, he always relished his work thereon, and he never missed a single day of oral argument! The jurist whom the senior correspondents of the press corps pronounced "our best friend on the Court since Hugo Black"[66] had penned some 300 opinions for the Court and another 350 in concurrence or dissent. He may well not be identified with many of the Court's landmark decisions–with the possible exceptions of his majority opinions in *Katz* v. *United States*[67] (an important 1967 case broadening the protection against wiretapping) and *Gregg* v. *Georgia*[68] (upholding capital punishment under carefully controlled circumstances in 1976); his concurring opinions in the 1972 *Furman* v. *Georgia* capital punishment cases[69] and the 1971 *Pentagon Papers* cases;[70] and his stirring dissenting opinion in the 1980 *Fullilove* v. *Klutznick* case that sanctioned a ten percent "set aside" racial quota for construction work on federally funded projects.[71] Yet he will be remembered as a principled constitutionalist who had that all-too-rare ability to write both simply and clearly. The seat he vacated not only provided President Reagan with his initial opportunity to nominate a Justice of the Supreme Court, but the President would make history that summer of 1981 by selecting the first woman to sit on the highest tribunal of the land, Sandra Day O'Connor.

Murdered on November 22, 1963, less than three years after he had assumed office at forty-three, John Fitzgerald Kennedy, the first Roman Catholic to be elected President, was not allowed sufficient time to establish a ratable record in office. Handsome, sensuous, urbane, and cultured and surrounded by a glamorous family, he set an elegant new tone and style for the country. His ringing phrases captured the imagination and the attention of the young; his cautious willingness to experiment and pioneer, at least on paper, roused the intellectual community to his side; his frequent open press conferences, replete with good-natured give and take, rendered him highly popular with the media. He was a master in the art of communicating, among modern Presidents probably second only to F.D.R. and, perhaps, Ronald Reagan. His Administration sparkled with ideas for a better and more constructive life for more people everywhere. Yet in most instances—the Peace Corps being a notable exception—their realization had to await the advent of his successor, who knew how to translate the Kennedy ideals and ideas into legislative reality—something that Kennedy had not generally mastered. Had he lived and been granted another term in office, chances are that he would have recouped a good many of his defeats at the hand of Congress—even as he had overcome those in foreign policy after the Bay of Pigs debacle in 1961. His courageously principled confrontation with Chairman Nikita S. Khrushchev of the U.S.S.R. over Soviet missile deployment in Cuba one year later was proof of his mettle, as was the establishment of the hot line to Moscow and the negotiation and ratification of the Nuclear Test Ban Treaty of 1963. On the other side of the developing ledger, however, was the emerging involvement in Vietnam, for which the Kennedy Administration must share a very real measure of blame.

John Kennedy was able to make two appointments to the Court, both going to members of his election and governmental team: Deputy Attorney General Byron R. White and Secretary of Labor Arthur J. Goldberg. He chose them preeminently because he knew them both well; because he was comfortable with them personally, professionally, and philosophically; because he trusted their dedication to the country and to the Constitution; because, in his brother Bobby's characterization, they were "his kind of people." It is conceivable that the President raised an eyebrow or two, given White's fairly prompt turn to the right on the bench on a good many issues; but he had little more than one term of Court to observe the two men. Goldberg of course, allowed himself to be coaxed off the high bench by Lyndon Johnson less than two years after Kennedy's death. It is tempting to muse how the shape of constitutional law might now be different had he lived and had Goldberg, as would almost surely have been the case, remained on the Court.

President Kennedy's first opportunity to fill a Court vacancy came with Justice Charles E. Whittaker's eager withdrawal, effective April 1, 1962. Primary responsibility for the search for a successor fell naturally to the Attorney General, Robert F. Kennedy. There was no dearth of excellent candidates–essentially there never is if the will to find them exists–and, in fact, the two brothers had already compiled a list of distinguished possibilities for contingency purposes. It consisted of six outstanding figures in governmental and legal circles: two (White and Goldberg) were high-ranking members of the Kennedy Cabinet; two were *the* then probably most highly regarded state supreme court Chief Justices (Walter B. Schaefer of Illinois and Roger J. Traynor of California); one was an able and effective member of the U.S. Court of Appeals for the Third Circuit (William H. Hastie); and one was one of the country's most renowned professors of constitutional law (Paul A. Freund of Harvard).

Because all of the individuals on the list more than amply met the Kennedy requirements of professional qualification, personal integrity, judicial temperament, intellectual capacity, public visibility, and experience and because all had evinced *real* politics more or less sympathetic to that of the Administration, Jack and Bobby Kennedy could afford to let other considerations govern. They were not especially concerned with age and geography (although they dealt with those factors collaterally) or with the presence or absence of judicial experience; they were, thus, able to indulge in the luxury of selecting someone with whom they would be truly comfortable, both professionally and personally. Ultimately their choices narrowed to Goldberg and White, and J.F.K. would send both to the Court in due course. There was potent pressure for the two outstanding state Chief Justices, but neither brother knew either one directly. Professor Freund, whom they did know well, was a strong candidate–in fact, some deemed him more in the running than Goldberg.[72] But Freund had some visible detractors in the legal fraternity and, more important, he was very much a "Frankfurter man" jurisprudentially (and, like Frankfurter, Jewish). There is considerable speculation that had Justice Frankfurter stepped down from the Court then rather than some five months later, Paul Freund would very likely have replaced him. Judge Hastie, the first black person to sit on a U.S. Court of Appeals, was an attractive candidate indeed. But the President had just encountered rough going in Congress with his embarrassingly unsuccessful attempt to create a Cabinet-level Department of Housing and Urban Development, with Robert C. Weaver, an able and experienced black public servant, as its Secretary; and he shied away from another potentially dangerous political confrontation. Thus, it came down to Goldberg or White. As a reporter would later record the events of the ultimate decision:

> The Attorney General tilted back in his chair and said, "You wanted someone who generally agreed with you on what role government should play in American life, what role the individual in society should have. You didn't think how he would vote in an apportionment case or in a criminal case. You wanted someone who, in the long run, you could believe would be best. You wanted someone who agreed generally with your views of the country." Both he and the President believed that White and Arthur Goldberg met that test. They could not be as sure of the others on the list.[73]

Byron White seemed perfectly suited and J.F.K. was even closer to him than to Goldberg. A youthful and vigorous forty-five, one of the younger appointees in the Court's history, White was born in Fort Collins, Colorado, and grew up in Wellington, a tiny town in a sugar-beet growing area near the Wyoming border. He knew poverty and hard work early; while still a young boy, he worked in the fields and on the railroad. Yet success was not long in coming. In 1938 he was graduated at the top of his class from the University of Colorado. He had been President of the student body, had earned an early *Phi Beta Kappa* key, and had been a popular All-American in football (called "Whizzer White"). He won a Rhodes scholarship to Oxford, but decided to delay enrollment for one term to accept a lucrative contract to play professional football for the Pittsburgh Steelers (where his $15,000 starting salary as a "driving halfback of matchless skills" was twice as much as anyone else in the National Football League was getting). At the end of the season he took his nest egg off to Oxford; in London he met and became a close friend of John F. Kennedy, whose father was then Ambassador to the Court of St. James. When war broke out late in 1939, all Rhodes scholars were sent home, and White entered the Yale School of Law (also concurrently playing outstanding football with the Detroit Lions). He enlisted in the Navy in 1942, serving in the Solomon Islands as PT-boat squadron skipper and intelligence officer; one of his fellow PT-boat officers was Jack Kennedy. It was White who wrote the official account of the battle events that were later portrayed in the movie *PT 109*. After the war, White returned to Yale, where he was graduated *magna cum laude,* served as law clerk to Chief Justice Vinson, and then began thirteen years of private practice in a prestigious Denver law firm. When in the late 1950s Jack Kennedy entered the Presidential race seriously, White became an effective and staunch supporter and organized the nationwide Citizens for Kennedy-Johnson in 1960. After the victorious election White was awarded with an appointment as Deputy U.S. Attorney General, a post in which he served with élan and distinction, especially in his personal command of the 600 federal marshals he sent to help quell racial disturbances in Montgomery, Alabama, in May 1961. A smiling President was observed pointing with obvious pleasure and pride to the front-page headline of the *New York Herald Tribune:* "WHIZZER WHITE TO SUPREME COURT–LAWYER, NAVAL OFFICER, FOOTBALL STAR." The subtitle read: "Kennedy Picks Friend, An Aide in Justice Dept."[74] White's confirmation on April 11, 1962, was by unanimous voice vote.

Almost at once it became clear that Justice White would embark on an independent and, arguably with the exception of the realms of race and gender litigation, an utterly nondoctrinaire career. It is one that defies categorization other than to note that it has been considerably more conservative in some realms of civil liberty than might have been anticipated by his nominator. Thus, during the remaining years of the Warren era, White could normally be found with Stewart, Harlan, and Clark on the side of governmental authority in many of the famed criminal-justice decisions, such as *Escobedo* v. *Illinois* (1964)[75] and *Miranda* v. *Arizona* (1966).[76] In First Amendment free-expression cases too (where the libertarians could usually count on Stewart, and especially so in freedom-of-the-press cases), White was to be found more often on the other side, as he also proved to be in certain symbolic speech[77] and, especially, in obscenity decisions. Thus, in the landmark 1973 obscenity cases he provided the decisive fifth vote by joining the four Nixon appointees in adopting a relatively tough regulatory posture.[78] Conversely, his posture on the race issue and, later, on that of gender was consistently far more activist or liberal than Stewart's.[79] Indeed, as the years went by, White turned into an all but predictable, certain ally of Justices Brennan and Marshall–usually joined by Justice Blackmun–in claims alleging racial or sexual or other class discrimination.[80]

Justice White's stance, and his centrist alliance with Stewart, both became more pronounced when the Warren Court turned into the Burger Court. On the latter, the two Justices clearly held, and appeared to be quite comfortable in being, the key or swing votes between the two generally predictable blocs as of 1971–1972, despite, or in spite of, the interesting fact that the two swing-centrists were not at all infrequently on opposite sides of decisions. This became particularly evident in such significant, emotion-charged issues as: abortion (1973, *et seq.*, here usually on opposite sides, Stewart pro and White anti by choice);[81] capital punishment laws–both were con (1972),[82] pro (1976),[83] and White, now without Stewart, was on *both* sides in 1983;[84] the 1971 *Pentagon Papers Case*[85] (involving the government's right to classify documents in the interest of national security *versus* the right of the press to publish them once they had fallen into its hands) as well as the *Texas Property Tax Case* (1973)[86] (where the two were on opposite sides); and in the *Richmond/Suburban*

Counties School Consolidation Case (1973)[87] (where they were, in all likelihood, again on opposite sides in a *per curiam* [unsigned] 4:4 tie decision). The swing-vote posture very likely represents a deliberate and deliberative jurisprudential role, clothed with often decisive power. It is a role that Justice White, now (late 1984) in his twenty-second year on the Court, evidently relishes. A diligent worker and admired colleague, perhaps somewhat less sophisticated and more blunt than Stewart and less elegant a stylist than his erstwhile center-swing colleague, White has been accorded a rating among the "average" Justices. Future events may well dictate a reassessment. In the meantime Justice White will in all probability continue along the not easily predictable, cautious centrist course he has charted for himself–which again cast him in the role of the "swing" man in the thirty-four cases in which the Court divided 5:4 in its 1982–1983 term.

On August 28, 1962, Felix Frankfurter, the brilliant jurist Judge Learned Hand once styled as "the most important single figure in our whole judicial system,"[88] bowed to the effects of a stroke suffered during the preceding April and, in a touching letter to President Kennedy, announced his retirement from "the institution whose concerns have been the absorbing interest of my life."[89] On the twenty-ninth, the President acceded to the request in a warm and sensitive reply. That afternoon he called a news conference in which he made the event public and announced that he had chosen Secretary of Labor Arthur J. Goldberg to fill the Holmes-Cardozo-Frankfurter seat. It did not come as a surprise to many. The fifty-four-year-old renowned labor expert had been more or less next in line after White for the post he very much wanted. Kennedy's regard and enthusiasm for Goldberg's ability and his warm personal feelings toward him were a matter of record. If there was any momentary hesitation in naming him to the Court at all, it was because of the President's reluctance to lose so close a personal and political adviser and so skillful a Cabinet member, one who had long been one of the country's most successful and most respected labor-management conciliators. But after momentarily pondering the possibility of nominating Abraham A. Ribicoff, his recently designated Secretary of Health, Education and Welfare and longtime supporter, he reasoned it was more important to have an individual of Goldberg's qualities on the Court than in the executive branch. Kennedy had discussed his intentions with both Chief Justice Warren and Justice Frankfurter himself and found wholehearted backing of his choice.[90] The nation's reaction was universally favorable and, after receiving the ready approval of the Senate Judiciary Committee, Arthur Goldberg was confirmed at the end of September. Only Senator Strom Thurmond of South Carolina recorded his opposition—albeit without giving a reason. Thus, the new Justice could take his seat in time for the October 1962 term of Court.

Like the man he succeeded, a Jew and of immigrant stock, Goldberg's rise to the top was in the best American tradition of *per aspera ad astra.* "America Sings in Goldberg Story," Ralph McGill headlined his column of September 8 in the *Washington Evening Star,* pointing to the appointee's passion for books and education, which aided his rise to the top. Goldberg was born on Chicago's West Side, one of eleven children of Russian-born parents, and he worked his way through Northwestern University Law School, graduating at the top of his class in 1929. For a time he worked for a firm that had him headed toward becoming a specialist on mortgage foreclosures. Goldberg loathed that task and ultimately opened his own law office, soon beginning to specialize in labor law. It became the center of his professional career that led him into a supremely successful thirteen-year role as general counsel of the United Steel Workers, the Congress of Industrial Organizations, and the American Federation of Labor, whence he entered the Kennedy Administration. Cultured and scholarly, he was a man of action as well as ideas, indeed, a worthy successor to Felix Frankfurter.

But Arthur Goldberg, as had been widely expected, pursued an entirely different jurisprudence than that practiced so tenaciously by Felix Frankfurter for almost a quarter of a century. The new Justice lost little time in demonstrating his attachment to the kind of judicial activism in the realms of civil rights and liberties that henceforth gave the Warren Court a usually solid libertarian wing. Thus, he and Justice White were frequently on opposite sides of the Court's lineup, although in his own perception of the judicial function, the President was pleased by the roles played by both men. During his less than three years on the Court, Justice Goldberg showed a zest for innovation in the law that left an imprint far out of proportion to the brief period he served—so brief that the Court's observers believed that an "average" ranking would be the only equitable one to bestow. But his energy and ability and his determined, activist pioneering in the world of new policy decisions contributed to changing American constitutional law. Thus, although he was no longer on the Court to see the ideas embraced at least in part by a majority, it was he who first raised the specter of the unconstitutionality of the application of the death penalty on the basis of the cruel and unusual punishment and due process of law clauses;[91] it was he, more than any other contemporary Justice except Douglas, who gave an expansive interpretation to the "additional fundamental rights" that he found in the Ninth Amendment;[92] it was he who spoke for the 6:3 Court that ruled the denial of passports to members of the Communist party and its fronts "unconstitutional on its face";[93] and it was he who authored the Court's landmark 5:4 decision in the coerced confession case of *Escobedo* v. *Illinois* (1964).[94] Why, then, did he leave the job he cherished so much so rapidly and amidst such universal astonishment to accept Lyndon B. Johnson's request *cum* offer to become Ambassador to the United Nations to succeed the deceased Adlai E. Stevenson? Surely, the President who, after all, had not been the one who appointed Goldberg to the Court, had no obvious leverage on him. Numerous highly speculative reasons have been advanced ever since, a good many of them contrived, implausible, and silly. According to L.B.J. himself, however, he had heard from economist John Kenneth Galbraith, among others, that Goldberg "would step down from his position to take a job that would be more challenging to him,"[95] one in which he would "speak for America before the nations of the world."[96] Arthur Goldberg, from his own vantage point, candidly asserted in an interview with the author—after wistfully asking, "Have you ever had your arm twisted by L.B.J.?"[97]—that he had agreed to leave the Court for two reasons: first, his deep conviction that he might be able to negotiate an end to the nightmare in Vietnam; second, his profound commitment to public service. Evidently he was also heavily influenced by a clearly implied understanding of an ultimate return to the Court.[98]

The tragic crime in Dallas brought one of the country's master politicians to the Presidency in the person of Lyndon Baines Johnson. Superb legislative leader, arm-twister, and I.O.U.-collector, he stepped into office and maneuvered some of the most far-reaching domestic legislation since the days of the New Deal. The nation had barely begun to recover from the wrench and trauma of President Kennedy's funeral when the tempestuous, mercurial man began to wheel and deal the languishing Kennedy program into enactment, adding a full measure of his own. In his first speech to Congress as President, he propelled legislators as well as citizens into action on the civil rights front: "We have talked for 100 years or more. It is now time to write it in the books of law." And so Congress did by passing the landmark Civil Rights Act of 1964, the most significant and certainly the most substantial statute on the subject in almost a century. Encouraged by his smashing defeat of Senator Barry Goldwater in the Presidential election of 1964–his 61.1 percent of the popular vote exceeding even that of F.D.R. in 1936–L.B.J. went on to post an impressive roster of legislative accomplishments. Among these were Medicare; improved social security benefits; higher minimum wages; environmental amelioration; the Voting Rights Act of 1965; the first massive federal aid to primary and secondary education; major housing programs. His motto of "come now, and let us reason together" succeeded everywhere along the line. America's blacks and America's poor had never had a better, nor a more effective friend at the nation's helm. L.B.J.'s mentor, F.D.R., would have been proud.

Yet Lyndon B. Johnson's Waterloo was foreign policy, Vietnam in particular. He was impatient with the intricacies of overseas diplomacy; his naïve belief that his internal *modus operandus* could be applied externally as well; his short temper and lack of patience; his emotional reactions to what he sensed were the foreign diplomats' sneering view of his manners and bearing; his craving for adulation; his ill-applied concept of national honor and sincere, yet almost puerile patriotism; and his unwillingness to accept defeat allowed him to be pulled deeper and deeper into the quagmire of Vietnam. By the beginning of 1968, with more than half a million American forces committed to Vietnam, with internecine warfare at home, with the campuses aflame, with Senator Eugene McCarthy ringing up astonishing numbers of votes in Presidential primary elections, the heartsick President went on the air to announce that he would not run again that fall. Instead, as he told the nation and the world, he would devote every waking moment of the balance of his term, and beyond, to the pursuit of peace. Yet his subsequent efforts were in vain–largely because he was basically incapable of shifting the gears of his *modi operandi* and his personality sufficiently; and in January 1969 L.B.J. went back to Texas and his beloved ranch in the Pedernales River Valley.

The final verdict on Lyndon Johnson must await more passage of time: how to weigh accomplished brilliance at home with abject failure abroad will prove to be no easy task. He had the perhaps macabre satisfaction of seeing his successor wrestle just as unsuccessfully with Vietnam until, one day before Mr. Johnson died on January 22, 1973, Richard M. Nixon's emissaries concluded a shaky settlement of the terrible war.

Lyndon B. Johnson made four nominations to the Court but he succeeded with only two. The first (Abe Fortas as Associate Justice in 1965) came as a result of coaxing Goldberg off the bench and into the U.N.; the second (Thurgood Marshall in 1967) was the first appointment of a black American citizen to the Court; the third (Fortas's projected promotion in 1968 to Chief Justice to replace Earl Warren) failed ignominiously; and, as a result, the fourth (Homer Thornberry's projected replacement of Fortas as Associate Justice) never materialized. With the exception of the Marshall appointment, which was as noble and timely as it was strategic, the Johnson nominations were sheer cronyism. Yet the nominees were not without qualifications. Judge Thornberry, although not outstanding, was a capable and experienced public servant; and not even Fortas's most advanced detractors would deny his uncanny ability, towering intellect, indeed brilliance. It is a pity that by his ill-conceived, arrogantly thoughtless, downright stupid, off-the-bench actions he found it necessary to resign after a few short years as Associate Justice.

Ironically, Abe Fortas had not at all sought a seat on the Court. In fact, he had demurred repeatedly, addressing, among others, the following letter to the President on July 19, 1965:[99]

> For The President:
>
> Again, my dear friend, I am obligated and honored by your confidence and generosity—to an extent which is beyond my power adequately to acknowledge.
>
> But after painful searching, I've decided to decline—with a heart full of gratitude. Carol thinks I should accept this greatest honor that a lawyer could receive—this highest appointive post in the nation. But I want a few more years of activity. I want a few more years to try to be of service to you and the Johnson family. And I want and feel that in justice I should take a few more years to stabilize this law firm in the interests of the young men who have enlisted here.
>
> This has been a hard decision—but not nearly as hard as another which had the virtue of continuing association with your trials and tribulations and greatness.
>
> I shall always be grateful.
>
> Abe

It took all of the President's persuasive powers during an entire week to get the balky Fortas to agree. In fact, Fortas never actually said yes: the President, having invited him to his White House office on July 28, simply informed him that he was about to go over to the theater in the East Wing "to announce his appointment to the Supreme Court," and that he could either stay in the office or accompany him.[100] Fortas opted for the latter course. But to the assembled reporters he appeared only slightly less disenchanted than had been the grim-faced Goldberg, who, with his tearful wife, Dorothy, and their son, Robert, by his side, had reluctantly agreed to become America's Ambassador to the U.N.: "I shall not, Mr. President, conceal the pain with which I leave the Court after three years of service. It has been the richest and most satisfying period of my career."[101] It was a veritable funereal ceremony–except for a broadly beaming L.B.J., who declared that "the job has sought the man–a scholar, a profound thinker, a lawyer of superior ability and a man of deeply compassionate feelings."[102]

President Johnson's regard for Abe Fortas was matched only by his regard for the Court as an institution itself. His choice may well have had its genesis seventeen years earlier: at that time, U.S. Representative Lyndon B. Johnson (D.-Tex.) was engaged in a bruising primary battle for the Texas Democratic Senatorial nomination with ex-Governor Coke Stevenson. Neither candidate had received an absolute majority in the initial race; thus, they faced a runoff. Almost one million votes were cast in the runoff, with Johnson emerging as victor by the hairbreadth margin of eighty-seven votes. Amid charges of gross irregularities, including ballot stuffing, an acrimonious legal battle ensued in which a federal district court issued a restraining order, affirmed by the U.S. Court of Appeals for the Fifth Circuit, against printing Johnson's name on the general election ballot in November. The frantic Johnson lawyers rushed to the nation's capital, where a thirty-eight-year-old attorney, an L.B.J. acquaintance from early New Deal days named Abe Fortas, filed an urgent appeal to the Supreme Court, contending that the federal judiciary had no jurisdiction in a Texas Senate election. The member of the Supreme Court in charge of the Fifth Circuit was Justice Hugo L. Black, who ordered a stay of the lower court's restraining order, thus enabling Johnson to get his name on that crucial ballot. "Landslide Lyndon," as he was jeeringly called, easily won the November election, and he never forgot Fortas's service. The two men–although an unlikely team: the huge, earthy, tough Johnson compared to the almost petite, sophisticated, cultured Fortas–became the closest of friends. Johnson often leaned heavily for advice and counsel on Fortas, for whom he felt a personal affection and respect bordering on adulation. Indeed, it was the President's stubborn unwillingness to forego those services even after he had sent Fortas to the Court that proved to be one of the key weapons in the hands of the opponents to the latter's proposed elevation to the Chief Justiceship. For, admittedly, Justice Fortas continued to serve the Chief Executive by participating in important military and diplomatic strategy conferences, by aiding in the drafting of delicate executive orders, by rendering advice on such delicate issues as racial controversies and street rioting, and by generally answering a host of Presidential calls for assistance. That sundry other members of the high bench throughout the Court's history had provided similar services to their President does not gainsay the compromising of separation of powers attending such practices. Yet, confident and proud, the two longtime associates could see no wrong in their continuing relationship.

The fifty-five-year-old Fortas, whose nomination the Senate quickly confirmed in early August—with only Republican Senators Carl T. Curtis (Nebraska), Strom Thurmond (South Carolina), and John J. Williams (Delaware) voicing opposition—brought with him a remarkable record of achievement. A native of Memphis, son of an Orthodox Jewish cabinetmaker who had migrated to Tennessee from England, Fortas—a superb violinist—had gone to Yale Law School, like many of his colleagues on the bench, following his scholarship undergraduate days at Presbyterian Southwestern College in his home city. A superb student—"with Abe," a brother once recalled, "it was study, study, study"[103]—and the editor of the *Yale Law Journal,* he was fascinated by the New Deal. He soon joined it—after a few years of teaching at Yale—initially under Chairman William O. Douglas of the Securities and Exchange Commission, the longtime friend who had been one of his Yale professors. Fortas eventually gravitated to governmental units that were then close to the policy center of the Roosevelt era, such as the Department of the Interior and the Public Works Administration (P.W.A.), whose General Counsel he became at twenty-nine. Just three years later, he was Undersecretary of the Interior, working with the redoubtable Harold L. Ickes, the department's head, who quickly joined the ranks of Fortas's enthusiasts. Fortas stayed in that post until 1946 when he joined two other well-known, successful New Deal figures, Thurman Arnold and Paul A. Porter, in establishing what became one of Washington's most prestigious and lucrative law firms (Arnold, Fortas & Porter). But it was also a public-spirited firm that became famous—or infamous—as the one firm willing to lend its talents, often *gratis,* to the many victims of the McCarthy era. Later the firm, one of whose partners would be Mrs. Abe Fortas (Carol Agger), who had met her husband at Yale, continued its aid to the underdogs of society. Thus, the future Justice Fortas was the attorney the Supreme Court assigned to represent Clarence Earl Gideon in his successful battle to win the right of counsel for indigents in noncapital as well as capital criminal cases.[104]

In his three and one-half years on the Court, Fortas showed himself to be a firm libertarian when it came to fundamental human rights. In that sense he filled Goldberg's shoes, although Goldberg tended to side with those who favored governmental-regulatory powers when it came to interpreting certain aspects of antitrust legislation. But Fortas's scholarly and structured style, his penchant for effective phrasemaking, and his additional year on the bench prompted the Court experts to give him a "near great" rating, an entire category higher than Goldberg. In view of his brief service the rating is probably rather generous. Yet it is arguably not surprising given such trailblazing Fortas opinions as that in the *Gault* case (1967), for example, which wrought a revolution in constitutional law by extending most of the Bill of Rights safeguards to juvenile offenders.[105] That seminal opinion accentuates the Fortas gift for poignant phrasemaking: "Under our Constitution, the condition of being a boy does not justify a kangaroo court."[106] It will long serve to associate decision and author. Nor is it surprising given his uncanny ability unfailingly to reach the heart of a complex legal matter, as he did in writing a stinging dissent in the *New York Textbook Case of 1968* (in which the Court upheld 6:3 the state's requirement to lend textbooks to students in private and parochial schools):

> Apart from the differences between textbooks and bus rides, the present statute does not call for extending to children attending sectarian schools the same service or facility extended to children in public schools. This statute calls for furnishing special, separate, and particular books, especially, separately, and particularly chosen by religious sects or their representatives for use in their sectarian schools. This is the infirmity. . . .[107]

But Fortas's promising career was to be cut short by a combination of political power plays and personal greed. When Chief Justice Warren wrote the President on June 13, 1968, announcing his intention to retire "effective at your leisure," Johnson—with the enthusiastic concurrence of Warren—two weeks later made Warren's decision public and, at the same time, nominated Fortas to succeed him. It was, of course, a logical choice. It was also just a few months before the Presidential elections of that year—one in which the Republican party had every reason to sense victory. Perhaps, with the apparently promised aid of such influential G.O.P. stalwarts as Minority Leader Everett McKinley Dirksen, and the L.B.J.-taken-for-granted support of his old friend, "Mr. Senate," namely Georgia's powerful Democrat Richard B. Russell, Fortas could have been confirmed. But L.B.J. committed three tactical errors: (1) he misjudged the firmness of Dirksen's support and/or ability to "deliver" the necessary Republican votes in what was a Presidential election year; (2) he had managed, uncharacteristically, to antagonize Russell by permitting his controversial Attorney General, Ramsey Clark, seriously to delay a federal judgeship for a Russell favorite, Alexander Lawrence, because of an allegedly racist speech he had made in the 1950s;[108] and (3) because of his unwise move of simultaneously nominating old crony Homer Thornberry for the resultant vacancy. That was simply too much for a good many objective and fair-minded Senators, such as William B. Spong, Jr. (D.-Va.). Thornberry was a onetime mayor of Austin, for eight terms the holder of L.B.J.'s former seat in the House, and a Johnson-appointed federal district and appellate judge preceding his nomination to the Supreme Court. The choice was obviously dictated by personal and political friendship. Judge Thornberry—one of those who would support the Nixon nomination of G. Harrold Carswell two years later—was a decent and experienced public servant of moderate ability, but he was hardly of the caliber that would have prompted a basically hostile Senate to overlook political factors.

Thus, cronyism, the timing of the nominations, the political climate, accumulated hostility to the Warren Court, Fortas's posture on some of the more controversial issues in which he participated (and some in which he did not), charges of judicial impropriety by his continuing extrajudicial active counseling of the President, and the revelation that he had accepted a then-huge lecture fee ($15,000) to conduct a series of university seminars during the summer of 1968 combined ultimately to doom the proposed Fortas promotion and with it the Thornberry nomination. Although the Senate Judiciary Committee did report Fortas's designation favorably, 11:6, it ran into a filibuster on the Senate floor, and a motion to terminate the latter by cloture failed by a wide margin. Shortly thereafter Fortas asked Johnson to withdraw his nomination; the President complied, disdaining any other attempted appointment. Thornberry's nomination was, thus, moot, and Earl Warren remained at the helm for another year.

It was not until May 4, 1969, that the final chapter in the Fortas tragedy began to be written with *Life* magazine's revelations that in 1966 the Justice had accepted, although several months later returned, a $20,000 fee from the family foundation of Louis E. Wolfson, the multimillionaire industrialist who had since been imprisoned for stock manipulations. Initially based on an arrangement that was intended to be a lifelong association in an advisory capacity with the foundation, the canceled agreement had provided for an annual stipend of $20,000, which would devolve on Mrs. Fortas in the event of the Justice's demise. On May 15, 1969, under heavy fire gleefully and subtly stoked by Attorney General Mitchell and the President himself,[109] the career of one of the most gifted individuals ever to sit on the Supreme Court ended. Abe Fortas resigned in a two-sentence missive to Nixon, to which the President consented in a one-sentence reply. In a long letter to Chief Justice Warren—a copy of which he sent to Nixon with Warren's consent—the devastated Fortas recounted in close detail the history of his involvement with Wolfson and avowed his complete innocence of any wrongdoing. Because of opposition by younger members of his old firm, Fortas did not return to it but, disdaining the life of a recluse, commenced a new career in private law practice. Less than two weeks after he had returned to the

U.S. Supreme Court for the first time in over twelve years, to argue a case, he succumbed to a ruptured aorta at seventy-one in April 1982.

Justice Tom C. Clark's retirement at the end of the Court's 1966–1967 term afforded President Johnson his last opportunity to fill a vacancy–and the chance to realize one of his repeatedly voiced dual goals: to send a nonwhite and nonmale to the high bench. His choice was as easy as it was obvious: his Solicitor General, Thurgood Marshall, previously a judge on the U.S. Court of Appeals for the Second Circuit and before that Counsel to the Legal Defense and Educational Fund of the National Association for the Advancement of Colored People (N.A.A.C.P.). "MARSHALL NAMED FOR HIGH COURT, ITS FIRST NEGRO" read the front-page headline in the *New York Times*. The subtitle elaborated: "Johnson Calls Nominee 'Best Qualified,' and Rights Leaders are Jubilant–Southerners Silent on Confirmation."[110] Following his dramatic announcement in the White House Rose Garden, with the nominee by his side, the President told reporters that he had been subjected to "very little pressure of any kind" on the fifty-eight-year-old Marshall's nomination, declaring that it was one clearly earned by the nominee's "distinguished record" in the law, and added: "He is best qualified by training and by very valuable service to the country. I believe it is the right thing to do, the right time to do it, the right place."[111] Only one other individual had, in fact, closely participated in the President's selection: his new Attorney General, Ramsey Clark, the son of the retiring Justice, Tom C. Clark. The nomination of another distinguished black jurist, William H. Hastie of the U.S. Court of Appeals for the Third Circuit–who, indeed, was senior to Marshall in the early civil rights battles and who had figured prominently as a candidate for the Whittaker vacancy in the Kennedy Administration in 1962–had been strongly urged on L.B.J. by bar and bench to become the first nonwhite nominee. But the President demurred: "Bill Hastie isn't known," he commented to a delegation of lawyers, headed by one of his Washington confidants, James Rowe.[112]

Marshall, the great-grandson of a slave, son of a Pullman-car waiter, and steward at an exclusive white country club on Chesapeake Bay, thus broke the racial barrier. If anyone was a logical and deserving choice to do so, it was this longtime champion of equality of opportunity. His parents had believed to the utmost in the value of education—his mother sold her engagement ring to pay for at least part of his college expenses at Lincoln University in Oxford, Pennsylvania. From there he went to Howard University Law School, ranking at the top of the class of 1933. Soon entering the field of civil rights, he won his first bittersweet victory in 1935 when his legal acumen and strategy compelled the University of Maryland (which had earlier denied him admission to its Law School) to accept Donald Murray as its first black law student.[113] (In fact, Murray was the first of his race to enter *any* state law school below the Mason-Dixon Line.) Marshall joined the N.A.A.C.P.'s legal department in 1936 and was named its chief counsel two years later. In 1961 President Kennedy appointed him to the Court of Appeals, and, late in 1965, President Johnson brought him back to active legal work by naming him Solicitor General of the United States (the third-highest post in the Department of Justice).

Thurgood Marshall's career as counsel for the N.A.A.C.P. mirrors the story of the upward climb of the fortunes of America's black men and women. Handling hundreds of cases, he tried thirty-two before the Supreme Court, winning all but three of them. His most notable victory of course was the Court's 1954 historic, unanimous decision banning compulsory racial segregation in the public schools throughout the nation.[114]

Predictably, the Marshall nomination ran into considerable and protracted opposition, led by Democratic Senators from the Deep South. They had recognized the inevitability of a black appointment for some time, but they were not about to accept it without a battle, concentrating their attacks on his well-known liberal philosophy and what some regarded as defective legal knowledge. Thus, Senator Strom Thurmond of South Carolina at one point read more than sixty complicated questions, studded with quotes from and about political figures of the 1860s, to the nominee during lengthy hearings before the Judiciary Committee. The vote on confirmation was delayed for two and one-half months until August 31. But when it came, it was by the decisive margin of 69:11. Of those Senators who were present and voting in opposition to Marshall all except one–Robert C. Byrd (D.-W. Va.)–were from the Deep South. And all but one–Strom Thurmond–were Democrats (Thurmond being a Democrat-turned-Republican).[115] A sign of the changing times was that among those casting affirmative votes were six Southern Senators: Democrat William J. Fulbright of Arkansas, Albert Gore of Tennessee, William B. Spong, Jr., of Virginia, and Ralph Yarborough of Texas; and Republicans Howard H. Baker, Jr., of Tennessee and John G. Tower of Texas. On October 2, 1967, Lyndon B. Johnson paid an unannounced visit to the Supreme Court, where he witnessed the swearing in of the broadly beaming Justice Thurgood Marshall, who took his oath in a private ceremony conducted by the Court's oldest member, eighty-one-year-old Hugo L. Black of Alabama.

The new appointee readily sided with Justices Douglas, Warren, Brennan, Fortas, and, somewhat less frequently, Black during the remaining two years of the Warren Court. When the latter turned into the Burger Court, Justice Marshall became an even more identifiable and predictable ally of the remaining libertarian activists on the Court, especially of Douglas and Brennan. With the former's health-dictated retirement in late 1975, Marshall and Brennan thus rendered themselves into *the* two most reliable, indeed, certain unified libertarian activists on the high bench. They voted together to the tune of ninety-seven percent in almost all cases involving claims of infractions of civil rights and liberties in general[116] and of allegations of denials of the equal protection of the laws in race and gender cases in particular.[117] So committed did Marshall prove to be to remedial, preferential, compensatory corrective action in the racial sector that, according to Douglas, who disapproved of "reverse discrimination" on the affirmative action front–such as in the *De Funis* case,[118] for example–Marshall told his colleagues: "You guys have been practicing discrimination for years. Now it is our turn."[119] In his seventeenth year on the Court now (late 1984), his career has been somewhat uneven participatorily. It has reached high points in the areas of his greatest concern and commitment–equal protection of the laws, due process of law, and First Amendment cases; not a judicial workaholic, however, Justice Marshall has evinced a rather indifferent, even demonstrably bored, attitude toward some of the more technical problems of statutory construction and constitutional interpretation in areas other than those of civil rights and liberties. Consequently, the Court's observers have quite properly given him merely an "average" rating. Yet he will always be remembered universally, if only because he broke the last remaining color barrier in high public service—save for the Presidency itself.

11

The Burger Court:

From Nixon to Reagan
1969-

The election of November 1968 brought to the Presidency one of the strangest phenomena on the American political scene, Richard M. Nixon, whose meteoric rise to the highest attainable public post in the land was destined to terminate in his resignation from that office in disgrace on August 9, 1974. It is the sole instance of its kind, just as the Nixon-applauded forced resignation of Justice Fortas five years earlier is a unique occurrence in its own cosmos. Controversy characterized the Nixon career from its inception in 1946. Then the future Chief Executive defeated a mild-mannered, kindly U.S. Representative from California, Jerry Voorhis, in the latter's quest for reelection in a race filled with what soon became characteristic of the Nixon style of dark insinuation, allegation, and attack. It continued in augmented compass when, but four years later, Nixon successfully challenged U.S. Representative Helen Gahagan Douglas for the U.S. Senate by categorizing her as a "pink lady" and by using charges of alleged pro-communism to telling effect, a device he was to employ with considerable success throughout his political life. In 1952, a mere four years after that, the visible, allegedly subversive-battling junior Senator from California was selected by Dwight D. Eisenhower's campaign strategists to become the war hero's Vice Presidential running mate. The less-than-enchanted Ike's doubts were heightened when the Republican ticket's success seemed acutely endangered by revelations of the existence of a *sub rosa* "Nixon fund" of some $18,000 contributed by a group of California businessmen to help defray Nixon's expenses as a U.S. Senator. But in what became known as the "Checkers" and/or "Republican Cloth Coat" television speech, an emotional Nixon persuaded both the public and Ike that he ought to be permitted to stay on the ticket. Sixteen years later he would head his own ticket, narrowly defeating Vice President Hubert H. Humphrey–who neither could, nor would, disavow his loyalty to President Johnson's embattled Vietnam policy. Nixon was reelected in 1972, defeating the ineffectual Democratic challenger, U.S. Senator George S. McGovern of South Dakota, with one of the largest popular percentage margins in the history of Presidential elections (60.7 percent), winning the electoral votes of every state in the Union except Massachusetts! Less than two years later he would become a private citizen. . . .

A proverbial Horatio Alger story type, Richard M. Nixon derived from humble origins, whence he rose to public service by virtue of hard work, discipline, and determination via Duke University's School of Law. Intelligent; capable of instant perception; possessed of a quick, lucid, rapierlike advocate's mind; not invariably concerned with the accuracy of proffered facts; often accused of a policy of self-serving and deliberate prevarication, he was quickly perceived as an ambitious, aggressive fighter who could be counted on to go to the mat in the causes of his personal and political welfare. Rarely had the public realm witnessed such an indefatigable worker for a political party or rarely a shrewder, more partisan fighting spirit. Yet these very qualities plus his endemic suspicions about the motives of others; his never-disappearing sense of social and economic insecurity; his omnipresent inferiority complex about his family background; and his paranoia regarding alleged enemies combined to catapult him into a craving, indeed a thirst, for the kind of ultimate power that would enable him to keep all "enemies" at bay. The 1972–1973 revelations of the outrage *cum* scandal, ever-thereafter to be known as Watergate (the Washington, D.C., building location of the 1972 Democratic National Committee campaign headquarters into which five men had broken, wearing surgical rubber gloves and carrying electronic eavesdropping equipment), was an event for which the basic responsibility would ultimately center in the tenor, climate, and scheming of the Oval Office.[1] Watergate proved to be Nixon's Waterloo. These revelations truncated the Nixon Presidency, following the Supreme Court's historic 8:0 decision in *United States* v. *Nixon*[2] and the House of Representatives's subsequent "acceptance," by a vote of 412:3, of its Judiciary Committee's unanimous conclusion that the President had engaged in "deliberate, repeated, and continued deception of the American people" in the Watergate syndrome.[3] Newspaper headlines throughout the world blazed the tidings of the Nixon resignation on that fateful August day, among them the Dublin *Irish Independent*'s cryptic "Nixon Out" and the *Times of London*'s equally laconic "President Ford Takes Over."[4] Nixon was saved from possible subsequent criminal prosecution by special prosecutor Jaworski's ruling that a President could not be indicted (the Watergate grand jury, however, citing him 19:0 as an "unindicted co-conspirator") and, ultimately and conclusively, by President Ford's precipitous September 1974 pardon of his predecessor.

President Richard M. Nixon's activities vis-à-vis the four Supreme Court vacancies that fate enabled him to fill between mid-1969 and the end of 1971 have been chronicled in considerable detail in Chapter 2, "The Nixon Era: A Turbulent Case Study."[5] Yet something more needs to be said concerning his professed criteria, his expectations, and of course the performances to date of his four appointees: Chief Justice Warren Burger and Associate Justices Harry A. Blackmun, Lewis F. Powell, Jr., and William H. Rehnquist, who commenced their services on the high tribunal in June 1969, June 1970, January 1972, and again January 1972, respectively. Nixon's repeatedly stated criteria were to select "strict constructionists" who would see "their duty as interpreting law and not making law"; who would follow a "properly conservative" course of judging that would, in particular, protect society's "peace forces" against the "criminal forces"; who would "see themselves as caretakers of the Constitution and servants of the people, not super-legislators with a free hand to impose their social and political viewpoints upon the American People."[6] The President articulated little additional criteria—although he consistently professed his desire to select not only "strict constructionists," but *Southern* strict constructionists. Yet geography was not really of major significance in his model (he appointed Minnesotan Blackmun despite the presence of Minnesotans Burger and Douglas, although the latter had resided in Connecticut when F.D.R. chose him). Nor did he seem to regard religion as a major consideration (he replaced the Jewish Fortas with the Protestant Blackmun—which would also have been the religious adherence of Nixon's erstwhile, but unsuccessful, nominees, Haynsworth and Carswell). Although his first two appointees (Burger and Blackmun) as well as Haynsworth and Carswell had prior judicial experience on lower federal benches—and quite extensive ones in the cases of his two successful selectees—neither of his last two (Powell and Rehnquist) had had any on either the federal or state level. Like almost every other President, Nixon was concerned with party affiliation: 93.7 percent of his judicial appointments came from the ranks of registered Republicans. Although Justice Powell had always been viewed as a Democrat, in his case Nixon was satisfied that Powell's *real* politics would vitiate his formal association—an educated guess that, like others similarly advanced, would prove to be only partly accurate.

With the major exception of Justice Blackmun's accelerating move to the Court's "liberal" wing, following his authorship of the contentious 1973 *Abortion Cases*[7] (from which appointees Burger and Rehnquist dissented) and Justice Powell's surprise authorship of "anti-Administration" decisions, for example, in the 1972 domestic subversive groups wiretapping holding,[8] Nixon's appointees followed a distinctly more cautious, more "conservative," jurisprudence than their predecessors, especially in the realm of criminal-justice controversies. Nonetheless, they quickly disappointed those who had predicted, or desired, wholesale reversals of the Warren Court positions. That was particularly true of cases involving claims of race and gender discrimination and major aspects of freedom of expression. Thus, the President was grievously disappointed, indeed, angered, by one of the Burger Court's early decisions, the 1971 "forced busing" ruling in *Swann* v. *Charlotte-Mecklenburg Board of Education,*[9] in which the Chief Justice, speaking for a surprisingly unanimous Court, upheld the use of court-ordered busing to desegregate public schools, even if it meant resorting to racial quotas.[10] Nor, of course, was Richard Nixon amused with the Court's 8:0 decision in *United States* v. *Nixon*[11] three years later, when all but Justice Rehnquist, who had recused himself, voted "against" the President's position in that famed "Nixon Tapes" ruling, which was prolegomenon to Nixon's resignation from the Presidency two weeks after the Supreme Court had filed its opinion on July 25, 1974. On the other hand, when the Court had voted 6:3 against the President's sweeping "national security" and "executive privilege" claims in the dramatic 1971 *Pentagon Papers Case,* the two Nixon appointees then serving on it both dissented along with Justice Harlan—the Chief Justice and Justice Blackmun both voicing strong support of the President's unsuccessful contentions.

Having postponed his announced retirement for one year—as a result of the misfired 1968 Fortas nomination to succeed him in the center chair—Earl Warren, true to his assurances to President Nixon, did retire at the close of the Court's business in June 1969. An era had come to an end, an era of unprecedented general judicial assertion of power but one—that of John Marshall's Court at the dawn of the Republic—specifically in the realms of civil rights and liberties, where the sixteen years of the Warren Court-stewardship knew no equal in our history. It was with undisguised glee that the President moved to select the next Chief Justice, who would be the fifteenth (counting the four-month recess service in the post by the Senate-rejected John Rutledge).[12] On May 21, 1969, with five weeks left in the last Warren Court term, Richard M. Nixon announced his choice. It devolved on the relatively little-known-outside-of-judicial-circles Judge Warren Earl Burger of the U.S. Court of Appeals for the District of Columbia, an on-the-record critic of Earl Warren's jurisprudence, in particular in matters of criminal justice. The then sixty-one-year-old silver-haired Midwestern Republican, with a *magna cum laude* degree from the St. Paul College of Law in Minnesota, was a Presbyterian of

Swiss-German origins and an experienced and dedicated political and judicial public servant. He had established the sort of "conservative" judicial record during his service on the bench below that, in his nominator's eyes, held high promise for a halt in the libertarian jurisprudence of the Warren Court and, perhaps, even a reversal of aspects thereof. That these hopes would only be fulfilled in part and arguably only in small measure—with the *a priori* exception of certain, but not all, aspects of the criminal-justice field—would not be due to a change in the new Chief's jurisprudence. Rather it reflected the ability of Warren Court holdovers, such as Douglas, Brennan, and Marshall, frequently to obtain the necessary fourth, fifth, and often sixth votes—sometimes including the Chief's in noncriminal justice cases—not only to preserve, but not-at-all-infrequently to expand on the libertarian decisions that had characterized Earl Warren's tribunal, especially in egalitarian issues[13] and on the new frontiers of privacy.[14]

President Nixon's choice of Judge Burger was one of those rare examples of an indisputably *bona fide* personal choice by a Chief Executive *qua* Chief Executive. Himself a lawyer, Richard Nixon was fully alive to the nature of the judicial process and the significance of the judicial role. By his own assertions, he considered his selection of Burger to be "the most personal choice of [my] Presidency to date."[15] He told a crowded news conference how he had ruled out "personal and political friends," among them prominent Washington attorney Charles S. Rhyne, largely because of his "lawyer's professional regard for the high court"[16] (which would not be exactly evident in his subsequent abortive putative nominees for the Fortas vacancy!). The President also acknowledged publicly that four prominent public figures had ruled themselves out from consideration: Justice Potter Stewart;[17] Attorney General John Mitchell; Ike's two-term Attorney General, Herbert Brownell; and former Governor Thomas E. Dewey of New York. Nixon insisted that he had refused to see Burger in advance and had also specifically declined to clear his name with any political leaders.[18] Naturally, however, in choosing Judge Burger, a jurist known to be hard-nosed on questions of law and order, the President made a political choice, and an understandable one. It was not so much political in the sense of party affiliation or Senatorial clearance, but in the broader sense that the Court's own function is indubitably political. Mr. Nixon, thus, deliberately selected an individual who would presumably act favorably on his often-expressed plaint that courts, led by the Warren Court, "have gone too far in weakening the peace forces as against the criminal forces."[19] He found concurrence in Warren Burger's comments, just a month prior to his nomination, in which he strongly criticized "the seeming anxiety of judges to protect every accused person from every consequence of his voluntary utterances."[20]

The choice of Warren Burger received generally warm public and private praise, and the man who was widely regarded as a "judge's judge" drew unrestrained approbation from Republicans and Southern Democrats in the U.S. Senate. Little confirmation difficulty, if any, was foreseen, and none developed. After he testified before the Senate Judiciary Committee, controlled by the Democrats–then the majority party in the upper house–the Committee unanimously (13:0) approved his nomination after one hour and forty minutes of hearings on June 1. Overriding an effort by liberals to delay action, the Senate itself confirmed Burger on June 9, after just three hours of debate, by the overwhelming margin of 74:3. While twenty-three Senators were absent or not recorded, only three cast negative votes: Eugene J. McCarthy (D.-Minn.), for what he termed "somewhat personal and political" reasons (apparently Burger, while he was Minnesota State Republican Chairman in 1952, had opposed McCarthy's reelection campaign for the House); Gaylord Nelson (D.-Wisc.), who said he did not know enough about the nominee and had been "mistaken" when he voted to confirm Fortas; and Stephen M. Young (D.-Ohio), who claimed that the Committee had not heard from an opposition witness.[21] On June 23, 1969, the future Chief Justice proudly took his oath of office from Earl Warren–who had been informed, but not consulted, by the President about his successor-choice just shortly prior to its announcement. It was an impressive Supreme Courtroom ceremony, attended by Nixon and senior members of the Administration and the legal profession.

Now (late 1984) in his fifteenth year in the Chief Justiceship of the United States, Warren Earl Burger has evinced the kind of adulation and love for the institution—and, incidentally, its magnificent building at 1 First Street, S.E., the beautification and modernized utilization of which has been his personal concern—that is rivaled only by that of Chief Justice William Howard Taft. It is the latter "Chief" after whom in many ways, particularly in the realm of judicial administration, Burger has patterned himself. Whatever some of his critics may think of his jurisprudential commitments, his internal Court leadership, or his literary style, none can gainsay the abiding commitment and incredibly hard, sustained, abiding, loving labors Chief Justice Burger has brought to the onerous, awe-inspiring, far-reaching responsibilities that being a conscientious and dedicated Chief Justice imposes. His annual State of the Judiciary Address quickly became an event of major significance and a platform for his never-ceasing endeavors to bring much-needed reforms to the overburdened and sometimes creaky judicial process, both on the trial and appellate levels. He toured the country, indeed, the world, in his untiring efforts to improve the machinery of justice and to introduce modes of caseload management that will hopefully render the judicial system more viable in both substantive and procedural terms. In that quest, he and his able staff of dedicated professionals have worked toward, and have seen the introduction of, such commendable and significant innovations on the frontiers of the judicio-administrative process, at times with congressional help, as the following: the creation of the Institute for Court Management (I.C.M.); the Circuit Court Executive Act of 1970, which provides for the appointment of circuit executives; the 1970 act's subsequent experimental extension in 1981 to the district court level as well as its provision for the utilization of statewide court administrators; the establishment of the Office of Administrative Assistant to the Chief Justice in 1972; the imaginative 1973 creation of the excellent Judicial Fellows Program; the Conference of Metropolitan Chief Judges; the revamping of the federal magistrates program; the Chief Justice's encouragement of jury reforms, especially reduction in the size of civil juries; and a host of innovative devices, techniques, and procedures in the federal courts. In addition, the Chief Justice has worked tirelessly to strengthen the state courts and reduce friction between state and federal courts, a program that resulted in such significant contributions as the National Center for State Courts in Williamsburg, Virginia, and the putative National Institute of Justice. Among his other achievements have been his support of, and programs for, the continuing education of judges and his assiduous furthering of the growth and activism of the Federal Judicial Center, whose Chairman of the Board he is (as well as being Chancellor of the Smithsonian Institution).[22]

Although Warren Earl Burger's tenure of Chief Justice may very well be remembered overridingly for the above-described reforms and innovations, it will undoubtedly also be recalled for his marginally successful attempts to pull or lead the Court reliably (or predictably) to the judicio-political center—or perhaps even right of center in some areas—away from its predictable liberal-left majoritarian position under his predecessor's leadership. In fact, it was not for want of trying on Burger's part, but that, with the exception of aspects of criminal justice, the fifth vote on behalf of the kind of conservative jurisprudence that Nixon (and, much later, Reagan) had hoped Burger could marshal proved to be elusive more often than not. Thus, as subsequent discussion of the post-Burger appointees will detail,[23] although Burger could frequently count on White and the early Blackmun in the criminal-justice realm, he would usually lose White and Blackmun to the Brennan-Marshall group in forced busing and racial quota cases. Whereas he could normally count on Powell in "political question" issues, he often lost his "swing/centrist" vote in such "conscience" or "can't help" cases as *Bakke*[24] and that of the South Dakota "habitual offender" law.[25] Douglas's departure gave promise of a shift in Burger's direction; however, his replacement, the Ford-appointed John Paul Stevens, although not as libertarian as Douglas, nonetheless soon began to evince a rather consistent allegiance to the Brennan-Marshall wing of the Court, except in racial quota cases—but those Douglas had opposed too. Stewart's replacement, Sandra Day O'Connor, would more often than not join the Burger-Rehnquist wing, but she proved libertarian-activist in certain gender and redistricting cases. In brief, perhaps oversimplifiedly—but not at all inaccurately–the "mature Burger Court" has been categorized widely as "more umpire than ideological player," given its sizable center group, and it has been labeled as "Going Thisaway and Thataway!"[26] Well might contemporary books on the Burger Court be titled *Neither Conservative nor Liberal*[27] and *The Burger Court: The Counter-Revolution That Wasn't*.[28] Still, antidote to the Warren Court or not, the Burger Court evinced its own brand of judicial activism, as many of its pioneering decisions manifest clearly. As one comment put it so well at the end of its eventful 1982–1983 term–which included such fateful holdings as the 6:3 *Chada* congressional veto case,[29] the 5:4 Arizona gender-equality retirement-pension decision,[30] and the 8:1 *Bob Jones* racial-discrimination/tax-exemption ruling[31]–"An activist court is one that regularly exercises the power of judicial review to enforce controversial as well as consensual norms."[32]

A verdict on Chief Justice Burger's stewardship must await developments that still lie in the lap of the future. The record of his prodigious labors on the frontiers of judicial administration and judicial reform will assuredly guarantee him a superior rating; that of his jurisprudential and Court-directional achievements probably one of average. Whatever that ultimate judgment of the Court watchers may be, he has earned the nation's gratitude for his dedication and his faith in the American system, which he has served so committedly.

The slight, sixty-one-year-old Minnesotan, who took the oath of office as the ninety-eighth Justice of the Supreme Court of the United States on June 9, 1970, in a simple seven-minute ceremony presided over by his longtime friend and sponsor, Chief Justice Warren E. Burger, had not been the President's first choice. But Harry A. Blackmun's nomination that April represented an "out" as well as profound relief to Richard Nixon, whose abortive efforts to move others into the slot vacated by Justice Fortas's resignation from the Court almost one year earlier were described in Chapter 2. The Senate was eager to confirm the experienced jurist, who had become Mr. Nixon's third choice; its Judiciary Committee recommended approval 17:0, noting that he was "thoroughly qualified" and that "not a single witness appeared in opposition." The full Senate happily concurred 74:0, delighted that the Fortas-Haynsworth-Carswell episode was over.

Judge Blackmun had served on the U.S. Court of Appeals for the Eighth Circuit (Missouri, Minnesota, Arkansas, Iowa, Nebraska, and the two Dakotas) for eleven years when the President's call came. A *summa cum laude* graduate of Harvard University with a *Phi Beta Kappa* key, a law degree from Harvard Law School, a record of public service, sixteen years of private practice, and an experienced teacher of law, he was readily found by the American Bar Association's (A.B.A.'s) Committee on Judiciary to meet "high standards of professional competence, temperament and integrity." His selection by the President was far from the directly involved, personal one that the Chief Executive had brought to his choice of Warren Burger. But Nixon was satisfied that Blackmun would comfortably fit his prerequisites of a jurist dedicated to judicial restraint and a "strict construction" of the Constitution. After all, he had been the Chief Justice's first choice for the Fortas vacancy—he was one of Burger's oldest and closest friends (he had been best man at Burger's wedding in 1933). He appeared to share Burger's jurisprudential philosophy, and he had frequently quoted Burger opinions with approval. Among others who urged Blackmun's nomination on the President were Attorney General John N. Mitchell and Deputy Attorney General Richard Kleindienst. Apparently Blackmun's only serious rival was U.S. District Judge Edward T. Gignoux of Maine, although the Attorney General had apparently compiled a list of 150 eligibles. Hubert H. Humphrey, a Minnesotan himself, and that state's two Democratic U.S. Senators, Eugene J. McCarthy and Walter F. Mondale, were pleased with, and entirely supportive of, their fellow Minnesotan's selection, but they had taken no active role in his identification. The country sighed a veritable relief that, at last, the now thirteen-month-old vacant slot on the highest bench of the land had been filled, and evidently filled with an unusually well-qualified jurist.

No one was more pleased than the Chief Justice, however. His boyhood friend from kindergarten and grade-school days in St. Paul brought to the Court a record of a judicial philosophy that, at least on the basis of most of his significant opinions on the federal tribunal below, gave every promise of dovetailing with his own. Most observers agreed. So shrewd and experienced a student of the Court as Fred P. Graham, for one, suggested that "Judge Blackmun appears strikingly like Mr. Burger in judicial philosophy . . . they will often see things the same way on the Supreme Court." And he added presciently that "they seem most alike in their reluctance to follow the Warren Court's lead in expanding the rights of criminal defendants."[33] Some second thoughts prompted him to caption an analysis five days later, "Blackmun May Prove to be a Surprise to Nixon."[34] He would and he did, in a host of ways and not only to Nixon!

But not at first: indeed, he voted so frequently, and seemingly so predictably, with the Chief Justice that the press soon dubbed them the "Minnesota Twins"—an appellation Blackmun began to resent fairly quickly. In First (and Fourteenth) Amendment free expression cases, the newest Justice was consistently at his old friend's "conservative" side, be that in speech, association, or belief cases, such as *Cohen* v. *California,*[35] *Gooding* v. *Wilson,*[36] *Coates* v. *Cincinnati,*[37] and *Lewis* v. *New Orleans,*[38] all in dissent; in governmental regulatory power questions allegedly impinging on free expression, such as *Baird* v. *Arizona*[39] and *Kleindienst* v. *Mandel*;[40] and in the obscenity field, highlighted by *Miller* v. *California.*[41] True to predictions, Blackmun also evinced a tough pro-state posture in criminal-justice cases,[42] in particular in those involving the exclusionary rule[43]—the downtoning or even elimination of which has been an abiding concern of Chief Justice Burger.[44] In most other areas of public law, too, Justice Blackmun ran true to predicted form during his first three or four terms of the "Minnesota Twin" characterization. Yet his bombshell opinion for the Court in the 1973 *Abortion Cases*[45] signaled a putative change in his approach to his presumably burgeoning "judicial restraint" commitments.

For whatever may be said concerning the merits of the decision in those seminal cases, Blackmun's opinion—the product of two years of excruciating labor of composition—is by all counts the leading candidate for the most patently "judicial activist" product of the Burger Court era. The holding, declaring that the fundamental right of privacy—which the 7:2 majority found (more or less) in the contours of the Fourteenth (and Ninth) Amendment concept of personal liberty—encompassed a woman's right to terminate her pregnancy by means of an abortion, engendered a raging controversy, with Blackmun at the center. The ruling in effect invalidated the abortion statutes in all but four of the fifty states and gave rise to what is arguably the most controversial decision of our time. The moral, philosophical, and theological issues engaged by the decision continue to rage, as do the attacks on its author. Among other emotion-triggering statements, he wrote that the fetus is not a "person" within the meaning of the equal-protection-of-the-laws guarantees of the Fourteenth Amendment (corporations *are,* however, and have been since 1886!)[46]—a view that is anathema to those who believe devoutly that life begins at conception. That Blackmun's opinion endeavored to soften the holding by ruling that the right to have an abortion was not absolute but could be regulated when the state's interest was "compelling," based on a "trimester" framework of substantive and procedural entitlements, did not do much to defuse the outcry. Even the world of academe, not at all generally hostile to the *results* of Blackmun's abortion ruling, was severely critical: a number of scholars contended, with considerable justice, that the decision was "a disingenuous excuse for usurpation of legislative prerogatives" and that his failure to "locate the constitutional underpinnings of the newly declared right would lead the Court once more down the road of substantive due process."[47]

As if stung by the attacks, including consistent charges of having created "ambiguous and uncertain" rights out of whole cloth, Blackmun's jurisprudence appeared to begin actively to change. With the possible exception of the criminal-justice sector, where he would still more often than not be found at Burger's side—although even there he left the proverbial reservation on occasion[48]—Justice Blackmun began to move toward the Court's liberal wing. As he celebrated his seventy-first birthday in 1979, he acknowledged his increasingly frequent disagreements with both the Chief Justice and the last of Nixon's four nominees, William H.

Rehnquist, who had joined the Court, together with Justice Powell, in January 1972. Commenting that he did not enjoy being characterized as a "Nixon judicial conservative," he elaborated bluntly: "I never met Mr. Nixon until I was called into the Oval Office. We had never met and he had no reason to know me. I am not obligated to him in any way. He didn't know me from Adam's off ox."[49] He added laconically that he will be evaluated best by time and history.

What that history will show conclusively is that, by the middle 1970s and thereafter—with seemingly increasing acceleration—Justice Blackmun became an almost, albeit not quite, wholly faithful ally of the Court's Brennan-Marshall libertarian wing, frequently joined by Justice Stevens and, somewhat less so, by Justice White. Blackmun's consistently sympathetic stance on allegations of racial[50] and gender[51] discrimination, particularly the former, became a cornerstone of his now liberal-activist jurisprudence in those aspects of egalitarianism, which frankly avows a posture that finds justification in remedial, preferential, compensatory policies, while expressing the hope of, and for, their "temporary" nature.[52]

Blackmun—a dedicated, scholarly, conscientious hard worker—is a warm human being, although not unenigmatic; now (late 1984) in his fourteenth year on the Court, he has often presented vistas of self-doubt, of Hamletlike approaches to justifying opinions. To cite one illustration: writing the majority opinion in an employment discrimination case in 1982, he turned around and wrote a separate plurality "addendum" to his own opinion![53] Although carefully researched, his opinions have often betrayed inconsistent reasoning and occasional lack of clarity. At times he has given indications of exasperation, not only with his tasks, but with at least some of his colleagues—to which his astonishing December 1982 televised interview with Daniel Schorr[54] and his extensive February 1983 *New York Times Sunday Magazine* interview with John A. Jenkins[55] bear witness, giving rise to speculations of retirement. But when the 1983–1984 Court opened its term, Justice Blackmun was in his chair.

Seated with Justice Blackmun on that Court were the two Nixon-selected brethren who had followed him to the bench early in January 1972: the President's fourth and last appointee, William H. Rehnquist, to his immediate left; the other, Lewis F. Powell, Jr., Nixon's third appointee–whose earlier confirmation date by the Senate had given him a bit of seniority over Rehnquist–placed on the other side of the alternating right-to-left order on the lovely Honduran mahogany bench immediately to the right of the then-number-four Justice in length of service, Thurgood Marshall. As described in some detail earlier,[56] it will be recalled how Mr. Nixon had at last turned to these two eminently qualified members of the legal profession, having tried but failed over a period of two months to teach the Senate and the A.B.A.'s Committee on Judiciary "a lesson" by endeavoring to foist on the country and Court nominees almost universally regarded as "mediocre . . . obscure and unsatisfactory"[57] to fill the seats of the distinguished Justices Black and Harlan. It was a clear-cut case of Presidential contempt, utter contempt, for the Court–especially coming so close on the heels of Nixon's abortive nominations of Judges Haynsworth and Carswell. Four of Nixon's September 1971 list of six putative nominees[58] that were allegedly "leaked" from the Bar's Committee on Judiciary (the Committee steadfastly denied it and pointed to the Justice Department as the culprit) were probably "throw ins." But there was little doubt that he fully intended to proceed with those of Little Rock lawyer Herschel Friday and California Court of Appeals Judge Mildred Lillie, after Congressman Richard H. Poff (R.-Va.), his first choice for one of the vacancies, had declined.[59]

All of those candidates were on a master list of some 100 names that Attorney General Mitchell's deputy, Richard Kleindienst, and Assistant Attorney General William H. Rehnquist had begun to assemble some time earlier to prepare for the probability of incumbency replacements, a list that had also included Clement Haynsworth and G. Harrold Carswell. Most but not all of the listees comprised sitting judges, of "appointable" age, with a compatible ideological philosophy. Ultimately, Kleindienst reduced the list to *circa* 30 names, with Mitchell–always reporting to Nixon–focusing on the now familiar, unsuccessful coterie. "The Six" became public and a firestorm of public outcry followed, punctuated tellingly by the A.B.A.'s Committee on Judiciary vote of 11:1 against Lillie and its 6:6 split on Friday. Nixon, Mitchell, and Kleindienst were advised by the White House congresssional liaison team that it would be "Haynesworth/Carswell all over again, only worse." Now positively livid, but nonetheless realistic, the President surrendered. Together with Mitchell he determined to focus on Powell, who had long been on the Administration's list; on Judge Arlin M. Adams of the U.S. Court of Appeals for the Third Circuit, an active Nixon backer and prominent Philadelphia Jewish Republican, who was also on the list; and on Rehnquist, who had worked on the list, but was not on it, and who had no intimation that he was under consideration—although he had strong ties to a highly supportive inner White House circle.

On Tuesday, October 19, 1971, Mitchell telephoned Lewis Powell in Richmond, advising him that the President wished to send him to the Court. That evening Nixon himself called, personally repeating the offer, urging the reluctant candidate—who had removed himself from consideration during the Haynsworth/Carswell period—to accept. Powell promised a response on the following day: it was positive, notwithstanding his serious and repeatedly publicly voiced reservations because of his age (sixty-four) and his satisfaction, comfort, and enjoyment in his professional and community work in Virginia's capital. Arlin Adams appeared to be next in line but, at the last moment, Mitchell voiced strong reservations because of what he viewed as Adams's questionable posture on the range and extent of the *Miranda Case*.[60] The two actors in the appointment drama now turned to Rehnquist, who, less than two days after Powell's selection, happily completed the dual ticket. It was a surprisingly well-kept secret: an obviously suspense-savoring Nixon relished making the official announcement in a nationally televised broadcast on October 21, which he began with a brief lecture on his commitment to "strict construction" and "judicial conservatism," then gleefully revealing the names of his unquestionably highly qualified choices to a totally surprised but relieved and generally approbative country.[61]

Universally admired and respected—indeed, loved—the reluctant designee Lewis F. Powell, Jr., to the manner born and educated, was one of America's most renowned and most principled attorneys and a descendant of distinguished old Virginia families—the first Powell, one of the original Jamestown colonists, arrived on Virginia's soil in 1607. A native of Suffolk, he attended Washington and Lee College in Lexington, Virginia, where he was graduated first in his class, with a *Phi Beta Kappa* key; received his law degree at Harvard; and then commenced a long and happy association with Richmond's powerful and large law firm of Hunton, Williams, Gay, Powell, and Gibson. He soon rose to influential positions in the community as well as the profession, including such prestigious plums as the chairmanships or presidencies of the A.B.A., the American College of Trial Lawyers, the Virginia State Board of Education, the Colonial Williamsburg Foundation, and the American Bar Foundation. Although an honored member of Virginia's conservative Democratic "establishment," he was no segregationist, and he denounced the Byrd organization's anti-desegregation doctrinal policy of "interposition" in what was for him uncharacteristic language as "a lot of rot."[62] Indeed, it was the patrician Lewis F. Powell, Jr., who led the opposition to, and ultimately defeated, the state's "massive resistance policy." As early as 1959, when he served as chairman of Richmond's Public School Board, he presided over the successful, disturbance-free integration of the city's schools—a delicate and difficult task a mere four years after *Brown II*.[63] Virginia's National Association for the Advancement of Colored People (N.A.A.C.P.) promptly endorsed his nomination. The tall, slim, impressive Powell ran into but marginal opposition during the ensuing confirmation hearings. The Senate Judiciary Committee recommended confirmation unanimously, and the Senate followed suit on December 6, 1971, by a vote of 89:1, the sole dissenter being retiring Senator Fred R. Harris (D.-Okla.). The latter said he opposed Mr. Powell because "he is an elitist [who] has never shown any deep feelings for little people"[64]—a patently false statement, as the gentle citizen's past record and his on-the-bench jurisprudence demonstrate with crystal clarity. "One wonders," commented Senator Henry M. Jackson (D.-Wash.), "why it has taken so long to propose a man of Mr. Powell's stature."[65] With predictable modesty, the new Justice, expressing his gratitude for Congress's "generous margin of approval," added: "I am too conscious of my own limitations to take it at face value. I am afraid I cannot live up to such high expectations."[66]

But, of course, he has! Now (late 1984) in his thirteenth year, probably the most revered and popular member of the Court, Lewis F. Powell, Jr., has manifested a role as its conscience. Cautious and conservative, yet moderate and nondoctrinaire by inclination and commitment, he has been comfortable in the Court's center, often side-by-side with such fellow-centrists as White and Stewart. Above all, he has been very much his own man, beholden only to his learning, his professionalism, and his conscience. He has lived up to some of his nominator's expectations, especially in his supportive stance on the role of the states in our federal system, usually joined by the Chief Justice and Justices Rehnquist and O'Connor–notably on the reach of the interstate commerce clause[67] and the state's power to administer criminal justice, where he and his aforementioned colleagues, sometimes joined by White or Blackmun, have tended to favor a good measure of state jurisdictional authority.[68] But he can also be found on the other side of that vexatious constitutional coin.[69] A particularly galling-to-Nixon Powell posture on the national security front was his opinion, for a unanimous Supreme Court, in *United States* v. *United States District Court for the Eastern District of Michigan* in 1972,[70] just shortly after Powell joined the high bench. As a private citizen Powell had publicly *supported* the Nixon Administration's claim of constitutional authority for wiretapping of radical domestic groups *without* a warrant; yet when the issue reached the Court, the Justices, led by Powell, declared that contention and practice to be an *unconstitutional* invasion of Fourth Amendment guarantees as well as being unauthorized under the applicable statute. In the freedom-of-expression realm, Nixon's third appointee would also follow a path of what he viewed as common sense. A devotee and defender of that freedom,[71] he nonetheless proved to be non-Pavlovian, constantly reminding the citizenry that rights and privileges do not stand alone, that there are also duties and responsibilities.[72] Like Justice Jackson, Justice Powell opposes the "turning of the constitutional Bill of Rights into a suicide pact."[73] That carefully structured "balancing" of individual and societal rights and obligations would also be demonstrated in Justice Powell's approach to the First Amendment's two religion clauses. There his measured oversight would, thus, enable him to write the Court's opinion striking down certain of New York's practices as violative of the establishment clause,[74] and to concur in a similar holding regarding Pennsylvania's practices.[75] Yet, nonetheless, Powell saw his way clear to join the Court's dramatic 5:4 upholding of Minnesota's tax-deduction statute that applies to children in parochial and other private elementary and secondary schools;[76] in a 1980 decision involving New York[77] that seemed to go counter to the aforementioned opinion affecting the same state;[78] and in the 5:4 approval in 1984 of Pawtucket, R.I.'s inclusion of a Nativity scene (a crèche) as part of an official Christmas display in a park in the teeth of bitter dissents that charged a crass violation of the constitutionally required separation of Church and State.[79]

A warm supporter of women in their struggle against invidious discrimination on the basis of gender,[80] Powell is, nonetheless, committed to a case-by-case approach that may well also find sporadic justification for the upholding of governmental authority to classify in noninvidious fashion on the basis of perceived legislative judgments in some instances, while denying it in others;[81] and in still others he may be critical of excessive governmental zealousness.[82] Although he did not write an opinion in the famed key 1973 *Abortion Cases,* headed by *Roe* v. *Wade*[83]–he joined Justice Blackmun's–he was the author of a group of cases growing out of *Roe*-engendered issues that reached the Court in 1983.[84] There, speaking in ringing tones from the bench, Justice Powell, prior to turning to the narrower issues of the litigation, noted that "arguments continue to be made [that] we erred in interpreting the Constitution," but that the now ten-year-old *Roe* holding "that the right of privacy grounded in the concept of personal liberty guaranteed by the Constitution, encompasses a woman's right whether to terminate her pregnancy" stands as the rule of law, as *stare decisis.* And he added firmly and sternly, to the relief and cheers of the decision's supporters everywhere: "We respect it today, and reaffirm *Roe* v. *Wade*."[85] The Court's vote was 6:3, with Justice O'Connor, who was not on the Court in 1973, writing a strong dissenting opinion on *Roe's* trimester approach, joined by Justices White and Rehnquist (who had both dissented in *Roe*).

Withal, there is but little doubt that Justice Powell's career on the Court will always be associated preeminently with his seminal dual holding in the emotion-charged, controversial *Bakke* decision of 1978.[86] Far from eager to bite the proverbial bullet of a definitive ruling on the affirmative action/reverse discrimination front, the Court had managed to avoid it, most recently in the 1974 *De Funis* case, which a 5:4 majority, including Powell, mooted.[87] But now the issue could no longer be avoided–the constitutional and statutory issues loomed too significant, and the polity clamored for a ruling by the land's highest tribunal. Typically, the assignment for the writing of that can of worms was assigned to Justice Powell, who, if anyone, was a logical, indeed, ideal choice given his centrist, thoughtful, cautious, articulate, conscience-prone stance in adjudicating issues before him. To that noble and responsible jurist the complex, wrenching case before him represented an anguished responsibility, to which he brought a good deal of a Holmesian "can't help" attitude. He also solved the riddle by some imaginative, flexible, internally persuasive and diplomatic moves, yielding neither patent winners nor losers–and that may well be what the engineer-manager of the ruling intended. That *Bakke* did not really settle the basic problem, and that the many dissenting and concurring opinions that accompanied the two controlling Powell holdings were as divisive as they were verbose, does not gainsay the service that the opinion's author performed.

Briefly,[88] what Justice Powell did in the two prongs of his *Bakke tour de force* was the following: *first,* he ruled (supported by the four votes of his colleagues Stevens, Burger, Stewart, and Rehnquist) that Alan Bakke–a rejected white applicant, who was admittedly more qualified to enter the University of California's Medical School at Davis than a 16-member minority group that had been admitted on the basis of a rigid 16-out-of-100 racial quota established by the University–would have to be admitted because that rigid racial quota constituted a *violation* of the Fourteenth Amendment's equal-protection-of-the-laws guarantees. That his four supporters, however, wanted the issue to be settled on *statutory* grounds—namely, that Title VI of the Civil Rights Act specifically barred discrimination on the basis of race to any governmentally subsidized institution, such as the University of California—did not dissuade Powell from forging his vote and controlling holding on *constitutional* grounds. For he feared that to accept the Stevens-led group's reasoning would too strictly harness affirmative action initiative and experimentation, such as the kind the second prong of his remarkable ruling propounded. In that *second* part (now joined by his colleagues Brennan, White, Marshall, and Blackmun) Powell *upheld* on constitutional grounds—bottomed on that very same equal-protection-of-the-laws provision of Amendment Fourteen on the basis of which he had ruled contrarily in his decision's first part—the significant concept *cum* practice of utilizing race "as a plus." He admonished, however, that it could only be used when a university had "a substantial interest" in a diverse student body "that legitimately may be served by a properly devised admissions program involving the competitive consideration of race and ethnic origin."[89] Thus, over the angry objections of the Stevens group, who contended that the Powell-led majority in part two of the opinion opened the door to purposeful violations of the specific language and prohibitions of Title VI of the governing Civil Rights Act of 1964, Justice Powell had in effect given the green light to a host of innovative actions on the affirmative action/reverse discrimination front, and this, as the dissenters had warned and feared, despite his striking down of rigid racial or ethnic quotas.

The future would prove those dissenters' dire prophecies to be generally correct. Indeed, Justice Powell himself would proffer serious objections to the expansive interpretations given to what he had clearly intended to be a narrow holding on the "race plus" frontier.[90] He would be particularly disturbed by some of the Court's broad-gauged backing of the use of racial quotas in involuntary school busing—crying out in separate dissenting opinions in two leading such cases (decided just one year after his *Bakke* opinions) that he was "profoundly disturb[ed]" by this "creation of bad constitutional law."[91] Yet, although he had never intended his *Bakke* holdings to give warrant to what he now decried and although it is of course possible to distinguish among and between sundry racial quota cases, there is no doubt that his Solomonlike *Bakke* resolution has resulted demonstrably in an embrace of its *permissive,* but very little of its *restrictive,* mandate.

A measure of the lovely human being and conscientious jurist that inform Justice Powell's cosmos is the following account of an event that took place in the Supreme Court of the United States on November 30, 1976. As reported by the Associated Press:

> Associate Justice Lewis F. Powell Jr. was wearing a business suit, and he was seated in the audience instead of on the bench, when he rose yesterday and motioned that Mary Lewis Sumner and Christopher Sumner be admitted to the Supreme Court bar. Justice Powell asured his colleagues that his daughter and son-in-law "possess the necessary qualifications" to argue cases before the nation's highest court. After the routine proceedings, Justice Powell donned his black judicial robes and went to the bench for the first case hearing of the week. A Supreme Court spokesman said that "so far as is recalled, this is the first time a sitting Justice has moved his child to admission of the Supreme Court Bar."

Lewis F. Powell, Jr., is an admirable example of Madison's prayer for "a bench happily filled." He has graced the Court.

President Nixon's fourth, and last, appointment, announced concurrently with that of Lewis Powell, was one of his Assistant Attorneys General, the Arizona-domiciled, Wisconsin-born William H. Rehnquist. In contrast to the former's smooth Senate confirmation hearings and all-but-unanimous approval, the Rehnquist nomination encountered rough sailing. As pointed out earlier,[92] the brilliant, youthful (at forty-seven almost two decades younger than Powell), ideologically conservative Republican had been a visible political activist, yet his legal credentials were impeccable as well as impressive. Nixon and Mitchell knew him well, although the following account, culled from the editorial page of the *Riverside California Press* of July 17, 1974, would seem to cast a bit of doubt on that conclusion with regard to the President:

SEND IN THE CLOWNS

Earlier this year, Oxford University Press published a book entitled "Justices and Presidents" dealing with presidential Supreme Court appointments over the years of our history.

At such time as there may be a revised edition, it is going to have to include the following, not known to author Henry J. Abraham or any of the rest of us, of course, at the critical time.

From a transcript prepared by the House Judiciary Committee of a recording in the President's office, July 24, 1971:[93]

President: . . . Nobody follows up on a goddamn thing. We've got to follow up on this thing; however, we, uh, we, uh, we had that meeting. You remember the meeting we had when I told that group of clowns we had around there. Renchburg and that group. What's his name?
Ehrlichman: Renchquist.
President: Yeah, Rehnquist.
Ehrlichman: Yeah.

From a nationally televised presidential speech, Oct. 21, 1971, announcing the nomination of assistant attorney general William H. *Rehnquist* to be an associate justice of the Supreme Court:

". . . guardian of our Constitution . . . the President's lawyer's lawyer . . . among the very best lawyers in the nation . . . at the very top as a constitutional lawyer and as a legal scholar . . . has been outstanding in every intellectual endeavor he has undertaken." [. . .]

Be that as it may, Bill Rehnquist himself had some doubts as to how well the President *really* knew him and he had no illusions about being in the running for either the Black or Harlan vacancy. When asked during that September 1971 whether he had any chance at all of landing one of the posts, he responded with a smile: "None at all, because I'm not from the South, I'm not a woman, and I'm not mediocre."[94] He did not meet these criteria—but more than any of the other four Nixon appointees would Rehnquist meet the President's desire and views of a "strict constitutional constructionist." Not even the generally philosophically empathetic Chief Justice Burger would amass such a pro-Nixon expectation record. Yet Rehnquist, ideologically even to the right of Nixon, of Burger, and certainly of Blackmun and Powell, was arguably the appointee with the quickest, most lucid, most intellectually alive mind, and he was possessed of a spontaneous, often-devastating sense of humor, qualities that would lace his opinions. An undergraduate *Phi Beta Kappa* at Stanford University and first in his class at Stanford's Law School—where he met Sandra Day O'Connor, who stood close to him in that same class—he clerked for Justice Robert H. Jackson during the incubation period of *Brown* v. *Board of Education.*[95] Demonstrating a superb grasp of the legal process, he settled down in Phoenix to enjoy the general practice of law. He would probably have been content to remain in his cherished Arizona surroundings but, a few years following his active involvement in the doomed Goldwater Presidential campaign of 1964, he yielded to his fellow Arizona Republican Nixonite, Richard Kleindienst, who persuaded him late in 1968 to join the President-elect's Department of Justice as Assistant Attorney General in charge of the Office of Legal Counsel (a position that accounts for Nixon's tape-comment reference to him as "the President's lawyer's lawyer").[96] As a vocal critic of the Warren Court's posture on criminal justice, a confirmed law-and-order man, a devoted supporter of strong national security, and a frequent outspoken opponent of the then-rampant student demonstrators—he styled them "the new barbarians"—the hard-line Rehnquist was bound to find firm approbation on the part of ideological conservatives and enraged opposition on the part of ideological liberals.

And so the turbulent confirmation hearings attested. No one challenged his legal credentials—they were of the highest caliber—but a firestorm of protest arose over what was widely predicted, hoped, or feared by respective protagonists would be his ideologically doctrinaire conservative approach to constitutional law on the Court. The hearings before the Senate Judiciary Committee were lengthy, intense, and stormy. Rancor reigned supreme, both during those hearings and the protracted emotional floor debate that followed, with Rehnquist being called "racist,"[97] "right wing zealot,"[98] and "another Carswell, only worse."[99] The American

Civil Liberties Union (A.C.L.U.) broke its time-honored tradition of fifty-two years' standing never to oppose a nominee for public office by calling publicly for Rehnquist's defeat as "a dedicated opponent of individual civil liberties."[100] On the other hand, the nominee was stoutly defended as "a man of the highest personal integrity,"[101] as a "shy, intellectual . . . public servant . . . blessed with honesty and straightforwardness,"[102] and as "superlatively qualified for service on the Court."[103] The Judiciary Committee's vote was 12:4, with Democratic Senators Bayh (Ind.), Hart (Mich.), Ted Kennedy (Mass.), and Tunney (Calif.) voting nay; 7 Republicans and 5 Democrats voted aye. Floor debate raged for a week, with Senator Bayh leading a filibuster against the nominee. A motion for cloture failed by 11 votes to attain the needed two-thirds vote; but it was now December 1971, Christmas loomed close, and 1972 would be a Presidential election year. Ergo, the opponents threw in the proverbial towel and agreed to a vote on December 10, after rejecting 70:22 Bayh's last-minute proposal to postpone a final vote. Confirmation came by a tally of 68:26, a comfortably wide margin but nonetheless constituting one of the highest total of nays in the history of Court nominations: 38 Republicans were joined by 30 Democrats in casting ayes, the latter including several noted Senate liberals, such as Adlai E. Stevenson III (Ill.), Thomas F. Eagleton (Mo.), Claiborne Pell (R.I.), and William Proxmire (Wisc.). The nays came from 23 Democrats and 3 liberal Republicans, Clifford P. Case (N.J.), Jacob K. Javits (N.Y.), and Edward W. Brooke (Mass.). On January 7, 1972, Chief Justice Burger administered the oath of office to Lewis F. Powell, Jr., and William H. Rehnquist as the 99th and 100th members of the Supreme Court of the United States. It was the first time since January 3, 1911, when Willis Van Devanter and Joseph R. Lamar had taken the oath together, that two Justices took their seats in a joint ceremony. Within minutes after a brief reception following the swearing in of the two new Justices, the Chief Justice led them into the conference room to commence a day-long session to act on pending petitions for review.

Now (late 1984) in his thirteenth year on the Court, Justice

Rehnquist has disappointed neither his nominator, nor his supporters, nor his opponents. He quickly became the leader of the "right" or "conservative" wing of the Court, most frequently joined in general by Chief Justice Burger and Justice O'Connor; less frequently, but more often than not, by Justice Powell in redistricting/reapportionment,[104] forced school busing,[105] and in a good many–although assuredly not all–criminal-justice rulings, usually joined by Justice White in that last category,[106] where he has also occasionally received Justice Blackmun's vote; and normally by Justice Stevens in "reverse discrimination" cases.[107] It is not inaccurate to note that unless the Court is unanimous–which, however, be it noted, *it is* between a quarter and a third of the *circa* 150 cases in which it usually renders formal opinions annually–Justice Rehnquist is never joined by Justices Brennan and Marshall, whose agreement on the "left" or "libertarian" wing of the Court has registered in the vicinity of ninety-six to ninety-eight percent in cases involving civil rights and liberties. A dramatic illustration of the polar-opposite stance by the Court's "left" and "right" wings on the central question of perceived constitutional and/or statutory support of the claims of individuals *versus* those of society on the civil rights and liberties front is the statistical dichotomy between the votes of Justice Douglas (then the leader of the Brennan-Marshall wing) and Justice Rehnquist during their last full term together, 1973–1974: in that term the Court handed down some 85 cases in the civil rights and liberties spectrum. Without in any way endeavoring to elucidate or evaluate the merits of the holdings in those 85 cases, and simply asking the question whether the Justice's vote went "for" or "against" the individual's libertarian claim, Douglas's score was 79:6 and Rehnquist's 16:69. Yet the two polar opposites heard the same cases, saw the same briefs and other documentation, took the same oath to the same Constitution, were both superbly qualified students and scholars of the law, both had earned *Phi Beta Kappa* keys, and both were graduated *summa cum laude*. Their respective reading of the Constitution, of statutes, their views on federalism, on governmental responsibility, on a host of other substantive and procedural aspects and elements of the judicial process, and, in particular, of aspects of the parameters of judicial power, obviously diverged fundamentally and conclusively in most, although naturally not in all, facets of their perceived role responsibilities and constitutional ideology.

An intensively hard worker; always thoroughly prepared for oral argument; intellectual, literate, and scholarly; ever ready with precise, quick, often difficult and trying questions for fellow Justices, Justice Rehnquist is a formidable advocate for his ideological view of the Constitution and the role of government thereunder. Blackstonian in commitment to popular rule, he not only embraces, but exceeds the Holmesian-Frankfurter creed of permitting legislatures, the people's representatives, wide discretion in forging public policy and public law, even if those representatives enact silly, stupid, asinine, unnecessary, even unfair and undemocratic legislation–so long as the latter is not unconstitutional. And for him that line, of course, is not reached nearly as soon as it is for the obvious contrary examples of Justices Brennan, Marshall, and almost, but not always, as quickly, for Justices Blackmun and Stevens.[108] A committed and consistent adherent to Federalism, Justice Rehnquist–here frequently in concord with the Chief Justice and Justice O'Connor and often with Justice Powell–will ride close and frequent herd on what he views as the intrusion of the national government on states' rights.[109] Devoted to the principle of deference to the other two branches of the government, especially the legislative, he is the Court's most consistent and most articulate exponent and defender of judicial restraint, here following what he views as the similar commitment of Justices Frankfurter and Harlan II.[110] Unlike Holmes, for example, Rehnquist does not adhere to a rule of less deference in the civil rights and liberties realm: to him, there are no such things as "preferred freedoms" and double standards between the judicial stance on "economic-proprietarian" and "fundamental" rights of freedoms.[111] Rehnquist, a connoisseur of language and literature, has an ideology and commitment to the judicial role and its obligations to the other institutions of government as well as the body politic that is perhaps best encompassed in his now famed, passionate, eminently *a priori* logical, dramatic, sarcastic, powerful dissenting opinion in the major 1979 affirmative action/reverse discrimination *Weber* case, which the Court decided one year after *Bakke.*[112]

At issue in that controversial decision, known as *United Steelworkers of American* v. *Weber,*[113] was an allegedly "voluntary" and "temporary" affirmative action plan devised by the Kaiser Aluminum and Chemical Corporation and the United Steelworkers of America for Kaiser's Gramercy, Louisiana, plant, under which at least one half of the available thirteen positions in an on-the-job training program had been reserved for blacks. Finding himself excluded solely because he was white, Brian Weber filed suit in federal district court, claiming a *prima facie* violation of Title VII of the Civil Rights Act of 1964. That provision categorically bans any racial discrimination in employment, no matter whether the individual's race be black, white (or any other color). It specifically states that its provisions are not to be interpreted "to require any employer . . . to grant preferential treatment to any individual or to any group because of the race . . . of such individual or group." Moreover, the congressional history of the statute's enactment made crystal clear that Congress meant precisely what it said and that the Civil Rights Act's proponents had so assured the doubters during the exciting eighty-three days of floor debate in 1964.[114] Basing their decisions on *both* the language of Title VII and that of the congressional debates, enshrined in the *Congressional Record,* the two lower federal courts that had adjudicated the case[115] upheld Weber's contentions and ruled the affirmative action plan at issue to be *illegal* under Title VII.

But in an astonishing decision, handed down during the last week of its 1978–1979 term, the Supreme Court reversed the courts below in a 5:2 holding, Justices Powell and Stevens abstaining (although it is fair to conjecture that, based on their records on the issue, they would have dissented). Writing for the majority, Justice Brennan (joined by Justices Marshall, Stewart, and White and, with reservations, by Justice Blackmun) frankly conceded that the rulings by the lower courts had *followed the letter* of the Civil Rights Act of 1964 but not its *spirit*. Justice Brennan suggested that Congress's primary concern had been with "the plight of the

Negro in our economy" and that it would be "ironic indeed" if Title VII would be used to prohibit "all voluntary private, race-conscious efforts to abolish traditional patterns" of discrimination.[116]

Chief Justice Burger and Justice Rehnquist dissented vehemently in separate opinions, charging that the majority had engaged in the crassest kind of judicial activism, which amounted to blatant judicial legislation, and that it had, in fact, "totally rewritten a crucial part" of the law. As a member of Congress, the Chief Justice admonished, he "would be inclined to vote for" the views expressed by the majority, but as a judge he had no business in writing legislation. "Congress," he explained with feeling, "expressly *prohibited* the discrimination against Brian Weber" that the five-member majority now approved.[117] And in what may well constitute one of the angriest dissenting opinions in recent times, Justice Rehnquist, joined by Chief Justice Burger, accused the Court majority of acting like Harry Houdini, the escape artist:

> Thus, by a *tour de force* reminiscent not of jurists such as Hale, Holmes, and Hughes, but of escape artists such as Houdini, the Court eludes clear statutory language, "uncontradicted" legislative history, and uniform precedent in concluding that employers are, after all, permitted to consider race in making employment decisions.[118]

Congress sought to require racial equality in government, Rehnquist contended:

> [T]here is perhaps no device more destructive to the notion of equality than . . . the quota. Whether described as "benign discrimination" or "affirmative action," the racial quota is nonetheless a creator of castes, a two-edged sword that must demean one in order to prefer the other.

He concluded:

> With today's holding, the Court introduces . . . a tolerance for the very evil that the law was intended to eradicate, without offering even a clue as to what the limits on that tolerance may be. . . . The Court has sown the wind. Later courts will face the impossible task of reaping the whirlwind.[119]

That dissent is vintage Rehnquist! Whatever one's personal views on the underlying issue, whatever one's sympathies, "it is simply unanswerable in terms of statutory construction and congressional intent," in the words of Philip B. Kurland, distinguished Professor of Constitutional Law at the University of Chicago.[120] It speaks to Rehnquist's manifold talents and to his ideological commitments, to his views of government under law and institutional obligations, in fine, to his perception of the nature and function of a judge under our written Constitution. A good many members of the Supreme Court have undergone demonstrable major ideological and process changes during their careers on the Court—contemporarily most obviously Justice Blackmun. But it would be a veritable revolutionary development were Justice William H. Rehnquist to alter his basic jurisprudential stance! His principles, his commitments, and his consistency are *res judicata*.

Gerald R. Ford's Presidency was destined to be confined to the relatively brief period between his predecessor's dramatic resignation on August 9, 1974, and his defeat by James E. "Jimmy" Carter in the close Presidential sweepstakes of 1976. Ford might well have been elected to a full term in his own right had it not been for the dual burden of the Watergate scandals—although he was not involved in them—and, arguably most decisively, of his precipitous unconditional pardon of Richard M. Nixon on September 8, 1974, barely one month after the latter's resignation. Few, if any, informed citizens doubted Ford's constitutional authority to take the action he did, but many questioned its moral propriety as well as its political wisdom. Ford of course was under intense personal pressure to do what he did for the man who had selected him to be his Vice President on Spiro T. Agnew's resignation in October 1973. (Agnew had been under federal investigation for possible violation of criminal laws dealing with extortion, bribery, tax evasion, and conspiracy.) Nonelected President Ford characteristically did what he regarded as appropriate.

Popular; likeable; appealingly, if not always informedly, candid; sociable; and athletic, the University of Michigan and Yale Law School alumnus had been a fixture in the U.S. House of Representatives, where he served as the Republican leader for many years.

A denizen possessed of basically decent instincts—notwithstanding his vendettas against Justice Douglas: he tried unsuccessfully to have him impeached for "moral turpitude"—President Ford devoted twenty-seven months as the nation's Chief Executive primarily to healing the nation's Watergate/Nixon wounds. It was an aim in which he largely succeeded, accompanied by the public's general approval. In sundry ways it was, thus, a pity that he was not enabled to demonstrate his mettle in a term of his own.

Notwithstanding his brief tenure, he did have an opportunity—unlike Jimmy Carter—to appoint one Justice of the Supreme Court. Although no intellectual, Ford emphasized a set of pondered criteria for candidates to the federal bench. The two predominant and repeatedly articulated ones were objective merit and ideologically acceptable "real politics," and he preferred at least some judicial experience for his nominees to the appellate level. Judge John Paul Stevens of Illinois seemed to fit the contours of the President's model as well as his moderate stance on public issues. But as the history of Presidential expectations has demonstrated so frequently, nominator Ford was in for a few jurisprudential surprises from the pen of Justice Stevens.

After receiving notice of the retirement of Associate Justice William O. Douglas from the Supreme Court on November 12, 1975, President Ford met with his able Attorney General, Edward H. Levi, and White House Counsel Philip Buchen to discuss possible successors. Ford asked Levi to compile a list of potential appointees and noted in his memoirs that he specifically told Levi, "don't exclude women from the list."[121]

The Ford Administration submitted such a list of eleven names to the A.B.A.'s Committee on Judiciary, thereby reviving a practice of A.B.A. review *before* nomination. (President Nixon had abandoned the practice in 1971—uttering his familiar expletive—after the A.B.A. Committee severely criticized two of his trial-balloon nominees.)[122] According to the *Washington Post*,[123] Ford's initial list comprised two members of Congress, Senator Robert P. Griffin (R.-Mich.) and Representative Charles E. Wiggins (R.-Calif.); Solicitor General Robert H. Bork; and five sitting U.S. Court of Appeals Judges (including Stevens, Arlin M. Adams,

Paul H. Roney, William H. Webster, and J. Clifford Wallace). The A.B.A. Committee on Judiciary pronounced the list "a good one, which was responsibly drawn"[124]–implying a welcome contrast to the Nixon era games.

Several days later, the Ford Administration submitted a second list:[125] the *New York Times* reported that two women, U.S. District Court Judge Cornelia Kennedy of Michigan and U.S. Court of Appeals Judge for the Ninth Circuit Shirley Hufstedler, were included, possibly also Secretary of Housing and Urban Development Carla A. Hills. In addition, law school professors Gerald Gunther of Stanford University, Philip B. Kurland of the University of Chicago, and Paul Mishkin of the University of California at Berkeley were allegedly on it.

During the selection process, the President's wife, Betty, put pressure on her husband publicly to nominate a woman. Her own voiced choice was Carla Hills. Senate G.O.P. leader Hugh Scott strongly endorsed his colleague Senator Griffin as well as (again) Judge Arlin M. Adams of the U.S. Court of Appeals for the Third Circuit, who had appeared on the initial list–and who had also been under serious consideration by Nixon for the Black and Harlan vacancies in late 1971.[126] Ford has recalled that the final choice was between Adams and Stevens and that it was "a close call," but that he selected Stevens after consulting again with Levi and Buchen.[127] Levi and his chief assistant had read all of Stevens's opinions and were very much impressed by their style and clarity. Of the four historically demonstrable major motivations in the Presidential selection process of future justices of the Supreme Court,[128] objective merit and political/ideological compatibility seem to have had the most influence on Ford's choice of Stevens. In announcing the Stevens nomination, Ford labeled him simply as "the best qualified." Indeed the A.B.A. Committee had given Stevens its top evaluation in stating that he met "the highest standards of professional competence, judicial temperament and integrity."

Certainly Stevens's background was demonstrably impressive. He was graduated *magna cum laude* and first in his class from the University of Chicago, where he was elected to *Phi Beta Kappa*.

He was also first in his class and coeditor of the law review at Northwestern University's Law School. After a clerkship with Supreme Court Justice Wiley B. Rutledge, Stevens entered private practice and became a specialist in antitrust matters. He served on the U.S. Circuit Court of Appeals for the Seventh Circuit during the five years prior to his selection for the highest bench.

Neither of the other two major factors, balancing "representation" nor personal and political friendship, appears to have played a role in Ford's choice. The President met Stevens for the first time at a White House dinner for the federal judiciary just four days prior to his decision to appoint him. According to Presidential Press Secretary Ron Nessen, Stevens's religion and party affiliation were unknown to the President and had not been considered at all in the selection process. Ideological compatibility seems to have been Ford's primary concern. In his memoirs he noted that he was looking for a Justice who would support Chief Justice Warren Burger's attempts "to limit federal jurisdiction and let state courts make more final judgments themselves."[129]

At the time of the Stevens appointment, the press, however, suggested more partisan factors that may well have affected Ford's decision–and with considerable credibility. The President may have shunned a controversial appointee to avoid having the Senate delay the confirmation until the election year of 1976. Moreover, it was already apparent that Ford was being challenged by G.O.P. conservatives for the Presidential nomination. That in effect limited the President's choices: Shirley Hufstedler, for example, although indubitably highly qualified, would have been far too liberal. Stevens was considered difficult to categorize, but "centrist" was the label most often attributed to him; he was professionally perceived as a "legal conservative." In hearings before the Senate Judiciary Committee, Stevens vowed to adhere to a policy of "judicial restraint" and "decide cases on the narrowest grounds possible." Despite criticism from woman's groups over Stevens's stand on the Equal Rights Amendment (E.R.A.), the nominee was confirmed unanimously (98:0) by a supportive Senate on December 17, 1975, just sixteen days after the President submitted his name to its Judiciary Committee, which had provided its unanimous endorsement after brief hearings.

Now (late 1984) in his ninth year on the Court, Justice Stevens–its junior Justice for almost six years (he termed it "an exceptionally long tenure"[130]) until Justice O'Connor replaced Justice Stewart in late 1981–has confounded prognosticators who thought they knew him as well as those who did not. Widely considered a "sure swing vote" in the Court's center–then generally composed of Justices White and Stewart, often joined by Justice Powell and occasionally by Justice Blackmun–he fairly rapidly proved to be found far more frequently with the "liberal bloc" of Justice Brennan and Marshall, increasingly so with the passing of time. Although not as predictably doctrinaire as the former two in all facets of the realm of civil rights and liberties and resolutely parting company with them on such contentious high-visibility issues as reverse discrimination,[131] his prorights or proindividual score has consistently been high, exceeded only by his two libertarian activist brethren and by Justice Blackmun in racial-discrimination litigation. The women's rights group who opposed his nomination because of his alleged "blatant insensitivity" to sex discrimination quickly began to hail him as both sensitive and free of preconceived notions.[132] Voting rights; free speech; free exercise of religion and separation of Church and State; civil rights for blacks, children, and prisoners; and not excluding the criminal justice sector–the Stevens record in all of these have drawn enduring praise from liberal constituencies.

Although some of these observations apply to Justice Blackmun as well, there are major differences between these two Justices who have so surprised their nominators. This is especially true with regard to their craftsmanship of opinions, with Stevens's consistently being tightly reasoned, if sometimes crochetlike; written with directness, forcefulness, and often blunt incisiveness; addressing statutory construction with literateness and literalness. A "gadfly to the brethren,"[133] a personal loner, a legal maverick, he forever challenges his colleagues without, however, triggering or adopting the sort of acrimony characteristic of some of them. Always well prepared and soft-spoken in his frequent colloquies with counsel in oral argument, he probes like a veritable explorer and is replete with novel legal theories. The latter is particularly notable in cases involving constitutional interpretation, where his jurisprudence permits him a great deal more latitude than in statutory construction problems. A student of history, and beholden to the tenets of *stare decisis,* he will nonetheless rationalize *cum* justify the moving finger of time's evolvement in accordance with his perception of the Holmesian "felt necessities of the time." Yet, as he demonstrated so fervently and outspokenly in such stream-of-consciousness cases as *Bakke* and *Weber,* he will not ignore legislative language or crystal-clear legislative intent in favor of judicial fiat.

But he has not been a Court leader, and it is doubtful that he will become one. Although respectful and courteous, he has found it difficult to subsume his own ideas and interpretations to others in order to forge not only a numerically united front, but also one that is jurisprudentially in concord. Although he is the Justice who, more than any other, has lamented the plethora of opinions handed down by the Court and the cascading number of cases accepted for review, he has written more dissenting and concurring opinions than any of his colleagues! Thus, he disagreed with the majority in fully fifty of ninety-one divided Court opinions in the 1983–84 term. To dissent, of course, is one thing; but to engage in the veritable flood of concurring opinions that have emanated from Justice Stevens's pen is quite another—for they all too often muddy the constitutional law waters and lay themselves open to the charge that they are ego trips. He has simply found it extremely difficult merely to join a majority or dissenting opinion without some comment—a regrettable habit in which he resembles Justice Frankfurter. Thus, in the delicate and difficult July 1983 holding in *Barefoot* v. *Estelle,*[134] in which a badly divided Court upheld the expedited handling of a death row case. Stevens *dissented* from Justice White's controlling opinion on the procedural issue involved but *concurred* in the majority's sanction of the prosecution's use of psychiatric testimony—thereby casting the Court's vote into a 5½:3½ equation! And early in 1984 he deemed it necessary not only to be the sole dissenter in an original jurisdiction case dispute, but he *also* filed a partial concurrence![135] That he is not the only one to engage in that questionable type of perfectionism does not gainsay the unfortunate effect it has on the judicial process, let alone the public's comprehension.

Yet Justice John Paul Stevens is patently a valuable addition to the Court. If he is not a jurisprudential or tactical on-bench leader, he is, nonetheless, an unceasing stimulator of reflection, of innovation, of disciplined literateness—witness his majority opinion for the 5:4 Court in the 1984 *Home Video Taping Case*—[136] of cerebral combat in constitutional law, logic, and theory. And his gift for elegant, pungent, memorable expression will always grace the Court's annals. An example of that enviable gift is his impassioned separate dissenting opinion—Brennan and Marshall joining Blackmun in another—in the 1980 *Regan* New York reimbursement-for-certain-expenses-incurred-by-nonpublic-schools case,[137] where he warned:

> The entire enterprise of trying to justify various types of subsidies to non-public schools should be abandoned. Rather than continuing with the Sisyphean task of trying to patch together the "blurred, indistinct, and variable barrier" described in *Lemon v. Kurtzman,* I would resurrect the "high and impregnable wall" [which Jefferson and Madison had envisaged].[138]

And in another notable dissent during that same term of Court, when the Court in *Fullilove* v. *Klutznick*[139] sustained Congress's ten percent "set aside" quota in federal construction contracts on behalf of "minority business enterprises," Stevens—again writing separately (Rehnquist joining the other dissent by Stewart)—read aloud from the bench on the day of the decision: he charged that the "minority set-aside" law represents a "perverse form of reparation,"[140] a "slapdash" law that rewards some who may not need rewarding and hurts others who may not deserve hurting.[141] Suggesting that such a law could be used simply as a patronage tool by its authors, he warned that it might breed more resentment and prejudice than it corrects,[142] and he asked what percentage of "oriental blood or what degree of Spanish-speaking skill is required for membership in the preferred class?"[143] Sarcastically, he said that now the government must devise its version of the Nazi laws that defined who is a Jew, musing that "our statute books will once again have to contain laws that reflect the odious practice of delineating the qualities that make one person a Negro and make another white."[144]

Fate did not permit Democrat Jimmy Carter to appoint a single Supreme Court Justice—the sole President in our history elected to a full four-year term of office in his own right never to have had that opportunity. Theoretically equipped with all the conventionally favorable accoutrements of the nation's leader—intelligence; public service experience (e.g., governor of Georgia); solid educational background; military service; good looks; an attractive, happy family; love of his land—in truth Carter had an unhappy and frustrating Presidency. He proved to be politically awkward and sometimes naïve; his was a poor public speaking and communication presence; he evinced a low boiling point; and he was both victim and perpetuator of a disastrous economy that resulted in the highest inflation and interest rates in history. Carter's Waterloo, however, was the seizure of the U.S. Embassy in Teheran on November 4, 1979, by Iranian militants and the painfully lengthy incarceration of more than sixty American hostages until January 1981—moments after Ronald Reagan had taken the oath of office, having defeated Jimmy Carter by a landslide.

Yet, although President Carter could not appoint a member of the highest court of the land, he was able to nominate and see appointed more members of the federal judiciary than any other President in the country's history. Owing to his Democratic Congress's present of the Omnibus Judgeship Act of 1978, he was enabled to fill 152 newly created judgeships in the U.S. District Courts and the U.S. Courts of Appeals. That huge plum, coupled with normal attrition, meant that at the end of his term, Jimmy Carter had appointed fully forty percent of the federal judiciary, close to 300 judges, not counting magistrates, bankruptcy judges, and administrative law judges. Thus, although there is no Carter Supreme Court Justice—and never will be—the Carter Administration's major legacy will undoubtedly be the stamp Carter appointees will have left on jurisprudence and the judicial process. And that will be particularly the case because of the Carter Administration's commitment to, and embrace of, a controversial, massive affirmative action program, which resulted in the installation of close to 100 women, blacks, and Hispanics, whose numbers had heretofore been small indeed.

In other words, Jimmy Carter adopted as his cardinal, overriding criterion for judicial selection none of the severally described traditional factors but rather the perceived political obligation of "representativeness," based on race and gender. To attain that goal, his Administration devised a series of imaginative procedural tools–such as the establishment of the U.S. Circuit Judge Nomination Commission[145]–all designed to increase dramatically the number of nonwhites and nonmales in the federal judiciary. As the President candidly admitted in a December 1978 press conference: "If I didn't have to get Senate confirmation of appointees, I could tell you flatly that twelve per cent of my judicial appointments would be black and three per cent would be Spanish-speaking, and forty per cent would be women, and so forth."[146] When questioned by both friendly and quizzical members of the Senate Judiciary Committee on the Administration's policy, Attorney General Griffin Bell had testified earlier that "Mr. Carter was prepared to appoint to the Federal bench a black, Hispanic, or woman lawyer who was found to be *less qualified* than a white male as long as the appointee was found qualified."[147] The policy constituted a veritable revolution with long-term consequences on which the verdict is still in doubt.

The Reagan Administration quickly made clear that its leader would return to traditional criteria in selecting Justices, and in April 1981 Attorney General William French Smith issued a "Memorandum on Judicial Selection Procedures"[148] to that effect. Its opening sentence emphasized that "in the process of judicial selection, the Department of Justice will work closely and cooperatively with the Senate leadership, the Judiciary Committee Chairman and individual members." In an oblique criticism of the predecessor Administration's policy, the Attorney General's memo went on to promise a firm commitment "to the principle that federal judges should be chosen on the basis of merit and quality."[149] And, unlike Jimmy Carter, Ronald Wilson Reagan would fairly soon have an opportunity to appoint a member of the Supreme Court: Justice Potter Stewart issued the surprise announcement of his unexpected retirement at the close of the Court's 1980–1981 term on July 3, 1981, after twenty-three years of service. It set the stage for President Reagan's selection of the first woman ever to mount the Supreme Court of the United States–Judge Sandra Day O'Connor of the Arizona Court of Appeals, that state's second highest tribunal. The surprise of the choice was exceeded only by the widespread acclaim it invoked.

During the 1980 Presidential campaign, Ronald Reagan had promised: "One of the first Supreme Court vacancies in my administration will be filled by the most qualified woman I can find, one who meets the high standards I will demand for all my appointments."[150] The opportunity to fulfill his campaign pledge and nominate the first woman member of the Court came within the initial six months of his Presidency. On June 18, 1981, in what constituted a major surprise in many normally knowledgeable circles, Justice Potter Stewart publicly announced his retirement from the Supreme Court. Members of the Reagan Administration, however, had known of Stewart's intention to step down since March and had, thus, informed the President on April 21, while the latter was still recovering from the assassination attempt one month earlier. Significantly, this advance notice of Stewart's departure gave the Administration three months to search quietly for a nominee without political pressure from outside and without media speculation.[151]

Attorney General William French Smith and White House Counselor Edwin Meese orchestrated the search for a suitable nominee in consultation with the then Deputy Secretary of State, William P. Clark, the President's close confidant, who had been Reagan's appointee to the California Supreme Court and possessed the most judicial experience of any member of the inner-circle Reagan team. All three men had themselves been considered possible candidates for the vacant Court seat but had removed their names from any genuine consideration.[152]

On June 23, Attorney General Smith provided the President with an initial list of *circa* twenty-five candidates, approximately half of whom were women—clearly a record to that date. Among the women in contention were: Arizona Court of Appeals Judge Sandra Day O'Connor; U.S. Court of Appeals Judge for the Sixth Circuit, Cornelia Kennedy; Chief Justice of the Michigan Supreme Court, Mary Coleman; and U.S. Court of Appeals Judge for the Second Circuit, Amalya L. Kearse, a youthful liberal black Carter appointee to that tribunal.[153]

By the end of June, the Attorney General had winnowed the "long list" of twenty-five to a "short list" of about five putative candidates. Judge O'Connor was among the names on that final roster, which also included Judge Kennedy and three men: Utah Supreme Court Judge and ex-President of Brigham Young University, Dallin H. Oaks; U.S. Court of Appeals Judge for the Ninth Circuit, J. Clifford Wallace; and Yale law professor and former U.S. Solicitor General, Robert H. Bork.[154]

On June 27, Attorney General Smith sent his chief counselor, Kenneth W. Starr, and Assistant Attorney General Jonathan Rose to Phoenix to interview Judge O'Connor as well as several Arizonans who were familiar with her personal and professional background. The Attorney General received a highly favorable report, and Judge O'Connor flew to Washington two days later for a secret meeting with Smith. During that same day she also met with President Reagan's three senior staffers—Meese, James Baker, and Michael Deaver. On July 1, those three plus the Attorney General gathered with Judge O'Connor and the President in the Oval Office. She quickly reminded Reagan that she had met him ten years earlier when he was governor of California and she was a member of the Arizona State Senate. The President and Judge O'Connor reportedly had a productive hour-long chat.[155] The Arizona jurist would be the only candidate to be interviewed directly by the President and his top aides for the Stewart vacancy.

In addition to that successful interview, the O'Connor candidacy was bolstered by the "Stanford connection." Dean Charles Myers of Stanford University's Law School, former Stanford Law Professor William Baxter (who had moved to the Justice Department as Assistant Attorney General to head its antitrust division), and Stanford Law alumnus U.S. Supreme Court Justice William H. Rehnquist all highly recommended O'Connor, who had taken her undergraduate and law degrees at that prestigious California institution. Senator Barry Goldwater (R.-Ariz.) also warmly urged Reagan to nominate O'Connor.[156] In addition, she received support from her home state's other U.S. Senator, Dennis De Concini, an influential moderate-to-conservative Democrat.[157]

With such powerful backing, O'Connor gained the inside track. On July 7, three weeks after Justice Stewart's retirement, President Reagan made his historic announcement that he would nominate the fifty-one-year-old Arizona judge to the Supreme Court. He had phoned Mrs. O'Connor on the previous afternoon to inform her of his intention to appoint her. In his statement, the President pronounced O'Connor "truly a 'person for all seasons,' possessing those unique qualities of temperament, fairness, intellectual capacity and devotion to the public good which have characterized the 101 'brethren' who have preceded her."[158]

Women's rights groups and prominent liberals, such as Senator Edward M. Kennedy (D.-Mass.) and Congressman Morris K. Udall (D.-Ariz.), were quick to announce their support for the first woman formally to be nominated to the highest court in the land. Udall commented of his fellow Arizonan, "She's about as moderate a Republican you'll ever find being appointed by Reagan."[159] Although members of the "Old Right" (most significantly its guru, Senator Goldwater) professed their support for Judge O'Connor, leaders of the "New Right," who had backed President Reagan so fervently in his 1980 campaign, unleashed a wave of protests against his first Supreme Court nominee. The Reverend Jerry Falwell, head of the fundamentalist Moral Majority, encouraged all "good Christians" to express concern over O'Connor's nomination. Falwell's opposition prompted a characteristically frank comment from Barry Goldwater: "Every good Christian ought to kick Falwell right in the ass."[160] Antiabortion groups also criticized O'Connor for several proabortion votes during her career as a state legislator.

As the abortion issue threatened a smooth confirmation, the

White House announced that O'Connor had assured the President that she is "personally opposed" to abortions, but that she believes abortion to be a legitimate matter for legislative regulation. During her Senate confirmation hearings, O'Connor called her vote in the Arizona legislature to decriminalize abortion a mistake. She quite properly refused, however, to state how she would vote on the abortion matter or any other issues that might come before the Supreme Court. Nevertheless, she expressed her personal feelings in favor of the death penalty and preventive detention and in opposition to busing to achieve racial integration. More generally, O'Connor explained her belief in a restrained role for the federal judiciary. She declared to the Senate Judiciary Committee: "I do not believe it is the function of the judiciary to step in and change the law because the times have changed. I do well understand the difference between legislating and judging." She continued: "As a judge, it is not my function to develop public policy."[161]

On September 15, 1981, the Senate Judiciary Committee approved Judge O'Connor's nomination by the unanimous vote of 17:0, with Senator Jeremiah Denton (D.-Ala.) voting "present" because O'Connor refused to criticize the 1973 *Roe* decision.[162] Six days later the full Senate voted 99:0 to confirm Sandra Day O'Connor as an Associate Justice of the U.S. Supreme Court. (The 100th Senator, Max Baucus [D.-Mont.], a strong supporter of the O'Connor nomination, was out of Washington when the vote was taken.) History had indeed been made!

In descending order of importance, balancing representation, political/ideological compatibility, and objective merit were the three main motivations in President Reagan's selection of O'Connor. (Personal and political friendship did not play a role in his choice, as he had met O'Connor only briefly prior to her nomination; but it was a factor among her supporters.) Clearly, gender was *the* primary concern of the Reagan Administration in choosing Judge O'Connor. In the 1980 election, Reagan had run relatively poorly among women voters and the so-called gender gap surfaced, a gap that was destined to widen during the ensuing term of office.

Still, although Reagan hoped to fulfill his campaign pledge to appoint a woman to the Supreme Court, he insisted that his nominee meet his political ideological criteria. Thus, the Reagan team had searched for a woman with demonstrable conservative political and judicial views. White House aides conducted an extensive examination of O'Connor's record as a legislator and judge. Apparently two precedents prompted such a thorough search–which included the use of a computer to trace O'Connor's personal and professional background. One was President Eisenhower's appointment in 1956 of Associate Justice William J. Brennan, Jr.; the other was Reagan's selection, while governor of California, of Donald R. Wright as Chief Justice of the California Supreme Court. Both selectees quickly developed into prime examples of judges who commenced to vote as committed and predictable liberals once on the bench, to the surprise and dismay of their conservative selectors.[163]

The Administration's painstaking research on O'Connor revealed a record of "mainstream pragmatic Republicanism" while a member of the Arizona State Senate from 1969 to 1974. After the President's announcement of her nomination, Attorney General Smith stated that Judge O'Connor shared Reagan's "overall judicial philosophy" of "restraint" and deference to the legislative branch in lawmaking. In an issue of the *William and Mary Law Review,* published just prior to O'Connor's nomination, the Arizona judge had referred with warm approbation to Supreme Court decisions that required federal judges to defer to some initial findings of fact by state courts.[164] Yet Judge O'Connor was by no means considered an extremist. One of her Democratic colleagues in the Arizona Senate described her as "a conservative in the conventional sense but beyond that she's extremely fair. She is not an ideologue. She is a perfectionist rooted in the law."[165]

Sandra O'Connor's less extreme brand of conservatism may have been a significant factor in President Reagan's decision to nominate her. According to one apparently accurate report, a member of the Supreme Court quietly told the Justice Department that some of his brethren were studying the selection closely. If Reagan appointed someone reasonable, they might be assured about his future nominations and be less reluctant to retire. Otherwise Marshall and Brennan, personifying the consistent core of the Court's liberal wing, might remain on the bench as long as physically possible.[166] (They would.)

In announcing Sandra Day O'Connor's nomination, the President stressed that he would not "appoint a woman merely to do so" and that he was convinced that she possessed those qualities necessary to serve on the Supreme Court.[167] Nevertheless, the A.B.A. Committee on Judiciary gave Judge O'Connor a qualified endorsement. Although declaring that she met "the highest standards of judicial temperament and integrity," the Committee expressed its concern over her limited experience as a judge and practicing attorney. The A.B.A. panel told the Senate Judiciary Committee that O'Connor's experience "has not been as extensive or challenging as that of some other persons who might be available for appointment."[168] Indeed, as University of Virginia Law Professor G. Edward White, among others, commented, a man with O'Connor's background would probably not be nominated to the Supreme Court.[169]

Nonetheless, although she lacked experience at the federal level before her nomination to the nation's highest tribunal, Judge O'Connor possessed impressive academic credentials. After a childhood on the family ranch on the Arizona-New Mexico border, Sandra Day was graduated from high school at the age of sixteen and enrolled at Stanford University. She completed her undergraduate work and her law degree in just five years, was graduated *magna cum laude,* and was accepted into the Society of the Coif, *the* honorary society for outstanding law students. She ranked near the top of her class (as did her future colleague William H. Rehnquist) and won a position on the *Stanford Law Review.*

Despite that outstanding record, Sandra Day was unsuccessful in finding a law firm that would hire a woman attorney. Her only job offer was for a legal secretary's position. She persisted, however, and began her legal career as Deputy County Attorney in San Mateo, California, a post she held for two years. In 1952 she married John O'Connor. For three years she worked as a civilian lawyer for the Quartermaster Corps in Frankfurt, West Germany, while her husband served in the Army's Judge Advocate General's

Corps. When they returned to the United States, she began raising their family of three sons, entered private practice, and subsequently became an assistant attorney general in Arizona. In 1969 she took a seat in the State Senate; three years later her Republican colleagues elected her majority leader—the first woman in the nation to hold such a position. She decided to pursue a judicial career in 1974 and won a seat on the Maricopa Superior Court. In 1980, Democratic Governor Bruce Babbitt nominated her to the Arizona Court of Appeals, one step below the state's Supreme Court. She had served on the Appeals Court for eighteen months when she received President Reagan's historic nomination to the U.S. Supreme Court.

In an appealingly frank statement (quoted in full in Chapter 1[170]) reflective of her selection as the first woman to serve on the highest tribunal in the land, the then-not-yet-two-year Associate Justice of the Supreme Court of the United States told the American Law Institute in May of 1983 why she thought lightning had struck her when it did:

> [W]hile there are many supposed criteria for the selection of a Justice, when the eventual decision is made as to who the nominee will be, that decision from the nominee's viewpoint is probably a classic example of being the right person in the right spot at the right time. Stated simply, you must be lucky. That certainly is how I view my nomination. . . ."

Now (late 1984), early in her fourth year on the Court, Justice O'Connor has generally met her nominator's expectations. In particular her jurisprudence has manifested a faithful, if not inevitably predictive, adherence to the gravamen of her testimony during her nomination hearings: the role of state courts and the attendant desirability as well as necessity for federal courts to respect that role by deferring to it, absent constitutional errors so blatant that they necessitate federal interference. Similar (if not the same) respect *cum* deference has informed her posture vis-à-vis actions by state legislatures, evincing a commitment to the proposition that, as a matter of basic democratic policy, the people's representatives must be granted the benefit of the doubt in setting and executing public policy and that judicial interference is justified only *in extremis*. Thus, she has been echoing the famed Holmesian creed that courts have no justifiable concern with legislative *wisdom*, only with its constitutionality; that a legislative enactment, or an executive action, may well be unwise, unjust, unfair, undemocratic, injudicious, or just plain stupid–yet still be constitutional.[171] It is a creed that Justice O'Connor has applied with particular fealty to the role of the states in our federal system. But that has by no means signaled either blind or Pavlovian support of state authority *versus* federal authority. She demonstrated that rapidly in one of her very first opinions, a concurrence in an Oklahoma capital punishment case in which, while writing separately, she joined the Court's 5:4 decision faulting the actions of the trial judge in the case,[172] carefully elucidating her reasons (here largely precedential). Whereas she went on to spend much of her first term (1981–1982) roundly denouncing encroachments on states' rights, she proved herself eminently capable of voting to invalidate state laws, even providing the decisive vote, as she did in the Court's 5:4 vote sustaining a man's equal-protection challenge to Mississippi's policy of excluding men from the Mississippi University for Women (M.U.W.) School of Nursing.[173] Her allies in a majority of other decisions, the Chief Justice, Justice Rehnquist, and Justice Powell, were among the four dissenters. And in her second term (1982–1983) she provided additional proof of her independence by writing opinions striking down California's vagrancy statute[174] and Minnesota's special tax on large newspapers.[175] Moreover, she left the "conservative" reservation three times during that term to enable a "liberal" 5:4 holding in a New Jersey redistricting case,[176] in a ruling holding a union liable to a member it failed to represent,[177] and in the seminal sex-discrimination case of *Arizona* v. *Norris*.[178] In the last she cast the decisive vote that henceforth required equal treatment of men and women in monthly annuity-benefit payments under insurance pension plans, such as those in her home state of Arizona, which was here at issue. But she *switched* to the Powell-Burger-Blackmun-

Rehnquist quartet of dissenters to deny claims of *retroactivity* of the ruling—thus, in a very real sense, providing a welcome bone *cum* breathing spell to the states.

Nonetheless, at least as of this writing, Justice O'Connor's opinions closely reflect the judicial philosophy portrayed in her confirmation hearings—including her notable dissenting opinion in the group of 1983 abortion decisions that confirmed the holdings of *Roe* v. *Wade* and its progeny.[179] She has evinced little sympathy for attempted infringement on state power, unless a clear showing of constitutional violation, in particular of the due process or equal protection clauses, is demonstrated. Although she voted against the states' legislative or judicial postures in nine of the forty-one opinions she authored during her first two terms, she was careful to articulate her reasons, obviously desirous of maintaining her allegiance to consistency in championing state power whenever constitutionally feasible. Three of these nine involved gender discrimination in which Justice O'Connor perceived due process or equal protection violations;[180] two concerned First Amendment problems;[181] and four dealt with instances in which she saw demonstrable denials of due process of law by virtue of state judicial or state legislative action.[182] Yet, in fine, she has stayed the announced jurisprudential course in approximately eighty percent of her *identifiable* votes—statistical[183] as well as substantive proof of her commitment to what, for want of a more appropriate characterization, we may regard as deference to the other branches of government, to the federal system, and to a basic role of judicial restraint.

The first woman to sit on the Supreme Court has, thus, indicated a resolute tendency, albeit not—as has been noted—an ironclad one, for example: to back state court jurisdiction in the realm of criminal-justice adjudication;[184] to respect the finality of state court judgments;[185] and to insist on exhaustion of all remedies at the state court level antecedent to permitting collateral review at the federal level;[186] to the presence and retention of certain essential components of state power and authority under the Tenth Amendment, not excluding the powerful congressional tool of the interstate commerce clause;[187] and to support state legislation and regulation under that same Amendment in the contentious obscenity sector.[188] It is always chancy to attempt to divine to what extent the on-Court record may be predictive of her future voting pattern. The pages of this tome are filled with illustrations of astonishing changes in the initially perceived jurisprudence of a host of members of the Supreme Court—to which Justice Blackmun's remarkable "switch" or "conversion" bears genuine witness. But, whatever else may lie ahead in Justice O'Connor's voting profile, it would seem highly unlikely that she would depart dramatically from what is an ably articulated, warmly embraced commitment to and recognition of the role of the states and their institutions, especially that of the state judiciary, in the American federal system.

Whatever forms Justice O'Connor's jurisprudence may take in the years ahead, her ascendancy to the Court as its first nonmale member has been a remarkably smooth one. She quickly became a respected and admired colleague; she has evinced commendable security and poise; her opinions testify to an able pen and a lucid mind; she is an assiduous worker (she wrote sixty-eight opinions in her first two terms, constituting written participation in twenty-three percent of the Court's decisions); she has been a disciplined, trenchant questioner of counsel. In short, she has manifested the collegiality, station, status, and ability that combine to have rendered the Supreme Court of the United States by and large "a bench happily filled," to reiterate Mr. Madison's fond hope of two centuries ago.

12
Epilogue

It may now be well to reflect briefly on some of the myths and truths that so often characterize public attitudes toward the Justices of the Supreme Court and that remarkable institution itself.

The Court does not operate in a vacuum, nor is it composed of Olympians. It functions as a legal, governmental, *and* political institution under a basic document that stands in constant need of interpretation against the backdrop of what Holmes referred to as the "felt necessities of the times."

Our Founding Fathers created a magnificent Constitution. But they could hardly foresee some of the contemporary problems that have found their way to the Court for resolution. Indeed, whereas for most of our history we have made laws to help solve public issues, in recent years the byword has been "let's go to court." It is a regrettable development but one that is here to stay.

The nine Supreme Court Justices who interpret the Constitution are steeped and trained in the law. But they respond to human situations; they are, in Justice Frankfurter's parlance "Men . . . not disembodied spirits, they respond to human emotions. . . ." "The great tides and currents which engulf the rest of mankind," in Justice Cardozo's beautiful and telling words, "do not turn aside in their course and pass the judges idly by."

Yet, notwithstanding the human factor, the Court operates in a setting that forces responsibility on it. Judges are bound within walls, lines, and limits that are often unseen by the layman—walls, lines, and limits built from the heritage of the law; the impact of the cases as they have come down through the years; the regard for precedent; the crucial practice of judicial restraint; the deference to the legislative process; in brief, the tradition of the law.

Moreover, the justices are well aware of two important facts of life: ultimately they do not have the power to enforce their decisions, for the purse is in the hands of the legislature and the sword in those of the executive; and the Court may be reversed by legislative action or by constitutional amendment.

We should recognize that much of our reaction to the Court's ruling is highly subjective. A "good" decision is one that pleases us; a "poor" one is one that does not. All too often our response depends on "whose ox is gored." Nor is that bit of wisdom confined to laypersons. It includes political leaders, such as President Nixon, whose frequent call for a "strict constructionist" on the bench was but a thinly disguised synonym for Justices who agreed with his philosophy of government and politics.

There is, of course, nothing wrong in a President's attempt to staff the Court with jurists who read the Constitution his way. All Presidents have tried to pack the Court, to mold it in their images. Nothing is wrong with this, provided, however, that the nominees are professionally, intellectually, and morally qualified to serve. Yet sloganeering and labeling, be they "strict constructionist" or "liberal" or "conservative," are as unhelpful to an understanding of the nature and function of the judicial process as they are misleading.

Is a Justice who upholds the Bill of Rights a liberal or a conservative? It depends on one's point of view. Were the three of the four "strict constructionists" President Nixon appointed to the Court under that label "strict" or "loose" constructionists when they joined in the majority decision to throw out abortion-control statutes in forty-five states early in 1973? The point is that there simply is no easy answer—and that one of the most difficult tasks in analyzing the judicial process is to be at once objective and consistent.

The Supreme Court of the United States is, indeed, engaged in the political process. But, in Justice Frankfurter's admonition, it is "the Nation's ultimate judicial tribunal, not a super-legal aid bureau." Neither is the Court, in the second Justice Harlan's words, "a panacea for every blot upon the public welfare, nor should this Court ordained as a judicial body, be thought of as a general haven for reform movements." In other words, the Constitution of the United States was simply not designed to provide judicial remedies for every social or political ill.

The Supreme Court is much better at saying yes or no to the government than in prescribing policy; indeed, it should resolutely shun *prescriptive* policymaking. It has quite enough to do in constitutional and statutory interpretation and application. The Court is much better at saying what the government may *not* do or what it *may* do than in prescribing what public policy the government ought to chart and how to go about doing it. Paraphrasing Professor Paul A. Freund, the question is not whether the Court can do everything, but whether it can do something in its proper sphere.

Of course, all judging involves decision making, and the Court can escape neither controversy nor criticism, nor should it. In Justice Holmes's oft-quoted words: "We are very quiet up there, but it is the quiet of a storm center, as we all know." As an institution at once legal, political, and human, it possesses both the assets and liabilities that attend these descriptive characteristics.

Yet when all is said and done, the Court is the "living voice of the Constitution," as Lord Bryce once phrased it. As such it is both arbiter and educator and, in essence, represents the sole solution short of anarchy under the American system of government as we know it. Within the limits of procedure and deference to the presumption of the constitutionality of legislation, the Court—our "sober second thought"—is the natural forum in American society for the individual and small groups, what Madison, the father of the Bill of Rights, fervently hoped it would always be. The Court is infinitely more qualified to protect minority rights than the far more easily pressured, more impulsive, and more emotion-charged legislative and executive branches. All too readily do these two yield to the politically expedient and the popular, for they are close indeed to what Judge Learned Hand once called "the pressure of public panic, and public greed."

In general, if not unfailingly, the Supreme Court of the United States has evinced a remarkable degree of common constitutional sense in its striving, as a voice of reason, to maintain the blend of continuity and change that constitute the *sine qua non* for desirable stability in the basic governmental processes of a democracy. In that role it will—because it must—live in history.

Notes

1. INTRODUCTORY REFLECTIONS: OF CRITERIA, EVALUATIONS, AND JUDGMENTS (pp. 3–12)

1. "Judicial Selection and the Qualities that Make a 'Good' Judge," 462 *Annals of the American Academy of Social and Political Science* 112 (July 1982), 113–114.
2. Restored Supreme Court Chamber, U.S. Capitol, April 30, 1982. Somewhat shortened and adapted, the address was published in 66 *Judicature* 7 (February 1983).
3. *Ibid.*, pp. 11–12.
4. As quoted by Judge Irving R. Kaufman, "Chartering a Judicial Pedigree," *New York Times*, January 24, 1981, p. A23.
5. See my *The Judicial Process: An Introductory Analysis of the Courts of the United States, England, and France*, 4th ed. (New York: Oxford University Press, 1980), pp. 65–80.
6. *New York Times*, March 2, 1932, quoting Senator Clarence Dill (R.-Wash.), p. 13.
7. Elmo Richardson, *The Presidency of Dwight D. Eisenhower* (Lawrence: Regents Press of Kansas, 1979), p. 108, quoting Ralph Cake, Oral History Transcript, OH 111, part 2, p. 38.
8. *Riverside California Press*, July 19, 1974, p. 11.
9. *Democracy in America*, trans. George Lawrence, ed. J. P. Mayer (Garden City, N.Y.: Doubleday, 1969), p. 149.
10. *Ibid.*, p. 150.
11. Albert P. Blaustein and Roy M. Mersky, *The First One Hundred Justices: Statistical Studies on the Supreme Court of the United*

States (Hamden, Conn.: Shoe String Press [Archon Books], 1978).

12. J. M. Dillon (ed.), *John Marshall: Complete Constitutional Decisions* (New York: Callaghan, 1903), p. 80.
13. Blanstein and Mersky, *op. cit.*, fn. 11, pp. 50–51.
14. 105 *University of Pennsylvania Law Review* (1957), 781.
15. *The* [New Orleans] *Times-Picayune,* July 30, 1978, p. 8, sec. 3.
16. Bernard Schwartz, "The Judicial Ten: America's Greatest Judges," *Southern Illinois University Law Journal* (1979), 405.
17. "The All-Time All-Star All-Era Supreme Court," 69 *American Bar Association Journal* (April 1983), 462–464.
18. *Ibid.*
19. *Ibid.*

2. THE NIXON ERA: A TURBULENT CASE STUDY (pp. 13–23)

1. Richard Harris, *Decision* (New York: E. P. Dutton, 1971), p. 11.
2. Quoted in Harris, *ibid.,* pp. 15–16.
3. *Congressional Record,* 91st Cong., 2d sess., Vol. 116, p. 7498.
4. *Ibid.,* p. 7487.
5. Harris, *op. cit.,* p. 16.
6. *Ibid.,* p. 56.
7. Presidential TV address, April 9, 1970. (Text in *New York Times,* April 10, 1970, p. 1.)
8. *New York Times,* September 4, 1977, p. A25.
9. 347 U.S. 483 (1954).
10. "The Southern Manifesto" was signed by nineteen U.S. Senators and eighty-two U.S. Representatives from the eleven Southern States of Alabama, Arkansas, Florida, Georgia, Louisiana, Mississippi, North Carolina, South Carolina, Tennessee, Texas, and Virginia. The six Border States of Maryland, Delaware, West Virginia, Kentucky, Missouri, and Oklahoma did not participate in "The Southern Manifesto."
11. As reported by James Goodman, "The Politics of Picking Federal Judges," *Juris Doctor,* June 1977, p. 26.

3. *HOW* THEY GET THERE: APPOINTING SUPREME COURT JUSTICES (pp. 24–48)

1. For a thorough and detailed analysis and discussion of the staffing of lower federal and state courts, see my *The Judicial Process:*

An Introductory Analysis of the Courts of the United States, England, and France, 4th ed. (New York: Oxford University Press, 1980), Ch. 2, "Staffing the Courts," especially pp. 23–41.

2. James Madison, *Notes of Debates in the Federal Convention of 1787* (Athens: Ohio University Press, 1966), pp. 67–68. Introduction by Adrienne Koch.
3. *The Advice and Consent of the Senate* (Berkeley and Los Angeles: University of California Press, 1953), pp. 28–30, 34.
4. *Congressional Record,* 82d Cong., 1st sess., Vol. 97, Pt. 10 (October 9, 1951), pp. 12838, 12840.
5. As quoted by Alpheus Thomas Mason, *William Howard Taft: Chief Justice* (New York: Simon & Schuster, 1965), p. 173.
6. Speech to the Annual Convention of the American Bar Association, Dallas, Texas, August 10, 1969.
7. See Ch. 2, *supra.*
8. See the detailed articles by Elliot E. Slotnick, "The ABA Standing Committee on Federal Judiciary: A Contemporary Assessment," Parts I and II, in 66 *Judicature* 8 and 9 (March and April 1983).
9. For a formal description, recently updated, of the Committee's procedures, see *The ABA's Standing Committee on Federal Judiciary: What It Is and How It Works* (Chicago: American Bar Association, 1983). Why its title insists on omitting the definite article "the" between "on" and "Federal" remains an intriguing quirk, at least to this observer!
10. Report of the Standing Committee on Federal Judiciary, 88 *American Bar Association Reports* (1963), p. 195.
11. *New York Times,* October 22, 1971, p. C24.
12. See Ch. 2, *supra.*
13. Interview with member Robert L. Trescher, Esquire (Third Circuit representative on the Committee), December 9, 1971.
14. *United Mine Workers* v. *Red Jacket Consolidated Coal and Coke Co.,* 18 F. 839 (1927).
15. *Hitchman Coal and Coke Co.* v. *Mitchell,* 245 U.S. 229 (1917).
16. *Hearings Before the Subcommittee of the Committee on the Judiciary, U.S. Senate, on the Confirmation of John J. Parker to be an Associated Justice of the Supreme Court of the United States,* 71st Cong., 2d sess., 1930, p. 74.
17. 165 F. 2d 387. (It sustained 72 F. Supp. 516.)
18. 133 F. Supp. 776.
19. 354 U.S. 449.
20. See Appendix A, *infra,* for the ranking—discussed in Chapter 1—of the first ninety-six Justices of the Supreme Court by sixty-five Court experts.

21. After barely fifteen months on the high bench, Byrnes resigned to become F.D.R.'s Assistant President for Domestic Affairs.
22. See Ch. 9, *infra,* for details.

4. *WHY* THEY GET THERE: QUALIFICATIONS AND RATIONALIZATIONS (pp. 49–70)

1. Frankfurter's one-time (1949–1956) colleague on the high bench, Sherman Minton, in a letter to F.F., fully seconded the latter's view on the point of judicial experience: "A copy of your letter should be sent to every member of Congress. Your statement explodes entirely the myth of prior judicial experience. I am a living example that judicial experience [he had had eight years on the lower federal judiciary] doesn't make one prescient." (Sherman Minton to Felix Frankfurter, April 18, 1957, Frankfurter Papers, Library of Congress.)
2. Frankfurter, "The Supreme Court in the Mirror of Justices," 105 *University of Pennsylvania Law Review* (1957), p. 781.
3. As quoted in *New York Times Magazine,* November 28, 1954, p. 14.
4. See Ch. 8, *infra,* for Taft's potent influence in the selection and nominating process, and Ch. 9 for the F.D.R.-Truman era.
5. One of the reviewers of the first edition of *Justices and Presidents* (Oxford University Press, 1974; Penguin Press, 1975) found that the twelve Justices rated "great" in the Blaustein and Mersky study (see Ch. 1, *supra,* and Appendix A, *infra*) had a total of but forty and one-half years of judicial experience prior to reaching the Supreme Court, with Holmes and Cardozo accounting for twenty-eight of those. But the fourteen rated either as "failure" or "below average" had accumulated sixty-four and one-half years!
6. Frankfurter, *op. cit.,* fn. 2, p. 793.
7. She had served on the Supreme Court of Arizona for six and one-half years and was confirmed by the U.S. Senate on September 21, 1981, by a vote of 99:0. (It was not until 1979 that *every* state of the Union had at least one woman judge.)
8. Paul J. Weber, "The Birth Order Oddity in Supreme Court Appointments," 13 *Presidential Studies Quarterly* 2 (Spring 1984), pp. 1–20.
9. Many of the earlier Supreme Court Justices "read" and/or were apprenticed in the law, without necessarily attending a formal school of law. Others were self-taught—but in both instances they

had to meet the bar's admission requirements and were, thus, full-fledged lawyers. Among recent members of the Courts, one who combined self-teaching of law with office experience was Justice James F. Byrnes. Neither Justice Robert H. Jackson nor Justice Stanley F. Reed finished law school. Yet the three ultimately met all necessary requirements for admission to the bar.

10. *New York Times,* June 29, 1949, p. 1.
11. See press conferences of May 22, 1969; March 22, 1970; and December 8, 1971, all referring at least partly to the point at issue.
12. *New York Times,* June 14, 1967, p. 1.
13. *Ibid.,* May 17, 1969, p. 1.
14. For details of Washington's approach and requirements see Ch. 5, *infra.*
15. Henry Cabot Lodge, *Selections from the Correspondence of Theodore Roosevelt and Henry Cabot Lodge, 1884–1918* (New York: Charles Scribner's Sons, 1925), Vol. 2, pp. 228, 230–231.
16. *Ibid.,* p. 229.
17. *The Supreme Court in United States History,* rev. ed. (Boston: Little, Brown, 1926), Vol. 2, p. 22.
18. 193 U.S. 197 (1904).
19. As quoted by James E. Clayton, *The Making of Justice: The Supreme Court in Action* (New York: E. P. Dutton, 1964), p. 47.
20. As quoted by Arthur Krock, *New York Times, October* 19, 1971, p. 43L.
21. Lecture at Columbia University, April 28, 1959.
22. As quoted in *Time Magazine,* May 23, 1969, p. 24.
23. Comment to Anthony Lewis, "A Talk with Warren on Crime, the Court, the Country," *New York Times Magazine,* October 19, 1969, pp. 128–29.

5. THE FIRST FORTY YEARS: FROM GEORGE WASHINGTON TO JOHN QUINCY ADAMS 1789–1829 (pp. 71–93)

1. See Appendix B, *infra,* for a tabular account of six well-publicized–and generally regarded as highly authoritative–Presidential performance evaluations, undertaken between 1948 and 1982. They produced remarkably similar judgments and results, except that a widely heralded reappraisal of President Eisenhower has caused him to be moved into a considerably higher slot, i.e.,

"near great," since his initial low "average" 1962 ranking. See, e.g., Fred I. Greenstein's work, *The Hidden Presidency: Eisenhower as Leader* (New York: Basic Books, 1982).

2. The twelve who were confirmed: Jay, John Rutledge, Cushing, Wilson, Blair, Iredell, Thomas Johnson, Paterson, Samuel Chase, Ellsworth; but two of these, Robert H. Harrison and Cushing (Chief Justiceship), declined postconfirmation. One, John Rutledge (Chief Justiceship) was rejected; one nomination, Paterson, was withdrawn, but successfully resubmitted. Three, Cushing, John Rutledge, and Paterson, had two nominations each, the first two serving as Associate Justices only. The fourteen nominations, thus, involved eleven different individuals: Jay, John Rutledge, Cushing, Robert H. Harrison, Wilson, Blair, Iredell, Thomas Johnson, Paterson, Samuel Chase, and Ellsworth. (For further details, see Charles Warren, *The Supreme Court in United States History,* Vol. 3, Appendix (Boston: Little, Brown, 1923).
3. Fred L. Israel, "John Blair," in Leon Friedman and Fred L. Israel (eds.), *The Justices of the United States Supreme Court, 1789–1969* (New York: Chelsea House, 1969), Vol. 1, p. 111.
4. Richard Barry, *Mr. Rutledge of South Carolina* (New York: Duell, Sloan & Pearce, 1942), p. 353.
5. As quoted by Marvin Meyerson and Dilys Pegler Winegrad, "Justice James Wilson," *Pennsylvania Gazette,* April 1978, p. 28.
6. Gertrude S. Wood, *William Paterson of New Jersey, 1745–1806* (Fair Lawn, N.J.: Fair Lawn Press, 1933), p. 101.
7. As quoted in Samuel Eliot Morison, Henry Steele Commager, and William E. Leuchtenburg, *The Growth of the American Republic,* 6th ed. (New York: Oxford University Press, 1969), Vol. 1, p. 346.
8. For an authoritative commentary and interpretation of Chase's travail see Richard Tillich, "The Chase Impeachment," 4 *American Journal of Legal History* (1960).
9. Fred L. Israel, "James Iredell," in Friedman and Israel (eds.), *op. cit.,* fn. 3, Vol. 1, p. 128.
10. See my *The Judicial Process: An Introductory Analysis of the Courts of the United States, England, and France,* 4th ed. (New York: Oxford University Press, 1980), pp. 328, 363.
11. *Ibid.,* p. 310.
12. As quoted by Charles Warren, *op. cit.,* fn. 2, Vol. 1, p. 178.
13. As quoted in Frank Monaghan, *John Jay: Defender of Liberty* (New York: Bobbs-Merrill, 1935), p. 425.
14. Robert J. Steamer, *The Supreme Court in Crisis: A History of Conflict* (Amherst: University of Massachusetts Press, 1971), p. 35.

15. *McCulloch* v. *Maryland,* 4 Wheaton 316 (1819), at 407.
16. *Osborn* v. *United States Bank,* 9 Wheaton 739 (1824), at 865.
17. 1 Cranch 137.
18. 4 Wheaton 315.
19. 4 Wheaton 518.
20. 9 Wheaton 1.
21. Benjamin N. Cardozo, *The Nature of the Judicial Process* (New Haven: Yale University Press, 1921), pp. 169–170.
22. J. M. Dillon (ed.), *John Marshall: Complete Constitutional Decisions* (New York: Callaghan, 1903), p. 77.
23. Fred L. Israel, "Thomas Todd," in Friedman and Israel (eds.), *op. cit.,* fn. 3, vol. 1, p. 409.
24. Letter to Thomas Ritchie, December 25, 1820, quoted in Andrew A. Lipscomb and Albert E. Bergh (eds.), *Thomas Jefferson, Writings* (Washington, D.C.: Thomas Jefferson Memorial Association, 1903), Vol. 15, pp. 297–298.
25. R. Kent Newmyer, "A Note on the Whig Politics of Justice Joseph Story," 48 *Mississippi Valley Historical Review* (December 1961), p. 482.
26. William O. Douglas, 41 when F.D.R. appointed him in 1939, would be the next youngest more than a century and one-quarter later.
27. 9 Wheaton 1.

6. THE NEXT FORTY YEARS: FROM ANDREW JACKSON TO ANDREW JOHNSON 1829–1869 (pp. 94–124)

1. 6 Peters 515.
2. Quoted widely by a host of commentators, for example, Charles Warren in his *The Supreme Court in United States History,* rev. ed. (Boston: Little, Brown, 1926), Vol. 1, p. 759. (See also his fn. 1, Ch. 1.)
3. *Register of Debates in Congress,* 22d Cong., 1st sess., 1832, Vol. 8, Pt. 3, Appendix, p. 76. (Italics added.)
4. *Dred Scott* v. *Sandford,* 19 Howard 393.
5. In an essay on "politically motivated judges," Alexander M. Bickel termed McLean "the most notoriously so." (*Politics and the Warren Court.* New York: Harper & Row, 1965, p. 135.)
6. In 1852 he had refused the Native American party's nomination, which would have been his fifth!
7. "Of Those Who Said 'No'," Note, 4 *Supreme Court Historical Society Quarterly* (Fall 1982), p. 10.

8. E.g.: *United States* v. *Gratiot,* 14 Peters 526 (1840); *Holmes* v. *Jennison,* 14 Peters 540 (1840); *Prigg* v. *Pennsylvania,* 16 Peters 539 (1842); the *Passenger Cases,* 7 Howard 283 (1849); and *Cooley* v. *Board of Port Wardens of the Port of Philadelphia,* 12 Howard 299 (1851).
9. Samuel Taylor, *Roger Brooke Taney* (Baltimore: J. Murphy, 1872), p. 223.
10. As quoted by Warren, *op. cit.,* fn. 2, Vol. 2, p. 10. (Italics added.)
11. *Dred Scott* v. *Sandford,* 19 Howard 393 (1857), at 454–455.
12. Others that might be cited plausibly: *Luther* v. *Borden,* 7 Howard 1 (1849), and *United States* v. *Southeastern Underwriters,* 322 U.S. 533 (1944).
13. Vol. 1 (1915), pp. 192–194. (Italics in original.)
14. *Cooley* v. *Board of Port Wardens of the Port of Philadelphia, op. cit.,* fn. 8, and others cited in that note.
15. See the account by Roy Franklin Nichols, *Franklin Pierce: Young Hickory of the Granite Hills* (Philadelphia: University of Pennsylvania Press, 1931), pp. 253, 276, 277.
16. Quoted by Philip Shriver Klein, *President James Buchanan* (University Park: Pennsylvania State University Press, 1962), pp. 401–402.
17. 17 Fed. Cases 144, No. 9487 (CCD Md.).
18. *The Supreme Court in the American System of Government* (Cambridge: Harvard University Press, 1955), p. 76.
19. 16 Wallace 36.
20. 4 Wallace 2 (1866).
21. 2 Black 635 (1863).
22. Carl Sandburg, *Abraham Lincoln: The War Years* (New York: Harcourt, Brace, 1939), Vol. 3; David M. Silver, *Lincoln's Supreme Court* (Urbana: University of Illinois Press, 1956), *passim.*
23. *Hepburn* v. *Griswold* (*First Legal Tender Cases*), 8 Wallace 603 (1870).
24. (*Second Legal Tender Cases*), 12 Wallace 457 (1871).
25. (New York: Pocket Books, 1957), especially Ch. 6 on Senator Ross, "I Looked Down into My Open Grave," pp. 107–128.
26. E.g., *Ex parte Milligan,* 4 Wallace 2 (1866); *Cummings* v. *Missouri,* 4 Wallace 277 (1867); and *Ex parte Garland,* 4 Wallace 333 (1867).
27. E.g., *Mississippi* v. *Johnson,* 4 Wallace 475 (1867); *Georgia* v. *Stanton,* 6 Wallace 50 (1867); *Ex parte McCardle,* 7 Wallace 506 (1869); and *Texas* v. *White,* 7 Wallace 700 (1869).

7. THE BALANCE OF THE NINETEENTH CENTURY: FROM ULYSSES S. GRANT TO WILLIAM McKINLEY 1869–1901 (pp. 125–53)

1. When the counting of the disputed votes had started, Tilden needed but one of the twenty votes, Hayes needed all of them to win. The congressionally established fifteen-member commission was composed of five Democratic and five Republican legislators and five Supreme Court Justices: Democrats Clifford and Field, Republicans Miller and Strong, and moderate "neutral" Republican Justice David Davis, who had been selected by his judicial colleagues. But Davis, afflicted with an arguable case of cold political feet, allowed himself to be elected to the U.S. Senate by the Illinois legislature, decisively by Democratic votes. Then, at Davis's own request and with the approval of both political parties, he was replaced on the commission by Bradley. The latter came through nobly for his party and its candidate!
2. *United States* v. *Reese,* 92 U.S. 214 (1876), and *United States* v. *Cruikshank,* 92 U.S. 542 (1876).
3. *United States* v. *Harris,* 106 U.S. 629 (1883), and the *Civil Rights Cases,* 109 U.S. 3 (1883), respectively.
4. As quoted by Howard Jay Graham, "The Waite Court and the Fourteenth Amendment," 17 *Vanderbilt Law Review* (March 1964), p. 525.
5. 16 Wallace 36 (1873).
6. *United States* v. *Cruikshank,* 92 U.S. 542 (1876), at 554.
7. 94 U.S. 113.
8. E.g., his dissenting opinions in such key cases as *Hurtado* v. *California,* 110 U.S. 516 (1884); *O'Neil* v. *Vermont,* 144 U.S. 323 (1892); *Plessy* v. *Ferguson,* 163 U.S. 537 (1896); *Maxwell* v. *Dow,* 176 U.S. 581 (1900); *Giles* v. *Kentucky,* 189 U.S. 475 (1903); *Berea College* v. *Kentucky,* 211 U.S. 45 (1908); and *Twining* v. *New Jersey,* 211 U.S. 78 (1908). See the excellent essay by Jacob W. Landynski, "John Marshall Harlan and the Bill of Rights," 49 *Social Research* (Winter 1982), pp. 899–926.
9. Fred Rodell, *Nine Men: A Political History of the Supreme Court of the United States from 1790–1855* (New York: Knopf, 1955), p. 143.
10. 163 U.S. 537, at 559.
11. March 13 and 15, 1881, p. 1.
12. Wilson allegedly suggested to the old-guard Republican Union League Club of Philadelphia that it might be well to find a place

for "Old Grover's" portrait in its elegant gallery reserved for the likenesses of *Republican* Presidents.

13. E.g., White's votes in the two *Income Tax Cases* of 1895 (157 U.S. 429 and 158 U.S. 601, both recorded as *Pollock* v. *Farmers' Loan and Trust Co.*).
14. 128 U.S. 1, at 20–21.
15. 156 U.S. 1.
16. *The Supreme Court Historical Society Quarterly* (Spring 1983), p. 2.
17. Bliss Perry, *And Gladly Teach* (Boston: Houghton Mifflin, 1935), pp. 146–147.
18. Allan Nevins, *Grover Cleveland: A Study in Courage* (New York: Dodd, Mead, 1932), p. 415.
19. 198 U.S. 45.
20. 10 *Railway and Corporation Law Journal* (October 10, 1891), p. 281.
21. *Lochner* v. *New York*, 198 U.S. 45.
22. *Holden* v. *Hardy*, 169 U.S. 366.
23. 163 U.S. 537.
24. Willard L. King, *Melville Weston Fuller: Chief Justice of the United States, 1888–1910* (New York: Macmillan, 1950; Phoenix, 1967), p. 181.
25. *Pollock* v. *Farmers' Loan and Trust Co.* 158 U.S. 601 (1895).
26. Quoted in 4 *Supreme Court Historical Society Quarterly* (Winter 1982), p. 8.

8. INTO THE TWENTIETH CENTURY: FROM THEODORE ROOSEVELT TO HERBERT HOOVER 1901–1933 (pp. 154–205)

1. *Theodore Roosevelt: An Autobiography* (New York: Macmillan, 1913), p. 406.
2. *Selections from the Correspondence of Theodore Roosevelt and Henry Cabot Lodge, 1884–1918*, H. C. Lodge and C. F. Redmond, eds. (New York: Charles Scribner's Sons, 1925), Vol. 2, p. 519.
3. "Annual Message to Congress," *Congressional Record*, 60th Cong., 2d sess., Vol. 43, Pt. 1, December 8, 1908, p. 21.
4. *Selections, op. cit.*, pp. 228–229.
5. Theodore Roosevelt, *Letters*, Elting E. Morison, ed. (Cambridge: Harvard University Press, 1952), Vol. 5, p. 396.
6. *Northern Securities Co.* v. *United States*, 193 U.S. 197. See Ch. 4, p. 69, *supra*.

7. 176 Mass. 492, at 505.
8. As told by Francis Biddle, *Justice Holmes, Natural Law, and the Supreme Court* (New York: Macmillan, 1961), p. 9.
9. Wallace Mendelson, *Capitalism, Democracy, and the Supreme Court* (New York: Appleton-Century-Crofts, 1960), p. 75.
10. As quoted by Charles P. Curtis in *Lions Under the Throne* (Boston: Houghton Mifflin, 1947), p. 281.
11. *Lochner* v. *New York,* 198 U.S. 45, at 74.
12. *Hammer* v. *Dagenhart,* 247 U.S. 251, at 280.
13. *Abrams* v. *United States,* 250 U.S. 616, at 630.
14. *Gitlow* v. *New York,* 268 U.S. 652, at 673.
15. *Olmstead* v. *United States,* 277 U.S. 438, at 469–470.
16. *Hammer* v. *Dagenhart,* 247 U.S. 251.
17. Paul T. Heffron, "Theodore Roosevelt and the Appointment of Mr. Justice Moody," 18 *Vanderbilt Law Review* (March 1965), p. 545.
18. 211 U.S. 78. The overruling came in 1964, in *Malloy* v. *Hogan,* 378 U.S. 1, by a vote of 5:4.
19. (New York: Columbia University Press, 1916), p. 144.
20. Judith Icke Anderson, *William Howard Taft: An Intimate History* (New York: W. W. Norton, 1981), p. 249.
21. Alpheus Thomas Mason, *William Howard Taft: Chief Justice* (New York: Simon & Schuster, 1965), p. 15.
22. As quoted by Henry F. Pringle in *The Life and Times of William Howard Taft* (New York: Farrar, & Rinehart, 1939), p. 531.
23. As quoted in Merlon J. Pusey, *Charles Evans Hughes* (New York: Macmillan, 1951), Vol. 1, p. 271.
24. *Ibid.*, p. 272. (Italics added.)
25. *De Jonge* v. *Oregon,* 299 U.S. 353 (1937), opinion for the Court, at 365.
26. Mark De Wolfe Howe (ed.), *Holmes-Pollock Letters* (Cambridge: Harvard University Press, 1941), Vol. 1, p. 170.
27. As quoted in Pringle, *op. cit.*, fn. 22, p. 534.
28. December 10, 1912, p. 1.
29. Pringle, *op. cit.*, fn. 22, p. 535.
30. As quoted in Mason, *op. cit.*, fn. 21, pp. 39, 34.
31. The six decisions discussed in the passage were, respectively: *Wilson* v. *New,* 243 U.S. 332 (1917); *Buttfield* v. *Stranahan,* 192 U.S. 470 (1904); *Pollock* v. *Farmers' Loan & Trust Co.,* 158 U.S. 601 (1865); *Northern Securities Co.* v. *United States,* 193 U.S. 197 (1904); *United States* v. *American Tobacco Co.,* 22 U.S. 106 (1911); and *Hammer* v. *Dagenhart,* 247 U.S. 251 (1918)–the federal labor law of 1916.
32. *McCabe* v. *Atcheson, Topeka, & Sante Fe Railroad,* 186 F. 966.

33. As quoted in both Mason, *op. cit.*, fn. 21, p. 213, and Pringle, *op. cit.*, fn. 22, p. 971.
34. As quoted by Louis W. Koenig, *The Chief Executive,* rev. ed. (New York: Harcourt, Brace & World, 1968), p. 302.
35. Josephus Daniels, *The Wilson Era, Years of Peace: 1910–1916* (Chapel Hill: University of North Carolina Press, 1944), p. 115.
36. As quoted in Mason, *op. cit.*, fn. 21, pp. 216–217.
37. *Ibid.*, p. 217.
38. 5 *Supreme Court Historical Society Quarterly* (Winter 1983), p. 6.
39. *Ibid.*, p. 167.
40. As quoted in Pringle, *op. cit.*, fn. 22, p. 971.
41. As reported by William O. Douglas in his *The Court Years: (1939–1975)–The Autobiography of William O. Douglas* (New York: Random House [Vintage Books], 1980), p. 15.
42. *Coppage* v. *Kansas,* 236 U.S. 1 (1915).
43. E.g., see his dissenting opinion on wiretapping in *Olmstead* v. *United States,* 277 U.S. 438 (1928).
44. 208 U.S. 412.
45. As quoted by Mason, *op. cit.*, fn. 21, p. 72. (Italics in original.)
46. E.g., *Abrams* v. *United States,* 250 U.S. 616 (1919), and *Gitlow* v. *New York,* 268 U.S. 652 (1925).
47. *Whitney* v. *California,* 274 U.S. 357 (1927), at 377.
48. Hoyt L. Warner, *The Life of Mr. Justice Clarke: A Testimony to the Power of Liberal Dissent in America* (Cleveland: Western Reserve University Press, 1959), p. 116.
49. *Bailey* v. *Drexel Furniture Co.*, 259 U.S. 20 (1922).
50. As quoted in Arthur M. Schlesinger, Jr., *The Age of Roosevelt: The Crisis of the Old Order, 1919–1933* (Boston: Houghton Mifflin, 1957), pp. 50–51.
51. *Ibid.*, p. 51.
52. *Ibid.*, p. 50, quoting from one of Alice Longworth's (T.R.'s daughter) cruelly frank epigrams.
53. *Adkins* v. *Children's Hospital,* 261 U.S. 525 (1923).
54. Alpheus Thomas Mason, "William Howard Taft," in Leon Friedman and Fred L. Israel (eds.), *The Justices of the United States Supreme Court, 1789–1969* (New York: Chelsea House, 1969), Vol. 3. p. 2113.
55. As quoted in C. Herman Pritchett, *The Roosevelt Court: A Study in Judicial Politics and Values, 1937–1947* (New York: Macmillan, 1948), p. 18.
56. Mason, *William Howard Taft: Chief Justice, op. cit.,* fn. 21, p. 167.

57. Pringle, *op. cit.*, fn. 22, p. 972.
58. Mason, *op. cit.*, fn. 21, pp. 77–78.
59. Fred Rodell, *Nine Men: A Political History of the Supreme Court of the United States from 1790–1855* (New York: Knopf, 1955), p. 189.
60. As quoted by Walter Clemons in *Newsweek,* October 5, 1981, p. 82.
61. It was drafted for the Senate Judiciary Committee largely by Justices Van Devanter, McReynolds, and Day, with the active assistance of Justice Sutherland and Chief Justice Taft himself.
62. Joel Francis Paschal, *Mr. Justice Sutherland: A Man Against the State* (Princeton, N.J.: Princeton University Press, 1951), p. 113.
63. *Ibid.* See biography's subtitle.
64. *Lochner* v. *New York,* 198 U.S. 45 (1905), at 74.
65. 287 U.S. 45.
66. E.g., *Panama Refining Co. v. Ryan,* 293 U.S. 388 (1935); *Schechter Poultry Corp.* v. *United States,* 295 U.S. 495 (1935); *United States* v. *Butler,* 297 U.S. 1 (1936); *Carter* v. *Carter Coal Co.,* 298 U.S. 238 (1936).
67. 299 U.S. 394 (1936).
68. For an informative account of the Butler nomination and appointment, see David J. Danelski, *A Supreme Court Justice Is Appointed* (New York: Random House, 1964), especially Chs. 6–8.
69. *Olmstead* v. *United States,* 277 U.S. 438.
70. *United States* v. *Schwimmer,* 279 U.S. 644.
71. *Gitlow* v. *New York,* 268 U.S. 652.
72. *Ibid.,* at 666.
73. As quoted in Pringle, *op. cit.,* fn. 22, p. 1043.
74. As quoted by Mason, *Harlan Fiske Stone: Pillar of the Law* (New York: Viking, 1956), p. 184.
75. *Ibid.,* pp. 182–185.
76. 297 U.S. 1. The famous quotes are on pp. 78 and 88.
77. The well-known account of his last moments is taken from Mason's biography of him, fn. 74, *op. cit.,* pp. 804–806. The citation is from one of three opinions he was about to read during the Court's session on that Opinion Monday (*Girouard* v. *United States,* 328 U.S. 61, at 79).
78. *United States* v. *Carolene Products,* 304 U.S. 144, at 152–153.
79. He went abroad for Truman in connection with war relief work; and he rendered valuable service as head of the Hoover Commissions between 1949 and 1955, which made important recommendations on the reorganization of the executive branch of the federal government.

80. As quoted by Mason, *William Howard Taft: Chief Justice, op. cit.*, fn. 21, p. 234.
81. For an authentic and detailed account of the often (and wrongly) disputed telephoned offer, see Frederick Bernays Wiener, "Justice Hughes' Appointment–the Cotton Story Re-Examined," *Yearbook 1981* (Washington, D.C.: Supreme Court Historical Society, 1981), pp. 79–91.
82. Although he hedges somewhat, that seems to be Mason's conclusion too. See his volumes on Taft, *op. cit.*, fn. 21, pp. 297–299, and especially that on Stone, *op. cit.*, fn. 74, pp. 277–283. It is also confirmed by Professor Samuel Hendel in his essay in Friedman and Israel, *op. cit.*, fn. 54, Vol. 3, pp. 1893–1915.
83. Pusey, *op. cit.*, fn. 23, *passim.*
84. *Congressional Record,* 71 Cong., 2d sess., Vol. 72, p. 3373.
85. E.g., *Of Law and Men* (New York: Harcourt, Brace, 1956), pp. 133, 148.
86. E.g., see his opinion for the 5:4 Court in 1934, upholding New York's milk price control law (*Nebbia* v. *New York,* 291 U.S. 502), and his joining of the Court's 5:4 Hughes opinion, again in 1934, in upholding Minnesota's statute against real estate foreclosures (*Home Building & Loan Association* v. *Blaisdell,* 290 U.S. 398).
87. (New Haven: Yale University Press, 1921.)
88. Mason, *Harlan Fiske Stone, op. cit.*, fn. 74, p. 336.
89. Claudius O. Johnson, *Borah of Idaho* (New York: Longmans, Green, 1936), p. 452.
90. Herbert Hoover, *The Memoirs of Herbert Hoover: The Cabinet and the President, 1920–1933* (New York: Macmillan, 1952), Vol. 2, p. 269.
91. "Mr. Justice Cardozo," *Harper's Magazine,* June 1932, p. 34.
92. Mason, *Harlan Fiske Stone, op. cit.*, fn. 74, p. 337.
93. February 16, 1932, p. 1. On a C.B.S. radio broadcast on March 1, 1932–the day Cardozo's confirmation was transmitted to the White House–Senator Clarence R. Dill (D.-Wash.) styled Hoover's act in appointing him as "the finest act of his career as President." *New York Times,* March 2, 1932, p. 13.
94. *Steward Machine Co.* v. *Davis,* 301 U.S. 548, and *Helvering* v. *Davis,* 301 U.S. 619.
95. 302 U.S. 319 (1937).
96. *Ibid.*, at 325–327.
97. As requoted in the *New Yorker,* "The Talk of the Town," April 4, 1970, p. 33.
98. *Dictionary of American Biography,* Vol. 22, Supp. 2, p. 95.

9. THE COURT ALTERS COURSE: F.D.R. AND TRUMAN 1933–1953 (pp. 206–247)

1. See, among others, the accounts by Leonard Baker, *Back to Back: The Duel Between F.D.R. and the Supreme Court* (New York: MacMillan, 1967); Joseph Alsop and Turner Catledge, *The 168 Days* (Garden City, N.Y.: Doubleday, Doran, 1938); and Robert H. Jackson, *The Struggle for Judicial Supremacy* (New York: Knopf, 1941).
2. 300 U.S. 379.
3. *N.L.R.B.* v. *Jones & Laughlin Steel Corporation,* 301 U.S. 1.
4. *Helvering* v. *Davis,* 301 U.S. 619, and *Steward Machine Co.* v. *Davis,* 301 U.S. 538, respectively.
5. *Jim Farley's Story* (New York: McGraw-Hill, 1948), p. 86.
6. As quoted by Virginia Van der Veer Hamilton, *Hugo Black: The Alabama Years* (Baton Rouge: Louisiana State University Press, 1972), p. 275. (Mrs. Hamilton is the source for the Minton claim.)
7. *Ibid.*, p. 274.
8. Hugo L. Black, Jr., *My Father: A Remembrance* (New York: Random House, 1975), pp. 16–17.
9. As the *Washington Post,* for one, put it in an editorial on August 13, 1937.
10. As quoted in 60 *Judicature* 7 (February 1977), p. 350.
11. Sixty Democrats and three Republicans–Robert La Follette (Wisconsin), Arthur Capper (Kansas), and Lynn J. Frazier (North Dakota)–voted aye; ten Republicans and six Democrats voted nay; and sixteen Senators abstained from voting.
12. John P. Frank, *Mr. Justice Black: The Man and His Opinions* (New York: Knopf, 1949), p. 105.
13. *New York Times,* October 2, 1937, p. 1.
14. Gerald T. Dunne, *Hugo Black and the Judicial Revolution* (New York: Simon & Schuster, 1977), p. 43.
15. *Ibid.*, p. 52.
16. As quoted by Frank, *op. cit.*, fn. 12, p. 102.
17. See Black's poignant valedictory publication, *A Constitutional Faith* (New York: Knopf, 1968).
18. "Mr. Justice Black and the Judicial Function," 14 *U.C.L.A. Law Review* 467 (1967), at 473.
19. "Hugo Lafayette Black: In Memoriam," 20 *Journal of Public Law* 359 (1971), at 362.

20. *Adamson* v. *California,* 332 U.S. 46.
21. *Palko* v. *Connecticut,* 302 U.S. 319.
22. For a detailed description, see my *Freedom and the Court: Civil Rights and Liberties in the United States,* 4th ed. (New York: Oxford University Press, 1982), Ch. 3: "The Bill of Rights and Its Applicability to the States," pp. 28–91.
23. See James J. Magee, *Mr. Justice Black: Absolutist on the Court* (Charlottesville: University of Virginia Press, 1980).
24. 372 U.S. 335.
25. *Betts* v. *Brady,* 316 U.S. 455 (1942).
26. *Chambers* v. *Florida,* 309 U.S. 227 (1940), at 241.
27. John P. Frank, "Hugo L. Black: He Has Joined the Giants," 58 *American Bar Association Journal* (January 1972), p. 25.
28. 328 U.S. 373.
29. 321 U.S. 649.
30. See the fascinating account by Alpheus Thomas Mason, *Harlan Fiske Stone: Pillar of the Law* (New York: Viking, 1956), pp. 614–615. See also my *The Judicial Process: An Introductory Analysis of the Courts of the United States, England, and France,* 4th ed. (New York: Oxford University Press, 1980), pp. 221–222.
31. See Liva Baker, *Felix Frankfurter* (New York: Coward-McCann, 1969), pp. 201–206.
32. As quoted by Eugene C. Gerhart, *America's Advocate: Robert H. Jackson* (Indianapolis, Ind.: Bobbs-Merrill, 1958), p. 165.
33. As quoted by Harold L. Ickes, *The Secret Diaries of Harold L. Ickes* (New York: Simon & Schuster, 1954), Vol. 2, p. 539.
34. *Felix Frankfurter Reminisces.* Recorded in talks with Harlan B. Phillips. (Garden City, N.Y.: Doubleday, 1962), pp. 328–329.
35. Fred Rodell, *Nine Men: A Political History of the Supreme Court of the United States from 1790–1855* (New York: Knopf, 1955), p. 271.
36. As quoted by Rodell, *ibid.,* p. 271.
37. 342 U.S. 165.
38. *Louisiana ex rel. Francis* v. *Resweber,* 329 U.S. 459 (1947).
39. As quoted by Marvin Braiterman, "Frankfurter and the Paradox of Restraint," *Midstream* (November 1970), p. 21.
40. For a controversial, yet substantially accurate, book-length study of that phenomenon, see Bruce A. Murphy, *The Brandeis/Frankfurter Connection: The Secret Political Activities of Two Supreme Court Justices* (New York: Oxford University Press, 1982).
41. *Minersville School District* v. *Gobitis,* 310 U.S. 586 (1940).
42. *West Virginia State Board of Education* v. *Barnette,* 319 U.S. 624 (1943).

43. *Ibid.,* at 646.
44. 369 U.S. 186.
45. *Ibid.,* at 270.
46. February 24, 1965, p. 40.
47. John P. Frank, "William O. Douglas," in Leon Friedman and Fred L. Israel (eds.), *The Justices of the United States Supreme Court, 1789–1969* (New York: Chelsea House, 1969), Vol. 4, p. 2453.
48. See *Go East, Young Man. The Early Years: The Autobiography of William O. Douglas* (New York: Random House, 1974), pp. 459–462.
49. *Ibid.,* pp. 462–463.
50. Frank, *op. cit.,* fn. 47, p. 2454.
51. *Griswold* v. *Connecticut,* 381 U.S. 479, at 481.
52. *Roe* v. *Wade* and *Doe* v. *Bolton,* 410 U.S. 113 and 410 U.S. 179, respectively.
53. *Sierra Club* v. *Morton,* 405 U.S. 727 (1972). For a discussion of "standing," see my *The Judicial Process, op. cit.,* fn. 29, Ch. 9.
54. As quoted in the *New York Times Magazine,* May 26, 1969, p. 26.
55. J. Woodford Howard, Jr. *Mr. Justice Murphy: A Political Biography* (Princeton, N.J.: Princeton University Press, 1968), pp. 215–216.
56. As quoted by Gerhart, *op. cit.,* fn. 32, p. 167.
57. 323 U.S. 214.
58. *Ibid.,* beginning at p. 233.
59. *In re Yamashita,* 327 U.S. 1.
60. *Ibid.,* at 29.
61. 332 U.S. 46. Murphy's dissent begins at p. 124.
62. *Ibid.,* at 75.
63. 5 *Supreme Court Historical Society Quarterly* (Winter 1983), p. 4.
64. *Ibid.,* p. 5.
65. James F. Byrnes, *All in One Lifetime* (New York: Harper & Bros., 1958), p. 130.
66. *The Nine Young Men* (New York: Harper & Bros., 1947), p. 243.
67. *Edwards* v. *California,* 314 U.S. 160 (1941).
68. Merlo J. Pusey, *Charles Evans Hughes* (New York: Macmillan, 1951), Vol. 2, pp. 787–788.
69. As quoted by Mason, *Harlan Fiske Stone, op. cit.,* fn. 30, p. 191.
70. *Ibid.,* p. 573.
71. As quoted by Gerhart, *op. cit.,* fn. 32, p. 191.
72. E.g., *West Virginia State Board of Education* v. *Barnette,* 319

U.S. 624 (1943); *Korematsu* v. *United States,* 323 U.S. 214 (1944); and *Thomas* v. *Collins,* 323 U.S. 516 (1945).

73. E.g., *Kunz* v. *New York,* 340 U.S. 290 (1951); *Dennis* v. *United States,* 341 U.S. 494 (1951); and *Adler* v. *Board of Education,* 342 U.S. 485 (1952).
74. *Terminiello* v. *Chicago,* 337 U.S. 1, at 37.
75. *West Virginia State Board of Education* v. *Barnette,* 319 U.S. 624 (1943), at 638, 642.
76. *Brown* v. *Board of Education of Topeka,* 347 U.S. 483, and *Bolling* v. *Sharpe,* 347 U.S. 497.
77. Gerhart, *op. cit.,* fn. 32.
78. As quoted by Joseph P. Lash, *From the Diaries of Felix Frankfurter* (New York: W. W. Norton, 1975), fn. 1, p. 239.
79. As quoted by David Fellman, letter to author, August 13, 1974.
80. 332 U.S. 46, at 124. (Italics added.)
81. 327 U.S. 1 (1946), at 43.
82. 330 U.S. 1 (1947), at 59.
83. As quoted by Louis H. Pollak, "Wiley Blount Rutledge: Profile of a Judge," 1979 *University of Illinois Law Forum* 2 (1979), p. 302.
84. Harry S. Truman, *Memoirs: Year of Decisions* (Garden City, N.Y.: Doubleday, 1955), pp. 5, 44.
85. *Youngstown Sheet & Tube Co.* v. *Sawyer,* 343 U.S. 579 (1952).
86. See pp. 244–245, *infra.*
87. *Louisiana ex rel. Francis* v. *Resweber,* 329 U.S. 459 (1947). Other pertinent illustrations of Burton's posture on the point were such cases as *Garner* v. *Board of Public Works of Los Angeles,* 341 U.S. 716 (1951), and *Joint Anti-Fascist Refugee Committee* v. *McGrath,* 341 U.S. 123 (1951).
88. E.g., *Everson* v. *Board of Education of Ewing Township,* 330 U.S. 1 (1947).
89. See the account by Frank, *Mr. Justice Black, op. cit.,* fn. 12, in Ch. 7, "The Chief Justiceship," pp. 123–131.
90. See C. Herman Pritchett, *The Roosevelt Court* (Chicago: Quadrangle, 1948), p. 26.
91. President Truman so asserted in his press conference of September 15, 1951. See the *New York Times,* September 16, 1951, p. 15. There exists controversy regarding Hughes's recommendation. Some observers, for example, his principal biographer, Merlo J. Pusey, hold that Hughes's first choice was really Jackson–a claim not necessarily incompatible with the Truman assertions however.
92. Richard Kirkendall, "Harold Burton," in Friedman and Israel, *op. cit.,* fn. 47, Vol. 4, p. 2641.

93. *Youngstown Sheet and Tube Co.* v. *Sawyer,* 343 U.S. 579.
94. *Dennis* v. *United States,* 341 U.S. 494.
95. *Sweatt* v. *Painter,* 339 U.S. 629, and *McLaurin* v. *Oklahoma State Regents,* 339 U.S. 637.
96. *Shelley* v. *Kraemer,* 334 U.S. 1, and *Hurd* v. *Hodge,* 334 U.S. 24.
97. See Dennis D. Dorin, "Truman's 'Biggest Mistake': Tom Clark's Supreme Court Appointment" (Paper presented at Hofstra University's International Conference on Harry S. Truman–The Man from Independence, Hofstra University, Hempstead, New York, April 16, 1983).
98. 120 (August 15, 1949), pp. 11–12.
99. *Youngstown Sheet and Tube Co.* v. *Sawyer,* 343 U.S. 579.
100. Professor Robert Jennings Harris reported that famed Princeton University Professor of Constitutional Law, Edward S. Corwin, told him that it was he, Corwin, who "supplied Clark's law clerk with the reasoning in the case" that was utilized by Clark in his controlling concurring opinion. (Robert Jennings Harris to author, June 18, 1974.)
101. Quoted by Merle Miller in his oral history biography of Truman, *Plain Speaking* (New York: Berkley, 1974), p. 242. (Italics in original.)
102. *Wieman* v. *Updegraff,* 344 U.S. 579.
103. *Burstyn* v. *Wilson,* 343 U.S. 195.
104. *Abington School District* v. *Schempp* and *Murray* v. *Curlett,* 374 U.S. 203.
105. 363 U.S. 643 (1961). See Dennis D. Dorin, " 'Seize the Time': Justice Tom Clark's Role in *Mapp v. Ohio,*" in Victoria L. Swigert (ed.), *Law and the Legal Process* (Beverly Hills, Calif.: Sage, 1982), pp. 21–72.
106. Dennis D. Dorin, "Criminal Justice Policy-Making at the Supreme Court Level: Tom Clark's Role in the Warren Revolution" (Paper presented at the 1974 Annual Meeting of the Southern Association of Criminal Justice Educators, Mobile, Alabama, October 17, 1974, p. 31). See also his "Tom C. Clark: The Justice as Administrator," 61 *Judicature* (December/January, 1978), pp. 271–277.
107. *The Court Years (1939–1975)–The Autobiography of William O. Douglas* (New York: Random House [Vintage Books], 1980), p. 245.
108. *New York Times,* Obituary, April 10, 1965, p. 29.
109. Richard Kluger describes Minton's habit in an amusing aside in his *Simple Justice* (New York: Knopf, 1975), p. 585.
110. *Brown* v. *Board of Education of Topeka,* 347 U.S. 483, and *Bolling* v. *Sharpe,* 347 U.S. 497.

10. THE WARREN COURT: FROM IKE TO L.B.J. 1953–1969 (pp. 248–91)

1. Harry S. Truman, *Memoirs: Years of Trial and Hope* (Garden City, N.Y.: Doubleday, 1956), pp. 384–385.
2. See Appendix B, *infra,* and Ch. 5, fn. 1, *supra.*
3. See his excellent *The Hidden Hand Presidency: Eisenhower as Leader* (New York: Basic Books, 1982).
4. See the *Washington Post,* February 21, 1983, p. A6, and Appendix B, *infra.* (A 1977 poll by the U.S. Historical Society had placed him fourteenth; a 1982 one conducted for the *Chicago Tribune Magazine* placed him ninth, just behind Truman and ahead of Polk.)
5. Dwight D. Eisenhower, *The White House Years: Mandate for Change, 1953–1956* (Garden City, N.Y.: Doubleday, 1963), pp. 226–227.
6. *Ibid.,* pp. 227–228.
7. *Ibid.,* p. 230.
8. *Ibid.,* p. 227.
9. *Ibid.,* p. 226.
10. Recounted by Joseph L. Rauh, Jr., "The Chief," *New Republic,* August 9, 1982, p. 31. F.F. was utterly disdainful of Vinson's intellectual and leadership prowess, and he did not like him personally.
11. *Ibid.,* p. 227.
12. *Ibid.,* p. 228.
13. As quoted in the *St. Louis Post-Dispatch,* April 19, 1974, p. 5A.
14. *Ibid.*
15. G. Edward White, *Earl Warren: A Public Life* (New York: Oxford University Press, 1982), pp. 127, 129.
16. Fn. 13, *supra.*
17. *Ibid.*
18. *Ibid.,* p. 152.
19. 347 U.S. 483.
20. White, *op. cit.,* fn. 15, Ch. 16, "Ethics and Activism," *passim.*
21. 347 U.S. 483. (*Bolling* v. *Sharpe,* 347 U.S. 497, applied the *Brown* ruling to the District of Columbia on the same day, but on "due process of law" grounds.)
22. J. P. Frank, *Marble Palace: The Supreme Court in American Life* (New York: Knopf, 1958), p. 86.
23. 354 U.S. 178. The sole dissenter was Tom Clark.
24. 377 U.S. 533, at 562.

25. 384 U.S. 436.
26. 395 U.S. 486.
27. 369 U.S. 186.
28. 377 U.S. 533.
29. 370 U.S. 421.
30. 376 U.S. 254 (1964).
31. 372 U.S. 335.
32. *New York Times,* October 21, 1969, p. 28.
33. 347 U.S. 483. The data concerning Jackson's health are from Eugene C. Gerhart, *America's Advocate: Robert H. Jackson* (Indianapolis, Ind.: Bobbs-Merrill, 1958), pp. 467–468.
34. 354 U.S. 298 (1957).
35. 377 U.S. 533, at 624–625. (Italics added.)
36. 163 U.S. 537.
37. As quoted by Anthony Lewis in the *New York Times,* November 4, 1972, p. 33.
38. Eisenhower, *op. cit.,* fn. 5, p. 230.
39. *Pennsylvania Gazette,* October 1977, p. 20.
40. Quoted by Elmo Richardson, *The Presidency of Dwight D. Eisenhower* (Lawrence: Regents Press of Kansas, 1979), p. 108.
41. *New York Times Co.* v. *Sullivan,* 376 U.S. 254.
42. E.g., *Roth* v. *United States* and *Alberts* v. *California,* 354 U.S. 476 (1957); *Freedman* v. *Maryland,* U.S. 51 (1965); *Ginzburg* v. *United States,* 383 U.S. 463 (1966); and *Ginsberg* v. *New York,* 390 U.S. 629 (1968).
43. The 1973 decisions, rendered that June by Chief Justice Burger for a narrowly divided 5:4 Court, were *Miller* v. *California* and *Paris Adult Theatre* v. *Slaton,* 413 U.S. 15 and 413 U.S. 49 (1976), respectively.
44. 374 U.S. 203.
45. 426 U.S. 736.
46. 403 U.S. 672.
47. *Regents of the University of California* v. *Bakke,* 438 U.S. 265.
48. *United Steelworkers of America* v. *Weber,* 443 U.S. 193.
49. 369 U.S. 186. Chief Justice Warren pronounced the *Baker* decision the most important of his time, outranking even the 1954 *Desegregation Cases.* Justice Douglas agreed. (October 30, 1973, interview.)
50. *Jencks* v. *United States,* 353 U.S. 657 (1957), at 660, majority opinion.
51. As quoted in the *Washington Post,* September 11, 1980, p. A16.
52. Whittaker's godson, John H. Bracken, Jr., told me in a phone interview on January 16, 1970, that, according to his godfather's

claim, Arthur Eisenhower was *the* key figure in the nomination.

53. *Congressional Record,* 86th Cong., 1st sess., May 5, 1959, p. 6693.
54. *New York Times,* May 6, 1959, p. 32.
55. *Ibid.*
56. *Ibid.*
57. Democratic Senators George Smathers of Florida, Estes Kefauver and Albert Gore of Tennessee, and Lyndon B. Johnson and Ralph Yarborough of Texas joined the entire Republican delegation in the Senate in supporting the nomination.
58. 378 U.S. 184, at 197, concurring opinion.
59. *Kingsley International Pictures Corporation* v. *Regents,* 360 U.S. 684 (1959), at 686.
60. *Terminiello* v. *Chicago,* 337 U.S. 1 (1949), at 37.
61. 378 U.S. 478 (1964).
62. 384 U.S. 436 (1966).
63. As reported in the *Philadelphia Bulletin,* May 28, 1969, p. 11.
64. *Time,* June 29, 1981, p. 48.
65. *3 Supreme Court Historical Society Quarterly* (Summer, 1981), p. 9.
66. James J. Kilpatrick, "Farewell to a Friend of the Press," [*Charlottesville, Virginia*] *Daily Progress,* June 26, 1981, p. A4.
67. 389 U.S. 347.
68. 428 U.S. 153.
69. 408 U.S. 238 (1972).
70. 403 U.S. 713.
71. 448 U.S. 448.
72. E.g., Anthony Lewis, then the *New York Times*'s Court expert, in an article in the *Times,* April 2, 1962, p. 17.
73. James E. Clayton of the *Washington Star* in his *The Making of Justice: The Supreme Court in Action* (New York: E. P. Dutton, 1964), p. 52. For a catalogue of Kennedy's criteria for nominees to the bench, see Ralph G. Martin, *A Hero for Our Time: An Intimate Story of the Kennedy Years* (New York: Macmillan, 1983), p. 371.
74. Saturday, March 31, 1962, p. 1.
75. 378 U.S. 478 (1964).
76. 384 U.S. 436 (1966).
77. E.g., *Adderley* v. *Florida,* 385 U.S. 39 (1966); *Street* v. *New York,* 394 U.S. 576 (1969); *Lehman* v. *Shaker Heights,* 418 U.S. 298 (1974).
78. He gave notice of that posture as early as *Ginzburg* v. *United States,* 383 U.S. 463 (1966). In the June 1973 cases (see n. 43, *supra*) he, thus, sided with the Chief Justice and Associate Jus-

tices Blackmun, Powell, and Rehnquist. The four dissenters were Douglas, Brennan, Stewart, and Marshall.

79. E.g., *Reitman* v. *Mulkey,* 387 U.S. 369 (1967).
80. E.g., *Regents of the University of California* v. *Bakke,* 438 U.S. 265 (1978); *United Steelworkers of America* v. *Weber,* 443 U.S. 193 (1979); *Fullilove* v. *Klutznick,* 448 U.S. 448 (1980).
81. *Roe* v. *Wade* and *Doe* v. *Bolton,* 410 U.S. 113 and 410 U.S. 179, respectively.
82. *Furman* v. *Georgia,* 408 U.S. 238.
83. *Gregg* v. *Georgia,* 428 U.S. 153 (1976).
84. *Autry* v. *Estelle,* 104 S. Ct. 20, review denied; and *Autry* v. *Estelle,* 104 S. Ct. 24, execution stayed by White.
85. *New York Times* v. *United States* and *United States* v. *Washington Post,* 403 U.S. 713.
86. *San Antonio School District* v. *Rodriguez,* 411 U.S. 980.
87. *Bradley* v. *School Board of the City of Richmond,* 411 U.S. 913.
88. *Time,* September 7, 1962, p. 15.
89. As quoted in the *New York Times,* August 30, 1962, p. C14.
90. As told to me by Meyer Feldman, ex-counsel to President Kennedy, in Philadelphia, Pennsylvania, May 7, 1965.
91. *Snider* v. *Cunningham* and *Rudolph* v. *Alabama,* 375 U.S. 889 (1963).
92. *Griswold* v. *Connecticut,* 381 U.S. 479 (1965), at 488, concurring opinion.
93. *Aptheker* v. *Secretary of State,* 378 U.S. 500 (1964).
94. 378 U.S. 478.
95. Lyndon B. Johnson, *The Vantage Point: Perspectives of the Presidency, 1963–1969* (New York: Holt, Rinehart & Winston, 1971), p. 543.
96. *Philadelphia Inquirer,* July 21, 1965, p. 1.
97. As told to me by Arthur J. Goldberg in Justice Brennan's home in Georgetown, Washington, D.C., May 24, 1969.
98. *Ibid.*
99. Johnson, *op. cit.,* fn. 93, pp. 544–545.
100. *Ibid.*
101. Televised Presidential news conference, July 20, 1965.
102. Rex Lee, "In Memoriam: Abe Fortas," *Yearbook 1983* (Washington, D.C.: Supreme Court Historical Society, 1983), p. 9.
103. Obituary, *Washington Post,* April 7, 1982, p. A10.
104. The story is well told by Anthony Lewis in his fine *Gideon's Trumpet* (New York: Knopf, 1964; Random House [Vintage Books], 1966).
105. *In re Gault,* 387 U.S. 1.
106. *Ibid.,* at 28.

107. *Board of Education* v. *Allen,* 392 U.S. 236, at 271. The other two dissenters were Justices Black and Douglas.
108. See the account by John Massaro, "L.B.J. and the Fortas Nomination for Chief Justice," 97 *Political Science Quarterly* 4 (Winter 1982–1983).
109. Their roles are discussed in Robert Shogan's *A Question of Judgment: The Fortas Case and the Struggle for the Supreme Court* (Indianapolis, Ind.: Bobbs-Merrill, 1972).
110. June 14, 1976, p. 1.
111. *Ibid.*
112. Interview with Francis L. Van Dusen, Judge of the U.S. Court of Appeals for the Third Circuit, Philadelphia, Pennsylvania, March 15, 1977.
113. *Pearson* v. *Murray,* 169 Md. 478 (1936). In 1980 the same University of Maryland dedicated its new library to Thurgood Marshall!
114. *Brown* v. *Board of Education of Topeka,* 347 U.S. 483, and *Bolling* v. *Sharpe,* 347 U.S. 497.
115. The other nine were: Eastland (Miss.), Ellender and Long (La.), Ervin (N.C.), Hollins (S.C.), Hill and Sparkman (Ala.), Holland (Fla.), and Talmadge (Ga.). Absent but paired against the nomination were McClelland (Ark.), Russell (Ga.), Smathers (Fla.), and Stennis (Miss.). Byrd (Va.) and Jordan (N.C.) were absent but unrecorded.
116. E.g., *Stanley* v. *Georgia,* 394 U.S. 557 (1967); *Orozco* v. *Texas,* 394 U.S. 324 (1969); *Brewer* v. *Williams,* 430 U.S. 387 (1977).
117. E.g., *Regents of the University of California* v. *Bakke,* 438 U.S. 265 (1978); *United Steelworkers of America* v. *Weber,* 443 U.S. 193 (1979); *Craig* v. *Boren,* 429 U.S. 190 (1976).
118. *De Funis* v. *Odegaard,* 416 U.S. 312 (1974).
119. As quoted by Fred Barbash in the *Washington Post,* September 11, 1980, p. 16.

11. THE BURGER COURT: FROM NIXON TO REAGAN, 1969–
(pp. 292–339)

1. Among the massive book-length commentaries on the historic event, see John J. Sirica, *To Set the Record Straight* (New York: W. W. Norton, 1979); Leon Jaworski, *The Right and the Power* (New York: Thomas Y. Crowell, 1976); Bob Woodward and Carl Bernstein, *All the President's Men* and *The Final Days* (New York: Simon & Schuster, 1975 and 1976, respectively);

and Theodore H. White, *Breach of Faith: The Fall of Richard Nixon* (New York: Atheneum, 1975).

2. 418 U.S. 683 (1974).
3. See Committee on the Judiciary, U.S. House of Representatives, *Impeachment: Selected Materials* and *Impeachment Inquiry* (Washington, D.C.: Superintendent of Documents, 1974 and 1975, respectively).
4. Friday, August 9, 1974, and Saturday, August 10, 1974, respectively.
5. *Supra,* pp. 13–23.
6. Campaign speech, November 2, 1968, quoted in *Congressional Quarterly, Weekly Report,* May 23, 1969, p. 798.
7. *Roe* v. *Wade* and *Doe* v. *Bolton,* 410 U.S. 113 and 410 U.S. 179, respectively.
8. *United States* v. *United States District Court for the Eastern District of Michigan,* 407 U.S. 297.
9. 402 U.S. 1.
10. There is considerable evidence, however, that the Court's unanimity was more apparent than real. Nonetheless, there were no recorded dissenting opinions. For an analysis of the former contention, see J. Harvie Wilkinson III, *From Brown to Bakke* (New York: Oxford University Press, 1979), Chs. 6–9, especially pp. 146–150. Wilkinson, who was Justice Powell's law clerk, claims that the initial conference vote was 6:3 *against* forced busing, with only Douglas, Brennan, and Marshall in its favor.
11. 418 U.S. 683 (1974). See fn. 2 and accompanying text (pp. 293–294), *supra.*
12. See Ch. 5, *supra,* pp. 72–73.
13. E.g., *Swann* v. *Charlotte-Mecklenburg Board of Education,* fns. 9 and 10 *supra; Runyon* v. *McCrary,* 427 U.S. 160 (1976); *Regents of the University of California* v. *Bakke,* 438 U.S. 265 (1978); *United Steelworkers of America* v. *Weber,* 443 U.S. 193 (1979); and *Fullilove* v. *Klutznick,* 448 U.S. 448 (1980). The Chief Justice dissented from these libertarian holdings only in the *Bakke* and *Weber* cases; Powell and Blackmun dissented in none (Powell did not participate in *Weber,* however); whereas Rehnquist dissented in all of them.
14. E.g., *Roe* v. *Wade* and *Doe* v. *Bolton,* fn. 7 *supra; Eisenstadt* v. *Baird,* 405 U.S. 438 (1972); and *Carey* v. *Population Services International,* 431 U.S. 678 (1977). Burger dissented in the latter two; Blackmun in none; Powell in part only in *Carey;* and Rehnquist in all three.
15. *Louisville Courier-Journal,* May 23, 1969, p. A1.
16. *Ibid.*

17. *Ibid.*, back page (unnumbered), col. 5.
18. *Ibid.*
19. E.g., the *New York Times,* May 22, 1969, p. 46.
20. *Ibid.*
21. *Philadelphia Inquirer,* June 10, 1969, p. 1.
22. See the Symposium article by Edward A. Tamm and Paul C. Reardon, "Warren Burger and the Administration of Justice," 1981 *Brigham Young University Law Review* 3, pp. 447–521.
23. See pp. 302ff., *infra.*
24. See fn. 13, *supra,* and accompanying text.
25. *Solem* v. *Helm,* 51 LW 5019 (1983).
26. *Time,* July 18, 1983, p. 39.
27. Francis Graham Lee (ed.), subtitled *The Burger Court on Civil Rights and Liberties* (Malabar, Fla.: Krieger, 1983).
28. Vincent Blasi (ed.) (New York: Columbia University Press, 1983).
29. *Immigration and Naturalization Service* v. *Chadha,* 51 LW 4907 (1983).
30. *Arizona* v. *Norris,* 51 LW 5243 (1983).
31. *Bob Jones University* and *Goldsboro Christian School* v. *United States,* 51 LW 4593 (1983).
32. *Time,* July 18, 1983, p. 39.
33. *New York Times,* April 15, 1970, p. 34.
34. *Ibid.*, April 19, 1970, Sec. 4, p. 10.
35. 403 U.S. 15 (1971).
36. 405 U.S. 418 (1972).
37. 402 U.S. 611 (1971).
38. 415 U.S. 130 (1974).
39. 401 U.S. 1 (1971).
40. 408 U.S. 753 (1972).
41. 413 U.S. 15 (1973).
42. E.g., *Furman* v. *Georgia,* 408 U.S. 238 (1972); *Gregg* v. *Georgia,* 428 U.S. 153 (1976); *Brewer* v. *Williams,* 430 U.S. 387 (1977); and *McKeiver* v. *Pennsylvania,* 403 U.S. 528 (1971).
43. E.g., *United States* v. *Calandra,* 414 U.S. 338 (1974); *Stone* v. *Powell,* 428 U.S. 465 (1976); *United States* v. *Peltier,* 422 U.S. 531 (1975); and *Bivens* v. *Six Unknown Agents,* 403 U.S. 388 (1971).
44. His lengthy dissenting opinions in *Bivens,* fn. 43, *supra,* spells out his views on the exclusionary rule, which he has vowed to see toned down to render admissibility of relevant, material, and probative evidence less complex.
45. *Roe* v. *Wade* and *Doe* v. *Bolton,* fn. 7, supra.

46. *Santa Clara County* v. *Southern Pacific Railroad Co.,* 118 U.S. 394.
47. Michael Pollet, "Harry A. Blackmun," in L. Friedman and F. L. Israel (eds.), *The Justices of the United States Supreme Court, 1789–1978,* Vol. 5 (New York: Chelsea, 1980), p. 14.
48. E.g., *Rizzo* v. *Goode,* 423 U.S. 362 (1976), and *Coker* v. *Georgia,* 433 U.S. 594 (1977).
49. As quoted in the *Miami Herald,* June 7, 1979, p. 14–AW.
50. E.g., *Regents of the University of California* v. *Bakke* (1978), *United Steelworkers of America* v. *Weber* (1979), *Fullilove* v. *Klutznick* (1980), and all of fn. 13, *supra.* See also *Runyon* v. *McCrary,* 427 U.S. 160 (1976); *Tillman* v. *Wheaton-Haven,* 410 U.S. 431 (1973); and *Griggs* v. *Duke Power Co.,* 401 U.S. 424 (1971).
51. E.g., *General Electric Co.* v. *Gilbert,* 429 U.S. 125 (1976); *Orr* v. *Orr,* 440 U.S. 268 (1979); *McCarty* v. *McCarty,* 453 U.S. 210 (1981); and *Craig* v. *Boren,* 429 U.S. 190 (1976).
52. See, e.g., his concurring opinion in *Bakke,* fn. 13, *supra,* and his acceptance of Marshall's opinion concurring in the judgment in *Fullilove* v. *Klutznick, ibid.*
53. *Logan* v. *Zimmerman Brush Co.,* 50 LW 4247.
54. Cable News Network, December 4, 1982.
55. "A Candid Talk with Justice Blackmun," February 20, 1983, pp. 20ff.
56. See Ch. 2, *supra,* especially pp. 18–23.
57. *Time,* November 1, 1971, p. 14.
58. See fn. 56, *supra.*
59. *Ibid.*
60. *Miranda* v. *Arizona,* 384 U.S. 436 (1966).
61. See the account in *Time,* fn. 57, *supra.* And an aside: a debate on a Philadelphia WCAU educational broadcast, in which I was scheduled to participate, was suddenly cancelled in late morning of October 21 in anticipation of "an important announcement."
62. *Ibid.,* p. 18.
63. *Brown* v. *Board of Education II,* 349 U.S. 294 (1955).
64. *New York Times,* December 7, 1971, p. 1.
65. *Ibid.,* p. 20.
66. *Ibid.,* p. 1.
67. E.g., *National League of Cities* v. *Usery,* 426 U.S. 833 (1976) and *EEOC* v. *Wyoming,* 103 S.Ct. 1054 (1983).
68. E.g., *Stone* v. *Powell,* 428 U.S. 465 (1976); *Rhode Island* v. *Innis,* 446 U.S. 291 (1980); and *Michigan* v. *Summers,* 452 U.S. 692 (1982).

69. E.g., *Brewer v. Williams,* 430 U.S. 387 (1977); *United States* v. *Henry,* 447 U.S. 264 (1980); and *Solem* v. *Helm,* 51 LW 5019 (1983).
70. 407 U.S. 297 (1972).
71. E.g., *Jenkins* v. *Georgia,* 418 U.S. 153 (1974); *Miami Herald Publ. Co.* v. *Tornillo,* 418 U.S. 241 (1974); and *Virginia Pharmacy Board* v. *Virginia Consumer Council,* 425 U.S. 748 (1976).
72. E.g., *Young* v. *American Mini Theatres,* 427 U.S. 50 (1976); *FCC* v. *Pacifica Foundation,* 438 U.S. 726 (1978); and *Elrod* v. *Burns,* 427 U.S. 347 (1976).
73. Jackson's famed opinion was penned in *Terminiello* v. *Chicago,* 337 U.S. 1 (1949), at 37.
74. *Committee for Public Education and Religious Liberty* v. *Nyquist,* 413 U.S. 756 (1973).
75. *Meek* v. *Pittenger,* 421 U.S. 349 (1975).
76. *Mueller* v. *Allen,* 51 LW 5162 (1983).
77. *Committee for Public Education and Religious Liberty* v. *Regan,* 444 U.S. 646 (1980).
78. *Nyquist,* fn. 74, *supra.*
79. *Lynch* v. *Donnelly,* 52 LW 4317.
80. E.g., *Frontiero* v. *Richardson,* 411 U.S. 677 (1973); *Craig* v. *Boren,* 429 U.S. 190 (1976); and *Stanton* v. *Stanton,* 421 U.S. 7 (1975).
81. E.g., *General Electric Co.* v. *Gilbert,* 429 U.S. 125 (1976), contrasted with *Mississippi University for Women* v. *Hogan,* 50 LW 5068 (1982); and *Arizona* v. *Norris,* 51 LW 5243 (1983).
82. E.g., *Grove City College* v. *Bell,* 52 LW 4283 (1984).
83. 410 U.S. 113.
84. *Akron* v. *Akron Center for Reproductive Health, Inc.,* 51 LW 4767; *Planned Parenthood Assn. of Kansas City, Mo.* v. *Ashcroft,* 51 LW 4783; and *Simopoulos* v. *Virginia,* 51 LW 4791.
85. *Akron* v. *Akron Center for Reproductive Health, Inc.,* 51 LW 4767, at 4768.
86. *Regents of the University of California* v. *Bakke,* 438 U.S. 265.
87. *De Funis* v. *Odegaard,* 416 U.S. 312.
88. For a detailed description and analysis of the case, see my *Freedom and the Court: Civil Rights and Liberties in the United States,* 4th ed. (New York: Oxford University Press, 1982), pp. 396–398.
89. *Bakke,* fn. 83, *op. cit.,* at pp. 321–324.
90. E.g., *United Steelworkers of America* v. *Weber,* 443 U.S. 193 (1979), *Fullilove* v. *Klutznick,* 448 U.S. 448 (1980), and *Firefighters Local Union* v. *Stotts,* 52 LW 4767 (1984).
91. *Columbus Board of Education* v. *Pennick,* 443 U.S. 449 (1979)

and *Dayton Board of Education* v. *Brinkman,* 443 U.S. 526 (1979). The two quoted references are at pp. 479 and 480, respectively, of *Pennick.*

92. See Ch. 2, *supra,* especially pp. 00–00.
93. July 24, 1971, tape: Conversation by Richard M. Nixon with John Ehrlichman and Egil (Bud) Krogh.
94. As quoted in *Time,* November 1, 1971, p. 10.
95. 347 U.S. 483 (1954).
96. See fn. 93, *supra,* and accompanying textual quotes.
97. The Rev. George Benjamin Brooks, as quoted in the *New York Times,* November 27, 1971, p. 54.
98. Andrew J. Biemiller, as quoted in the *Philadelphia Evening Bulletin,* November 10, 1971, p. 1.
99. Bayard Rustin, as quoted in the *New York Times,* December 12, 1971, p. E7.
100. Documented in its own publication, 283 *Civil Liberties* (January 1972), p. 8. The A.C.L.U. had sent a letter detailing its opposition to all members of the Senate in early November 1971.
101. Barry M. Goldwater, guest column in the *New York Times,* November 17, 1971, p. B45.
102. Kevin P. Phillips, syndicated column in the *Philadelphia Evening Bulletin,* November 15, 1971, p. 17.
103. James J. Kilpatrick, syndicated column in the *Washington Evening Star,* October 28, 1971, quoted in *Congressional Record* S 17550.
104. E.g., *Rogers* v. *Lodge,* 50 LW 5041 (1982); *Mobile* v. *Bolden,* 446 U.S. 55 (1980); *Brown* v. *Thomson,* 51 LW 4883 (1983) and *Karcher* v. *Daggett,* 51 LW 4853 (1983).
105. See fn. 93, *supra,* and accompanying textual quotes.
106. E.g., *Rhode Island* v. *Innis,* 446 U.S. 291 (1980); *Jenkins* v. *Anderson,* 447 U.S. 231 (1980); and *Taylor* v. *Alabama,* 102 S. Ct. 2664 (1982).
107. E.g., *Bakke,* fn. 86, *op. cit.,* and *Washington* v. *Davis,* 426 U.S. 229 (1976).
108. E.g., *Jefferson* v. *Hackney,* 406 U.S. 535 (1972); *Personnel Administrator of Massachusetts* v. *Feeney,* 442 U.S. 256 (1979); and *Craig* v. *Boren,* 429 U.S. 190 (1976).
109. *National League of Cities* v. *Usery,* 426 U.S. 833 (1976); *FERC* v. *Mississippi,* 546 U.S. 742 (1982); and *EEOC* v. *Wyoming,* 103 S. Ct. 1054 (1983).
110. See Chs. 9 and 10, *supra, passim.*
111. See Ch. 2, "The Double Standard," in my *Freedom and the Court, op. cit.,* fn. 88, pp. 8–27.
112. See fn. 86, *op. cit.*

113. 443 U.S. 193 (1979).
114. Thus, an exchange between the C.R.A.'s floor manager, Senator Hubert H. Humphrey (D.-Minn.), and a principal opponent, Senator Willis Robertson (D.-Va.): "If the Senator can find in Title VII . . . any language which provides that an employer will have to hire on the basis of percentage or quota related to color . . . I will start eating the pages, one after another, because it is not in there." (110 *Congressional Record* 7420.) Senator Ed Muskie (D.-Maine) insisted that the provision calls for "Not equal pay, not racial balance. Only equal opportunity." (*Idem,* at 12617.) Senator Leverett Saltonstall (R.-Mass.) insisted that § 703(j.) ". . . provides no quotas. It leaves an employer free to select whomever he wishes to employ." (*Idem.,* at 13080.) "In fact, it specifically prohibits such treatment." (*Idem,* at 12691.)
115. 415 F. Supp. 761 and 563 F. 2d 216 (1977).
116. *Weber, op. cit.,* fn. 113, at 201.
117. *Ibid.,* at 219. (Italics in original.)
118. *Ibid.,* at 222.
119. *Ibid.,* at 255.
120. Letter to author, July 7, 1979.
121. Gerald R. Ford, *A Time to Heal* (New York: Harper & Row and Readers Digest Association, 1979), p. 335.
122. As reported by James Goodman, "The Politics of Picking Federal Judges," *Juris Doctor,* June 1977, p. 26. See also Ch. 2, *supra,* especially pp. 20–21.
123. November 14, 1975, p. A2.
124. *New York Times,* November 17, 1975, p. 18.
125. *Ibid.,* November 19, 1975, p. C16.
126. See this chapter's discussion in connection with the Rehnquist nomination, *supra,* pp. 313ff.
127. Ford, *op. cit.,* fn. 121, p. 335.
128. See Ch. 1, *supra.*
129. Ford, *op. cit.,* fn. 121, p. 335.
130. "Remarks" to the Annual Banquet of the American Judicature Society, San Francisco, August 6, 1982.
131. E.g., *Bakke, op. cit.,* fn. 86, and *Fullilove* v. *Klutznick,* 448 U.S. 448 (1980).
132. *Wall Street Journal,* January 26, 1978, p. 1.
133. *Time,* July 21, 1980, p. 76.
134. 51 LW 5189 (1983), at 5196.
135. *South Carolina* v. *Regan,* 52 LW 4232, at 4241.
136. *Sony Corporation of America* v. *Universal City Studios,* 52 LW 4090.

137. *Committee for Public Education and Religious Liberty* v. *Regan,* 444 U.S. 646.
138. *Ibid.,* at 671.
139. *Bakke, op. cit.,* fn. 129, at 532–554.
140. *Ibid.,* at 538.
141. *Ibid.,* at 539.
142. *Ibid.,* at 545.
143. *Ibid.,* at 547, 552.
144. *Ibid.,* at 534.
145. Executive Order 11972, February 14, 1977. For a discussion and analysis see my *The Judicial Process: An Introductory Analysis of the Courts of the United States, England, and France,* 4th ed. (New York: Oxford University Press, 1980), Ch. 2, "Staffing the Courts," especially pp. 30–32.
140. White House Press Conference, December 7, 1978.
147. *New York Times,* February 13, 1979, p. A16. (Italics added.)
148. Reprinted in 64 *Judicature* 9 (April 1981), p. 428.
149. *Ibid.,* § 1, sent. 2.
150. *New York Times,* October 15, 1980, p. A24.
151. *Washington Post,* July 8, 1981, p. A1.
152. *Ibid.,* pp. A1, A6.
153. *Time,* July 20, 1981, p. 11.
154. *New York Times,* July 8, 1981, p. A12.
155. *Time, op. cit.,* fn. 153, pp. 11–12.
156. *Ibid.,* pp. 10–11.
157. *New York Times, op. cit.,* fn. 154.
158. As quoted in the *New York Times, op. cit.,* fn. 154, pp. A1, A12.
159. As quoted in the *Washington Post, op. cit.,* fn. 151, p. A7.
160. As quoted in *Time, op. cit.,* fn. 153, p. 10.
161. As quoted in the *Washington Post, op. cit.,* fn. 151, p. A1.
162. *New York Times,* September 16, 1981, p. A16.
163. *Ibid.,* July 8, 1981, p. A12.
164. Summer 1981, Vol. 22, pp. 801–815.
165. As quoted in the *New York Times,* July 8, 1981, p. A13.
166. *Time, op. cit.,* fn. 153, p. 11.
167. *New York Times,* July 8, 1981, p. A12.
168. As quoted in the *Washington Post,* September 9, 1981, p. A1.
169. *The* [Charlottesville, Virginia] *Daily Progress,* July 8, 1981, p. A8.
170. *Supra,* pp. 6–7.
171. See my *The Judicial Process, op. cit.,* fn. 145, pp. 394–395, and *passim.*
172. *Eddings* v. *Oklahoma,* 102 S.Ct. 869 (1982); her concurring

opinion begins at p. 877. (Dissenting were Burger, Rehnquist, White, and Blackmun.)

173. *Mississippi University for Women v. Hogan,* 102 S.Ct. 333 (1982).
174. *Kolender* v. *Lawson,* 103 S.Ct. 1855 (1983).
175. *Minneapolis Star and Tribune Co.* v. *Minnesota Commissioner of Revenue,* 103 S.Ct. 1365 (1983).
176. *Karcher* v. *Daggett, op. cit.,* fn. 105.
177. *Bower* v. *U.S. Postal Service,* 51 LW 4051–4061 (1983).
178. *Arizona Governing Committee for Tax Deferred Annuity and Deferred Compensation* v. *Norris,* 103 S.Ct. 3492 (1983).
179. See fns. 83–85, *op. cit.*
180. *Arizona v. Norris, op. cit.,* fn. 178; *Mississippi University for Women* v. *Hogan, op. cit.,* fn. 173; and *Patsy* v. *Board of Regents of Florida,* 102 S.Ct. 2557 (1982).
181. *Globe Newspapers Co.* v. *Superior Court of Norfolk,* 102 S.Ct. 2613 (1982), and *Minneapolis Star and Tribune Co.* v. *Minnesota Comissioner of Revenue, op. cit.,* fn. 175.
182. *Eddings* v. *Oklahoma,* 102 S.Ct. 869 (1982); *Mills* v. *Hapleutzel,* 102 S.Ct. 1549 (1982); *Bearden* v. *Georgia,* 103 S.Ct. 2064 (1983); and *Zobel* v. *Williams,* 102 S.Ct. 2309 (1982).
183. I am indebted for these statistics to Richter H. Moore, Jr., "Justice O'Connor and the States." (Unpublished paper, presented to the 1983 Annual Meeting of the Southern Political Science Association, Hyatt-Birmingham, Birmingham, Alabama, November 3, 1983.)
184. E.g., *California* v. *Ramos,* 103 S.Ct. 3446 (1983), and *Michigan* v. *Long,* 103 S.Ct. 3469 (1983).
185. E.g., *Engle* v. *Isaac,* 102 S.Ct. 1558 (1982), and *Edmund* v. *Florida,* 102 S.Ct. 3368 (1982).
186. E.g., *Rose* v. *Lundy,* 102 S.Ct. 1198 (1982), and *Taylor* v. *Alabama,* 102 S.Ct. 2664 (1982).
187. E.g., *Federal Energy Regulatory Commission* v. *Mississippi,* 102 S.Ct. 2126 (1982), and *EEOC* v. *Wyoming,* 103 S.Ct. 1054 (1983).
188. *New York* v. *Ferber,* 102 S.Ct. 3348 (1982).

Appendix A

Rating Supreme Court Justices

In June 1970, sixty-five law school deans and professors of law, history, and political science (including myself), whose expertise lay in the judicial process, were asked by law professors Albert P. Blaustein (Rutgers University) and Roy M. Mersky (University of Texas) to evaluate the performance of the ninety-six Justices who had served on the Supreme Court from 1789 until 1969, just prior to the appointment of Chief Justice Burger. We were requested to use a survey model that would employ the categories of "great," "near great," "average," "below average," and "failure"—but no other criteria, yardsticks, or measuring rods were provided. Our only other specific instruction was to "select the nine outstanding Justices of both centuries"—a stipulation that ultimately resulted in the selection of twelve "great" Justices (see fn. 11, Ch. 1, *supra*). In 1978, the results were published in book form by the project's originators as *The First One Hundred* [*sic*] *Justices: Statistical Studies on the Supreme Court of the United States* (Hamden, Conn.: Shoe String Press [Archon Books]).

The following categories are arranged *chronologically* (see Appendixes C and D and Ch. 4 for convenient tabular data on all Justices, indicating a variety of background information). (The numbers in parentheses refer to those used in Appendix D, *infra.*)

"GREAT" (12)

J. Marshall (14)
Story (19)
Taney (25)
Harlan I (45)
Holmes (59)
Hughes (63) and (76)
Brandeis (69)
Stone (75) and (85)
Cardozo (78)
Black (79)
Frankfurter (81)
Warren (92)

"NEAR GREAT" (15)

W. Johnson (15)
Curtis (33)
Miller (37)
Field (39)
Bradley (42)
Waite (44)
E. D. White (56) and (64)
Taft (71)
Sutherland (72)
Douglas (82)
R. H. Jackson (86)
W. B. Rutledge (87)
Harlan II (93)
Brennan (94)
Fortas (99)

"AVERAGE" (55)

Jay (1)
J. Rutledge (2)
and (9)
Cushing (3)
Wilson (4)
Blair (5)
Iredell (6)
Paterson (8)
S. Chase (10)
Ellsworth (11)
Washington (12)
Livingston (16)
Todd (17)
Duval (18)
Thompson (20)
McLean (22)
Baldwin (23)
Wayne (24)
Catron (27)
McKinley (28)
Daniel (29)
Nelson (30)
Woodbury (31)
Grier (32)
Campbell (34)
Clifford (35)
Swayne (36)
Davis (38)
S. P. Chase (40)
Strong (41)
Hunt (43)
Matthews (47)
Gray (48)
Blatchford (49)
L. Q. C. Lamar (50)
Fuller (51)
Brewer (52)
Brown (53)
Shiras (54)
Peckham (57)
McKenna (58)
Day (60)
Moody (61)
Lurton (62)
J. R. Lamar (66)
Pitney (67)
J. H. Clarke (70)
Sanford (74)
Roberts (77)
Reed (80)
Murphy (83)
T. C. Clark (90)
Stewart (96)
B. R. White (97)
Goldberg (98)
T. Marshall (100)

"BELOW AVERAGE" (6)

T. Johnson (7)
Moore (13)
Trimble (21)
Barbour (26)
Woods (46)
H. E. Jackson (55)

"FAILURE" (8)

Van Devanter (65)
McReynolds (68)
Butler (73)
Byrnes (84)
Burton (88)
Vinson (89)
Minton (91)
Whittaker (95)

Appendix B
Rating Presidents

The Presidential "rating game" commenced in earnest in 1948 when *Life* commissioned and published (see table footnote) a poll of fifty-five scholars, chiefly historians, under the chairmanship of Arthur M. Schlesinger, Sr., who conducted a similar poll in 1962. Between that time and late 1983, four additional major polls were undertaken, as

Schlesinger Poll 1948 (No. 1)	Schlesinger Poll 1962 (No. 2)	Maranell and Dodder Poll 1970 (No. 3)
		Accomplishments of Administrations
Great	*Great*	
(1) Lincoln	(1) Lincoln	(1) Lincoln
(2) Washington	(2) Washington	(2) F. Roosevelt
(3) F. Roosevelt	(3) F. Roosevelt	(3) Washington
(4) Wilson	(4) Wilson	(4) Jefferson
(5) Jefferson	(5) Jefferson	(5) T. Roosevelt
(6) Jackson		(6) Truman
		(7) Wilson
Near Great	*Near Great*	(8) Jackson
(7) T. Roosevelt	(6) Jackson	(9) L. Johnson
(8) Cleveland	(7) T. Roosevelt	(10) Polk
(9) J. Adams	(8) Polk	(11) J. Adams
(10) Polk	(8) Truman	(12) Kennedy
	(9) J. Adams	(13) Monroe
	(10) Cleveland	(14) Cleveland
		(15) Madison
Average	*Average*	(16) Taft
(11) J. Q. Adams	(11) Madison	(17) McKinley

described herein. None of the polls rated Presidents William Henry Harrison or James A. Garfield because of their brief tenures in office. One of the polls' remarkable results is their general agreement on Presidential performance, although some differences are notable.*

DiClerico Poll 1977 (No. 4)	*Chicago Tribune* Poll 1982 (No. 5)	Murray Poll 1982 (No. 6)
Ten Greatest Presidents	*Ten Best Presidents*	*Presidential Rank*
(1) Lincoln	(1) Lincoln (best)	(1) Lincoln
(2) Washington	(2) Washington	(2) F. Roosevelt
(3) F. Roosevelt	(3) F. Roosevelt	(3) Washington
(4) Jefferson	(4) T. Roosevelt	(4) Jefferson
(5) T. Roosevelt	(5) Jefferson	(5) T. Roosevelt
(6) Wilson	(6) Wilson	(6) Wilson
(7) Jackson	(7) Jackson	(7) Jackson
(8) Truman	(8) Truman	(8) Truman
(9) Polk	(9) Eisenhower	(9) J. Adams
(10) J. Adams	(10) Polk (10th best)	(10) L. Johnson
		(11) Eisenhower
		(12) Polk
	Ten Worst Presidents	(13) Kennedy
		(14) Madison
	(1) Harding (worst)	(15) Monroe
		(16) J. Q. Adams
	(2) Nixon	(17) Cleveland

Schlesinger Poll 1948 (No. 1)	Schlesinger Poll 1962 (No. 2)	Maranell and Dodder Poll 1970 (No. 3)
(12) Monroe	(12) J. Q. Adams	(18) J. Q. Adams
(13) Hayes	(13) Hayes	(19) Hoover
(14) Madison	(14) McKinley	(20) Eisenhower
(15) Van Buren	(15) Taft	(21) A. Johnson
(16) Taft	(16) Van Buren	(22) Van Buren
(17) Arthur	(17) Monroe	(23) Arthur
(18) McKinley	(18) Hoover	(24) Hayes
(19) A. Johnson	(19) B. Harrison	(25) Tyler
(20) Hoover	(20) Arthur	(26) B. Harrison
(21) B. Harrison	(20) Eisenhower	(27) Taylor
	(21) A. Johnson	(28) Buchanan
		(29) Fillmore
Below Average	*Below Average*	(30) Coolidge
(22) Tyler	(22) Taylor	(31) Pierce
(23) Coolidge	(23) Tyler	(32) Grant
(24) Fillmore	(24) Fillmore	(33) Harding
(25) Taylor	(25) Coolidge	
(26) Buchanan	(26) Pierce	
(27) Pierce	(27) Buchanan	
Failure	*Failure*	
(28) Grant	(28) Grant	
(29) Harding	(29) Harding	

No. 1 Arthur M. Schlesinger, Sr., "The U.S. Presidents," *Life,* November 1, 1948, p. 65. Fifty-five scholars polled.
No. 2 Arthur M. Schlesinger, Sr., "Our Presidents: A Rating by Seventy-five Scholars," *New York Times Magazine,* July 29, 1962, pp. 12ff.
No. 3 A poll of 571 historians, the results published by Gary Maranell and Richard Dodder, "Political Orientation and Evaluation of Presidential Prestige," *Social Science Quarterly,* 51 (September 1970), p. 418.
No. 4 First published by Robert E. DiClerico in his book *The American President,* Prentice-Hall, 1979, p. 332. Ninety-three historians were polled.
No. 5 A survey of forty-nine leading scholars conducted by the *Chicago*

DiClerico Poll 1977 (No. 4)	*Chicago Tribune* Poll 1982 (No. 5)	Murray Poll 1982 (No. 6)
	(3) Buchanan	(18) McKinley
	(4) Pierce	(19) Taft
	(5) Grant	(20) Van Buren
	(6) Fillmore	(21) Hoover
	(7) A. Johnson	(22) Hayes
	(8) Coolidge	(23) Arthur
	(9) Tyler	(24) Ford
	(10) Carter (10th worst)	(25) Carter
		(26) B. Harrison
		(27) Taylor
		(28) Tyler
		(29) Fillmore
		(30) Coolidge
		(31) Pierce
		(32) A. Johnson
		(33) Buchanan
		(34) Nixon
		(35) Grant
		(36) Harding

Tribune, as analyzed by *US News and World Report,* January 25, 1982, p. 29.

No. 6 A survey conducted by Robert K. Murray, Professor of History at Pennsylvania State University, for which 953 historians completed a seventeen-page questionnaire containing 155 questions. Professor Murray's study was published in *The Journal of American History,* December 1983.

* Adapted from Arthur B. Murphy, "Evaluating the Presidents of the United States," 14 *Presidential Studies Quarterly* (Winter 1984), pp. 117–126. Permission granted by the Center for the Study of the Presidency, publisher.

APPENDIX C

TABLE OF SUCCESSION OF THE JUSTICES OF THE SUPREME COURT OF THE UNITED STAT

Showing Years of Active Service on the Court

	Judiciary Act of 1789 provided for a Chief Justice and 5 Associate Justices					
1789 1790	John Jay 1789–1795	John Rutledge 1789–1791	William Cushing 1789–1810	John Blair 1789–1796	James Wilson 1789–1798	James Irede 1790–179
	John Rutledge 1795 Oliver Ellsworth 1796–1800	Thomas Johnson 1791–1793 William Paterson 1793–1806		Samuel Chase 1796–1811	Bushrod Washington 1798–1829	Alfred Moo 1799–180
1800	John Marshall 1801–1835	Henry B. Livingston 1806–1823				William John 1804–183
1810			Joseph Story 1811–1845	Gabriel Duval 1811–1836		
1820		Smith Thompson 1823–1843			Henry Baldwin 1830–1844	
1830	Roger B. Taney 1836–1864			Philip P. Barbour 1836–1841		James M. Wa 1835–186
1840		Samuel Nelson 1845–1872	Levi Woodbury 1846–1851	Peter V. Daniel 1841–1860	Robert C. Grier 1846–1870	
1850			Benjamin R. Curtis 1851–1857 Nathan Clifford 1858–1881			
1860	Salmon P. Chase 1864–1873			Samuel F. Miller 1862–1890	William Strong 1870–1880	Act of July 23, 1866, provided for reduction of the Court to 7 members as vacancies should occur.
1870	Morrison R. Waite 1874–1888	Ward Hunt 1872–1882			William B. Woods 1880–1887	
1880	Melville W. Fuller 1888–1910	Samuel Blatchford 1882–1893	Horace Gray 1881–1902	Henry B. Brown 1890–1906	Lucius Q. C. Lamar 1888–1893	
1890		Edward D. White J 1894 CJ 1910–1921			Howell E. Jackson 1893–1895 Rufus W. Peckham 1895–1909	
1900	Edward D. White J 1894 CJ 1910–1921	Willis Van Devanter 1911–1937	Oliver Wendell Holmes, Jr. 1902–1932	William H. Moody 1906–1910 Joseph R. Lamar 1911–1916	Horace H. Lurton 1909–1914	
1910				Louis D. Brandeis 1916–1939	James C. McReynolds 1914–1941	
1920	William H. Taft 1921–1930 Charles E. Hughes 1930–1941					
1930	Harlan F. Stone J 1925 CJ 1941–1946	Hugo L. Black 1937–1971	Benjamin N. Cardozo 1932–1938 Felix Frankfurter 1939–1962	William O. Douglas 1939–1975		
1940	Fred M. Vinson 1946–1953				James F. Byrnes 1941–1942 Wiley B. Rutledge 1943–1949 Sherman Minton 1949–1956	
1950	Earl Warren 1953–1969				William J. Brennan, Jr. 1956–	
1960	Warren E. Burger 1969–		Arthur J. Goldberg 1962–1965 Abe Fortas 1965–1969 Harry A. Blackmun 1970–			
1970		Lewis F. Powell, Jr. 1972–		John Paul Stevens 1975–		
1980						

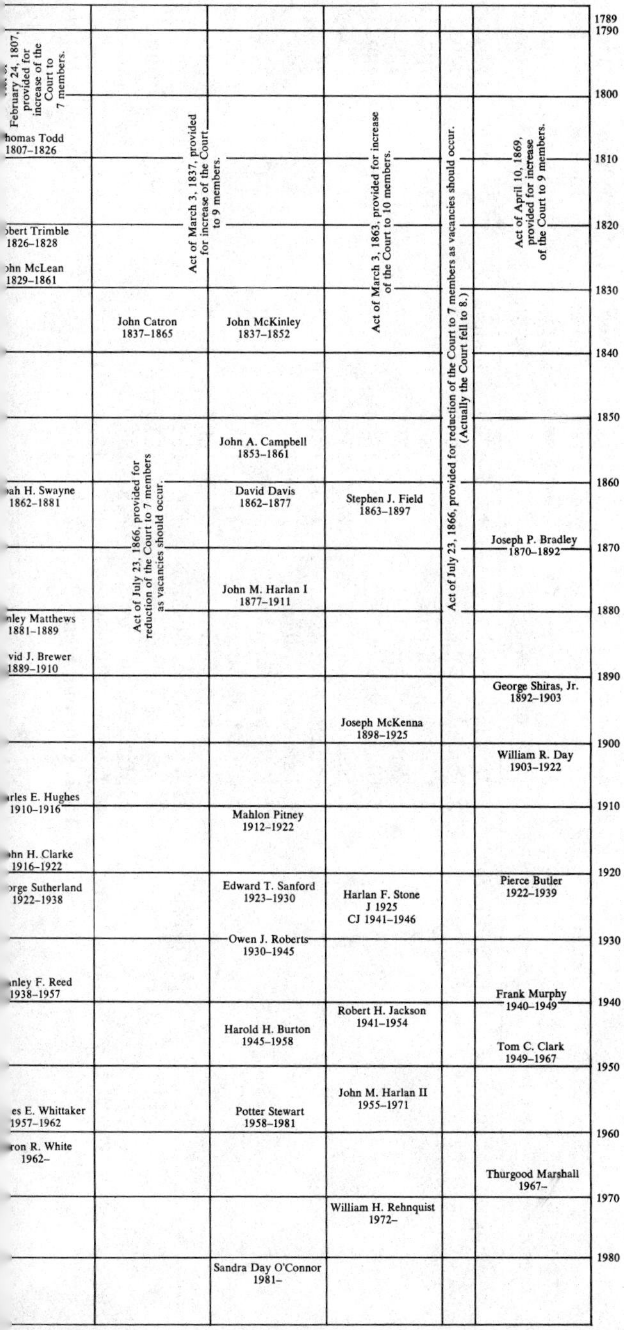

...February 24, 1807, provided for increase of the Court to 7 members.

...homas Todd
1807–1826

...bert Trimble
1826–1828

...hn McLean
1829–1861

...ah H. Swayne
1862–1881

...nley Matthews
1881–1889

...vid J. Brewer
1889–1910

...rles E. Hughes
1910–1916

...hn H. Clarke
1916–1922

...rge Sutherland
1922–1938

...nley F. Reed
1938–1957

...es E. Whittaker
1957–1962

...ron R. White
1962–

Act of March 3, 1837, provided for increase of the Court to 9 members.

John Catron
1837–1865

Act of July 23, 1866, provided for reduction of the Court to 7 members as vacancies should occur.

John McKinley
1837–1852

John A. Campbell
1853–1861

David Davis
1862–1877

John M. Harlan I
1877–1911

Mahlon Pitney
1912–1922

Edward T. Sanford
1923–1930

Owen J. Roberts
1930–1945

Harold H. Burton
1945–1958

Potter Stewart
1958–1981

Sandra Day O'Connor
1981–

Act of March 3, 1863, provided for increase of the Court to 10 members.

Stephen J. Field
1863–1897

Joseph McKenna
1898–1925

Harlan F. Stone
J 1925
CJ 1941–1946

Robert H. Jackson
1941–1954

John M. Harlan II
1955–1971

William H. Rehnquist
1972–

Act of July 23, 1866, provided for reduction of the Court to 7 members as vacancies should occur. (Actually the Court fell to 8.)

Act of April 10, 1869, provided for increase of the Court to 9 members.

Joseph P. Bradley
1870–1892

George Shiras, Jr.
1892–1903

William R. Day
1903–1922

Pierce Butler
1922–1939

Frank Murphy
1940–1949

Tom C. Clark
1949–1967

Thurgood Marshall
1967–

1789
1790
1800
1810
1820
1830
1840
1850
1860
1870
1880
1890
1900
1910
1920
1930
1940
1950
1960
1970
1980

Appendix D
Statistical Data on Supreme Court Justices

Appointing President	President's Political Party	Dates of President's Service	Name of Justice	Dates of Birth and Death	Justice's Nominal Party Allegiance on Appointment	State from Which Justice Was Apptd.*	Dates of Service on Supreme Court
Washington	Federalist	1789–1797	1. Jay, John†	1745–1829	Federalist	N.Y.	1789–1795
"	"	"	2. Rutledge, John	1739–1800	"	S.C.	1789–1791‡
"	"	"	3. Cushing, William	1732–1810	"	Mass.	1789–1810
"	"	"	4. Wilson, James	1742–1798	"	Pa.	1789–1798
"	"	"	5. Blair, John, Jr.	1732–1800	"	Va.	1789–1796
"	"	"	6. Iredell, James	1751–1799	"	N.C.	1790–1799
"	"	"	7. Johnson, Thomas	1732–1819	"	Md.	1791–1793
"	"	"	8. Paterson, William	1745–1806	"	N.J.	1793–1806
"	"	"	9. Rutledge, John†	1739–1800	"	S.C.	1795§
"	"	"	10. Chase, Samuel	1741–1811	"	Md.	1796–1811
"	"	"	11. Ellsworth, Oliver†	1745–1807	"	Conn.	1796–1800
Adams	"	1797–1801	12. Washington, Bushrod	1762–1829	"	Va.	1798–1829
"	"	"	13. Moore, Alfred	1755–1810	"	N.C.	1799–1804
"	"	"	14. Marshall, John†	1755–1835	"	Va.	1801–1835
Jefferson	Dem.-Rep.	1801–1809	15. Johnson, William	1771–1834	Dem.-Rep.	S.C.	1804–1834
"	"	"	16. Livingston, Henry B.	1757–1823	"	N.Y.	1806–1823

Appointing President	President's Political Party	Dates of President's Service	Name of Justice	Dates of Birth and Death	Justice's Nominal Party Allegiance on Appointment	State from Which Justice Was Apptd.*	Dates of Service on Supreme Court
"	"	"	17. Todd, Thomas	1765–1826	"	Ky.	1807–1826
Madison	"	1809–1817	18. Duval, Gabriel	1752–1844	"	Md.	1811–1835
"	"	"	19. Story, Joseph	1779–1845	"	Mass.	1811–1845
Monroe	"	1817–1825	20. Thompson, Smith	1768–1843	"	N.Y.	1823–1843
J. Q. Adams	"	1825–1829	21. Trimble, Robert	1777–1828	"	Ky.	1826–1828
Jackson	Democrat	1829–1837	22. McLean, John	1785–1861	Democrat	Ohio	1829–1861
"	"	"	23. Baldwin, Henry	1780–1844	"	Pa.	1830–1844
"	"	"	24. Wayne, James M.	1790–1867	"	Ga.	1835–1867
"	"	"	25. Taney, Roger B.†	1777–1864	"	Md.	1836–1864
"	"	"	26. Barbour, Philip P.	1783–1841	"	Va.	1836–1841
"	"	"	27. Catron, John‖	1786–1865	"	Tenn.	1837–1865
Van Buren	"	1837–1841	28. McKinley, John	1780–1852	"	Ala.	1837–1852
	"	"	29. Daniel, Peter V.	1784–1860	"	Va.	1841–1860
Tyler	Whig	1841–1845	30. Nelson, Samuel	1792–1873	"	N.Y.	1845–1872
Polk	Democrat	1845–1849	31. Woodbury, Levi	1789–1851	"	N.H.	1846–1851
	"	"	32. Grier, Robert C.	1794–1870	"	Pa.	1846–1870
Fillmore	Whig	1850–1853	33. Curtis, Benjamin R.	1809–1874	Whig	Mass.	1851–1857
Pierce	Democrat	1853–1857	34. Campbell, John A.	1811–1889	Democrat	Ala.	1853–1861
Buchanan	"	1857–1861	35. Clifford, Nathan	1803–1881	"	Maine	1858–1881

Appointing President	President's Political Party	Dates of President's Service	Name of Justice	Dates of Birth and Death	Justice's Nominal Party Allegiance on Appointment	State from Which Justice Was Apptd.*	Dates of Service on Supreme Court
Lincoln	Republican	1861–1865	36. Swayne, Noah H.	1804–1884	Republican	Ohio	1862–1881
"	"	"	37. Miller, Samuel F.	1816–1890	"	Iowa	1862–1890
"	"	"	38. Davis, David	1815–1886	"	Ill.	1862–1877
"	"	"	39. Field, Stephen J.	1816–1899	Democrat	Calif.	1863–1897
"	"	"	40. Chase, Salmon P.†	1808–1873	Republican	Ohio	1864–1873
Grant	"	1869–1877	41. Strong, William	1808–1895	"	Pa.	1870–1880
"	"	"	42. Bradley, Joseph P.	1813–1892	"	N.J.	1870–1892
"	"	"	43. Hunt, Ward	1810–1886	"	N.Y.	1872–1882
"	"	"	44. Waite, Morrison R.†	1816–1888	"	Ohio	1874–1888
Hayes	"	1877–1881	45. Harlan, John M., I	1833–1911	"	Ky.	1877–1911
"	"	"	46. Woods, William B.	1824–1887	"	Ga.	1880–1887
Garfield	"	Mar.–Sept. 1881	47. Matthews, Stanley	1824–1889	"	Ohio	1881–1889
Arthur	"	1881–1885	48. Gray, Horace	1828–1902	"	Mass.	1881–1902
"	"	"	49. Blatchford, Samuel	1820–1893	"	N.Y.	1882–1893
Cleveland	Democrat	1885–1889	50. Lamar, Lucius Q. C.	1825–1893	Democrat	Miss.	1888–1893
"	"	"	51. Fuller, Melville W.†	1833–1910	"	Ill.	1888–1910
Harrison	Republican	1889–1893	52. Brewer, David J.	1837–1910	Republican	Kans.	1889–1910
"	"	"	53. Brown, Henry B.	1836–1913	"	Mich.	1890–1906

Appointing President	President's Political Party	Dates of President's Service	Name of Justice	Dates of Birth and Death	Justice's Nominal Party Allegiance on Appointment	State from Which Justice Was Apptd.*	Dates of Service on Supreme Court
"	"	"	54. Shiras, George, Jr.	1832–1924	"	Pa.	1892–1903
"	"	"	55. Jackson, Howell E.	1832–1895	Democrat	Tenn.	1893–1895
Cleveland	Democrat	1893–1897	56. White, Edward D.	1845–1921	"	La.	1894–1910
"	"	"	57. Peckham, Rufus W.	1838–1909	"	N.Y.	1895–1909
McKinley	Republican	1897–1901	58. McKenna, Joseph	1843–1926	Republican	Calif.	1898–1925
T. Roosevelt	"	1901–1909	59. Holmes, Oliver Wendell, Jr.	1841–1935	"	Mass.	1902–1932
"	"	"	60. Day, William R.	1849–1923	"	Ohio	1903–1922
"	"	"	61. Moody, William H.	1853–1917	"	Mass.	1906–1910
Taft	"	1909–1913	62. Lurton, Horace H.	1844–1914	Democrat	Tenn.	1909–1914
"	"	"	63. Hughes, Charles E.	1862–1948	Republican	N.Y.	1910–1916
"	"	"	64. White, Edward D.†#	1845–1921	Democrat	La.	1910–1921
"	"	"	65. Van Devanter, Willis	1859–1941	Republican	Wyo.	1911–1937
"	"	"	66. Lamar, Joseph R.	1857–1916	Democrat	Ga.	1911–1916
"	"	"	67. Pitney, Mahlon	1858–1924	Republican	N.J.	1912–1922
Wilson	Democrat	1913–1921	68. McReynolds, James C.	1862–1946	Democrat	Tenn.	1914–1941
"	"	"	69. Brandeis, Louis D.	1856–1941	Republican**	Mass.	1916–1939
"	"	"	70. Clarke, John H.	1857–1945	Democrat	Ohio	1916–1922
Harding	Republican	1921–1923	71. Taft, William H.†	1857–1930	Republican	Conn.	1921–1930

Appointing President	President's Political Party	Dates of President's Service	Name of Justice	Dates of Birth and Death	Justice's Nominal Party Allegiance on Appointment	State from Which Justice Was Apptd.*	Dates of Service on Supreme Court
"	"	"	72. Sutherland, George	1862–1942	"	Utah	1922–1938
"	"	"	73. Butler, Pierce	1866–1939	Democrat	Minn.	1922–1939
"	"	"	74. Sanford, Edward T.	1865–1930	Republican	Tenn.	1923–1930
Coolidge	"	1923–1929	75. Stone, Harlan F.	1872–1946	"	N.Y.	1925–1941
Hoover	"	1923–1933	76. Hughes, Charles E.†	1862–1948	"	N.Y.	1930–1941
"	"	"	77. Roberts, Owen J.	1875–1955	"	Pa.	1930–1945
"	"	"	78. Cardozo, Benjamin N.	1870–1938	Democrat	N.Y.	1932–1938
F. D. Roosevelt	Democrat	1933–1945	79. Black, Hugo L.	1886–1971	"	Ala.	1937–1971
"	"	"	80. Reed, Stanley F.	1884–1980	"	Ky.	1938–1957
"	"	"	81. Frankfurter, Felix	1882–1965	Independent	Mass.	1939–1962
"	"	"	82. Douglas, William O.	1898–1980	Democrat	Conn.	1939–1975
"	"	"	83. Murphy, Frank	1890–1949	"	Mich.	1940–1949
"	"	"	84. Byrnes, James F.	1879–1972	"	S.C.	1941–1942
"	"	"	85. Stone, Harlan F.†#	1872–1946	Republican	N.Y.	1941–1946
"	"	"	86. Jackson, Robert H.	1892–1954	Democrat	N.Y.	1941–1954
"	"	"	87. Rutledge, Wiley B.	1894–1949	"	Iowa	1943–1949
Truman	"	1945–1953	88. Burton, Harold H.	1888–1965	Republican	Ohio	1945–1958
"	"	"	89. Vinson, Fred M.†	1890–1953	Democrat	Ky.	1946–1953
"	"	"	90. Clark, Tom C.	1899–1977	"	Tex.	1949–1967
"	"	"	91. Minton, Sherman	1890–1965	"	Ind.	1949–1956

Appointing President	President's Political Party	Dates of President's Service	Name of Justice	Dates of Birth and Death	Justice's Nominal Party Allegiance on Appointment	State from Which Justice Was Apptd.*	Dates of Service on Supreme Court
Eisenhower	Republican	1953–1961	92. Warren, Earl†	1891–1974	Republican	Calif.	1953–1969
"	"	"	93. Harlan, John M., II	1899–1971	"	N.Y.	1955–1971
"	"	"	94. Brennan, William J., Jr.	1906–	Democrat	N.J.	1956–
"	"	"	95. Whittaker, Charles E.	1901–1973	Republican	Mo.	1957–1962
"	"	"	96. Stewart, Potter	1915–	"	Ohio	1958–1981
Kennedy	Democrat	1961–1963	97. White, Byron R.	1917–	Democrat	Colo.	1962–
"	"	"	98. Goldberg, Arthur J.	1908–	"	Ill.	1962–1965
L. Johnson	"	1963–1969	99. Fortas, Abe	1910–1982	"	Tenn.	1965–1969
"	"	"	100. Marshall, Thurgood	1908–	"	N.Y.	1967–
Nixon	Republican	1969–1974	101. Burger, Warren E.†	1907–	Republican	Va.	1969–
"	"	"	102. Blackmun, Harry A.	1908–	"	Minn.	1970–
"	"	"	103. Powell, Lewis F., Jr.	1907–	Democrat	Va.	1972–
"	"	"	104. Rehnquist, William H.	1924–	Republican	Ariz.	1972–
Ford	"	1974–1977	105. Stevens, John Paul	1920–	"	Ill.	1975–
Reagan	"	1981–	106. O'Connor, Sandra Day	1930–	"	Ariz.	1981–

* Not necessarily, but often, state of birth.
† Chief Justice.
‡ Resigned without sitting.
§ Unconfirmed recess appointment, rejected by Senate, December 1795.
|| Nominated by Jackson, but not confirmed until after Van Buren had assumed office.
\# Promoted from Associate Justice.
** Many—and with some justice—consider Brandeis a Democrat; however, he was in fact a registered Republican when nominated.

Bibliography

Selected Biographies, Autobiographies, and Related Works of, and by, Justices of the Supreme Court of the United States

The sources and related readings for a book of this type are numerous, eclectic, and sometimes elusive. *Primary* information, which consists largely of personal and official papers of the principals, can be especially elusive. A good many of these documents are not readily available because some Justices have provided for the deliberate destruction or partial sealing off from publication of sundry notes and papers. Nor does the Freedom of Information Act reach papers of Justices in the same manner and to the same degree as it does those of Presidents. Public repositories, however, such as the Library of Congress, the National Archives, the *Congressional Record,* the Reports of the Committee on the Judiciary of the U.S. Senate, and the burgeoning Presidential libraries provide much valuable data. So do obituaries in the public press and the Court's tributes to its departed members.

Secondary sources pertaining to Justices, Presidents, and other public and private personages apposite to the subject are indeed vast. Autobiographies and biographies of the individuals discussed or mentioned in this book are not only readily obtained, but are often separately catalogued in special bibliographical publications and anthologies, some of which are annotated. The following listings, which are confined to publications dealing with Justices only, are divided into two source groups: the first catalogues appropriate general works and those that deal with multiple judicial personages. The second, arranged in alphabetical order, cites publications by, or about, individual Justices. The dates following each Justice's name refer to his or her life span; their years of service on the Supreme Court are noted in Appendixes C and D as well as in the textual material.

I. *General or Multi-applicable Works*

Abraham, H. J. *Freedom and the Court: Civil Rights and Liberties in the United States.* 4th ed. Oxford, 1982.

———. *The Judicial Process: An Introductory Analysis of the Courts of the United States, England, and France.* 4th ed. Oxford, 1980.

Acheson, P. C. *The Supreme Court: America's Judicial Heritage.* Dodd, Mead, 1961.

Asch, S. H. *The Supreme Court and Its Great Justices.* Arco, 1971.

Barbar, J. *The Honorable Eighty-Eight.* Vanguard, 1957.

Barnes, C. *Men of the Supreme Court: Profiles of the Justices, 1945–1976.* Facts on File, 1979.

Bates, E. S. *The Story of the Supreme Court.* Bobbs-Merrill, 1936.

Blandford, L. A., and P. R. Evans, eds. *Supreme Court of the United States, 1789–1980: An Index to Opinions Arranged by Justice.* Supreme Court Historical Society, 1983.

Blaustein, A. P., and R. M. Mersky. *The First One Hundred Justices: Statistical Studies on the Supreme Court of the United States.* Shoe String [Archon Books], 1978.

Brown, J. M. *Through These Men.* Harper, 1956.

Cahn, E., ed. *The Great Rights.* Macmillan, 1963.

Campbell, T. W. *Four-Score Forgotten Men.* Pioneer, 1950.

Cannon, M., and D. M. O'Brien, eds. *Views from the Bench.* Chatham, 1984.

Carson, H. L. *The Supreme Court of the United States: Its History.* Huber, 1891.

Congressional Quarterly. Guide to the U.S. Supreme Court. 1979– .

Crosskey, W. W. *Politics and the Constitution in the History of the United States.* University of Chicago, 1953.

Danelski, D. J. *The Chief Justices of the Supreme Court.* Ph.D. diss., University of Illinois, 1961.

Dunham, A., and P. B. Kurland, eds. *Mr. Justice.* Rev. and enl. Phoenix, 1964.

Ewing, C. A. M. *The Judges of the Supreme Court, 1780–1937.* University of Minnesota, 1938.

Fairman, C. *Reconstruction and Reunion, 1864–88.* Macmillan, 1971.

Flanders, H. *The Lives and Times of the Chief Justices of the Supreme Court of the United States.* Lippincott, 1858.

Frank, J. P. "The Appointment of Supreme Court Justices: Prestige Principles and Politics." *Wisconsin Law Review,* vol. 1941: March (172), May (343), July (461).

———. *Marble Palace: The Supreme Court in American Life.* Knopf, 1958.

Freund, P. A. *On Law and Justice.* Harvard University, 1968.

———, ed. *The Oliver Wendell Holmes Devise: History of the Supreme Court of the United States* (various volumes). Macmillan, 1971– .

Friedman, L., and F. L. Israel, eds. *The Justices of the United States Supreme Court, 1789–1978*. 5 vols. Chelsea House, 1980.

Goebel, J. *Antecedents and Beginnings to 1801*. Macmillan, 1971.

Grossman, J. B. *Lawyers and Judges: The ABA and the Process of Judicial Selection*. Wiley, 1965.

Harris, J. P. *The Advice and Consent of the Senate*. University of California, 1953.

Harris, R. *Decision*. Dutton, 1971.

Haynes, E. *Selection and Tenure of Judges*. National Conference of Judicial Councils, 1944.

Howell, R. F. "Conservative Influence on Constitutional Development, 1923–1937–The Judicial Theories of Justices Van Devanter, McReynolds, Sutherland, and Butler." Ph.D. diss., Johns Hopkins University, 1952.

Lewis, W. E. *Seven Great American Lawyers*. Lippincott, 1909.

Lieberman, J. K. *Milestones! 200 Years of American Law*. West, 1976.

London, E., ed. *The World of Law: The Law in Literature and The Law as Literature*. Simon & Schuster, 1960.

Mason, E., ed. *Chief Justices of the United States*. [Columbus, Ohio] Dispatch Co., 1977.

McCloskey, R. G. *The American Supreme Court*. University of Chicago, 1960.

McCune, W. *The Nine Young Men*. Harper, 1947.

McHargue, D. S. "Factors Influencing the Selection and Appointment of Members of the United States Supreme Court, 1789–1932." Ph.D. diss., UCLA, 1949.

Merryman, J. H. *The Civil Law Tradition*. Stanford University, 1970.

Murphy, B. A. *The Brandeis/Frankfurter Connection: The Secret Political Activities of Two Supreme Court Justices*. Oxford, 1982.

Noonon, F. T. *Persons and Makers of the Law: Cardozo, Holmes, Jefferson, and Wythe*. Farrar, Straus & Giroux, 1976.

Pritchett, C. H. *The Roosevelt Court: A Study in Judicial Politics and Values, 1937–1947*. Macmillan 1948.

Rodell, F. *Nine Men: A Political History of the Supreme Court of the United States from 1790–1855*. Knopf, 1955.

Schmidhauser, J. R. *Judges and Justices: The Federal Appellate Judiciary*. Little, Brown, 1979.

———. *The Supreme Court: Its Politics, Personalities, and Procedures*. Holt, Rinehart & Winston, 1960.

Schubert, G. A. *The Judicial Mind: The Attitudes and Ideologies of the Supreme Court, 1943–1963*. Northwestern University, 1965.

Seagle, W. *Men of Law: From Hammurabi to Holmes*. Macmillan, 1947.

Simon, J. F. *In His Own Image: The Supreme Court in Richard Nixon's America.* McKay, 1973.

Steamer, R. J. *The Supreme Court in Crisis: A History of Conflict.* University of Massachusetts, 1971.

Thompson, D. C. *The Supreme Court of the United States: A Bibliography.* University of California, 1959.

Tresolini, R. J. *Justice and the Supreme Court.* Lippincott, 1962.

Umbreit, K. B. *Our Eleven Chief Justices: A History of the Supreme Court in Terms of Their Personalities.* Harper, 1938.

Vanderbilt Law Review. Symposium: "Studies in Judicial Biography." Vol. 10, no. 2 (1957).

Van Santvoord, G. *Sketches of the Lives and Judicial Services of the Chief Justices of the Supreme Court of the United States.* Scribner's, 1854.

Warren, C. *The Supreme Court in United States History.* Little, Brown, 1922, 1926, 1935.

Westin, A. F., ed. *The Supreme Court: Views from Inside.* Norton, 1961.

White, G. E. *The American Judicial Tradition. Profiles of Leading American Judges.* Oxford, 1976.

Woodward, B., and S. Armstrong. *The Brethren: Inside the Supreme Court.* Simon & Schuster, 1979.

II. *Works About or by Individual Justices*

HENRY BALDWIN (1780–1844):

Baldwin, H. *A General View of the Origin and Nature of the United States.* Lippincott, 1837.

PHILIP P. BARBOUR (1783–1841):

Baldwin, H. *A General View of the Origin and Nature of the Constitution and Government of the United States.* J. C. Clark, 1837.

Cynn, P. P. "Philip Pendleton Barbour." 4 John P. Branch Historical Papers of Randolph-Macon College 67 (1913).

Scott, W. W. *History of Orange County.* Waddey, 1907.

HUGO LAFAYETTE BLACK (1886–1971):

Ball, H. *The Vision and the Dream of Justice Hugo L. Black: An Examination of a Judicial Philosophy.* University of Alabama, 1975.

Black, H. L. *A Constitutional Faith.* Knopf, 1968.

Black, H. L., Jr. *My Father: A Remembrance.* Random House, 1975.

Davis, H. B. *Uncle Hugo: An Intimate Portrait of Mr. Justice Black.* Privately published, Amarillo, Texas, 1965.

Dennis, E. E., et al., eds. *Justice Hugo Black and the First Amendment*. Iowa State University, 1978.

Dilliard, I. *One Man's Freedom: Mr. Justice Black and the Bill of Rights*. Knopf, 1963.

Dunne, G. T. *Hugo Black and the Judicial Revolution*. Simon & Schuster, 1977.

Frank, J. P. *Mr. Justice Black: The Man and His Opinions*. Knopf, 1949.

Hamilton, V. V. de V., ed. *Hugo Black and the Bill of Rights*. University of Alabama, 1978.

———. *Hugo Black: The Alabama Years*. Louisiana State University, 1972.

Magee, J. J. *Mr. Justice Black: Absolutist on the Court*. University of Virginia, 1980.

Mason, G. L. *Hugo Black and the United States Senate*. University of Kansas, 1964.

Meador, D. J. *Mr. Justice Black and His Books*. University of Virginia, 1974.

Mendelson, W., ed. *Justices Black and Frankfurter: Conflict in the Court*. 2nd ed. University of Chicago, 1966.

Silverstein, M. *Constitutional Faiths: Felix Frankfurter, Hugo Black, and the Process of Decision-Making*. Cornell University, 1984.

Strickland, S. P., ed. *Hugo Black and the Supreme Court: A Symposium*. Bobbs-Merrill, 1967.

United States Congress, Joint Committee on Printing. *Hugo Lafayette Black, 1886–1971: Memorial Addresses and Tributes*. U.S. Government Printing Office, 1972.

Williams, C. *Hugo L. Black: A Study in the Judicial Process*. Johns Hopkins, 1950.

Yale Law Journal. Symposium: "Mr. Justice Black." (February 1956.)

HARRY A. BLACKMUN (1908–19):

Pollett, M. "Harry A. Blackmun." In *The Justices of the United States Superior Court, 1789–1978,* edited by L. Friedman and F. L. Israel, p. 2, vol. 5. Chelsea House, 1980.

JOHN BLAIR, JR. (1732–1800):

Drinard, J. E. "John Blair, Jr." 39 *Proceedings of Virginia State Bar Association* 436 (1927).

SAMUEL BLATCHFORD (1820–1893):

Paul, A. M. "Samuel Blatchford." In *The Justices of the United States Supreme Court, 1789–1978,* edited by L. Friedman and F. L. Israel, p. 2, vol. 2. Chelsea House, 1980.

JOSEPH P. BRADLEY (1813–1892):

Bradley, C., ed. *Miscellaneous Writings of Joseph P. Bradley.* Harham, 1901.

Bradley, J. P. *Family Notes Respecting the Bradley Family of Fairchild.* Newark, N.J.: privately published, 1894.

Fairman, C. "Mr. Justice Bradley." In A. Dunham and P. B. Knowland, *Mr. Justice.* University of Chicago, 1964.

LOUIS DEMBITZ BRANDEIS (1856–1941):

Baker, L. *Brandeis and Frankfurter: A Dual Biography.* Harper & Row, 1984.

Bickel, A. M. *The Unpublished Opinions of Mr. Justice Brandeis: The Supreme Court at Work.* Harvard University, 1957; Phoenix, 1967.

DeHaas, J. *Louis D. Brandeis.* Block, 1929.

Dilliard, I., ed. *Mr. Justice Brandeis: Great American.* Modern View Press, 1941.

Fraenkel, O. K., ed. *The Curse of Bigness: Miscellaneous Papers of Louis D. Brandeis.* Viking, 1934.

Frankfurter, F. *Mr. Justice Brandeis.* Yale University, 1932; Da Capo, 1972.

Freund, P. A. *The Writings of Louis D. Brandeis.* Bobbs-Merrill, 1966.

Gal, A. *Brandeis of Boston.* Harvard University, 1980.

Goldman, S., ed. *The Words of Mr. Justice Brandeis.* Schuman, 1953.

Konefsky, S. J. *The Legacy of Holmes and Brandeis: A Study in the Influence of Ideas.* Macmillan, 1956; Da Capo, 1974.

Lief, A., ed. *Brandeis: The Personal History of an American Ideal.* Stackpole, 1936.

———. *The Social and Economic Views of Mr. Justice Brandeis.* Viewpoint, 1930.

Mason, A. T. *Brandeis–A Free Man's Life.* Viking, 1946.

———. *Brandeis and the Modern State.* National Home Library, 1936.

———. *Brandeis: Lawyer and Judge in the Modern State.* Princeton University, 1933.

———. *The Brandeis Way.* Princeton University, 1938.

Noble, I. *Firebrand for Justice: A Biography of Louis Dembitz Brandeis.* Westminster, 1969.

Paper, L. J. *Brandeis: An Intimate Biography of America's Truly Great Supreme Court Justice.* Prentice-Hall, 1983.

Peare, C. O. *The Louis D. Brandeis Story.* Crowell, 1970.

Pollack, E. H., ed. *The Brandeis Reader.* Oceana, 1956.

Strum, P. *Louis D. Brandeis: Justice for the People.* Harvard University, 1984.

Todd, A. L. *Justice on Trial: The Case of Louis D. Brandeis.* McGraw-Hill, 1964.

Urofsky, M. I. *Louis D. Brandeis and the Progressive Tradition.* Little, Brown, 1981.

———. *A Mind of One Peace: Brandeis and American Reform.* Scribner's, 1971.

——— and D. W. Levy, eds. *Letters of Louis D. Brandeis,* Vol. 1, 1870–1897: *Urban Reformer;* Vol. 2, 1897–1912: *People's Attorney;* Vol. 3, 1912–1916; Vol. 4, 1916–1921; Vol. 5, 1921–1941. State University of New York, 1972–1978.

Yale Law Library. *Louis Dembitz Brandeis, 1856–1941: A Bibliography.* Yale University, 1958.

WILLIAM J. BRENNAN, JR. (1906–):

Friedman, S. J. *William J. Brennan, Jr.: An Affair with Freedom.* Atheneum, 1967.

DAVID J. BREWER (1837–1910):

Lardner, L. A. "The Constitutional Doctrines of Justice David Josiah Brewer." Ph.D. diss., Princeton University, 1938.

HENRY BILLINGS BROWN (1836–1913):

Kent, C. A. *Memoir of Henry Billings Brown.* Dunfield, 1915.

Paul, A. M. *Conservative Crisis and the Rule of Law.* Cornell University, 1960.

WARREN E. BURGER (1907–):

Norman, A. E. "Warren E. Burger." In *The Justices of the United States Supreme Court, 1789–1978,* edited by L. Friedman and F. L. Israel, p. 2, vol. 5. Chelsea House, 1980.

HAROLD H. BURTON (1888–1965):

Berry, M. F. *Stability, Security, and Continuity: Mr. Justice Burton and Decisionmaking in the Supreme Court, 1945–1948.* Greenwood, 1978.

Hudson, E. G., ed. *The Occasional Papers of Mr. Justice Burton.* Bowdoin College, 1969.

Marquardt, R. G. "The Judicial Justice: Mr. Justice Burton and the Supreme Court." Ph.D. diss., University of Wisconsin, 1973.

Provine, D. M. *Case Selection in the United States Supreme Court.* University of Chicago, 1980.

PIERCE BUTLER (1866–1939):

Brown, F. J. *The Social and Economic Philosophy of Pierce Butler.* Catholic University, 1945.

Danelski, D. J. *A Supreme Court Justice Is Appointed.* Random House, 1964.

JAMES F. BYRNES (1879–1972):

Byrnes, J. F. *All in One Lifetitme.* Harper, 1958.

Petit, W. "Justice Byrnes and the Supreme Court." 6 *South Carolina Law Quarterly* 423 (1954).

JOHN A. CAMPBELL (1811–1889):

Conner, H. G. *John Archibald Campbell, Associate Judge of the United States Supreme Court,* 1853–1861. Houghton Mifflin, 1920.

Holt, J., Jr. "The Resignation of Mr. Justice Campbell." 12 *Alabama Law Review* 105 (1959).

BENJAMIN N. CARDOZO (1870–1938):

Bender, N., ed. *The Benjamin N. Cardozo Memorial Lectures.* Bender, 1971.

Cardozo, B. N. *The Growth of the Law.* Yale University, 1924.

———. *Law and Literature and Other Essays.* Harcourt, Brace, 1931.

———. *The Nature of the Judicial Process.* Yale University, 1921.

———. *Paradoxes of the Legal Science.* Columbia University, 1928.

Hall, M. E., ed. *Selected Writings of B. N. Cardozo.* Fallon, 1947.

Hellman, G. S. *Benjamin N. Cardozo–American Judge.* Whittlesey, 1940.

Levy, B. H. *Cardozo and Legal Thinking.* Oxford, 1938.

———. *Cardozo and the Frontiers of Legal Thinking: With Selected Opinions.* 2nd ed. Case-Western Reserve University, 1970.

Pollard, J. P. *Mr. Justice Cardozo: A Liberal Mind in Action.* Yorktown Press, 1935.

Sainer, A. L. *Law Is Justice: Notable Opinions of Mr. Justice Cardozo.* Ad Press, 1938.

JOHN CATRON (1786–1865):

Gass, E. C. "The Constitutional Opinions of Justice John Catron." 8 *East Tennessee Historical Society's Publications* 54 (1936).

SALMON PORTLAND CHASE (1808–1873):

Chase, S. P. *Diaries and Correspondence.* Da Capo, 1971.

Hart, A. B. *Salmon Portland Chase.* Houghton Mifflin, 1899.

Johnson, B. T. *Reports on Cases Decided by Chief Justice Chase in the Circuit Court of the United States for the Fourth Circuit.* Da Capo, 1972.

Schuckers, J. W. *The Life and Public Services of Salmon Portland Chase.* Appleton, 1874.

SAMUEL CHASE (1741–1811):

United States Senate. *Trial of Samuel Chase, an Associate Justice of the Supreme Court Impeached by the House of Representatives for High Crimes and Misdemeanors Before the Senate of the United States.* 1805, 8th Cong., 2d sess.

Warren, C. *The Supreme Court in United States History*. Rev. ed. Little, Brown, 1937.

TOM C. CLARK (1899–1977):

Dorin, D. D. "Justice Tom Clark and the Right of Defendants in State Courts." Ph.D. diss., University of Virginia, 1974.

Dutton, C. B. "Mr. Justice Tom Clark." 26 *Indiana Law Journal* 169 (1951).

Kirkendall, R. J. *The Truman Period as a Research Field*. Columbia University, 1967.

JOHN H. CLARKE (1857–1945):

Levitan, D. M. "The Jurisprudence of Mr. Justice Clarke." 7 *Miami Law Quarterly* 44 (1952).

Warner, H. L. *The Life of Mr. Justice Clarke: A Testimony to the Power of Liberal Dissent in America*. Western Reserve University, 1959.

NATHAN CLIFFORD (1803–1881):

Clifford, P. G. *Nathan Clifford, Democrat*. Putnam's, 1922.

Magrath, C. P. *Morrison R. Waite: The Triumph of Character*. Macmillan, 1963.

BENJAMIN ROBBINS CURTIS (1809–1874):

Curtis, B. R., Jr. *A Memoir of Benjamin Robbins Curtis, L.L.D.* Little, Brown, 1897.

Leach, R. H. "Benjamin R. Curtis: Case Study of a Supreme Court Justice." Ph.D. diss., Princeton University, 1951.

WILLIAM CUSHING (1732–1810):

Cushing, J. D. "A Revolutionary Conservative: The Public Life of William Cushing, 1732–1810." Ph.D. diss., Clark University, 1960.

PETER V. DANIEL (1784–1860):

Frank, J. P. *Justice Daniel Dissenting: A Biography of Peter V. Daniel, 1784–1860*. Harvard University, 1964.

Hendricks, B. M. *Bulwark of the Republic: A Biography of the Constitution*. Little, Brown, 1957.

DAVID DAVIS (1815–1886):

Fairman, C. *Mr. Justice Miller and the Supreme Court,* 1862–1890. Harvard University, 1939.

King, W. L. *Lincoln's Manager: David Davis*. Harvard University, 1960.

Kutler, S. I. *Judicial Power and Reconstruction Politics*. University of Chicago, 1968.

WILLIAM RUFUS DAY (1849–1923):

McLean, J. E. *William Rufus Day, Supreme Court Justice from Ohio*. Johns Hopkins University, 1947.

WILLIAM O. DOUGLAS (1898–1980):

Ashmore, H. S., ed. *The William O. Douglas Inquiry into the State of Individual Freedom*. Westview, 1979.

Bosmajian, H. *Justice Douglas and Freedom of Speech*. Scarecrow, 1980.

Countryman, V., ed. *Douglas of the Supreme Court: A Selection of His Opinions*. Doubleday, 1959.

———. *The Douglas Opinions*. Random House, 1977.

———. *The Judicial Record of Justice William O. Douglas*. Harvard University, 1974.

———. *The Right of the People*. Arena, 1972.

Douglas, W. O. *The Anatomy of Liberty: The Rights of Man Without Force*. Trident, 1963.

———. *The Bible and the Schools*. Little, Brown, 1966.

———. *The Court Years (1939–1975). The Autobiography of William O. Douglas*. Random House [Vintage Books], 1980.

———. *Democracy and Finance*. Yale University, 1940.

———. *Go East, Young Man*. Random House, 1974.

———. *International Dissent*. Random House [Vintage], 1974.

———. *A Living Bill of Rights*. Doubleday, 1961.

———. *Of Men and Mountains*. Harper & Row, 1950.

———. *The Supreme Court and the Bicentennial*. Associated University Press, 1978.

———. *We the Judges*. Doubleday, 1956.

———, ed. *Courts, Law and Judicial Process*. Free Press, 1981.

Duram, J. C. *Justice William O. Douglas*. G. K. Hall, 1981.

Keller, R. H., Jr., ed. *In Honor of Justice Douglas: A Symposium on Individual Freedom and the Government*. Greenwood, 1981.

Simon, J. F. *Independent Journey: The Life of William O. Douglas*. Harper & Row, 1980.

University of Chicago Law Review. "Justices Frankfurter and Douglas." (Autumn 1958.)

Wolfman, B. J., L. F. Silver, and M. A. Silver. *Dissent Without Opinion: The Behavior of Justice William O. Douglas in Federal Tax Cases*. University of Pennsylvania, 1975.

GABRIEL DUVAL (1752–1844):

Dilliard, I. "Gabriel Duval." In *The Justices of the United States Supreme Court, 1789–1978,* edited by L. Friedman and F. L. Israel, p. 2, vol. 1. Chelsea House, 1980.

OLIVER ELLSWORTH (1745–1807):

Brown, W. G. *The Life of Oliver Ellsworth*. Macmillan, 1905; Da Capo, 1970.

STEPHEN J. FIELD (1816–1899):

Field, S. J. *Personal Reminiscences of Early Days in California*. Privately published, Washington, D.C., 1893; Da Capo, 1968.

Swisher, C. B. *Stephen J. Field: Craftsman of the Law*. Brookings, 1930; Phoenix, 1969.

Turner, W. R., *Documents in Relation to the Charges Preferred by Stephen J. Field and Others*. San Francisco: privately published, 1853.

ABE FORTAS (1910–1982):

Fortas, A. *Concerning Dissent and Civil Disobedience*. New American Library, 1968.

Heckart, R. J. "Justice Fortas and the First Amendment." Ph.D. diss., SUNY, Albany, 1973.

Shogan, R. *A Question of Judgment: The Fortas Case and the Struggle for the Supreme Court*. Bobbs-Merrill, 1972.

FELIX FRANKFURTER (1882–1965):

Aronson, M. J. "The Juristic Thought of Mr. Justice Frankfurter." *Journal of Social Philosophy* (1940).

Baker, L. *Brandeis and Frankfurter: A Dual Biography*. Harper & Row, 1983.

———. *Felix Frankfurter*. Coward, McCann, 1969.

Frankfurter, F., ed. *The Business of the Supreme Court*. Macmillan, 1927.

———. *The Case of Sacco and Vanzetti: A Critical Analysis for Lawyers and Layman*. Little, Brown, 1927, 1961, 1962.

———. *The Commerce Clause Under Marshall, Taney and Waite*. University of North Carolina, 1937.

———. *Extrajudicial Essays on the Court and Constitution*, edited by P. B. Kurland. Harvard University, 1970.

———. *Of Law and Men*. Harcourt, Brace, 1956.

———. *Mr. Justice Brandeis*. Yale University, 1932; Da Capo, 1972.

———, ed. *Mr. Justice Holmes*. Coward, McCann, 1931.

———. *Mr. Justice Holmes and the Constitution*. Harvard University, 1938.

———. *Mr. Justice Holmes and the Supreme Court*. 2nd ed. Atheneum, 1965.

———. *The Public and Its Government*. Beacon, 1964.

Freedman, M. *Roosevelt and Frankfurter: Their Correspondence, 1928–1945*. Little, Brown, 1968.

Hirsch, H. N. *The Enigma of Felix Frankfurter*. Basic Books, 1981.

Jacobs, C. E. *Justice Frankfurter and Civil Liberties*. Berkeley, 1961; Da Capo, 1974.

Konefsky, S. J., ed. *The Constitutional World of Mr. Justice Frankfurter*. Macmillan, 1949.

Kurland, P. B., ed. *Felix Frankfurter on the Supreme Court*. Harvard University, 1970.

———. *Mr. Justice Frankfurter and the Constitution.* University of Chicago, 1971.

———. *Of Law and Life and Other Things That Matter: Papers and Addresses of Felix Frankfurter, 1956–1963.* Harvard University, 1965.

Lash, J. P. *From the Diaries of Felix Frankfurter.* Norton, 1975.

MacLeish, A., and E. F. Prichard, Jr., eds. *Law and Politics: Occasional Papers of Mr. Justice Frankfurter.* Harcourt, Brace, 1939.

Mendelson, W., ed. *Felix Frankfurter: A Tribute.* Reynal, 1964.

———, ed. *Felix Frankfurter: The Judge.* Reynal, 1964.

———. *Justices Black and Frankfurter: Conflict in the Courts.* 2nd ed. University of Chicago, 1966.

Parrish, M. E. *Felix Frankfurter and His Times: The Reform Years.* Free Press, 1982.

Phillips, H. B., ed. *Felix Frankfurter: Scholar on the Bench.* Johns Hopkins University, 1960.

Silverstein, M. *Constitutional Faiths: Felix Frankfurter, Hugo Black, and the Process of Judicial Policy-Making.* Cornell University, 1984.

University of Chicago Law Review. "Justices Frankfurter and Douglas." (Autumn 1958).

Yale Law Journal. Symposium: "Mr. Justice Felix Frankfurter." (December 1957.)

MELVILLE WESTON FULLER (1833–1910):

King, W. L. *Melville Weston Fuller: Chief Justice of the United States, 1888–1910.* Macmillan, 1950; Phoenix, 1967.

Wade, W. E. "Chief Justice Fuller, The Individualist on the Bench." 10 *Maine Law Review* 77 (1917).

ARTHUR J. GOLDBERG (1908–):

Goldberg, A. J. *Equal Justice: The Supreme Court in the Warren Era.* Northwestern University, 1971.

———. *The Supreme Court of the United States.* Northwestern University, 1971.

Moynihan, D. P., ed. *The Defenses of Freedom: The Public Papers of Arthur J. Goldberg.* Harper & Row, 1966.

HORACE GRAY (1828–1902):

Mitchell, S. R. "Mr. Justice Horace Gray." Ph.D. diss., University of Wisconsin, 1961.

ROBERT C. GRIER (1794–1870):

Jones, F. R. "Robert Cooper Grier." 16 *Green Bag* 221 (1904).

JOHN MARSHALL HARLAN (I) (1833–1911):

Clark, F. B. *The Constitutional Doctrine of Justice Harlan.* Johns Hopkins University, 1915; Da Capo, 1969.

Kentucky Law Journal. Symposium: "John Marshall Harlan, 1833–1911." (Spring 1958.)

Latham, F. B. *The Great Dissenter–John Marshall Harlan*. Cowles, 1970.

Porter, M. C. A. "John Marshall Harlan and the Laissez-Faire Courts." Ph.D. diss., University of Chicago, 1970.

JOHN MARSHALL HARLAN (II) (1899–1971):

Harvard Law Review. Symposium: "Mr. Justice John Marshall Harlan." December 1971.

Levin, M. "Justice Harlan: The Full Measure of the Man." 58 *American Bar Association Journal* 579 (1972).

Shapiro, D., ed. *The Evolution of a Judicial Philosophy: Selected Opinions and Papers of Justice John M. Harlan*. Harvard University, 1969.

OLIVER WENDELL HOLMES, JR. (1841–1935):

Bander, E. J., comp. *Justice Holmes Cathedra*. Michie, 1966.

Bent, S. *Justice Oliver Wendell Holmes*. Vanguard, 1932.

Biddle, F. *Justice Holmes, Natural Law, and the Supreme Court*. Macmillan, 1961.

———. *Mr. Justice Holmes*. Scribner's, 1942.

Bowen, C. D. *A Yankee from Olympus: Justice Holmes and His Family*. Little, Brown, 1944.

Burton, D. H., ed. *The Holmes-Sheehan Correspondence*. Kennikat, 1976.

———, ed. *Oliver Wendell Holmes, Jr., What Manner of Liberal?* Krieger, 1979.

———, ed. *Progressive Masks: Letters of Oliver Wendell Holmes, Jr., and Franklin Ford*. University of Delaware, 1981.

Frankfurter, F., ed. *Mr. Justice Holmes*. Coward, McCann, 1931.

———. *Mr. Justice Holmes and the Supreme Court*. 2nd ed. Atheneum, 1965.

Holmes, O. W., Jr. *Collected Legal Papers*. Harcourt, 1920.

———. *The Common Law*. Little, Brown, 1881; new ed., Harvard, 1962, edited by Mark de Wolfe Howe.

———. *Speeches*. Little, Brown, 1891, 1896, 1913.

Howe, M. de W., ed. *The Holmes-Laski Letters, 1916–1935*. Harvard University, 1953; Atheneum, 1963.

———, ed. *The Holmes-Pollock Letters, 1874–1932*. Rev. ed. Harvard University, 1941; Atheneum, 1963.

———, ed. *Justice Holmes to Dr. Wu: An Intimate Correspondence, 1921–1932*. Central Books, 1935.

———. *Justice Oliver Wendell Holmes: The Proving Years, 1870–1882*. Harvard University, 1963.

———. *Justice Oliver Wendell Holmes: The Shaping Years, 1841–1870.* Harvard University, 1957.

———, ed. *The Occasional Speeches of Justice Oliver Wendell Holmes.* Harvard University, 1963.

———, ed. *Touched with Fire: Civil War Letters and Diary of Oliver Wendell Holmes, Jr., 1861–1864.* Da Capo, 1969.

Hurst, W. J. *Justice Holmes and Legal History.* Macmillan, 1964.

Konefsky, S. J. *The Legacy of Holmes and Brandeis: A Study in the Influence of Ideas.* Macmillan, 1956; Da Capo, 1974.

Lerner, M., ed. *The Mind and Faith of Justice Holmes.* Little, Brown, 1943.

Lief, A., ed. *The Dissenting Opinions of Mr. Justice Holmes.* Vanguard, 1943.

———. *Representative Opinions of Mr. Justice Holmes.* Greenwood, 1976.

Marke, J., ed. *The Holmes Reader.* 2nd ed. Oceana, 1964.

Morse, J. T., Jr., ed. *Life and Letters of Oliver Wendell Holmes.* Houghton Mifflin, 1896.

Peabody, J. B., ed. *Holmes-Einstein Letters.* Macmillan, 1964.

Shriver, H. C., ed. *Justice Oliver Wendell Holmes: His Book Notice and Uncollected Letters and Papers.* Da Capo, 1973.

Wu, J., ed. *Justice Holmes to Dr. Wu: An Intimate Correspondence.* Central Books, 1947.

CHARLES EVANS HUGHES (1862–1948):

Danelsik, D. J., and J. S. Tulchin, eds. *The Autobiographical Notes of Charles Evans Hughes.* Harvard University, 1973.

Hendel, S. *Charles Evans Hughes and the Supreme Court.* Columbia University, 1951.

Hughes, C. E. *Addresses.* 2nd ed. Harper, 1916.

———. *The Supreme Court of the United States.* Columbia University, 1928.

Hughes, H. L. "They Don't Make Them Like That Anymore." *New York Review of Books,* May 30, 1974.

Kornberg, H. R. "Charles Evans Hughes in the Supreme Court: A Study in Judicial Philosophy and Voting Behavior." Ph.D. diss., Brown University, 1972.

Perkins, D. *Charles Evans Hughes and American Democratic Statesmanship.* Little, Brown, 1956.

Pusey, M. J. *Charles Evans Hughes.* Macmillan, 1951.

Ransom, W. L. *Charles Evans Hughes: The Statesman as Shown in the Opinions of the Jurist.* Dutton, 1916.

Warren, E. *Hughes and the Court.* Colgate University, 1962.

Wesser, R. F. *Charles Evans Hughes: Politics and Reform in New York, 1905–1910.* Cornell University, 1967.

WARD HUNT (1810–1886):

Obituaries: *New York Times* and *New York Daily Tribune*. March 25, 1886.

Wyman, T. B. *Genealogy of the Name and Family of Hunt*. Wilson, 1862.

JAMES IREDELL (1751–1799):

Connor, H. G. "James Iredell: Lawyer, Statesman, Judge, 1751–1799." 60 *University of Pennsylvania Law Review* 225 (1911–1912).

McRee, G. F., ed. *The Life and Correspondence of James Iredell*. Peter Smith, 1949.

HOWELL E. JACKSON (1832–1895):

Doak, H. M. "Howell Edmunds Jackson." 1897 *Proceedings of the Bar Association of Tennessee* 76.

Schiffman, H. E. "Howell E. Jackson." In *The Justices of the United States Supreme Court, 1789–1978,* edited by L. Friedman and F. L. Israel, p. 2, vol. 2. Chelsea House, 1980.

ROBERT H. JACKSON (1892–1954):

Desmond, C. S., et al. *Mr. Justice Jackson: Four Lectures in His Honor*. Columbia University, 1969.

Gerhart, E. C. *America's Advocate: Robert H. Jackson*. Bobbs-Merrill, 1958.

———. *Robert H. Jackson: Lawyer's Judge*. "Q" Corp., 1961.

Jackson, R. H. *Full Faith and Credit: The Lawyer's Clause in the Constitution*. Columbia University, 1945.

———. *The Struggle for Judicial Supremacy: A Study of a Crisis in American Judicial Power*. Knopf, 1941.

———. *The Supreme Court in the American System of Government*. Harvard University, 1955.

Schubert, G., ed. *Dispassionate Justice: A Synthesis of the Judicial Opinions of Robert H. Jackson*. Bobbs-Merrill, 1969.

Seymour, W. N., P. Stewart, P. A. Freund et al., eds. *Mr. Justice Jackson: Four Lectures in His Honor*. Columbia University, 1969.

Stanford Law Review. Symposium: "Mr. Justice Jackson." (December 1955.)

Steamer, R. J. "The Constitutional Doctrine of Mr. Justice Robert H. Jackson." Ph.D. diss., Cornell University, 1954.

JOHN JAY (1745–1829):

Jay, W. *The Life of John Jay*. Harper, 1833.

Johnston, H. P., ed. *The Correspondence and Public Papers of John Jay*, 1763–1826. Putnam's, 1890, 1893.

Monaghan, F. *John Jay: Defender of Liberty*. Bobbs-Merrill, 1935.

Morris, R. B., ed. *John Jay, the Making of a Revolutionary: Unpublished Papers, 1745–1780*. Harper & Row, 1975.

———. *John Jay, the Nation and the Court*. Boston University, 1967.

THOMAS JOHNSON (1732–1819):

Delaplaine, E. S. *The Life of Thomas Johnson*. Hitchcock, 1927.

WILLIAM JOHNSON (1771–1834):

Morgan, D. G. *Justice William Johnson, the First Dissenter: The Career and Constitutional Philosophy of a Jeffersonian Judge*. University of South Carolina, 1954.

Schroeder, O., Jr. "Life and Judicial Work of Justice William Johnson, Jr." 95 *University of Pennsylvania Law Review* 164 (1946–1947).

JOSEPH RUCKER LAMAR (1857–1916):

Lamar, C. P. *The Life of Joseph Rucker Lamar, 1857–1916*. Putnam's, 1926.

LUCIUS Q. C. LAMAR (1825–1893):

Cate, W. A. *Lucius Q. C. Lamar*. University of North Carolina, 1935.

Mayes, E. *Lucius Q. C. Lamar*. Barbee, 1895.

Merrill, H. S. *Bourbon Leader*. Little, Brown, 1957.

HENRY BROCKHOLST LIVINGSTON (1757–1823):

Livingston, E. B. *The Livingstons of Livingston Manor*. Knickerbocker, 1910.

HORACE H. LURTON (1844–1914):

Obituaries: 59 *Ohio Law Bulletin* 389, 1914; 12 *Ohio Law Register* 223, 1914; *New York Times*, July 13, 1914.

JOSEPH MCKENNA (1843–1926):

McDevitt, M. B. *Joseph McKenna: Associate Justice of the United States*. Catholic University, 1946; Da Capo, 1974.

JOHN MCKINLEY (1780–1852):

Hicks, J. "Associate Justice John McKinley: A Sketch." 18 *Alabama Law Review* 227 (1965).

JOHN MCLEAN (1785–1861):

Weisenburger, F. P. *The Life of John McLean: A Politician on the United States Supreme Court*. Ohio State University, 1937; Da Capo, 1974.

JAMES CLARK MCREYNOLDS (1862–1946):

Blaisdell, D. P. "Mr. Justice James Clark McReynolds." Ph.D. diss., University of Wisconsin, 1948.

Early, S. T., Jr. "James Clark McReynolds and the Judicial Process." Ph.D. diss., University of Virginia, 1954.

Gilberts, S. P. *James Clark McReynolds*. Privately published, 1946.

McCraw, J. B. "Justice James Clark McReynolds and the Supreme

Court, 1914–1941." Ph.D. diss., University of Texas, Austin, 1949.

JOHN MARSHALL (1755–1835):

Adams, J. S., ed. *An Autobiographical Sketch by John Marshall.* University of Michigan, 1837.

Baker, L. *John Marshall: A Life in Law*. Macmillan, 1974.

Beveridge, A. J. *The Life of John Marshall.* Houghton Mifflin, 1916.

Corwin, E. S. *John Marshall and the Constitution: A Chronicle of the Supreme Court*. Yale University, 1921.

Cotton, J. P., Jr., ed. *The Constitutional Decisions of John Marshall.* Putnam's 1905; Da Capo, 1969.

Cullen, C. T., and H. A. Johnson. *The Papers of John Marshall.* University of North Carolina, 1977.

Dillon, J. M., ed. *John Marshall: Complete Constitutional Decisions*. Callaghan, 1903.

Faulkner, R. K. *The Jurisprudence of John Marshall.* Princeton University, 1968.

Gunther, G., ed. *John Marshall's Defense of McCulloch* v. *Maryland*. Stanford University, 1969.

Haskins, G. L., and H. A. Johnson. *Foundations of Power: John Marshall, 1801–1815*. Macmillan, 1981.

Johnson, H. A., ed. *The Papers of John Marshall,* vol. 1, *Correspondence and Papers, Nov. 10, 1775–June 23, 1788*. University of North Carolina, 1974.

Jones, W. N., ed. *Chief Justice John Marshall: A Reappraisal.* Cornell University, 1956; Da Capo, 1971.

Konefsky, S. J. *John Marshall and Alexander Hamilton: Architects of the American Constitution*. Macmillan, 1964.

Loth, D. G. *Chief Justice: John Marshall and the Growth of the Republic*. Norton, 1949.

Mason, F. N. *My Dearest Polly: Letters of Chief Justice Marshall to His Wife, 1779–1831*. Garret & Massie, 1961.

Oliver, A. *The Portraits of John Marshall.* University of Virginia, 1976.

Palmer, B. W. *Marshall and Taney: Statesmen of the Law*. University of Minnesota, 1939.

Rhodes, I. S. *The Papers of John Marshall: A Descriptive Calendar.* University of Oklahoma, 1969.

———. *The Papers of John Marshall: A Descriptive Calendar.* University of Oklahoma, 1970.

Roche, J. P., ed. *John Marshall: Major Opinions and Other Writings*. Bobbs-Merrill, 1966.

Services, J. A. *A Bibliography of John Marshall.* U.S. Commission for Celebration of 200th Anniversary of Birth of John Marshall, 1956.

Severn, B. *John Marshall: The Man Who Made the Court Supreme.* McKay, 1969.

Stinchombe, W. C., and C. Cullen, eds. *The Papers of John Marshall.* Vols 1, 2, 3. University of North Carolina, 1975.

Stites, F. *John Marshall: Defender of the Constitution.* Little, Brown, 1981.

Surrency, E., ed. *The Marshall Reader.* Oceana, 1955.

Sutherland, A. E. *Government Under Law.* Harvard University, 1956.

Swindler, W. F. *The Constitution and Chief Justice Marshall.* Dodd, Mead, 1979.

Thayer, J. B. *John Marshall.* Houghton Mifflin, 1901; Phoenix, 1967; Da Capo, 1974.

THURGOOD MARSHALL (1908–):

Bland, R. W. *Private Pressure on Public Law: The Legal Career of Justice Thurgood Marshall.* Kennikat, 1973.

Fenderson, L. H. *Thurgood Marshall.* McGraw-Hill, 1969.

STANLEY MATTHEWS (1824–1889):

Greoe, C. J. "Stanley Matthews." In W. D. Lewis, ed. *Seven Great American Lawyers.* Lippincott, 1909.

SAMUEL FREEMAN MILLER (1816–1890):

Fairman, C. *Mr. Justice Miller and the Supreme Court, 1862–1890.* Harvard University, 1939.

Gregory, C. N. *Samuel Freeman Miller.* State Historical Society of Iowa, 1907.

Miller, S. F. *Lectures on the Constitution.* Banks & Bros., 1891.

SHERMAN MINTON (1890–1965):

Wallace, H. L. "Mr. Justice Minton–Hoover Justice on the Supreme Court." 34 *Indiana Law Journal* 145 (1959).

WILLIAM HENRY MOODY (1853–1917):

Weiner, F. B. *The Life and Judicial Career of William Henry Moody.* Harvard University, 1937.

ALFRED MOORE (1755–1810):

Friedman, L. "Alfred Moore." In *The Justices of the United States Supreme Court, 1789–1978,* edited by L. Friedman and F. L. Israel, p. 2, vol. 1. Chelsea House, 1980.

FRANK MURPHY (1890–1949):

Fine, S. *Frank Murphy: The Detroit Years.* University of Michigan, 1975.

———. *Frank Murphy: The New Deal Years.* University of Chicago, 1979.

Howard, J. W., Jr. "Frank Murphy: A Liberal's Creed." Ph.D. diss., Princeton University, 1959.

———. *Mr. Justice Murphy: A Political Biography*. Princeton University, 1968.

Lunt, R. D. *The High Ministry of Government: The Political Career of Frank Murphy*. Wayne State University, 1965.

Michigan Law Review. Symposium: "Mr. Justice Frank Murphy." (April 1950.)

Norris, H. *Mr. Justice Murphy and the Bill of Rights*. Oceana, 1965.

SAMUEL NELSON (1792–1873):

Countryman, E. "Samuel Nelson." 19 *Green Bag* 329, 1927.

SANDRA DAY O'CONNOR (1930–):

Moore, R. H., Jr. "Justice O'Connor and the States." Paper presented at the annual meeting of the American Political Science Association, Birmingham, Alabama, November 3, 1983.

Time "Justice–At Last." July 20, 1981.

WILLIAM PATERSON (1745–1806):

Wood, G. S. *William Paterson of New Jersey, 1745–1806*. Fair Lawn Press, 1933.

RUFUS W. PECKHAM (1838–1909):

Duker, W. F. "Mr. Justice Rufus W. Peckham: The Police Power and the Individual in a Changing World." 47 *Brigham Young Law Review* (1980).

Hall, A. O. "Mr. Justice Peckham." 8 *Green Bag* (1896).

MAHLON PITNEY (1858–1924):

Breed, A. R., "Mahlon Pitney." Senior Thesis, Princeton University, 1932.

LEWIS F. POWELL, JR. (1907–):

Richmond Law Review. Symposium: "Hon. Lewis F. Powell, Jr." (1977.)

Wilkinson III, J. H. *Serving Justice: A Supreme Court Clerk's View*. Charterhouse, 1974.

STANLEY F. REED (1884–1980):

Fitzgerald, M. J. "Justice Reed: A Study of a Center Judge." Ph.D. diss., University of Chicago, 1950.

O'Brien, F. W. *Justice Reed and the First Amendment: The Religion Clauses*. Georgetown University, 1958.

WILLIAM H. REHNQUIST (1924–):

Rehnquist, W. H. "The Notion of a Living Constitution." 54 *Texas Law Review* 693 (1976).

———. "Political Battles for Judicial Independence." 50 *Washington Law Review* 835 (1975).

OWEN J. ROBERTS (1875–1955):

Leonard, C. A. *A Search for a Judicial Philosophy: Mr. Justice Roberts and the Constitutional Revolution of 1937*. Kennikat, 1971.

Roberts, O. J. *The Court and the Constitution*. Harvard University, 1951.

JOHN RUTLEDGE (1739–1800):

Barnwell, R. W. "Rutledge, 'The Dictator.' " 7 *Journal of Southern History* 215 (1941).

Barry, R. *Mr. Rutledge of South Carolina*. Duell, Sloan and Pearce, 1942.

WILEY B. RUTLEDGE (1894–1949):

Harper, F. W. *Justice Rutledge and the Bright Constellation*. Bobbs-Merrill, 1965.

Iowa Law Review. Symposium: "Wiley B. Rutledge." (Summer 1950.)

Rutledge, W. B. *A Declaration of Legal Faith*. University of Kansas, 1947; Da Capo, 1971.

EDWARD T. SANFORD (1865–1930):

Cook, S. A. "Rath to the High Bench: The Pre-Supreme Court Career of Justice Edward Terry Sanford." Ph.D. diss., University of Tennessee, 1977.

Sanford, E. T. *Blount College and the University of Tennessee*. University of Tennessee, 1894.

GEORGE SHIRAS, JR. (1832–1924):

Shiras III, G., ed. *Justice George Shiras, Jr., of Pittsburgh*. University of Pittsburgh, 1953.

JOHN PAUL STEVENS (1920–):

Orland, L. "John Paul Stevens." In *The Justices of the United States Supreme Court, 1789–1978,* edited by L. Friedman and F. L. Israel, p. 2, vol. 5. Chelsea House, 1980.

POTTER STEWART (1915–):

Barnett, H. M., and K. Levine. "Mr. Justice Stewart." 40 *New York University Law Review* 526 (1965).

Frank, J. B. *The Warren Court*. Macmillan, 1964.

HARLAN FISKE STONE (1872–1946):

Konefsky, S. J. *Chief Justice Stone and the Supreme Court*. Macmillan, 1946.

Mason, A. T. *Harlan Fiske Stone: Pillar of the Law*. Viking, 1956.

Stone, H. F. *Law and Its Administration*. Columbia University, 1915.

———. *Public Control of Business*. Howell, Soskin & Company, 1940.

JOSEPH STORY (1779–1845):

Commager, H. S. "Joseph Story." In A. N. Holcombe et al., eds. *Gaspar G. Bacon Lectures on the Constitution of the United States*. Boston University, 1953.

———. *The Writings of Justice Joseph Story*. Bobbs-Merrill, 1966.

Dunne, G. F. *Justice Joseph Story and the Rise of the Supreme Court*. Simon & Schuster, 1970.

McClellan, J. *Joseph Story and the American Constitution*. University of Oklahoma, 1971.

Schwartz, M. D., and J. C. Hogan. *Joseph Story: A Collection of Writings by an Eminent American Jurist*. Oceana, 1959.

Story, Joseph. *Commentaries on the Constitution of the United States*. C. C. Little & Brown, 1833.

Story, W. W., ed. *Life and Letters of Joseph Story*. Little, Brown, 1851.

———. *The Miscellaneous Writings of Joseph Story*. Little, Brown, 1852.

Warren, C. *The Story-Marshall Correspondence*. New York University, 1942.

WILLIAM STRONG (1808–1895):

Kutler, S. I. "William Strong." In *The Justices of the United States Supreme Court, 1789–1978,* edited by L. Friedman and F. L. Israel, p. 1, vol. 2. Chelsea House, 1980.

GEORGE SUTHERLAND (1862–1942):

Paschal, J. F. *Mr. Justice Sutherland: A Man Against the State*. Princeton University, 1951.

Sutherland, G. *Constitutional Power and World Affairs*. Columbia University, 1919.

NOAH H. SWAYNE (1804–1884):

Silver, D. M. *Lincoln's Supreme Court*. University of Illinois, 1956.

Swayne, N. W., comp. *The Descendants of Francis Swayne and Others*. Lippincott, 1921.

WILLIAM HOWARD TAFT (1857–1930):

Anderson, J. I. *William Howard Taft: An Intimate History*. Norton, 1981.

Mason, A. T. *William Howard Taft: Chief Justice*. Simon & Schuster, 1965.

McHale, F. *President and Chief Justice: The Life and Public Services of William Howard Taft*. Dorrance, 1931.

Pringle, H. F. *The Life and Times of William Howard Taft*. Farrar & Rinehart, 1939.

Taft, W. H. *The Anti-trust Act and the Supreme Court*. Harper & Bros., 1914.

———. *Liberty Under Law, an Interpretation of the Principles of our Constitutional Government*. Yale University, 1922.

———. *Our Chief Magistrate and His Powers.* Columbia University, 1916.

———. *United States Supreme Court the Prototype of a World Court.* American Society for Judicial Settlement of International Disputes, 1915.

ROGER BROOKE TANEY (1777–1864):

Lewis, W. *Without Fear or Favor: A Biography of Chief Justice Roger Brooke Taney.* Houghton Mifflin, 1965.

Palmer, B. W. *Marshall and Taney: Statesmen of the Law.* University of Minnesota, 1939.

Smith, C. W., Jr. *Roger B. Taney: Jacksonian Jurist.* University of North Carolina, 1936; Da Capo, 1973.

Steiner, B. C. *Life of Roger Brooke Taney, Chief Justice of the United States Supreme Court.* Williams & Wilkins, 1922.

Swisher, C. B. *Roger B. Taney.* Macmillan, 1935.

———. *The Taney Period, 1836–64.* Macmillan, 1974.

Taylor, S. *Memoir of Roger Brooke Taney: Chief Justice of the Supreme Court of the United States.* J. Murphy, 1872; Da Capo, 1973.

SMITH THOMPSON (1768–1843):

Roper, D. M. *Mr. Justice Thompson and the Constitution.* Ph.D. diss., Indiana University, 1963.

THOMAS TODD (1765–1826):

O'Rear, E. C. "Justice Thomas Todd." 38 *Register of the Kentucky State Historical Society* 113 (1940).

ROBERT TRIMBLE (1776–1828):

Goff, J. T. "Mr. Justice Trimble of the United States Supreme Court." 58 *Register of the Kentucky Historical Society* 6 (1960).

WILLIS VAN DEVANTER (1859–1941):

Gould, L. L. "Willis Van Devanter in Wyoming Politics, 1884–1897." Ph.D. diss., Yale University, 1966.

Howard, J. O. B. "Constitutional Doctrines of Mr. Justice Van Devanter." Ph.D. diss., State University of Iowa, 1937.

FRED M. VINSON (1890–1953):

Bolner, J. "Chief Justice Vinson: A Study of His Politics and His Constitutional Law." Ph.D. diss., University of Virginia, 1962.

Frank, J. P. "Fred Vinson and the Chief Justiceship," 21 *University of Chicago Law Review* 212 (1954).

Pritchett, C. H. *Civil Liberties and the Vinson Court.* University of Chicago, 1954.

MORRISON R. WAITE (1816–1888):

Magrath, C. P. *Morrison R. Waite: The Triumph of Character.* Macmillan, 1963.

Trimble, B. R. *Chief Justice Waite: Defender of the Public Interest.* Princeton University, 1938.

EARL WARREN (1891–1974):

Bozell, L. B. *The Warren Revolution.* Arlington House, 1966.

Christman, H. M., ed. *The Public Papers of Chief Justice Earl Warren.* Simon & Schuster, 1959.

Frank, J. P., with Y. Karsh. *The Warren Court.* Macmillan, 1964.

Katcher, L. *Earl Warren: A Political Biography.* McGraw-Hill, 1967.

Pollack, J. H. *Earl Warren: The Judge Who Changed America.* Prentice-Hall, 1979.

Schwartz, B. *Super Chief Earl Warren and His Supreme Court: A Judicial Biography.* Columbia University, 1983.

Stone, I. *Earl Warren.* Prentice-Hall, 1948.

Warren, E. "All Men Are Created Equal." Association of the Bar of the City of New York, 1970.

———. *Hughes and the Court.* Colgate University, 1962.

———. *The Memoirs of Chief Justice Warren.* Doubleday, 1977.

———. *A Republic . . . if You Can Keep It.* Quadrangle, 1972.

Weaver, J. D. *Warren: The Man, the Court, the Era.* Little, Brown, 1967.

White, G. E. *Earl Warren: A Public Life.* Oxford, 1982.

BUSHROD WASHINGTON (1762–1829):

Binney, R. *Bushrod Washington.* Sherman, 1858.

Washington, C. B. "Justice Bushrod Washington." 9 *Green Bag* 329 (1897).

JAMES MOORE WAYNE (1790–1867):

Lawrence, A. A. *James Moore Wayne: Southern Unionist.* University of North Carolina, 1943.

BYRON R. WHITE (1917–):

Israel, F. L. "Byron R. White." In *The Justices of the United States Supreme Court, 1789–1978,* edited by L. Friedman and F. L. Israel, p. 2, vol. 4. Chelsea House, 1980.

EDWARD DOUGLAS WHITE (1845–1921):

Highsaw, R. B. *Edward Douglas White: Defender of Conservative Faith.* Louisiana State University, 1981.

Hill, A. B. "The Constitutional Doctrine of Chief Justice White." Ph.D. diss., University of California, 1922.

Klinkhamer, Sister M. C. "Edward Douglas White, Chief Justice of the United States." Ph.D. diss., Catholic University, 1948.

CHARLES E. WHITTAKER (1901–1973):

Friedman, L. "Charles Whittaker." In *The Justices of the United States Supreme Court, 1789–1978,* edited by L. Friedman and F. L. Israel, p. 2, vol. 4. Chelsea House, 1980.

James Wilson (1742–1798):

McCloskey, R. G., ed. *The Works of James Wilson.* Harvard University, 1967.

Smith, C. H., *James Wilson, Founding Father.* University of North Carolina, 1956.

Wilson, J. *Commentaries on the Constitution of the United States.* Extracted from debates, published in Philadelphia by T. Lloyd, 1792.

———. *The Works of the Hon. James Wilson.* Bronson & Chaunch, 1804.

Levi Woodbury (1789–1851):

Woodbury, C. L., ed. *Writings of Levi Woodbury.* Little, Brown, 1852.

William B. Woods (1824–1887):

Proceedings of the Bench and Bar of the Supreme Court of the United States in Memoriam William B. Woods. 123 U.S. 761 (1887).

Proceedings of the Bench and Bar . . . William B. Woods. 15 *Washington Law Reporter* 357 (1887).

Index

I. NAME INDEX

II. COURT CASE INDEX